UNDERSTANDING COMMUNICATION

A Workbook Approach

Second Edition

Douglas B. Hoehn

Community College of Philadelphia

KENDALL/HUNT PUBLISHING COMPANY
2460 Kerper Boulevard P.O. Box 539 Dubuque, Iowa 52004-0539

ABOUT THE AUTHOR

Douglas B. Hoehn is an Associate Professor of Speech at the Community College of Philadelphia. He received his B.A. degree from Dakota Wesleyan University, his M.A. from the University of Maryland, and his Ph.D. degree from New York University. Dr. Hoehn held teaching positions at Eisenhower Jr. High School in New Jersey, the University of Maryland, and New York University. He has also taught at Montclair State College, Kean State College, Bergen Community College, and Passaic Community College.

Contents

3   The Process of Communication   30

4   Listening   44

5   Putting Your Ideas Into Words   58

6   Verbal and Nonverbal Communication   76

7   Communicating in Social Encounters   94

8   Communicating in Your Career   108

9   Communicating in Small Groups   122

10   Researching Your Ideas   150

11   Understanding Your Listeners   172

12   Preparing a Speech   190

13   Presenting a Speech   208

14   Argumentation and Debate   234

Appendix and Answers to Exercises   255

Index   259

Preface

Understanding Communication has been used by thousands of students in hundreds of courses. This second edition owes its creation to each of those students and teachers whose suggestions and guidance have helped to make this new edition possible. Some chapters have been added, some changed, a few deleted. All have been revised to make the book more understandable, more readable, and more interesting for the student of the nineties. To all of them this book is dedicated.

TO THE INSTRUCTOR

Understanding Communication is a text designed for the introductory speech communication course. Units covered in the text include communication theory, listening, language, verbal and nonverbal message sending, research skills, audience analysis, interpersonal communication, group discussion, public speaking, and argumentation and debate. The book is replete with critique sheets, tear-out exercises and worksheets to aid in learning. Hopefully this text will serve as a "complete package" providing student and teacher alike with everything needed to successfully fulfill all course requirements.

Material is presented in a logical order. While individual instructor needs will vary, material is presented in a building order from more general to more specific. Beginning chapters establish a basic understanding of how communication works. Immediate following chapters present the fundamental units of listening, language, and verbal and nonverbal communication. More specific chapters discuss communication in one's social life, career, and in small groups. Subsequent chapters cover public speaking in terms of research, audience analysis, preparation, and presentation. A final chapter discusses argumentation and debate for those instructors who wish to include this unit in their course.

Numerous activities are listed. Believing that students can best learn by doing, the text is "rich" in activities and exercises. All in-class activities are carefully timed to occur within the confines of a standard classroom period. Take home exercises are designed to reinforce learning and "drive home" essential concepts and ideas. To increase flexibility, many chapters include several varied exercises providing instructors with the option to choose those most appropriate.

Current examples are used. Recognizing that students best appreciate that which they can most easily understand, this edition uses present day examples whenever appropriate. Communicators used to illustrate a point include people like Jesse Jackson, George Bush, Geraldine Ferraro, Diane Sawyer, Ronald Reagan, and Gloria Steinem just to name a few. Sometimes people like these can get across a point just as effectively as a Kennedy or a Lincoln. Likewise, illustrations relate to current everyday social concerns: A.I.D.S., homelessness, working mothers, teenage pregnancy, drug abuse and the like.

Interesting communication facts are included. Part of the appreciation of communication comes from an understanding that communication is all around us, all the time. To help reinforce this concept interesting issues and communication facts are boxed-off within chapters. What are the most frequent complaints of bosses? How can people practice empathic listening? What's the best way to control nervousness? How can one measure the power of words? Inserts like these tend to make chapters more interesting to read, more enjoyable to understand.

Ease of reading is stressed. Chapters are designed to make wading through content more exciting than tedious. Frequent use is made of pictures, drawings, charts, and graphs to help break up reading and illustrate a point. Actual content is made as readable as possible. Whenever possible a conversational tone is used, employing easily identifiable words—nervousness replaces stage fright, touch instead of tactile, interview in place of dyadic, taste rather than gustatory. When needed, reference is made to the technical term, but the easily understood term dominates the discussion. Likewise, all words and sentences are kept basic and simple to understand.

Changes in the Second Edition

The second edition of *Understanding Communication* fluctuates from the first edition in the following ways:

- Nervousness, being an immediate concern of students, is dealt with in a lively discussion in the first chapter. Similarly, a new section on being an ethical communicator has been added to Chapter 1.
- The discussion of communication models in Chapter 3 has been simplified. A typical model is now described in step by step order, adding each element as the model is completed.
- Chapter 4 on listening has been completely revised and now includes a discussion of the eight skills needed to become a better listener. A new section provides methods for taking careful notes.
- A brand new chapter on language has been added. Language is discussed in terms of its use, impact, and understanding. A challenging language worksheet involves students in the process of using language appropriately and vividly.

- Chapter 8, Communicating in Your Career, has been revised to more specifically discuss the employment interview. Based on student need, added to the discussion has been a section on speaking over the telephone and giving oral reports.
- Since many beginning students are weak in research skills, a chapter on research and information collecting has been included. This chapter gives the basics of doing library research, interviewing for information, and conducting survey research.
- A separate self-contained chapter on audience analysis is now included. A section of this chapter suggests to students the methods for collecting information about their listeners. A blank and filled out audience analysis form are included.
- Chapter 12 lists ten simple steps for preparing a speech, and five simple steps for delivering a speech. Included in this chapter are examples of four types of speeches and an example of a typical first speech.
- A new section on speech delivery has been written for Chapter 13. Included are beefed up sections on using visual aids and persuasive speaking.
- In both the small group and debate chapters, new, more timely topics have been added, while dated topics have been deleted.

TO THE STUDENT

You are about to embark on an exciting adventure. Taking a communication course presents you with many challenges, a few thrills, and a lot of experiences. Unlike many courses, what you learn in this class will be used by you in every hour of every day for the rest of your life. Communication classes are one of the few places where you'll be able to see the results almost immediately. Suddenly speaking up in other classes will seem easier, talking to a stranger will seem less stressful, and listening to others will now become a skill you'll be able to polish. So begin this class with an open mind, keep your spirits up, and let the journey begin.

About the Book

As thousands of students have experienced before you, look at *Understanding Communication* as a guide, a friend to help take you through this course. Probably everything you need to know exists right between its covers. Don't look at reading it like a chore, relish it as you would a novel, curious about what might be revealed on the next page. The worksheets and exercises are there to be used; do so. Let them help in your planning, focusing your outline, bringing out your concerns, and developing your skills. Likewise read boxed off inserts, examine all charts, explore all graphs, digest all photo captions. All these things are there to help make your learning experience as meaningful and pleasurable as possible. Here are some tips to make your job easier as you begin to work your way through this book.

Using this Book

- At the start of each chapter are three "questions for retention." Read them aloud, planting in your mind's eye the important information to be revealed in that upcoming chapter. Then when you discover the answer, underline it, copy it in your notes, and file it away in you memory.
- At the end of each chapter is a summary. Always read it. It will help to refresh important concepts discussed in the chapter. It is also helpful to reread chapter summaries while prepping for an upcoming test.

- Look at the exercises at the end of each chapter. Can you answer all the questions? If not go back and find the answers. You'll be amazed at how this will underscore key facts.
- Fill out all the exercise sheets at the end of each chapter. These will focus on important points, while helping you to build a communication inventory about yourself.
- Save all the critique sheets your instructor returns to you. These will help establish a road map for you of your work and growth as a communicator throughout the course.
- Underline and take notes on all information presented as communication facts in boxed-off inserts. Remember that this information might be asked on a test as well.
- Work ahead. It's usually a good idea to at least glance at an upcoming chapter a week ahead. Then if you have a question about an assignment, you can ask your instructor when the chapter is assigned.
- Need to find an answer to an exercise? Consult the appendix located on page 255 at the end of the book.
- Looking for a particular subject? Refer to the index starting on page 259 at the very end of the book. If you can't find what you're looking for under that term, look under similar descriptors. For example, ''group discussion'' can be found under ''small groups''. If not sure where something might be located, consult the Table of Contents in the front of the text. Many listings in the index refer back to chapter titles.
- Keep this book. Don't think once you finish this course you'll never need to give a speech again, be interviewed, or appear in a group discussion. By keeping this text you'll be able to refer back to subjects and know what to do and how to prepare yourself. Just as you'll never outgrow the need to communicate, this book will never outgrow you. Let it serve as a lifetime resource.

Name _____   Course _____

Student Data Sheet
(Fill out and give to your instructor)

Campus Address _____

Home Address _____

Home Phone _____   Best Times to Call _____

Work Phone _____   Best Times to Call _____

Year in College (circle one)   1   2   3   4   other

Age ____ Year of High School Graduation ____ Married? ____

Reason for Taking This Course _____

_____

Major _____   Minor(s) _____

Probable Vocation _____

Present Employment _____

Past Job Experience _____

_____

Present Co-Curricular Activities _____

_____

Hobbies _____

Previous Speech Courses Taken (if any) _____

Prior Speaking Experience _____

_____

Describe your general reaction to a speaking situation _____

_____

_____

_____

_____

_____

List any special concerns or difficulties you have in a communication situation _____

_____

_____

_____

_____

_____

_____

In the space below, write a paragraph about yourself which will help your instructor know you as an individual:

Name _____   Course _____

Goals in this Course

Rank in order of priority the top ten goals you want to accomplish by taking this course:

____   to organize my thoughts in a clearer way

____   to communicate more effectively

____   to deliver a speech properly

____   to gain confidence

____   to persuade others to my point of view

____   to improve upon my research skills

____   to make myself more marketable for a job

____   to improve my voice and articulation

____   to work effectively in small groups

____   to increase my spoken vocabulary

____   to become a better listener

____   to be more successful in interview situations

____   to speak in a clearer way

____   to learn about communication theories

____   to become more aware of how others perceive me

____   to use nonverbal communication (gestures, facial expressions, movement, etc.) more effectively

____   other (write in)

Communication Concerns

Rank in order of priority the top ten concerns you have about the way you communicate with others:

_____ I tend to speak too rapidly

_____ I often speak before I think

_____ I tend to interrupt others while they are speaking

_____ I frequently misunderstand what others tell me

_____ People often misinterpret what I have said

_____ I tend to repeat myself

_____ I sometimes have problems organizing my thoughts in a logical order

_____ I often think about what I should have said after I have spoken

_____ I tend to speak rather than listen to what others are saying to me

_____ I notice that people often lose interest in what I am saying

_____ I tend to be shy rather than outgoing

_____ I usually let others do most of the talking

_____ I frequently get nervous when I first meet someone

_____ When I speak I tend to use more gestures than most people

_____ I have trouble looking at someone when I talk to them

_____ I feel I express my thoughts better by writing than speaking

_____ I show my anger too easily when I speak

UNDERSTANDING COMMUNICATION

Second Edition

1 Introduction

Speaking to others represents a privilege as well as a responsibility.

QUESTIONS FOR RETENTION

Before reading this chapter, ask yourself the following questions:

1. What are the major benefits to be gained by taking a course in speech communication?
2. How can I overcome nervousness?
3. What does it mean to be an ethical communicator?

Think of the conversations you've participated in. They're pretty fantastic, aren't they? They can be short or they can be long; they can honor the noteworthy or they can mark the routine; they can suggest what should be or they can defend what has been. Yet the common ingredient of all conversations, from the bland to the memorable, is that they possess a tempo all their own. You can read a conversation or hear it repeated, but you can never recapture the magic it held at the moment that it occurred.

A conversation is never just a collection of words and ideas either. For when a spoken message is delivered words and ideas come to life and take on a special power. Think of some of the world's great communicators—Abraham Lincoln, Susan B. Anthony, Martin Luther King, John F. Kennedy. The messages these people presented came to represent more than just a passing moment. Instead they marked a generation and became the touchstone of an era. Each of your spoken messages will also come to mark the highlights of your life and serve as the guideposts to your future.

So what is speech communication? It's not writing, or acting, or talking—yet it has something in common with all three. Speaking means creating a special chemistry between you and your listeners. When you build such a relationship you have a chance to make a difference in the world. Speech lets you transfer a plan, a dream, an idea, an experience from your mind into the minds of your listeners. With spoken comments you can instruct, convince, or inspire. Being instructed is a satisfaction; being convinced is a challenge; being inspired is downright exciting. Therefore in an artistic sense, communication has the same goal as other art forms, be it literature, music, or architecture—to give pleasure, to enrich the lives of others, to make a difference in the world. It is through the practice of speech communication that you'll be able to hone the skills necessary to master this art form. But in order to really understand speech you must experience it firsthand—just as generations of others have done before you.

AN HISTORICAL OVERVIEW

Historians have long recognized the importance of the spoken word. Research suggests, for example, that among our earliest ancestors, those who could communicate best and were the most intelligent were those who survived and passed on their intelligence to their children.[1] And in the eighteenth century a French philosopher in his treaty on human knowledge speculated that human beings developed rationality together with the capacity for speaking. Grecian orator and rhetorician Isocrates recognized the importance of speech when he wrote 2500 years ago, "... *generally speaking, there is no institution devised by human beings which the power of speech has not helped us to establish.*"

Since the dawn of humankind speech has been unequaled by any other form of communication. Earliest humans first established a chain of command, through tribal councils and individual leaders, based upon the power of speech. Later, in the city republics of Greece all issues were discussed in open assemblies. Two thousand years ago speeches made in the Roman Forum affected the whole empire comprising the then discovered world.

Renaissance Italy, imperial Spain, democratic England, and revolutionary France all experienced the affects of speech communication upon their historical destinies. Freedom seeking colonists in early America were influenced by forceful orators in the Colonial Congresses and Constitutional Convention. The political movements that led to Bolshevik Russia and Fascist Germany were directed by powerful public speakers. Religious thought and dictum was expressed chiefly through public speaking by such teachers as Jesus, Buddha, and later Mohammed.[2] In fact, we could generalize and say that all great movements, social, religious, and political, have been conveyed to the populous primarily through the orchestration of the spoken word. Even a demagogue such as Adolf Hitler recognized the power of speech when he wrote in *Mein Kampf*, "*The power which has always started the greatest religious and political avalanches in history rolling has from time immemorial been the magic power of the spoken word, and that alone.*"[3]

Today you're probably exposed to more spoken messages in a single week than the average person heard in a lifetime just one hundred years ago. Through television, radio, forums, conferences, debates, and open meetings, you have access to any number of communicators on all sorts of topics. At any given time you're likely to hear accomplished speakers such as Coretta Scott King, Billy Graham, Gloria Steinem, George Bush, Jesse Jackson, Robert Schuller, Mario Cuomo, and Jean Kirkpatrick, just to name a few. On a typical day, in the average American city or college campus, speakers can be heard discussing women's rights, foreign policy, child abuse, or literally thousands of other subjects.

Most of the men and women who speak about the timely issues of the day were not born as great communicators either. Rather, they perfected and polished their skills through effort and practice. Nevertheless you might care to ask, "*What does all this have to do with me?*" "*After all, what do I have in common with a Graham, a Bush, or a Steinem?*"

Indeed, you may not desire to become a religious leader, become President of the United States, or devote your life to a social cause—but you do want to make a difference. By learning how to communicate with energy and confidence you can make your dreams come true, your thoughts come alive, your plans become real. As you shall see, a course in speech communication offers untold benefits.

BENEFITS OF TAKING A COMMUNICATION COURSE

Speech courses are amazingly popular among college students. A survey of communication students at one major university found that 89 percent of them would recommend that their friends take the same course in speech. At another school two-thirds of all speech students felt that a course in communications should be required of students in every curriculum. Students at community colleges felt similarly about the value of speech courses. Nearly three out of four thought that the communication course they were taking was the most valuable of all their classes.[4]

Surprised? You shouldn't be. For where else will you have a better opportunity to explore an interesting issue, be confronted with a challenging question, or weigh a competing viewpoint? Likewise, remember that the skills you learn in this course will not desert you after the final exam; rather they will travel with you, no matter where you go, no matter what you do. Therefore, it's little wonder that when recent graduates are asked to look back upon all the courses they took while in college they inevitably rank speech as one of the most valuable.[5] Here are some reasons why:

This course will help to make you a more effective day-to-day communicator. Many of the skills you'll learn can be used in everyday conversation. For communicating means relating to others, and that's just what you must do countless times each day. If you're typical, you speak over 30,000 words per day, and by the time you were 18 had already spoken at least 60 million words.[6] You use speaking three times more than writing to convey your messages, and probably speak twice as often on the telephone as someone living just 20 years ago. In fact, you spend 7 out of every 10 hours that you're awake in some form of communication! By using the principles learned in this class you'll not only become a better speaker, but also a more self-aware and assured communicator.

This course will make it easier for you to express yourself in other classes. Have you ever wanted to say something in a class but just couldn't quite find a way to get it out? Have you ever wanted to ask an instructor a question but felt hesitant to do so? Or, have you ever said something in a class but couldn't get anyone else to really understand your point? If you've had these experiences you're not at all unusual—in fact most students have had these same feelings at one time or another. By taking this class you'll find it easier to speak up, to ask a tough question, or make an important point. A course in speech communication teaches you how to organize your thoughts, how to express yourself clearly, and how to carefully listen to others. Upon completing this course you'll feel a renewed sense of strength and confidence which will help you in every class, every day of the year. No wonder good speech skills are considered by many educators to be a student's most prized asset.

This course will help you to get a job. Many students are amazed to find out that the skills they learned in communication class *"pay back"* so quickly in terms of helping them to land a job. Research shows this to be no illusion—good communication skills are considered extremely important by employers. For example, when college recruiters from 45 large corporations were asked to rank the most important skills they were looking for in new employees, they overwhelmingly ranked the ability to speak effectively as number one. And 125 questionnaire responses from chief executives of the largest corporations in the United States mentioned communication skills—specifically the ability to speak well and listen intelligently—as especially important in terms of what they were looking for in new employees.[7] Just as being a good speaker can help you to get a job, being a poor communicator can stand in our way. When 170 business and industrial companies were asked to list the most common reasons for rejecting job applicants, they almost universally replied that poor communication skills were the number one reason. It's no coincidence that employers consider communication skills so important. They realize that people who can communicate effectively perform more efficiently and reduce the likelihood of costly errors. Without a doubt, the skills you learn in this class will be just as important in the office, as they are at the podium.

This course will help you to succeed in your career. No matter what career you choose, you'll have to communicate with others. The world of business is a world of messages, directives, and personal interactions. Reports, position papers, memos, interviews, discussions, speeches, conferences, and oral presentations are all vital avenues of the work world. The Department of Labor estimates that speech is essential for about eight out of every ten jobs, and that at least 35 percent of the time of managers, secretaries, and technicians is spent in direct face-to-face communication. When executives with more than 500 employees were asked what they felt was the major deficiency or need of their supervisors, managers, and professionals, they responded that it was in their employee's inability to communicate their ideas well either orally or in writing. Not surprisingly, studies have established a high correlation between a manager's ability to communicate and their on-the-job success.

Think of this in terms of your own career goal. Are you interested in a career in the law? A recent symposium on the legal profession concluded that effective speech skills are essential for the practice of the law. Plan to go into a technical field? According to *Engineering Education* magazine, 500 leaders in engineering said that being a good communicator was the most important skill required of civil and electrical engineers. Hope to be promoted in your career? A report entitled, *College Education and Employment* discovered that as people were promoted in their jobs they were required to place an increasing reliance on communication skills. Want to be successful in business? Top managers in business identified communication skills as the most important to their own success. They specified those skills as speaking effectively to groups, working efficiently with individuals, communicating within an organization, and in carefully listening to coworkers. Still not convinced? Think of what you'll learn in this class: how to prepare a message, how to get your ideas across, how to relate to others, and how to sound clear and convincing. What skills could possibly be more important in your career? Indeed, as professionals from art to zoology have discovered before you, being a good communicator is essential for one's success no matter what their choice of career.[8]

This course will encourage you to accept new challenges. Having the ability to communicate with confidence will certainly broaden your horizons and encourage you to accept new opportunities at every turn. For being able to effectively communicate a message gives you the power to make a difference about the things you care about. A study of one group of average working class people found, for example, that 43 percent of them had given at least one speech in the past two years![9] You too, will probably have the opportunity to do so in the near future. Think of this as you begin your studies this semester. A speech class is rewarding, it is challenging, but most of all—it is fun.

DEALING WITH NERVOUSNESS

If you're like most people, you're probably a bit nervous about communicating in public. But as you'll soon see, **nervousness is normal, can be logically explained**, and actually **can be used to make you a better communicator**. And, just what is speaker nervousness? It's any feeling which hampers you from clearly expressing yourself to other people.[10] You can show your nervousness in many different ways: maybe you stammer or pause; maybe you fidget or squirm; maybe you forget what you want to say or cut your messages short. Whatever you do, you're not alone—for just about everyone gets nervous.

Your Nervousness is Normal

What one thing do Fidel Castro, Terry Bradshaw, Jane Fonda, Kris Kristofferson, and Peter Jennings all have in common? If you guessed that they get nervous when speaking before others you're absolutely right. Winston Churchill once said that whenever he spoke in public he felt like he had a block of ice in the pit of his stomach. And President and Civil War General Ulysses S. Grant said giving a speech was worse than leading troops into battle. What these people expressed is not at all unusual. When 3,000 Americans were asked to name their greatest fear they said they were more afraid of communicating in public than of heights, sickness, or even death![11]

If you associate speaking with ice cubes, battle, and death you're not alone. In fact, it's been estimated that about 8 out of every 10 Americans get nervous about communicating in public.[12] College students reported that they were more afraid of speaking in public than of going on a job interview, being questioned by someone in authority, or meeting a stranger on a blind date! All types of people get nervous too. Studies have shown that nervousness has nothing to do with your grade point average, major of study, or place of upbringing.

In simple truth, everyone who has to perform in front of the public gets a sense of unease. Actors get cold feet before going out on stage; athletes get the locker room jitters; and politicians seldom enjoy a pre-speech dinner. But people who succeed learn to put their nervousness to work. When tennis star Boris Becker was at the 1986 U.S. Open he said he was so tense he felt he could get sick. But all he did was put his energy to work and blow his opponent away two sets to none. Surprised? You shouldn't be. For once you understand why you get nervous, you'll be able to put your nervousness to work too.

Why You Get Nervous

Mark Twain once said, *"Humans are the only animal that blushes. Or needs to."* Unfortunately, Mark Twain's observation is all too correct. As human beings we set up all sorts of barriers that help to make us nervous. Let's now review the four main reasons why speaking before the public can be such a nerve-wracking experience.

Because your body sends you messages.

Here's how Jane, a beginning speech student, described her feelings when giving a speech: *"I get butterflies in my stomach, my heart starts to pound, I get short of breath, my legs tremble, and I feel weak all over."* Peter, another student, put it this way: *"I get cold and clammy hands. Worse yet, I get a terrible dryness in my mouth—it almost feels like I'm chewing cotton."*

What Jane and Peter described is purely natural. It's your body's way of helping you to deal with a stressful situation.[13] Athletes call it adrenalin and use it to help them run faster and perform better. Even though you're not running a 100-meter race, however, you can put this excess energy to good use by being more animated, using a lively delivery, and being more energetic. And foremost, don't get upset when your body sends you these messages. Bear in mind that shortness of breath is caused by an increased heartbeat; dizziness by rapid breathing; tightness by muscle tension; cold and clammy hands by your circulation and a change in the secretion of fluids; and dryness in the mouth from an increased release of sugar and the secretion of fluids. By understanding why your body is reacting, you'll be able to concentrate more on what you're saying, and less on the way you're feeling.

Because you're the center of attention.

Ever wondered why animals in the wild cluster together, seldom standing apart? It's because there's safety in numbers and animals herd together for mutual support and protection. Like animals, most of us feel comfortable when we're members of a group—teams, clubs, fraternities, sororities, classes, audiences. But when you communicate in public you're no longer just part of a group. Now you're forced to stand alone—looking out at the group and the group looking back at you. Feeling like a goldfish in a bowl can be awfully distressing. That is until you realize that you must be a pretty special person. After all, you're the one everybody's listening to.

Because you think you're shy.

A lot of students think that because they're shy it's automatic that they'll get nervous when speaking before others. Actually this is far from the truth. Many people who are admittedly shy speak in front of the public all the time—Johnny Carson, Barbara Walters, and Michael Jackson just to name a few. There are lots of differences between being nervous and being shy. Shyness is partly inborn, and mostly developed during childhood. Nervousness, on the other hand, is often caused because you lack sufficient experience.[14] Therefore shyness will cause nervousness only to the extent that you let it. If you think you're certain to get nervous because you're shy—the chances are you'll get your wish. But if you realize that even shy people can be effective communicators, you'll be able to put this concern to rest.

Because you're afraid you won't meet your listener's expectations.

Many speakers feel they'll never be able to satisfy their listeners. Before speaking they'll implant negative thoughts like: my topic isn't interesting enough; my content isn't challenging enough; or my delivery isn't smooth enough. When you're sure your listeners won't be pleased, you've set in motion several good reasons for being nervous. How unfortunate this is—for studies show that listeners are almost never as critical of a speaker as he or she thinks they'll be. Keep your expectations realistic—probably what you're most worried about won't even be noticed by your audience.

Using Nervousness to Your Advantage

Being the keynote speaker at a New York luncheon honoring celebrity women of the 1980's, newswoman Diane Sawyer felt very nervous. Just before her speech she slipped into the hall and psyched herself up. By the time she faced the audience she was relaxed, confident, and articulate. What impressed her audience most was how she was in such control, so totally prepared.

How did Diane Sawyer overcome her nervousness? She put her fears at ease, she concentrated on the task at hand, and she planted positive ideas in her mind. Good communicators do this all the time. Once you understand your fears, and why you have them, put them in perspective. Remember that you probably

CONTROLLING NERVOUSNESS

Speech consultant Dorothy Sarnoff suggests the following simple exercise to control the pre-speech jitters. It's been used by thousands of speakers and is reported to work most every time. Sarnoff claims that by contracting your rectus abdominous muscles, as you do in this exercise, you're preventing the production of noradrenaline or epinephrine—the fear-producing chemicals in your system. The beauty of this procedure is that it can be done right in your seat before you get up to speak. Here's how it works:

While sitting straight up in your chair lean slightly forward. Now put your hands together out in front of you, move your elbows apart, and push your fingertips upward together. As you do you'll feel a force in the heels of your palms and under your arms.

Next say ssss, like a hiss. While exhaling the s contract your muscles by moving your arms like you were pulling the oars of a boat. Relax the muscles at the end of your exhalation, then inhale gently. Do this a couple of times and you'll suddenly feel relaxed.

know more about your topic than any one of your listeners—think of all the time and effort you've put into preparing your message. And bear in mind that your listeners want you to succeed—audiences always feel empathy with the person doing the speaking.

Of course you still will feel somewhat nervous. Put this energy to work. How often have you heard professors who were so calm while giving a lecture that they never varied their voice one octave? By being excited your voice will naturally rise and fall— use it! Bring in gestures, expressions, and movements to get rid of physical tenseness. Burn off extra energy by being an animated, dynamic communicator. It may be helpful to **develop a pre-speaking regimen** to be practiced before every performance. Some people like to take a brisk walk before speaking in public. Others like to use various isometric and aerobic exercises to relax tense muscles. Some even like to lean back and breathe in and out several times in rapid succession. Find a regimen that works for you through simple trial and error. Once you've found one, use it before every performance.

Finally, be comforted in the fact that your confidence will grow with every class. One helpful way to improve is to concentrate on one aspect of your nervousness with every assignment. Once you've conquered one, move on to the next. By the time the course is completed, clammy hands and trembling knees should be a memory of the past.[15] Your teacher probably has some useful suggestions for reducing tension and increasing your confidence. Here are some others:

Figure 1.1
Demosthenes. Demosthenes was probably the greatest of the old Athenian orators. He overcame a speech defect by practicing his orations at the seaside, shouting against the noise of the rolling waves. He also talked with pebbles in his mouth to improve his enunciation. (Courtesy, Bettmann Archive)

Be Prepared

The better you research and organize your presentation the more confidence you'll have when you deliver it. Remember, preparation does more than just familiarize you with your material—it starts you "thinking communication."

Rehearse Your Speaking Performances

Practice may not always make perfect, but it sure helps! The more you rehearse your presentation the more familiar, and thus comfortable you'll feel with its content.

Familiarize Yourself with Your Surroundings

Know the room and conditions for your presentation. Many speakers find it helpful to practice under conditions as close to the actual speaking situation as possible.

Think Positive

Don't focus on your weaknesses or on negatives. Think of your strengths and why your presentation is bound to be a success. Look at the chance to speak as an opportunity, not a burden.

Be Ready for Your Presentation

Get enough rest and avoid eating a heavy meal before a performance. The person who stays up all night and smokes five cigarettes before class is only increasing his or her sense of uneasiness.

Appear Confident

If you make a mistake the chances are that no one will know it but yourself. Look and act like you've prepared for this presentation all your life—confidence is contagious!

Think Communication

Focus on conversing with your listeners. Look at your audience, speak clearly, and be expressive. Put all your energies in a positive direction.

Be Yourself

No two people are exactly alike—so too, no two communicators are the same. What worked for Abe Lincoln, John Kennedy, or a classmate may not work for you. Your listeners want to hear you—the real you. The most successful communicators are those who are themselves.

You've already taken the first step for becoming a successful communicator—you've enrolled in this class. By dedicating yourself to this challenge you're certain to realize your goals and satisfy your dreams; indeed, your speaking horizons are limitless.

BEING AN ETHICAL COMMUNICATOR

There's an awesome power in the spoken word. Throughout history some people have abused this power and the results have been dreadful. Adolf Hitler led a nation and a people to ruin. Jim Jones caused hundreds of his cult followers to commit mass suicide in the jungles of South America. Joseph Goebbels persuaded a people to continue a hopeless war. And Saddam Hussein threatened the use of poison gas.

Today, due to the magic of television, hardly a day goes by that we aren't confronted with communicators with a less than noble purpose. Terrorists describe public bombings, kidnappers openly discuss terms for the release of hostages, and highjackers endanger the lives of hundreds while voicing their grievances.[16] Closer to home, ethical questions leap out at us at every turn—Watergate, the S & L scandal, insider trading on Wall Street, Laetrile, Iran-Contra, and the list could go on and on.

Perhaps at no time in history has there been as great a need for every responsible communicator to follow an ethical code of behavior. And what is it to be ethical? It means to be honest with your listeners, concerned for their welfare, and conscious of their vulnerabilities. As a communicator these ethical questions usually focus on your *methods* and *goals*. Are your methods ethically valid? Hitler and Goebbels distorted facts and appealed to a false sense of nationalism in preserving a 1000 year Reich; Jim Jones led his followers to believe he spoke with righteous wisdom; and Saddam Hussein claimed he spoke for the whole Arab world. Certainly most of us would agree that these methods were on ethically questionable ground. And what of your goals? Are they really designed for the benefit of your listeners, or is there an ulterior motive? Without doubt a person who leads a nation to ruin or a people to mass suicide is hardly being ethical. But think of some of the communicators we've observed in this chapter—Billy Graham speaks about the value of leading a good life, Coretta Scott King stands up for racial equality, and Gloria Steinem argues for women's rights. Few of us would find the goals of these communicators unethical.

How do you practice ethical communicating? Experts have concluded that there are four basic things you need to do to be an ethical communicator:

Demonstrate Good Will

Show your listeners you're honest and well informed. Search out both sides of an issue, don't distort information, and explore all aspects of your subject. Listeners appreciate communicators who blend their personal integrity with the integrity of their ideas. When you demonstrate that you're presenting a sincere message your listeners are more likely to accept what you have to say.

Present A Complete Message

Both your means and your ends should be ethically valid. Make your means acceptable staying away from questionable material from a biased source. Discussing abortion? Pro-Life will give you information, but what about the other side? Right-to-Life will tell you what they think, but is it totally objective? Research both sides of an issue, select objective information, properly arrange your ideas and support, and use a clear, understandable delivery. And what about the ends? Does your solution present a quick fix, but pose the potential of long-term harm? If your listeners accept your suggestions will they really accomplish what they think? Remember that the ends don't always justify the means.

Be a Responsible Communicator

Present the best reasons for your argument, not just those you think will work. Likewise avoid using faulty reasoning. Don't pander to a fear or prejudice, avoid setting up straw targets, scapegoating, or jumping to hasty generalizations. Being responsible means stating your message in clear, noninflammatory terms.

Respect Your Listeners

Look at your listeners as *coparticipants* in your communication. Involve them in your message and react to their wants, needs, and concerns. Allow them the time to make rational choices, giving them an opportunity to reflect and weigh your arguments. If any change is brought about, make it voluntary rather than due to coercion or indoctrination.

By taking this course you'll have numerous opportunities to practice ethical communication. You'll be quick to realize that your most effective message is almost always rooted in truth. As the great Roman teacher Quintilian so aptly summarized it, *"The perfect orator is a good person speaking well"*—and that doctrine is as true today as it was over 2,000 years ago.

CHAPTER SUMMARY

Communicating with others means more then just stating words in sequence. It includes our ideas, feelings, and sense of the world around us. The best way to learn how to communicate more effectively is to experience it firsthand.

The study of communication goes back thousands of years. Speech played an important part in the historical development of Greece, Rome, Europe, and in an emerging America. Religious thought and political movements have primarily been expressed to the public through the use of speech.

There are many benefits to taking a course in communication. This course will help to make you a better day-to-day communicator; make it easier to express yourself in class; help you to get a job; make you more successful in your career; and will encourage you to accept new challenges.

Most people get nervous when thinking about speaking to the public. However, nervousness is normal, since about 80% of all Americans have some feelings of nervousness when communicating with others. We get nervous because our body sends us messages, because we feel we're the center of attention, because we think we're shy, and because we're afraid we won't meet our listener's expectations. We should try to use our nervousness to our advantage. We can do this by being prepared, rehearsing, becoming familiar with our surroundings, thinking positively, being ready to speak, appearing confident, thinking of communicating, and most of all—by being ourselves.

Ethics are important in communication. Ethical communicators are honest with their listeners, concerned for their welfare, and conscious of their vulnerabilities. We can practice ethical communicating by demonstrating good will, presenting a complete message, being responsible, and respecting our listeners.

EXERCISES FOR REVIEW

1. Choose a political, religious, or social movement in history and write a short essay on how speech communication played an important role in its development. Be prepared to discuss this in class.
2. Prepare a list of ten reasons why being a good communicator will help you in your career. Likewise, list ten reasons why being a poor communicator could hinder you in your career.
3. Write a 200 word paper on what happens to you when you get nervous. Do your knees shake, does your voice quiver, do you sweat a lot, and so on. Then assess the reasons why you get

nervous and why your body reacts as it does. You may find it helpful to meet with a group of four or five classmates to discuss your concerns and the way these nervous mannerisms can be overcome.

4. Be prepared to take part in a class discussion on the reasons why communicators get nervous. Particularly be ready to answer the following questions: How is the fear felt by a communicator the same as that felt by a parachute jumper? How is it different? How does the fear of speaking in public compare with the tension felt by an athlete before a big game? How is it different? Why are many successful actors and actresses able to play a role but find it difficult to speak in public?

5. Form a group called *"Nervous Anonymous"* with several classmates. Meet when needed and share concerns over the anxiety of speaking before others. Particularly discuss ways to defeat nervousness in steps—starting with something quite simple and working up to presenting a full-fledged speech.

NOTES

1. Although it is impossible to know the exact date that humans began to speak, it is generally presumed to be one million years ago. This particular theory has been expressed by many anthropologists, for instance Ernest Mayr of Harvard.

2. Jesus communicated by teaching the parables and the gathering of 12 disciples; Gautama Buddha journeyed up and down the Ganges Valley in Northern India building up teaching monastic orders, their message was transmitted orally by disciples as, *"Thus, I have heard;"* Mohammed taught his message persuasively from Mecca to Taif and Yathrid, doing his most persuasive speaking at Medina. All three movements were begun with oral, not written communications.

3. Adolf Hitler, *Mein Kampf*, Houghton Mifflin, New York, 1971, pp. 106–107. Actually Hitler came under some criticism for this statement in volume 1 and went into further detail concerning the power of speaking over writing in all great movements in volume 2, pages 469–477. Hitler particularly illustrates his point with the examples of the French Revolution and communist revolution in Russia; for instance, stating that it was not the *Communist Manifesto* by Karl Marx, but the speaking of Lenin and Trotsky which furthered the revolution to the masses. Hitler's view might best be illustrated by his own movement however; Otto Strasser recounts in his book, *Hitler and I*, that he once inquired of Hitler's top henchmen whether they had read *Mein Kampf*, the so-called Nazi bible: Goebbels, Goering, and all others present admitted they had not. Most historians concur that while *Mein Kampf* was the second largest selling book in German history, it was never read by more than a few thousand people.

4. For a summary of these findings, see Douglas B. Hoehn, *A Survey of Speech Courses* (New York: New York University, 1978).

5. For a summary of several studies that support this conclusion, see A.R. Weitzel and Paul C. Gaske, "An Appraisal of Communication Career-Related Research," *Communication Education* 33 (April, 1984), pp. 181–194.

6. Estimates vary as to the exact number; however, in our present oral society this seems like a reasonable prediction. Paul Soper, *Basic Public Speaking*, Oxford University Press, New York, 1963, p. 8.

7. The studies cited are just two of many which support this view. See D.H. Swenson, "Relative Importance of Business Communication Skills for the Next Ten Years," *Journal of Business Communication* 17 (1980), pp. 41–49 and M.S. Kessler, "Communicating Within and Without: The Work of Communication Specialists in American Corporations," *Association for Communication Administration Bulletin* 35 (1981), pp. 45–47.

8. For a sampling of some of this research see S.L. Becker and L.R. Ekdom, "That Forgotten Basic Skill," *Association for Communication Administration Bulletin* 33 (1980), pp. 12–25; V. DiSalvo, D.C. Larson and W.J. Seiler, "Communication Skills Needed by Persons in Business Organizations," *Communication Education* 25 (1976), pp. 269–282; H. Jaffe, "Symposium on the Legal Profession," *Newark Star Ledger* (October 21, 1984), p. 15; and William R. Kimel and Melford E. Monsees, "Engineering Graduates; How Good Are They? " *Engineering Education* (November, 1979), pp. 210–212.

9. These speaking opportunities included union meetings, church gatherings, day-care centers, bowling banquets, and driver-safety classes. See Kathleen Kendall, "Do Real People Ever Give Speeches?" *Central States Speech Journal* (Fall, 1974), p. 233–235.

10. Speaker nervousness is also referred to as stage fright, speech anxiety, and communication apprehension. For a definition and thorough discussion of speaker nervousness see, Joe Ayres, "Perceptions of Speaking Ability: An Explanation for Stage Fright," *Communication Education* 35 (July, 1986), pp. 275–287.

11. Bruskins Associates, "What Are Americans Afraid of?" *The Bruskin Report: A Market Research Newsletter* 53 (July, 1973).

12. This figure is supported by several studies which consistently show that between 70 and 85 percent of the public suffer from some degree of speaker nervousness. For the cited 80 percent figure see Amy Mereson, "When All Eyes Are On You: Stage Fright Is Surprisingly Common—and Surprisingly Treatable," *Science Digest* (May, 1985), p. 21.

13. This is known as the James-Lange theory of emotion. This theory suggests that a heightening of emotion leads to a perception of fear. Once the mind reaches a state of fear, the body responds, which in turn, causes an even increased sense of disorder.

14. Temperamentally shy people (naturally inhibited people) have a tougher time overcoming nervousness than those who become shy during adolescence. Most of the work studying shys comes from the work of Jerome Kagan of Harvard and Philip Zimbardo of Stanford. The conclusions stated are drawn from J.K. Burgoon and J.L. Hale, "A Research Note of the Dimensions of Communication Reticence," *Com-

munication Quarterly 37 (1983), pp. 238–248 and S.R. Glazer, "Oral Communication Apprehension and Avoidance: The Current Status of Treatment Research," *Communication Education* 30 (1981), pp. 321–341.

15. This is premised on the psychological therapy called desensitization. With this therapy you defeat a fear one step at a time. For instance if afraid of speaking in public you might first watch others deliver a speech, then deliver a speech to an empty room, next stand in front of an audience without speaking, and last deliver a speech. This therapy has proven successful with people suffering from speech phobias.

16. This a value judgement on the part of the author; indeed what is one person's terrorist is another's patriot. The standard used for the present volume interprets good or evil based on the ultimate consequences of the speaker's actions. This can be classified as a utilitarian or teleological view of ethical behavior— the result or probable outcome of the message determines its ethical qualities. Obviously this determination could change with a different time, different place, or different author.

Name _____   Course _____

Test of Knowledge

Circle the correct true or false answer for each question:

1. T F Most of our communication time is spent listening.

2. T F An extemporaneous speech is one given with no preparation.

3. T F A good tension reliever when speaking in public is to hold a pen or paper clip.

4. T F The study of speech communication dates back to ancient times.

5. T F We can comprehend (listen) at a faster rate than we can speak.

6. T F It is important to consider time limits when preparing a speech.

7. T F How you say something is more important than what you say.

8. T F Most actors and experienced public speakers have some nervousness before speaking before an audience.

9. T F When preparing a speech your first step should be to prepare an outline.

10. T F First impressions are very important in interviews.

11. T F Eye contact is important in all interpersonal interactions.

12. T F The average American spends more time reading than writing.

13. T F Gestures can help to bring out what you want to say.

14. T F The proper way to close a speech is to say "I thank you."

15. T F Effective communicators are born, not made.

16. T F Feedback should have no effect on the way we communicate with our listeners.

17. T F Most Americans spend about 70% of their waking time communicating with others.

18. T F All messages either inform or entertain.

19. T F Research shows that communication is essential for most lines of work.

20. T F The greatest fear of most Americans is the fear of snakes.

(correct answers are provided in the Appendix)

The World of Communication

All of us communicate many times each day.

Before reading this chapter, ask yourself the following questions:

1. What are the three purposes of communication?
2. What are the four levels of communication?
3. How can I define the word "communication?"

Sound

Many kinds of animals communicate with sounds. You have probably heard, for instance, the songs of birds in spring. Male birds, such as these two song sparrows, establish breeding territories by singing. Each male bird perches in his territory and sings for hours. His song warns rivals away from his territory. The song also attracts females.

Sight

Some animals use visual signals. Fireflies' bodies produce light. Each male firefly flies through the air blinking his light in a series of flashes. Every species, or kind, of firefly has a different pattern of blinks. The female stays on the ground and blinks when she sees the right pattern from a male. Males fly to females that respond to their signal. Then they mate.

Touch

Many animals that live in groups, such as baboons, rely on touch as one important way of communicating. Adults, as well as young animals, spend many hours a day grooming one another. In grooming, the animals clean dirt and parasites from each other's fur. The touch of grooming strengthens bonds among the animals.

Smell

Animals send many different messages with body odors. Some odors serve as warnings. For example, when a mother mule deer sees an enemy and becomes frightened, she bounds away. At the same time, she releases alarm scents from glands on her legs (arrows, small picture). The strong odors immediately tell her fawns to begin running after her.

Figure 2.1
Ways Animals Communicate. (Permission granted by *National Geographic World* [Washington, D.C.] February 1985, Number 114, p. 26. Artist: Dorothy Michelle Novick.)

HOW ANIMALS COMMUNICATE

Every living creature uses some form of communication. Animals communicate through the use of sounds, positions, movements, appearance, expressions and the like to send messages such as, *"Leave me alone!" "Stay away!" "Come closer!" "I need help!"* or *"Follow me in this direction!"* More elaborate messages include information such as, *"Fly south with me until I turn due east"* or *"Swim in a northeastern direction until we reach a new feeding supply."*

The very survival of a species is dependent upon a keen sense of communication. Non-human animals generally use communication to attract or repel and to maintain some form of social organization. Accurate communication allows for an informational exchange which permits a species to select its subsequent activities with a greater degree of certainty. This process allows animals to survive and prosper within their respective environments.

Animals communicate using a range of methods for a variety of purposes. Tree toads frequently send sounds which indicate mating. Crickets and grasshoppers produce sounds by rubbing one body part against another to signify a desire for mating or combat.[1] Birds use flight patterns to specify rank and status

The Dance of Bees

Bees communicate by conducting a "dance" to impart information to other bees of the hive. The type of dance the bee does dictates to member bees the general distance to the located food source. The dance consists of wagging or rounded which indicates distance, the frequency of turning which indicates distance in terms of direction, and vigor of the dance which indicates the richness of the food source.

The bee indicates the direction of the food source from the hive by using the sun. The bee dances so that the horizontal line which connects the two halves of the dance hits the rays of the sun at the same angle that the rays of the sun hit the line connecting the hive with the food supply. In this way fellow bees know exactly the angle to fly so as to locate the food source. If there is an obstacle between the line and the food source (say a tree) directional signals are given.

Bees also communicate about where a new hive can be located. When a new hive is needed scouts go out and search for a new hivesite. When a homesite is located the scout bee returns and does a dance to communicate the advantages of the site. Other scouts also report back with their findings. Considerations include the size of the home, the protection it affords from wind and rain, and the availability of a food supply. Since there is only one queen all bees must agree on which hive-site to select, were the bees to split up only those with the queen would survive. Therefore, a dance serves as a debate with each bee imparting essential information and advantages of each site. When all factors are considered only one site is agreed upon and all bees depart for the new location.

---

and remain in perfect flying formation even when shifting direction.

Most of the communication used by non-human animals is **species-specific**. This means that messages are intended for individuals within the same species; any flow of communication to other species is irrelevant. Some species of birds use songs to communicate that they are males, are in a breeding condition, and are unmated so that female birds will form a pair-bond with the male. Vocal displays used by geese usually precede flight and inform other members of the family to depart as a unit. Birds migrating in flocks use signals to inform one another of their position in the night sky, so other members of the flock can compensate for possible navigational errors. Studies have shown that vocalizations made by hatching baby chicks influence the rate of the hatching of sibling chicks so that all may hatch simultaneously. The return call of a female nocturnal frog indicates whether she has laid her eggs or is ready for breeding.

Appearance is equally important in the animal kingdom. To the average human being all seagulls look very much the same. However, other gulls are able to distinguish species by a combination of eye color and the degree of contrast with a white head.

Female birds of many species are less distinctively colored than males, because it is the female who only selects a mate with the correct plumage.

Dolphins are especially noted for their intelligence and ability to communicate. Dolphins are mentioned in stories from early Grecian times to the present for heroic deeds in the rescuing of maritime travelers. Research shows that dolphins acutely send and receive messages through ultrasonic pulses.[2] This allows them to catch fish in murky water or to make fine discriminations of objects even when blindfolded.

Some of the most interesting communication is that of ants. All 8,000 species of ants are **social in habit** which means that they live together in organized colonies. Within a colony the workers are females who do the work of the nest, while larger males defend the colony as soldiers. Each colony consists of three castes—queens, males, and workers. Messages are sent by tapping a complex series of codes with antennae. Information that is communicated includes role, status, and assignments. Ants also send messages by secreting pheromones forming a trail by leaving an odor. The odor trail communicates to other ants whether they are to follow it for a food supply or to escape danger. Pheromones left for a

Teaching Primates to Talk

In many behavioral patterns chimpanzees are the most similar to man of all non-humans. However, despite many noble experiments, most attempts to get chimps to talk have met with failure. Recently several people have had at least minimal success in teaching chimpanzees to speak.

The Kelloggs were the first couple to record their efforts to teach a chimp to talk. The Kelloggs raised Gua, a 7 1/2 month old chimp with their son Donald who was 9 1/2 months old. Gua was treated just like Donald with no special effort made to teach her to speak. Gua did learn to produce several different sounds to mean different things. Also, she did manage to comprehend 70 different sentences. At one point she even surpassed Donald in her understanding of sentences. But Gua could never understand sentences that she was not explicitly taught. Donald, on the other hand, like most human children, could comprehend these sentences and soon surpassed her.

Thinking that raising a chimp practically from birth might make a difference, the Hayes bought the chimp Viki home at only 6 weeks. Viki was treated like a special child and was given specific lessons in language. Viki learned to speak three words and could make many utterances. However, that was the limit of Viki's language development.

The most advanced of all chimp learning in language occurred with Sarah. Sarah was taught by psychologist David Premack. Premack taught Sarah language by using plastic pieces which would stick to a magnetic board. Each piece corresponded to a word. In learning the language Sarah had to place the correct piece representing a word as she would if it were a sentence. Thus, if she wanted a banana Sarah had to choose the proper piece that represented a banana and place it on the board. Sarah is reported to have learned 21 verbs, 8 people's names, 6 colors, and 27 concepts (table, key etc.). She was also able to learn several complex sentences. The most significant of her accomplishments was to learn the meaning of "the name of." By this knowledge Sarah could learn countless names since she understood what she was being taught. It is hoped by Premack that Sarah could then pass down this information to her offspring.

Most experts conclude that despite these worthwhile experiments chimps are limited in what they can learn in language. This is thought to be so because they are unable to physiologically produce the sounds necessary for speech. Intellectual ability may also be a factor, however. The chimp Washoe was taught not speech, but sign language. He was able to learn 300 two word signs but that was the limit and the experiment had to be abandoned.

Gorillas may have a somewhat greater potential for language development than chimpanzees. The 12 year old gorilla Koko has been taught over 500 words in sign language and has the intelligence of a 3 year old child. More significant than language ability, gorillas may have the capacity to understand more complex concepts.

In 1983 Koko communicated in sign language that she wanted a pet. Animal trainer Penny Patterson first gave her stuffed pets which Koko ignored until she was given her choice of a new litter of kittens. Koko chose one kitten without a tail and carried it around with her as if it were a baby. Koko named her kitten "All Ball."

Unfortunately, in January 1985, Koko's kitten was run over by a car and she had to be told of the death. When informed of the tragedy Koko cried actual tears for over two days. Dr. Ron Cohn, secretary of the Gorrilla Foundation in Wood-side, California, believes that Koko understood the concept of death after seeing some dead birds several years before.

trail to escape danger evaporate much sooner than those leading to a food source.

Monkeys and apes communicate to indicate travel, relationships, and behavior. Female rhesus monkeys receive signals on their hands with specialized touches from the male. Among chimpanzees and apes a leader settles disputes within the group and decides upon travel distance and direction for that day. Primates also have intricate social hierarchies which define status and privilege.

But, regardless of how complicated the communication of even the highest primates, it is simple when compared to that of human beings.

HUMAN COMMUNICATION

Every organism needs communication to adapt to its environment. When a species has failed to develop a working system of communication, it has become extinct. Many social scientists speculate that primitive human beings created speech as a result of their need to quickly send messages so as to pool their intellectual and physical resources. People, therefore, have been communicating since the earliest roots of civilization.

Speech is a method of communication **unique to human beings**. While animals send messages in many forms, none use speech. Animal sounds which superficially resemble human speech, such as words mimicked by parrots, are strictly imitations of sounds and not speech. Those members of the animal kingdom which come closest to being genetically similar to human, the primates, have proven highly resistant to the acquisition of speech.

The chief difference between human and animal communication is that animals **vocalize** but only human beings can **verbalize**. Vocalizing can be done by most animals and includes yelps, grunts, growls, songs, calls, moans, and the like. Verbalization, on the other hand, includes sound symbols in the form of words. Consequently, only humans can transfer opinions, judgments, attitudes, and abstract thoughts.

Anthropologists have generally concurred that human beings passed through a vocalization stage early in our development. It was not until humans were able to verbalize words that they became clearly superior to other animal forms. This enabled humans to pass on stored knowledge to succeeding generations, called **time-binding**.

Figure 2.2
Humans and animals both share a need to communicate.

Time-binding is unique to human beings. When an animal dies, only essential survival information is passed forward, all else is lost forcing each generation to learn anew this information. Humans, on the other hand, are able to build upon their store of information with each new generation. Libraries serve as excellent examples of this stored knowledge.

Humans communicate in many different ways. We send messages through gestures, facial expressions, vocal intonations, tone, language, movements and the like. However, with every message—regardless of how sophisticated, we must have a purpose.

PURPOSE OF COMMUNICATION

Every message that we elect to send has a single primary purpose: to **inform**, to **persuade**, or to **entertain**. When our purpose is to inform we attempt to teach someone about something new. College instructors do this every day. For instance we might give a stranger directions, teach a friend chess, or coach a classmate for an upcoming test. When our purpose is persuasive we try to convince someone else to our point of view. Fund raisers, political candidates, and sales personnel do this all the time. We might try to persuade a friend to see a movie we enjoyed, talk a professor into a higher grade, or convince a police officer not to give us a ticket. When our purpose is to entertain we seek to delight and bring pleasure to others. Any standup comedian tries to accomplish this. We might entertain others with anecdotal stories, tell a classmate a joke, or imitate a funny voice to make a child laugh.

Sometimes our **purposes may merge**. We might, for example, tell some friends about the fun ski trip we took last weekend, try to convince them to join the ski club, and entertain them with colorful stories all at the same time. However the key to remember is that we should always have one main reason, or purpose for every message. For once we clearly understand our purpose, we can go about preparing our message in the most effective way possible. Now that we understand the purpose of every communication, let's see how we get it across.

COMMUNICATION SITUATIONS

Most of our "communication life" will be spent interacting with others in three arenas. These include **social contexts**, **work situations**, and in **public forums**. Here's a review of each.

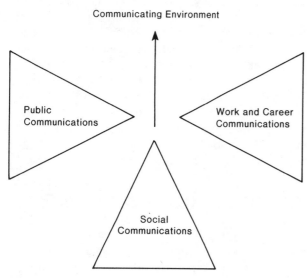

Figure 2.3
The World of Communication.

Social Situations

A good portion of our interactions will be with others in social situations. We have conversations with friends, share the latest gossip, or ask an important question. Sometimes this includes communicating with total strangers, anything from visiting with another rider on the bus to buying a newspaper from the man on the corner. While most of the messages shared in this context tend to be rather simple, it's important to get our ideas across clearly, without misinterpretation. One could argue that the essence of living itself is linked with our ability to socially interact with others.

Figure 2.4
All of our personal relationships and friendships are based on our ability to communicate with others.

Work Situations

Chances are a great portion of our lives will be spent in our work environment. One estimate suggests that most people spend one quarter of their lives at their place of business. How important is our communication at work? Research shows that our ability to communicate is tied to our promotions, income, happiness, and general contentment.[3]

The world of work is a world of discussions, conversations, presentations, reports, and directives. Whether we like it or not, almost any career that we choose will require spoken communication.

Public Situations

Public communication means speaking before a group of other people. This can range from giving a speech to addressing a panel of fellow discussants. Many people find public communication as the most stressful, and least natural. But even though it can be considered the most difficult, speaking before others presents great opportunities. In public communication we get the chance to instruct, to change views, and to entertain large groups of people. Probably few things will be as memorable in our lives as the messages we send in a public forum.

LEVELS OF COMMUNICATION

Just as we communicate in different situations, we communicate on different levels. For the purpose of this book, we will categorize the four levels as **intrapersonal, interpersonal, public**, and **mass communication**. Let's take a look at each.

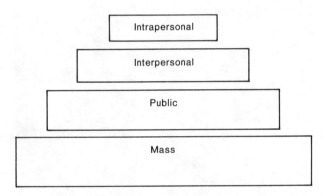

Figure 2.5
The Four Levels of Communication. Each level of communication involves more individuals playing the role of the receiver.

Intrapersonal Communication

Intrapersonal communication means **communicating within oneself**. This is the process which includes our taking in raw data from observation and experience and interpreting it according to our view of the world. Consequently, since no two of us are alike, no two of us will interpret the same occurrence in exactly the same way.

How do we communicate intrapersonally? One way is to daydream. We do this hundreds of times a day, most of the time not even realizing that this is what we are doing. In addition, every day we sort out all sorts of interests and fantasies by thinking them through.

Figure 2.6
When we daydream or think to ourselves, we are engaging in intrapersonal communication.

Intrapersonal communication is the foundational level of all communication. Without first communicating within ourselves, we would be unable to communicate to others. Once messages are digested internally, we are prepared to share some of our thoughts and ideas with the outside world. Here are two important factors to remember about intrapersonal communication:

1. *It occurs entirely within the person; no one else can take part in the interaction.*
2. *It is the first level that must be reached before any subsequent communication can take place.*

Interpersonal Communication

Interpersonal communication means **interacting with a small group** of other people. This could include a conversation with one, to a discussion with half a dozen people. In order for true interpersonal communication to take place each person must be directly engaged in the conversation. Talking to a friend about your weekend plans is a form of interpersonal communication; so is discussing the food in the cafeteria with several classmates.

One major advantage of interpersonal communication is that it allows for immediate feedback. We can quickly see if our ideas are getting across. Likewise, interpersonal communication allows us to personalize our messages—we can refer to people by name or refer to a common experience. Here are three points to remember about interpersonal communication:

1. *It can only occur with one other person or a small group of about six people or less.*
2. *It lets us personalize our messages and permits immediate feedback.*
3. *It must be direct, person-to-person interaction.*

Public Communication

Public communication is when we communicate to a **large group of people**. In order for this to occur only one person can be the speaker, and everyone else must be listeners. A public speech is a perfect example of public communication. Another ingredient of public communication is that all listeners must have some physical proximity to the speaker. In other words, listening to a speech over television would not be public communication, while listening to one in an auditorium would be.

A major disadvantage of public communication is that it does not allow us to personalize our message. After all, it would be very difficult to name every person in an audience numbering in the hundreds. Similarly, public communication allows for little adjustment to audience feedback. While some fine-tuning can take place, it is certainly more difficult than in a direct face-to-face conversation. Finally, in public communication delivery and preparedness are far more important than in interpersonal communication. Here are some major points to bear in mind:

1. *It must include one person speaking to a large group of listeners.*
2. *All listeners must have some physical proximity to the speaker.*
3. *It allows for little adjustment and personalization.*

Mass Communication

The last level of communication is mass communication, which means the **mass distribution of identical copies of the same message** to people unknown by the communicator. When the President speaks over television, it is an example of mass communication. Many times communications are mass produced and are heard or seen by people far into the future. This would include video copies of speeches, books, movies, magazines and the like.

When we send messages through mass communication we have no control over who hears or sees our message. This allows for no feedback. Likewise audiences that witness the communication have little in common. Many times in public com-

Figure 2.7
Oftentimes, mass communications involves the sending or receiving of a message through an electronic signal.

Figure 2.8
One way people send messages is through music.

munication audiences gather for a common concern or reason; this is often not the case in mass communication. Finally, mass communication allows for no personalization whatsoever.

Frequently mass communication is not in spoken words, but is in the form of pictures, paintings, theatre, music, or dance. While mass communication allots the communicator the least control, it also provides the opportunity for greatest impact.

Here are some things to keep in mind about mass communication:

1. *It allows for an audience of unlimited size.*
2. *It gives the communicator no control over who sees or hears the message.*
3. *It allows a message to be heard many times over.*

Now that we understand the levels of communication, let's take a look at the characteristics of all messages.

CHARACTERISTICS OF COMMUNICATION

There are six basic characteristics of communication which are based on the propositions of Dean Barnlund.[4] While they are largely applicable to interpersonal communication, they can also be employed to the four levels of communication just discussed.

The six characteristics include: (1) **communication is dynamic**; (2) **communication is continuous**; (3) **communication is circular**; (4) **communication is unrepeatable**; (5) **communication is irreversible**; and (6) **communication is complex**. Let's examine each in turn.

1. **Communication is Dynamic.** The process of communication is ongoing and ever-moving. When we examine the way people communicate we recognize that communication never stands still, but is in a constant state of change. A communicative act cannot be studied like a portrait, rather to be truly appreciated it must be experienced firsthand.
2. **Communication is Continuous.** There is never a clear beginning or ending to a communicated message. Although we may stop and review the process, in reality it must continue to flow to really be understood.
3. **Communication is Circular.** When two people communicate, one does not just send messages and the other receive them. Rather each person influences the other. While only one may be speaking, the other will be returning nonverbal cues which impart information. Therefore both participants are sending and receiving information at the same time.
4. **Communication is Unrepeatable.** Once something is said it can never be precisely imitated. No matter how many times it may be repeated, it can never recapture the magic it held at the moment of delivery. This is because no two people or situations are ever exactly the same.[5]

5. **Communication is Irreversible.** Once something is said it is done. Some processes can be reversed. For example water can be frozen into ice and then thawed back to water again. This is a reversible system. Communication, however, is irreversible in that once something is said it can be amended, but never completely retracted.
6. **Communication is Complex.** The process of communication includes numerous components. Every communicative act possesses different purposes, is spoken in a different context, includes different messages, and involves different communicators. This is why communication is among the most difficult processes to study.

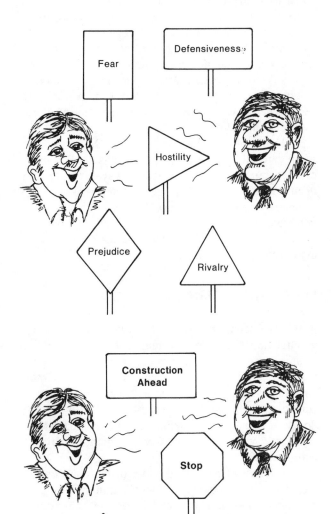

Figure 2.9
Barriers to Communication. Anything that interferes with the proper reception of our messages is a barrier to communication.

BARRIERS TO COMMUNICATION

What is a barrier? It's something that **stands in the way of effective communication.** Barriers come in all sizes, forms and shapes. They can take place through prejudice, hostility, rivalry, fear, defensiveness, confusion, misunderstandings, and so on. Sometimes barriers are perfectly innocent. Let's say you ask a woman for directions to Third Street, but she thinks you said Third Avenue. An innocent error, but a barrier to effective communication nevertheless—if you doubt this, just think how you would feel after driving two miles in the wrong direction! Sometimes, however, barriers are more intentional. We may not listen to someone who seems too young, or too old, or looks too disheveled, or appears too untrustworthy. Barriers sometimes occur out of downright bigotry or close-mindedness. We might turn someone off who is from a certain ethnic group, from another race, who speaks with a certain accent, or is from another neighborhood. Regardless of the reason, barriers are usually needless and always get in the way of effective communication.

How do we overcome barriers? One way is to listen carefully, an entire chapter in this book is dedicated to just that skill. Another way is to remain open-minded—avoid prejudgments and making snap decisions about other people. Finally, try and phrase your questions and answers as precisely as you can. An articulate, organized communicator does a lot to avoid setting up potential barriers.

DEFINING COMMUNICATION

In this chapter we've come a long way toward getting a better understanding of communication. We have a clearer sense of how animals communicate, we know the major differences between animal and human communication, and we have a firmer grasp on how communication occurs. But one thing we still need to do is to work out a definition of communication. After all, what does the word **"communication"** really mean?

Authorities have long debated this question. In fact, there are probably as many definitions as there are authorities! But for the purpose of this course let's define communication in this way: **Communication is the process whereby a sender sends a message to a receiver with the intention of achieving a desired response.**

What does this definition tell us? First, it reminds us that communication is a process. Second, it lets us know that in order for communication to take place there must be a sender and a receiver. And third, it makes clear that every message should reach

a desired outcome. While this provides a good working definition for this class, following are ten additional definitions taken from speech experts. Read and rank them, one to ten, one being the best in your opinion, ten the worst.

10 Definitions of Communication

1. ____ "In its broadest perspective, communication occurs whenever an individual assigns significance or meaning to an internal or external stimulus."

2. ____ "A communicates B through channel C to D with effect E. Each of these letters is to some extent an unknown and the process can be solved for any one of them or any combination."

3. ____ "Communication means that information is passed from one place to another."

4. ____ ". . . The process of sending and receiving messages. . . . In the sense used here, the word 'message' does not mean 'idea' or 'thought' or 'information,' it means only the physical signals (ordinarily light waves and air pressure waves) transmitted between message-sender and message-receiver."

5. ____ "All communication proceeds by means of signs, with which one organism affects the behavior of another (or more generally the state of another).

6. ____ "The word communication will be used here in a very broad sense to include all of the procedures by which one mind may affect another. This, of course, involves not only written and oral speech but also music, the pictorial arts, the theatre, the ballet, and in fact all behavior."

7. ____ "When someone gains certain impressions of someone else the latter is communicating something to the former . . . the man who allows junk to accumulate in his front yard communicates something to his neighbor whether he knows it or not."

8. ____ "Communication does not refer to verbal, explicit, and intentional transmission of messages alone. The concept of communication would include all those processes by which people influence one another. This definition is based upon the premise that all actions and events have communicative aspects, as soon as they are perceived by a human being; it implies, furthermore, that such perception changes the information which an in-

dividual possesses and therefore influences him.''

9. ____ "This definition says that communication occurs when some environmental disturbance impinges on an organism and the organism does something about it. If the stimulus is ignored by the organism, there has been no communication.''

10. ____ "Communication is the assignation of meaningfulness or significance to one's perception of an arbitrary sign.''

As you can see, each of these definitions paints communication in a slightly different way. Do you like a broad definition, one that brings in all behavior? Or do you like a narrower, more precise definition which limits the way we view communicative behavior? Whatever your view, be prepared to discuss your ideas in class. If you wish to see how your rankings compare with those of one hundred communication experts, turn to the appendix at the end of this book where their answers are listed.

CHAPTER SUMMARY

Every living creature uses some form of communication. Animals communicate through the use of sounds, positions, movements, appearance, expressions, and so on. Of all animals, primates come the closest to duplicating human beings in their ability to communicate.

Speech is a method of communication unique to human beings. While many animals can vocalize, only humans can verbalize. Verbalizing means putting thoughts and ideas into words. Every message that we send has one of three purposes: to inform, to persuade, or to entertain.

We communicate in three basic situations. These include social situations, work situations, and public situations. The four levels of communication include intrapersonal communication, interpersonal communication, public communication, and mass communication.

The six characteristics of communication are that communication is dynamic, continuous, circular, unrepeatable, irreversible and complex. Any obstacle to effective communication is called a communication barrier. Barriers can be perfectly innocent, or can be caused by intentional or closed-minded actions. While communication is difficult to define, our working definition is: Communication is the process whereby a sender sends a message to a receiver with the intention of achieving a desired response.

EXERCISES FOR REVIEW

1. Pick a non-human animal and research the way it communicates. Write some of the pertinent facts down and come to class prepared to discuss the animal's communication, including how it adapts to its environment.

2. Write a 200 word paper on one of the following three questions: What affect has time-binding had on the development of world civilization? How has time-binding directly affected your life? Do you think that time-binding is the single major distinction between the development of humans and primates? Also be prepared to discuss in class your answer to the question you've chosen.

3. Cut out pictures and advertisements from magazines which depict each of the four levels of communication. Bring them to class and show each picture explaining how it serves as an example for that level of communication.

4. On a sheet of paper draw three columns; label column one *Social Situations*, column two *Work Situations*; and column three *Public Situations*. For each of the cases listed below, note in which column it would most likely occur in your life. Be prepared to discuss your answers in class.
   a. *asking for a ride to work*
   b. *telling a friend you like her new dress*
   c. *accidentally dialing a wrong number*
   d. *ordering at a restaurant*
   e. *asking a coworker how you should ask for a raise*
   f. *discussing last nights ball game on the bus to college*
   g. *yelling at an umpire at a baseball game*
   h. *presenting a book report in class*
   i. *talking to a classmate about a missed assignment*
   j. *yelling at the driver of a car that just cut you off*

5. Re-enact a communication event with another class member. Incorporate some barriers that occur in everyday life into your transaction. Have other class members pick out the barriers and then discuss why they occur.

NOTES

1. This is called stridulation.
2. This is referred to as echolocation.
3. This information can be found in N. Ochsner and C. Lewis, *College Education and Employment—The Recent Graduates* (Bethlehem, Pa.: The College Placement Foundation, 1979).
4. Dean C. Barnlund, *Interpersonal Communication: Survey and Studies* (Boston: Houghton Mifflin Co., 1968).
5. Linguists refer to this as novel communications.

COMMUNICATION FACTS

Mating of the Wolf Spider

The male wolf spider is engaged in a risky business when it comes to mating with a female. If he fails to understand his communication accurately the results will be deadly. When the male is ready to mate he charges his palpi and begins to look for a female. When he comes across the silken thread left by the female (she drags this behind her) he checks the odor to make sure she is a wolf spider and then follows it. Danger occurs when he reaches her—for the female wolf spider is extremely dangerous; she will pounce on anything near her that moves and kill it. If the male is not very careful, this will happen to him unless he is able to communicate effectively.

When he overtakes her the male keeps just out of her reach and begins a dance of identification. In this rhythmic dance he throws his front legs up in movements and moves in an alternating dance fashion. He continues to stomp his legs as he gets ever closer to the female. As he becomes more excited the hairs on his front legs become erect and he moves closer to the female. Gradually, the female becomes more receptive until the male is able to touch the female. Eventually she allows him to insert the palpi and the mating occurs.

Should the male move close to the female too soon the female will attack and kill him immediately. Therefore, the male wolf spider must use effective communication with his rhythmic dance or he will lose his life!

Communication Stress Test

Answer each question by circling a yes or no response; generally, the most accurate results are achieved if you put down your immediate answer to each question without spending a great deal of time thinking about it.

1. YES NO   I give and receive affection from others regularly.

2. YES NO   I don't try to evade conversations with others.

3. YES NO   I consider myself to be in good to excellent health.

4. YES NO   I go out of my way to meet new people.

5. YES NO   I am the appropriate weight for my height and age.

6. YES NO   I usually am the first person to say hello to someone I meet in passing.

7. YES NO   I have a broad network of friends with whom I am acquainted.

8. YES NO   I have at least one very close personal friend.

9. YES NO   When I drive or ride in a car I notice that other drivers are more aggressive than I am.

10. YES NO   I talk on the telephone at least 5 times a week.

11. YES NO   If someone else is in the house I usually let them answer the telephone when it rings.

12. YES NO   I enjoy discussing current events with others.

13. YES NO   I seldom sit alone when I go to the movies.

14. YES NO   I enjoy background noise when I work.

15. YES NO   When the doorbell rings I usually let someone else answer it.

16. YES NO   I would prefer to live in a heavily populated area rather than in the country.

17. YES NO   I am able to speak openly about my thoughts and feelings.

18. YES NO   I regularly attend club and social meetings.

19. YES NO   I usually sit near or next to other students in class or people at work.

20. YES NO   I have daily conversations with the people I live with.

21. YES NO   I exercise regularly.

22. YES NO   I do not smoke more than a couple of cigarettes a day.

23. YES NO   I never have an alcoholic drink before I meet someone.

24.   YES   NO   I drink less than two cups of coffee (or cola) a day.

25.   YES   NO   I have no trouble falling asleep at night.

Count the number of yes answers; the more yes answers the less vulnerable you are to communication stress. Compare your responses with the scale below:

  20 or more yes answers   -   Low Stress

  19 to 15 yes answers   -   Average Stress

  14 to 10 yes answers   -   High Stress

  9 or fewer yes answers   -   Very High Stress

Communicating 10,000 Years in the Future

In 1982 the United States passed the Nuclear Waste Policy Act which necessitated the planning of huge underground waste dumps where the deadly byproducts of nuclear-power and weapons plants could be isolated. During this planning the Department of Energy considered nine sites in six states where the radioactive garbage could be stored. Since the material will remain toxic for 10,000 years, the Department of Energy created a special 13 member panel in 1980 to explore how future inhabitants of the earth might be protected from hazardous waste sites. The Human Interference Task Force was composed of linguists, psychologists, anthropologists, engineers, and nuclear physicists. The assignment of the task force was to come up with suggestions on how to communicate with the inhabitants of the earth in the 120th century.

The panel had to devise a way to communicate with human beings who would live 300 generations in the future. A significant difficulty for the panel was to consider the unpredictable ways that languages evolve; since any language used at that time would be virtually unintelligible to today's vernacular. One suggestion was to create a waste repository with raised earth barriers built around it in a triangular pattern. Within the wedge would be monument-like markers, as durable as the pyramids. These monolithic structures would bear triangular warning symbols or cartoons which would be very simple in design; as simple as the cave drawings by Cro-Magnon man 17,000 years ago. One suggested sequence would entail the drawing of three human beings standing by a well site; one of them drinks from a bubbling well and falls dead.

Thomas Sebeok, a professor of semiotics (the study of the relationship of signs in language) at Indiana State University had an intriguing proposal. Sebeok proposed an "atomic priesthood" to pass along rituals and legends which would explain dangers of these waste dumps. Such forms of communication would pass along for millenniums the message that to ignore the mandate would be tantamount to inviting some sort of supernatural disaster. Such a message would be conveyed by an example as the following triangular picture:

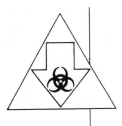

The task force cautioned that there is considerable controversy over the efficacy of spoken messages over many thousands of years. Historians have predicted that the oral transmissions are inaccurate conveyers of information over such a long period of time. However, the task force suggested further study on the problem.

How are we going to communicate with humans in 10,000 years? The task force designed to tackle this problem is still working to come up with something better. The one thing these experts have discovered is that it is no easy task.

The Process of Communication

Most people enjoy sharing their thoughts and feelings with others.

QUESTIONS FOR RETENTION

Before reading this chapter, ask yourself the following questions:

1. What does ''meaning'' mean in communication?
2. What are the eight elements of communication?
3. How is communication transactional?

In order to understand how communication operates as a process we must first become familiar with certain concepts. In this chapter we shall review the concept of meaning, the workings of the communication process, the elements in the process, the transactional nature of every communicative act, and the basics of communication models. In this way we will come to clearly understand the workings of this most complex system.

THE CONCEPT OF MEANING

Figure 3.1
All of us need to interact with those around us.

The art of communicating means *exchanging symbols* with other people. Symbols are words which people give different meanings to according to their own set of values, culture, and experience. For example, we might tell our employer that we'll be in late the next day, interpreting the word *"late"* to mean within one hour after our usual time. The employer, however, might interpret *"late"* to mean that we won't be in for several hours, necessitating the hiring of a temporary worker to take our place. Such confusions often occur in the world of communication.

Meaning also has a far more emotional connotation. When we say something the words we use can have many different meanings. Listeners assign meaning to our statements based upon their impressions of us. In other words, two people can say the exact same statement, and the same listener can assign two entirely different interpretations to the message. What could be considered a complement by one could be viewed as an insult by another. Many people who study communication explain this with the often

quoted statement, "Meanings are in people, not in words."[1]

How do our assignments of meaning vary? Theorists have determined that people assign meaning based chiefly upon their culture, social system, attitudes, knowledge, and experiences. We can easily see how culture leads to different interpretations. If someone were to spit in our face we would consider it a great insult. The Masai tribe of South Africa, however, would consider it a sign of affection for a member of the opposite sex. If the person spits back the affection is shared. In American society the social system in which we live gives different shades of meaning to the same word or term. In some communities the term *"the man"* means an adult male, in others the police, and still in others a person who leads a criminal group. Attitudes vary greatly with different people. Referring to someone as *"a jock"* can mean to some that the person is not very bright, while to others it just means an accomplished athlete. Certainly all of us vary in our knowledge on different issues. To a computer wiz *"a mouse"* has one meaning, to the rest of us it's just a rodent. Lastly, all of us share different experiences. What seems significant to one, might seem trivial to another.

What does all this tell us about communication? It means we must choose our words and examples carefully. It means to understand our listeners. And it means to always remember that words are powerful things which flash with a burst of energy. The right word used in the right place is perfect, the wrong word in the wrong place can be downright offensive. As effective communicators we should always try to create a *shared meaning* with our listeners. This means seeing the world as they see it, feel the sense of the moment as they feel it, and to understand an issue as they understand it. When this is accomplished we have successfully utilized meaning in our communicative interactions.

HOW COMMUNICATION WORKS AS A PROCESS

A process implies continuous change. As communicators our world, our experiences, our view of life changes every day. Our trip to college today was different than the same trip yesterday, and will never be quite the same again. A Greek philosopher, Heraclitus, recognized this four thousand years ago when he said, *"A man can never step in the same river twice."* The man has changed and is a different man, the river will never be exactly the same again.

We need to recognize, therefore, that the act of communicating is one of constant dynamic change. In order to deal with this change we must learn to adapt to each environment in which we send and receive messages. We do this every day. We don't speak to a child as we do to an adult, we don't interact with a stranger as we do with a friend, we don't treat a parent the same as a spouse. Consequently it's important to remember that by its very nature communication is an **adaptive process**.

Communication is also **systemic**. Communication works as a system in that numerous elements must all operate for the process to take place. If one element does not work, then the entire process is jeopardized. There are eight important elements involved in most communicative acts—we'll now take a look at each.

ELEMENTS IN THE COMMUNICATION PROCESS

Every communicative transaction includes four essential elements—a **sender**, a **receiver**, a **channel**, and a **message**. Four additional elements also can be added. These include **feedback, interference**, the **situation**, and **listener-to-listener communication**. As we review the elements in the process, we'll also build them into a model—a pictorial way of showing how communication takes place. Let's now review each in turn.

The Sender

All communication begins with the sender. When you communicate a message you don't just do it by your voice alone, but also with your nonverbal actions—expressions, movements, vocal tone, gestures and the like. All of these actions and reactions convey important information to your receivers. Effective senders don't just work alone, rather they work in tandem with their receivers. They react to the way their listeners smile, nod, and frown. When you receive this kind of information from your listeners you are also serving as a receiver.

The Receiver

The person who receives the message sent by the sender is the receiver. Receivers can vary in size—from one to several million listening to a television address. How your receivers interpret your message will determine its success or failure. This is why it's often said that every communicative act really takes place in the minds of your listeners. Good communicators are sensitive to the cues sent by their receivers. This means being **listener-centered**. If your listeners have a question, answer it; if they want more

detail, provide it; if they seem curious about a point, explain it. A listener-centered sender is an effective communicator.

The Channel

The channel is the medium used to send a message. Communicators use a variety of channels: television, radio, video tape, microphones, public address systems, and direct face-to-face interactions. Usually we speak without electronic assistance. You might, however, bring in other communicative channels—taste, touch, or smell. If demonstrating something, for example, you might have your listeners taste or touch it. By using a variety of channels you can often make a message more memorable and appealing, helping it to stick in the minds of your listeners. Once you've selected a channel, you'll need to create a message.

The Message

The message is the content of what you say to your listeners. As figure 3.2 shows, the message travels in a circular channel between sender and receiver. Messages are both intentional and unintentional. Intentional messages are what you intend to convey. Unintentional messages, on the other hand, are what you don't intend to convey, but what your listeners think you meant. Sometimes these unintentional messages can pose real problems for a communicator, since they belie the actual words used. Say, for instance, someone wishes to discuss the harm caused by the prolonged use of marijuana; but, while speaking shifts her eyes, smirks, and uses a sarcastic tone. As a listener you'd likely ask, *"What's she really saying?"* This is why it's always important to create a message that replicates what you really believe—not just what you think others want to hear.

Feedback

It can be said that feedback serves as the lifeblood of any communicative interaction—it's the information sent by a receiver which signals whether your message is hitting its target, or missing its mark. Since it's clear that most interactions involve a constant give-and-take between sender and receiver, feedback provides you with a lot of information about your listeners. Are they looking out the window while you're speaking? Are they glancing at their watch? Do they smile and nod in agreement? Are they leaning forward in their seats, trying to catch every word? Messages like these suggest, *"I'm bored,"* *"I really*

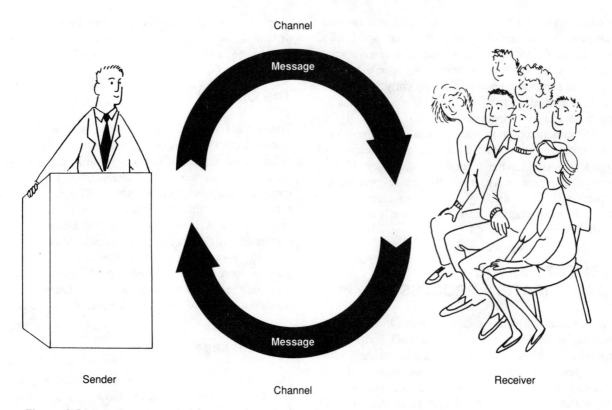

Channel

Message

Message

Sender

Channel

Receiver

Figure 3.2
The Communication Cycle: The Message. Communication is an exchange of information between the sender and the receiver. Notice that every message must travel through a channel.

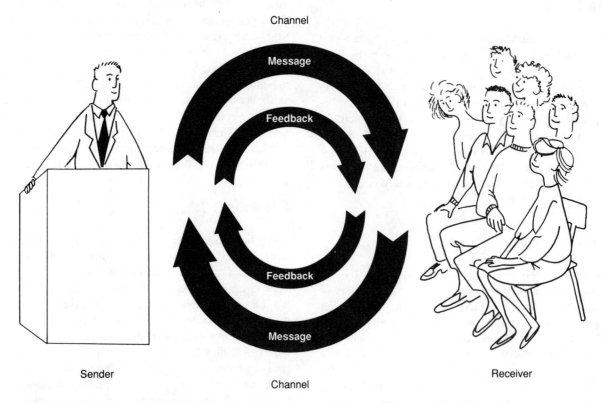

Channel

Message

Feedback

Feedback

Message

Sender

Channel

Receiver

Figure 3.3
The Communication Cycle: Feedback. We've now included the element of feedback in our model. Observe that feedback is exchanged between sender and receiver.

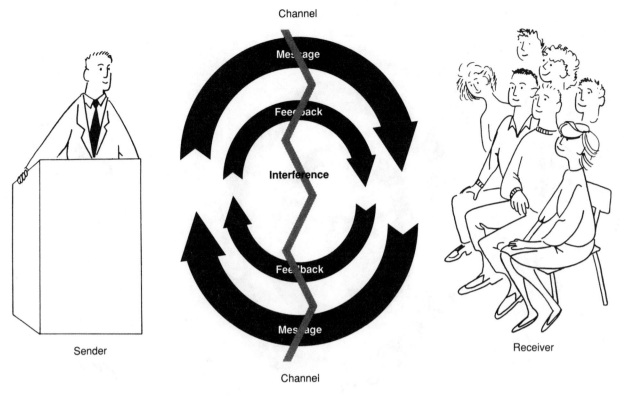

Channel

Message

Feedback

Interference

Feedback

Message

Sender

Receiver

Channel

Figure 3.4
The Communication Cycle: Interference. We've now included the element of interference to our model. Notice how interference hinders all communication between sender and receiver.

should be someplace else," "I like what you're saying," or "This is great stuff, give me more." The more alert you are to these messages, the better you can adapt your message to meet the needs of listeners. Sometimes, however, feedback is not so immediate. A speech or panel discussion broadcast over television won't let you know for days, or even weeks how it hit your listeners. Eventually some form of delayed feedback may filter in, however. Consequently feedback is an important part of communication. We've added feedback in our model, as shown in figure 3.3. The next element we'll examine is interference.

Interference

Every interaction involves some form of interference. Interference is anything that gets in the way of ideal communication. It can be a clanging noise that makes it hard to hear; a stuffy room which makes it hard to concentrate; or a time of day which makes listeners wish they were someplace else. Often interference comes from within your listeners. They might be daydreaming, paying attention to someone else, or ready to jump to a quick conclusion before you've had a chance to state your case. At other times interference is the fault of the speaker. You might speak in a soft voice that's hard to hear, use unfamiliar

words, or present a disorganized, jumbled set of ideas. Regardless of how it occurs, interference always serves as a barrier between sender and receiver. We've now added interference in figure 3.4. We now just have two elements left to make our model complete.

Situation

The situation is the why, the when, and the where of a message. Why is it taking place? When is it being given? Where will it be? The why measures the reason for the interaction—is it to make a date, or break an appointment; to convince an audience to take a stand, or to teach them something new? The when measures the time of your message. Is it communicated early in the morning, or late at night? Research shows it's harder to keep people's attention before they've had a chance to wake up. The where measures the place of your message. Is it delivered in a classroom or in a subway station? To a group of two, or an audience of twenty? Once your able to gage the situation of a communication, you can prepare a more fitting message. Now take a look at figure 3.5. You'll notice we've added one more element to our model—the situation of the interaction. This leaves but one additional element to make our

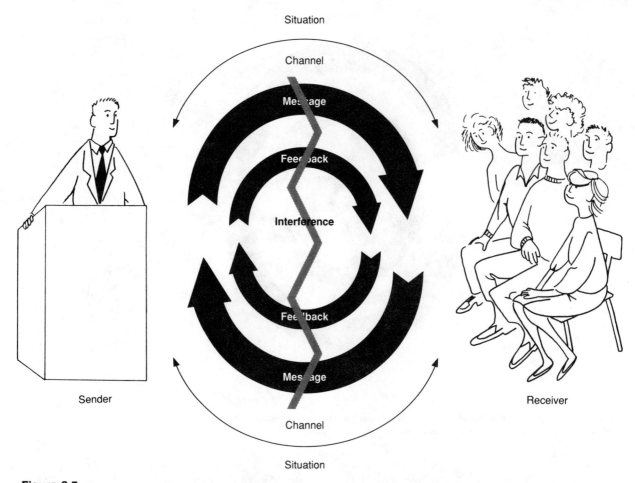

Situation

Channel

Message

Feedback

Interference

Feedback

Message

Channel

Situation

Sender

Receiver

Figure 3.5
The Communication Cycle: Situation. Notice that the situation—the why, the when, and the where of communication is now added to our model. This situation affects the whole process of communication.

model complete; and that's the interaction that happens between listeners themselves.

Listener to Listener Communication

Often you communicate to more than one person at a time. Whenever this happens you're bound to have some form of listener to listener communication. And what is listener to listener communication? It's any information shared between listeners themselves. Don't confuse this with feedback—feedback only refers to information sent back to you as the sender. How do groups of listeners communicate? They wink, smile, nod, frown, mutter comments, and whisper asides. How often have you noticed that the reaction

of one person in a group soon becomes the reaction of many? Inter-group communication is hard to grasp, and difficult to deal with. You're best bet is to be an alert communicator. If you spot a problem, head it off; if you see something is working, keep it up; if you notice a few listeners seem distracted, don't give up. Now take a look at our finished model in figure 3.6. As you can see, some listeners are listening in rapt attention, others are looking away, one seems half asleep. This is one of the reasons why every communicative transaction is so unique—because while you might be the same, the reaction of your listeners almost never is. And this reminds us that all communication is transactional.

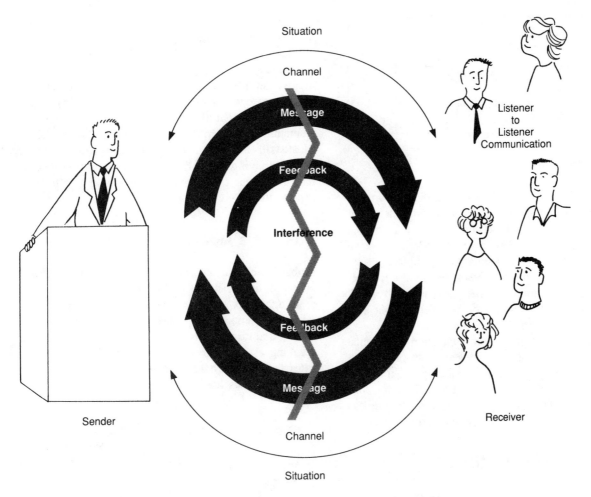

Situation

Channel

Message

Feedback

Interference

Feedback

Message

Channel

Situation

Sender

Receiver

Listener to Listener Communication

Figure 3.6
The Communication Cycle: Listener. This is our completed model of the communication process. Just as every communication is different, so is every listener.

TRANSACTIONAL COMMUNICATION

What do we mean by transactional communication? It means that all our behaviors, all our actions, and all our perceptions have message value. Everything we do, everything we say, everything we don't say, and everything we don't do communicates something. How do we communicate something by not doing or saying anything? Let's imagine we pass someone in the hall and ignore them, not saying *"Hello,"* *"How are you,"* or even moving slightly aside. Have we communicated anything? You bet we have! We've told that person we don't wish to interact with them, we're angry with them, or that we just wish to be left alone. Situations like these happen quite often. Someone doesn't wave, a friend decides not to return your call, a classmate gives you a dirty look. This is why an often quoted premise in communication is: *"You cannot, not communicate."*[2] Whatever you do or don't do, whatever you say or don't say, however you act or don't act, has message value. Transactional

communication, therefore, means that all actions and inactions alike communicates information to others.

Communication is also transactional in the sense that we never just play the role of sender or receiver separately. Instead, we are continually doing both simultaneously. Years ago, communication theorists had a hard time explaining this premise. Often a communicative exchange was explained by comparing it to a ping pong ball game. The person serving the ball was the sender, the person receiving the ball was the receiver, the ball was the message, and hitting it with a paddle was the channel. The net served as interference and the actions of the other player represented feedback. Once the ball was received, the process was reversed with the sender hitting the ball back to the receiver and so on.

However what this explanation failed to take into account was that we never act strictly as senders or receivers of information. While hitting the ball we also are receiving information. We observe how the other player is standing, the position of the paddle, the angle of the extended arm, and any last minute

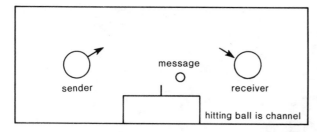

Figure 3.7
Ping Pong Ball Game.

movements. Similarly, while awaiting the ball we are sending this information, not just receiving cues from the other player. This can be understood by imaging a classmate, Maria, delivering a speech. While speaking Maria observes some students taking notes, a few whispering comments, and several listening attentively. As a good communicator Maria is not only sending information—the content of her speech—but also receiving it—the actions of her audience.

This is true of every communication experience we have. We are constantly in a process of sending and receiving messages, even though we might not be consciously aware of it at the time. Therefore all communication is transactional, and all communication models should represent this important concept.

COMMUNICATION MODELS

We already went through the process of building a communication model step by step with our eight basic elements. As we saw, each element can really only be understood when it interrelates with each other element in a model. And what exactly is a communication model? It's a **visualization of the communication process**. Models allow us to "take a picture" of an interaction, study its strengths and flaws, and make corrections for the future.

We already recognize that communication is ongoing and continuous, and therefore in reality, it's impossible to really stop a communicative act and examine it. But with a model we can "freeze" the process for study and review. If two people have difficulty communicating with each other is it because the sender doesn't understand the receiver? Is there a problem with the channel? Could the message be more articulate? Is feedback being ignored? Is the situation right? What kind of interference is operating? Is listener to listener communication a problem? Questions like these can only be answered through the use of a communication model. Whether preparing a communicative chain for an entire organization, or putting together a simple classroom speech, communication models are invaluable for effective understanding.

There are hundreds of different communication models. Some models emphasize interpersonal communication, others public speaking, and many mass communication. We will review a few basic models to give an idea of what communication models do, and to demonstrate how they can be effectively used. Keep in mind that all models must have four essential elements—a sender, receiver, channel, and message. Most will also include interference and feedback. While studying the following communication models remember that the purpose of any model is to help explain the nature of a communicative act.

Aristotle's Model

Probably the earliest model of communication was prepared by Aristotle in his *Rhetoric* written 2300 years ago. This model is very basic, including five essential elements: the speaker, message, audience, occasion, and effect. This model is best suited for public speaking as Aristotle advises the speaker on how to construct a speech to gain a desired effect on different audiences for varied occasions.

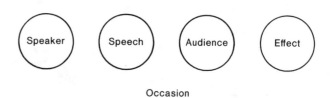

Occasion

Figure 3.8
Aristotle's Model of Communication.

Lasswell's Model

One of the earliest models was created by political scientist Harold Lasswell. This model is really a series of five questions, and is similar to that of Aristotle. In Lasswell's model the sender is the *"who,"* the receiver is the *"to whom,"* the message is *"what,"* the channel is *"says,"* interference is *"with what,"* and feedback is *"what effect."* Thus, this simple model includes six elements.

WHO—SAYS WHAT—TO WHOM—THROUGH WHAT CHANNEL—WITH WHAT EFFECT?

Figure 3.9
Lasswell's Model of Communication.

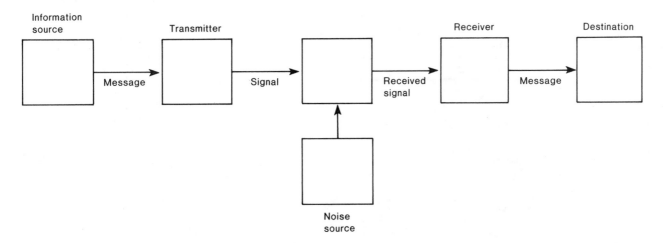

Figure 3.10
Shannon and Weaver's Model of Communicatio (Source: Claude E. Shannon and Warren Weaver, THE MATHEMATICAL THEORY OF COMMUNICATION [Urbana, Illinois: University of Illinois Press, 1949] p. 5.

Shannon and Weaver's Model

One of the most famous models was created in the late 1940's by two mathematicians from M.I.T., Claude Shannon and Warren Weaver. This model was developed to elicit desired information from early computers. According to this model communication follows a simple left to right process. There are five elements: an information source, transmitter, channel, receiver, and destination all arranged in linear order. The information source selects a message from all possible messages, transmits the message through a channel using signals (sound, sight, touch, taste, or smell), the message is received, and transmitted back. Interference occurs when an intended part of the message is not transmitted by the source. This model is most often used for mass communications, depicting television, radio, art, music, print and the like. If representing a telephone conversation, for instance, the elements could be: (1) a person talking on the phone; (2) the mouthpiece of the phone; (3) the words used; (4) the electrical impulses allowing the message to travel; (5) the earpiece of the phone; and (6) the receiver of the message. **Entropy** was also introduced with this model. Entropy in a principal derived from physics which is analogous to interference in a message. Entropy could be, for example, audio or visual static that reduces the clarity of the message.

Berlo's Model

David Berlo's SMCR model clearly depicts the four essential elements of communication—source, message, channel, and receiver. This model also focuses on encoding and decoding which occurs during any communicative interaction. Five personal factors are listed which influence both sender and receiver. These include communication skills, attitudes, knowledge, social system, and culture. Berlo also lists the five senses for the channel, and has a good breakdown of the components of a message. Notice that both sender and receiver reflect identical attributes; this reminds us that both are sending and receiving messages simultaneously.

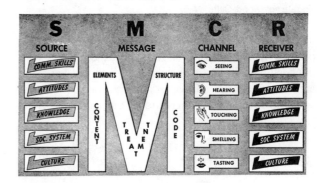

Figure 3.11
Berlo's SMCR Model of Communication. (From PROCESS OF COMMUNICATION: AN INTRODUCTION TO THEORY AND PRACTICE by David K. Berlo. Copyright © 1960 by Holt, Rinehart and Winston, Inc. and renewed 1988 by David K. Berlo, reprinted by permission of the publisher.)

McCroskey's Model

A simple model to follow is that by James Mc-Croskey. According to this model a sender (source) investigates, encodes, and sends a message through a channel in which there is interference (noise), to a receiver who decodes the message using two senses, interpretations, evaluations, and response skills. Note, also, that there are subsequent effects to the message—reactions might be delayed for hours or days.

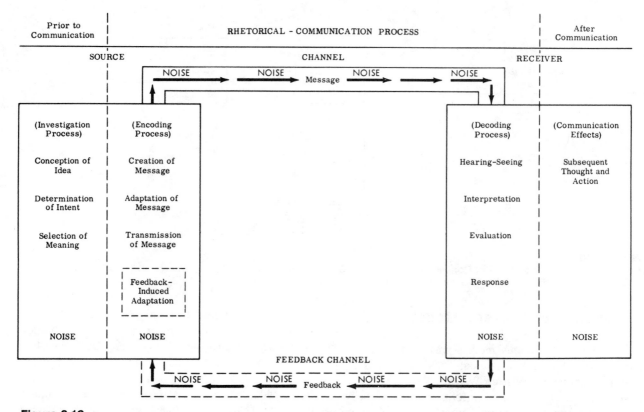

Figure 3.12
McCroskey's Model of Communication. (Source: James C. McCroskey, AN INTRODUCTION TO RHETORICAL COMMUNICATION: The Theory and Practice of Public Speaking, 5/e, © 1986, p. 6. Reprinted by permission of Prentice-Hall, Inc., Englewood Cliffs, N.J.)

In the feedback channel there is interference (noise), because feedback is never received exactly as it was intended. An interesting aspect of this model is that it includes feedback-induced adaptations which usually occur in face-to-face interactions, but can happen in any communicative act.

Schramm's Model

This model is interesting in that it shows communication as a circular process. In the Schramm model no distinction is made between message and feedback, and both participants are depicted as acting jointly as sender and receiver. This model, likewise, includes the element of interpreter. Basically, the interpreter involves creating meaning as discussed earlier in this chapter.

Dance's Model

The model by Frank Dance simply depicts communication in the form of a helical spiral. Dance's model emphasizes that every interaction has no clear observable beginning or ending; as a result the spiral continues indefinitely. Communication has no fixed

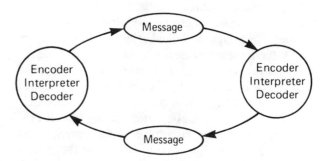

Figure 3.13
Schramm's Model of Communication. (Source: Wilbur Schramm, "How Communication Works," in THE PROCESS AND EFFECTS OF MASS COMMUNICATION, Wilbur Schramm and Donald F. Roberts, ed. [Urbana, Illinois: University of Illinois, 1971]).

boundaries, and this model demonstrates its infinite parameters.

Hoehn's Model

The last model we'll review highlights the fact that communication is transactional in nature—both sender and receiver are communicating at the same time. The sender creates a message based on those attributes which make each of us unique. Meaning is given to the

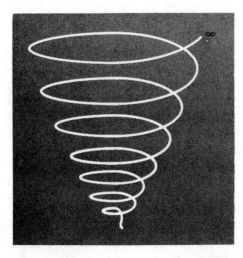

Figure 3.14
Dance's Helical Spiral. (Source: Frank E.X. Dance, "Toward a Theory of Human Communication," in HUMAN COMMUNICATION THEORY: ORIGINAL ESSAYS, F.E.X. Dance, ed. [New York: Holt, Rinehart & Winston, 1957], p. 296.)

sender's ideas and they are encoded—put into words and actions that the sender thinks the receiver will understand. Both verbal (V) and nonverbal (NV) messages travel through a channel to the receiver. The receiver decodes the sender's messages and assigns meaning to them according to those attributes which make each receiver unique. Feedback is likewise sent through a channel using both verbal and nonverbal means. Notice that feedback is also given meaning and needs to be encoded and decoded. Interference exists at all levels and is replete throughout the process. The situation of the interaction affects both sender and receiver, and listener to listener communication influences the receiver. With this model we can see all eight elements at play. We have a sender, receiver, channel, message, feedback, interference, situation, and listener to listener communication.

With this model we have come full circle—from the simplest representation of the communication process to the most complex. But all models do

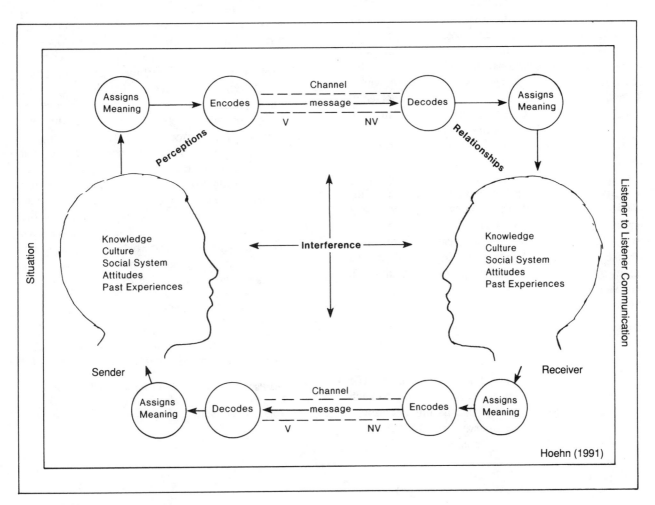

Figure 3.15
Hoehn Transactional Model of Communication.

basically the same thing: they show how communication works and operates. So as you study the magic of the spoken word, think about how you can use a model to depict the process. For the best way to understand communication, is to study it firsthand.

CHAPTER SUMMARY

An adage in communication teaches us that "Meanings are in people, not in words." Meaning refers to the way we assign significance to what is communicated to us. We base these perceptions in large part on our culture, social system, attitudes, knowledge, and experiences. This is why effective communicators carefully choose the words and examples they use.

Communication works as a process in that it is in continuous, dynamic change. Communication also works as a system. In the system there are four essential elements, and another four elements that usually apply. The four essential elements of any communicative interaction are that there must be a sender, receiver, channel, and message. The four elements that usually apply include feedback, interference, the situation, and listener to listener communication.

All of our interactions are transactional. Communication is transactional in that all of our behaviors, actions, and perceptions have message value. This is why it's often said, "You cannot, not communicate." The transactional nature of communication also means that we never are just a sender or a receiver; rather we constantly play both roles simultaneously.

A communication model is a way of depicting the process of communication in a visual way. This allows us to "freeze" the process and study how it applies. Models we reviewed include those by Aristotle, Lasswell, Shannon and Weaver, Berlo, McCroskey, Schramm, Dance, and Hoehn. All models allow us to appreciate the magic of communication firsthand.

EXERCISES FOR REVIEW

1. Review the following situations, and then write down the "meaning" you would apply to each example. Be prepared to discuss this in class:
   a. *A used car salesperson tries to sell you a car calling it a "creampuff."*
   b. *A faculty member warns you to leave the building due to a bomb scare.*
   c. *A classmate you hardly know asks for a $10 loan.*
   d. *A former F.B.I. agent comes to class to discuss the F.B.I. fingerprint file in Washington.*
   e. *A classmate from Viet Nam pulls back when you greet her with a hug.*
   f. *A black student from South Africa discusses the pain of racial segregation.*

2. Greek philosopher Heraclitus said, "A man can never step in the same river twice." Write a 200 word paper explaining what this statement means to you. Particularly relate your discussion to the topic of communication.

3. Look at national magazines such as *Time*, *Newsweek*, or *Life*. Cut out pictures from the magazines which reflect each of the eight elements of communication. For instance a picture of telephone wires could represent the channel, a baby's smile feedback, a messy desk interference, and so on.

4. What does the statement, "You cannot, not communicate" mean? Sift through personal experiences to find examples to support your interpretation. Discuss your thoughts with a group of four other classmates.

5. Review the eight communication models represented in this chapter. Then make your own communication model integrating, adding, or eliminating elements as you see fit. Make your model on poster board using a magic marker or pictures from a magazine, and then sitting in a circle, explain it to the rest of the class. Someone, for example, might explain how a fire alarm works as a model, another might describe the hand signals of a football referee, or someone else the workings of an engine as a model. Be as original and creative as possible.

NOTES

1. This statement is attributed to many communicologists, chiefly to David K. Berlo who first coined the term.
2. See Paul Watzlawick, Janet Beavin, and Don Jackson, *The Pragmatics of Human Communication*, (New York: W. W. Norton, 1967).

PROCESS WORKSHEET

Below is a model of communication. Label each of the eight elements of communication used in the model.

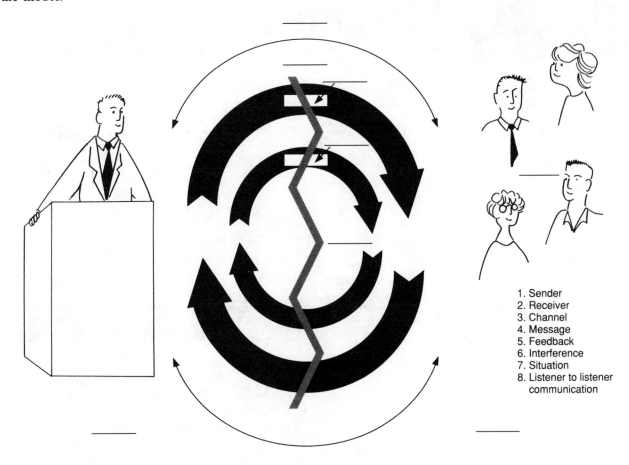

1. Sender
2. Receiver
3. Channel
4. Message
5. Feedback
6. Interference
7. Situation
8. Listener to listener communication

4 Listening

Even when listening to the radio, we tend to filter out distracting noises.

QUESTIONS FOR RETENTION

Before reading this chapter, ask yourself the following questions:

1. Why is listening important?
2. How can I become a better listener?
3. How can I take careful notes?

Several years ago a college professor wanted to learn if students were listening to his lectures. To find out he conducted an experiment where a gun was fired at random intervals during his class. At the sound of the shot students wrote down whatever they were thinking. Throughout the nine week course the gun was fired twenty-one times, sometimes catching the professor in mid-sentence. Much to his dismay, he learned that only one student in five was paying any attention to him, and that just 12 percent were actively listening to the content of his lectures. The remaining 80 percent were pursing erotic thoughts, reminiscing about past events, or daydreaming about lunch or religion.[1]

What the professor observed points out a rather disturbing fact—most of us are surprisingly poor listeners. Even when we're listening carefully, as to a classroom lecture, we're only able to recall about 50 percent of what was said. And after two days we can remember only half of that, or but 25 percent of the original message.[2] In other words, three out of every four things that are said to us go in one ear and right out the other.

Sometimes we act like we're listening, when we really aren't. We fake listening by smiling, nodding, or muttering things like *"You don't say."* We even give nonverbal hints when we're not listening—looks at our watch, movements back and forth, doodles on a pad, glances in another direction. This is why experts have consistently stated that people need to be trained to become better listeners. For without a doubt, listening is our most neglected skill.

WHY IT'S IMPORTANT TO BE A GOOD LISTENER

Not listening doesn't mean we haven't *heard* what someone has said to us. Hearing is the physical process of receiving sound waves and transmitting them to the brain. Listening, on the other hand, means making sense out of what was transmitted. This is because hearing comes naturally while listening takes hard work. As George Burns said in the movie OH GOD, "I can't help hearing, but I don't always listen."

How important is listening in your life? As a student you're in an arena where information is constantly being presented to you through lectures, discussions, conferences, and reports. In fact you spend seven out of every ten hours in the classroom engaged in some form of listening.[3] The world of business is no different. The average executive spends 60 to 80 percent of a typical workday listening to clients, customers, and coworkers. A poll of top-flight managers reported that they thought listening was "super critical" for anyone going into management, and they ranked it as the number one skill for business.[4] Listening is equally important in all relationships—parent and child, husband and wife, roommate and friend, teacher and classmate. None of this is surprising when you consider that you spend more time listening than communicating in any other way—more than reading, more than writing, and even more than speaking.[5] No matter what your personality or choice of career, few things will be as important in your life as the ability to listen.

How do you become a better listener? One way is to become one with the person speaking. Think with the speaker, feel with the speaker, work with the speaker. English poet John Milton once said, *"A good teacher is one whose spirit enters the soul of the pupil."* What Milton advised for teachers also applies to listeners. For a good listener is one "whose spirit enters the soul of the speaker." And without a doubt, when speaker and listener are joined in harmony, everybody benefits.

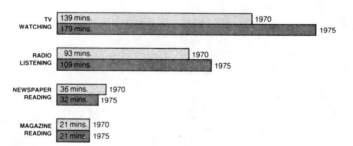

Figure 4.1
The Increase in Daily Time Spent With Television, Radio, Newspapers, and Magazines Between 1970 and 1975.
(Statistics are from the television Bureau of Advertising; reported in Brown, Brown, and Rivers, 1978.)

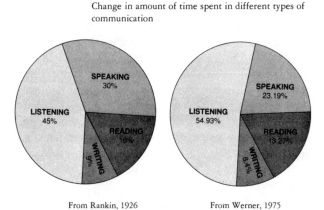

Change in amount of time spent in different types of communication

SPEAKING 30%
LISTENING 45%
READING 16%
WRITING 9%

From Rankin, 1926

SPEAKING 23.19%
LISTENING 54.93%
READING 13.27%
WRITING 8.4%

From Werner, 1975

Figure 4.2
Change in Amount of Time Spent in Different Types of Communication.

EIGHT SKILLS FOR BECOMING A BETTER LISTENER

Nothing is preventing you from becoming a better listener. Good listening is not tied to intelligence, grade point, upbringing, or experience. Like the skill of speaking itself, it can only be learned through effort and practice. Let's now review the skills which can make you a better listener and allow you to "enter the soul of the speaker."

Skill 1: Be An Active Listener

Think back to the last time you listened to the radio or watched television. Can you remember much of what you heard? The chances are you can't. That's because listening for relaxation is a passive activity which requires little effort or concentration. Whether you remember what was said, or forget it five minutes later doesn't really matter. But listening to a lecture or a speech is an entirely different situation. Here you'll want to remember everything you heard so it can become firmly etched in your mind. This means becoming an *active listener*, putting energy and concentration into the effort.

Active listening is hard work. Famed trial attorney Clarence Darrow said that after a day of courtroom listening he'd often feel exhausted and be wringing wet with perspiration. And noted listening authority Ralph Nichols explains that listening is characterized by faster heart action, a quicker circulation of the blood, and a small rise in body temperature. Recent evidence even suggests that active listening is beneficial to your physical well-being and is as important to your cardiovascular health as exer-

cise or diet.[6] This is why people who practice active listening sometimes say it's like taking a "mental lap around a track."

Being an active listener means putting forth at least fifty percent of the energy that's poured into every message. To do this you've got to be motivated to work with the person doing the speaking. And how do you practice active listening? First weigh the speaker's evidence—is it relevant, objective, and credible? Second follow the speaker's organization—are his or her thoughts presented in a logical order? Third evaluate the speaker's ideas—are they sensible and reasonable? And last observe the person's delivery—is it lively and animated? By working with the communicator you'll be astonished at the results. One student who practiced active listening described her reaction this way: "I was amazed at how much I learned. I found that every message offered tidbits of information which I otherwise might have missed. On top of that, I now listen better everywhere—to my friends, in other classes, to my husband." No wonder listening experts conclude, "An active listener is a good listener."

EAR
EYES
UNDIVIDED ATTENTION
HEART

Figure 4.3 Notice how these characters in the Chinese language that mean "to listen" signify the important skills necessary for effective listening.

Skill 2: Concentrate On What Is Being Said

President Franklin Roosevelt suspected that people who passed through receiving lines at the White House weren't really concentrating on what he said. His suspicions were confirmed one night when he commented to one dignitary, while shaking hands, *"I shot my grandmother this morning,"* and the dignitary replied, *"How lovely! What a splendid celebration!"*

What Franklin Roosevelt observed in a receiving line happens to listeners all the time. Sometimes people think they heard one thing, when just the opposite was said. At other times people listen for one message, missing everything else that's been described. None of this is too shocking when we realize that listening takes mental discipline and concentration. After all we can't absorb information like a sponge, expecting to soak in every little detail that comes our way.

While listening to someone it's awfully easy to daydream, fantasize, and think about unrelated events. Whenever we focus on tomorrow or yesterday, instead of the moment at hand, we're bound to miss a lot of what's being said. As incredible as it seems, the major reason why it's so tough to concentrate is because the brain is amazingly efficient. Although we speak from 125 to 150 words a minute, the brain can process three times that amount, or about 500 words per minute. This would seem to make concentration very easy, but actually it has just the opposite effect. That 75 percent of spare "brain power" makes it easy for us to mentally wander—thinking about totally unrelated events.

How do you target your concentration and keep your mind from wandering? First prepare for every speaker. Make yourself comfortable and get psyched up for what you're about to hear. Second clear your mind of extraneous thoughts—pour all your energies into the message at hand. And third use your spare "brain time" to think along with the speaker. Anticipate coming thoughts, review those just made, and evaluate those currently being expressed. When you use all your mental capabilities in a positive way, you'll be amazed to see how easy it is to concentrate and remain mentally alert.

Skill 3: Resist Distractions

Pete Crosby was excited. In two days he'd be graduating from college with a degree in journalism. But what especially made Pete delighted was that he'd just learned the person delivering the commencement address was the same woman he'd written about in his senior thesis. Pete quickly called home and told his mother the good news.

On the day of the graduation the outdoor stadium was filled to capacity as Pete prepared to listen to every word of the commencement address. But after the woman had spoken for about ten minutes, a clap of thunder echoed overhead. *"Oh-Oh,"* thought Pete, *"I sure hope it doesn't rain."* The thunder continued and fifteen minutes later a drenching rain came down, just as the speaker concluded her address.

Arriving home, the first thing Pete's mother asked was how he liked the speech. Pete thought for a second and replied, *"I don't remember much about the speech, but wait till you hear about the thunderstorm!"*

As Pete discovered, we live in a world full of distractions. Even when we really want to hear what someone has to say, as Pete did with the commencement address, it's often difficult to block out annoying distractions. Sometimes distractions can be heard—voices in the hall, construction work going on outdoors, the annoying buzz of a fly. At other times distractions can be seen—activities going on outside, a poster on the wall, actions by someone else in the audience. Distractions may even be physical—a bad cold, headache, or room that feels too hot or too cold. In an ideal world none of these distractions would exist, but in the real world they all too often do.

How do you resist distractions? The best way is to focus on the message, and the message alone. For example think of an Olympic figure skater. Have you ever wondered why skaters don't get dizzy when they spin around? It's because they focus on the spin, ignoring everything that's not related to the task at hand. Listening to a speaker takes much the same thing. Simply override intrusions by becoming totally absorbed in one message, by one speaker, at one moment. Students who live in dormitories manage to block out distractions all the time. As a listener follow this advice: hear an annoying sound? ignore it; see something outside that's intriguing? overlook it; feel uncomfortable in your seat? disregard it. As one student who worked hard to rule out distractions while listening said, *"I worked at focusing on the speaker alone. I learned to shut everything else out, much like I do when studying for a big test."* Just like this student, focus on every message just as you would if studying for a "big test."

Table 4.1
Eight Skills for Becoming a Better Listener

Listening Technique	Poor Listener	Good Listener
Be An Active Listener	Lets the speaker do all the work	Works with speaker to gain understanding of content
Concentrate On What Is Being Said	Thinks of things not related to message; fills mental void with daydreams	Anticipates with speaker; realizes thought is faster than speech
Resist Distractions	Allows mind to wander	Focuses on main ideas; filters out outside noise and thoughts
Be Open-Minded	Allows bias and prejudice to interfere with message	Overrides negative thoughts and prejudice; listens with empathy
Overlook Appearance and Delivery	Focuses more on looks and style than content	Places emphasis on substance of message, not on image or performance
Hold Your Judgment	Jumps to premature conclusions; mentally argues with speaker	Avoids making snap judgments before message is concluded; weighs evidence and argument
Show Interest in Content	Fails to relate content to personal experience	Uses meaningful analogies and examples to illustrate value of message
Take Careful Notes	Concentrates more on notetaking than message; copies down unimportant information	Gleans only essential information from message

Skill 4: Be Open-Minded

Ever met someone who wouldn't listen to you no matter what you said? If you have, the chances are that person had a closed-mind. Closed-mindedness is especially disruptive when listening to someone. Maybe you don't like someone because of a political belief or because of a stand on a controversial issue. Maybe you resent a person's accent or type of mannerisms. Whatever the reason, closed-mindedness sets up impossible barriers between speaker and listener. Closed-mindedness is not only silly, it's destructive. Failing to listen to someone because of ignorance or prejudice only prevents a listener from overcoming his or her own ignorance. That's why a closed-mind is often called an empty mind.

How can you keep an open-mind? The best way is to listen with **empathy**. When you empathize with others you feel as they feel, you see the world as they see it, you imagine things as they imagine things. This doesn't mean you must agree with others; instead it means you listen giving the speaker every benefit of the doubt. As the author of the book *Human Be-ing* advises, *"Real listening 'means tuning in' to what the other person is feeling so that we listen to emotions, not simply to 'ideas.' "* Remember, a speaker is much more than just someone presenting a collection of ideas. It's a real person who thinks and feels just like you.

Skill 5: Overlook Appearance and Delivery

Suppose you were a member of an audience that heard Abraham Lincoln deliver a speech in 1856. According to one eye witness this is what you would have seen:

> *"On his head he wore a somewhat battered 'stovepipe' hat. His neck emerged, long and sinewy, from a white collar turned down over a thin black necktie. His lank, ungainly body was clad in a rusty black dress coat with sleeves that should have been longer; but his arms appeared so long that the sleeves of a 'store' coat could hardly be expected to cover them all the way down to the wrists. His black trousers, too, permitted a very full view of his large feet. . . . I had seen, in Washington and in the West, several public men of rough appearance; but none whose looks seemed quite so uncouth, not to say grotesque, as Lincoln's."*[7]

Although unpleasant in appearance, Abraham Lincoln was one of the greatest speakers in history. But if people hadn't been willing to overlook the way he appeared, his forceful message about the evils of slavery would never have been heard.

As a good listener it's important to pay more attention to the content of a message rather than the package it comes in. Many speakers with an important message—people who changed the course of history—were individuals who were unlikely to impress anyone with their delivery or appearance. Patrick Henry was tall and awkward; Eleanor Roosevelt had a shrill, unpleasant voice; Mahatma Ghandhi was frail and soft spoken; George Washington was stiff and upright; Albert Einstein looked unkept and disheveled; and Teddy Roosevelt had a speech impediment and was tonguetied. Yet, imagine what the world would be like if no one had listened to these speakers.

While it takes a greater effort to listen to unpleasant sounding or appearing speakers, you owe it to yourself to do so. Listening to someone means concentrating on what they say, not just focusing on the way they say it. Of course the flip side of this issue is not to become mesmerized by smooth and attractive speakers. Throughout history many people have been fooled and misled by speakers who sounded good but concealed an evil and dangerous message. Try and keep an objective balance between delivery and content, so you can judge the entire message, not just the eloquence of its transmission.[8]

Skill 6: Hold Your Judgement

Whenever you make a snap decision about a subject before you've heard someone out, you've jumped to a conclusion. This is sometimes hard to avoid. Unless you're only exposed to speakers who mirror everything you think and feel, you're likely to run into some arguments that cause you to disagree. Poor listeners jump to conclusions all the time. As soon as they hear something they don't like, a red flag goes up and they stop listening to anything else the person has to say. Good listeners, on the other hand, hold their fire and hear someone out.

Even when we try to keep an open-mind, it's sometimes difficult to prevent ourselves from reaching a hasty conclusion. After all, there are lots of explosive issues where people have pretty strong views—sex education, abortion, capital punishment, prayer in school, just to name a few. As one listener said, *"Some topics make you just want to boo, hiss, and rattle around in protest."* Open-minded or not, some people have a tough time listening to someone they think's all wrong:

What can we do to prevent ourselves from making snap decisions? Listening experts recommend the best thing is not to mentally argue with the speaker. Instead listen to the whole message, and then decide whether or not it has merit. When we start to mentally debate we end up spending more time on our own arguments, and less on the person's points. Rather than arguing, weigh each contention, evaluate the evidence, and measure its logic. Listen to get a full understanding and intelligently evaluate at the end. As writer Kurt Luedtke wisely advises: "It will not be a week, and certainly not a month, before you will become aware that someone in your own circle of influence is saying something or thinking something very wrong. I think you have to do something about that. I think you have to help them be heard. I think you are required to listen."

Skill 7: Show Interest in the Content

Francis Bacon once said, *"All knowledge and wonder is an impression of pleasure in itself."* Bacon was right, for the pleasure of every message is in the wealth of knowledge it possesses. Ask any listener and they'll be hard pressed to think of a message that didn't teach them at least one thing. Even topics which sound simple and boring often turn out to be instructive and challenging. Thomas Edison recognized that there's a value in everything. One time he was mocked for trying some twelve hundred materials for the filament of his great dream, the incandescent light bulb. *"You have failed 1200 times,"* he was told. To this Edison replied, *"I haven't failed. I've discovered 1200 materials that won't work."*

Like Edison, don't focus on what a message isn't telling you, instead concentrate on what it is. One helpful way to remember content is to use reference points. This means taking something out of the speaker's frame of reference, and putting it into your own. For instance if a speaker is discussing the problems of off-shore dumping, you might post a reference point for each main idea. Suppose the speaker says: *"The great majority of dumping occurs off the Mid-Atlantic coast"* (my vacation last summer was at Cape Cod and I saw barges being towed out to sea); *"Those primarily responsible are cities and chemical companies"* (my brother works for a chemical company in Boston); *"This continued dumping has polluted many waters and contaminated shell fish"* (I remember we couldn't order clams in a restaurant). In this way each of these points will stick in your mind because you've made them relevant to your life.

Skill 8: Take Careful Notes

Ever observed someone who's life work depends on listening? You'll notice one striking thing—they take careful notes. Interviewers jot down details about an applicant; counselors note observations after a session; executives write out remarks at a board meeting. Observe your speech teacher. Many students are amazed at how accurately their teacher can pinpoint every detail after a speech presentation. Of course having lots of practice and knowing what to look for helps; but notice your teacher during your next speaking assignment. Chances are he or she will be poised with a pen or pencil at the ready. As research consistently reveals, note taking is one well-tested way of "locking in print" the content of a spoken message.[9]

Unfortunately note taking is not as simple as it seems. Some people take down too much, some too little, and some pay more attention to their notes than the message itself. Listeners who try to copy down every little detail are running a losing race. Not only is it next to impossible to keep up with the rapid pace of a speaker, but an awful lot of energy is spent copying down unimportant information. People who put down too little end up five minutes later with words and phrases that make little or no sense. And listeners who spend too much time concentrating on their notes end up with beautiful looking notes, but can't remember a thing the speaker said. Obviously none of these strategies works very well.

How do you use a system of note taking that gives you principles and facts, but doesn't interfere with listening comprehension? One recommended method is the **Cornell System**. In this system you jot down main ideas in a right-hand *"Record"* column, and summarize key ideas, phrases, and questions in a left-hand *"Recall"* column. Later on you can go back and reconstruct the speaker's message in your own words. Suppose you were listening to this student's speech on roller coasters:

Imagine tortuous twists and corkscrews, free falls and backward loops. That's what I love—a roller coaster. And I'm not alone. Last year over five million people rode on roller coasters in the United States. Roller coasters are not only a lot of fun, they're a part of our culture, and are more exciting than ever.

There's nothing like a ride on a coaster. Sharp twists, bends, and 85 degree drops are nothing unusual. After one or two rides your heart's pounding, your head's spinning, and your adrenalin's pumping.

Roller coasters are an important part of our culture. In the 1920's and 1930's there were over 1500 coasters in the country. Today there are less than 300. Like the great baseball stadiums of yesterday, old roller coasters are a thing of the past. There's not one wooden coaster left anywhere.

But don't lament. Coasters are coming back! Some of the best coasters today are the Beast and Vortex outside Cincinnati; Master Twister in Denver; Mindbender in Atlanta; Ultratwister in New Jersey; and of course the Cyclone in New York.

So the next time you visit an amusement park try something different. Hop on a coaster and take a twist and a turn. You'll never be the same again.

Your notes would look like this:

Record	Recall
Topic: Roller Coasters	*5 million ride*
1. *Fun of coasters*	*twists & bends*
2. *Part of culture*	*1500 in 1930*
	300 today
	Are they endangered?
3. *More exciting—*	*Beast & Vortex*
are coming back	*Ultratwister*
	Cyclone, N.Y.—is it best?

This speech was about 200 words long. By using this simple outline we were able to jot down all the main points, key ideas, and questions in less than 30 words. Of course you'd want to review these notes later, adding information while it's still fresh in your mind. The questions are helpful as well, since you might want to ask the speaker for more information later on.

Use a system of note taking that works best for you. It will not only help when listening to a speech, but will prove invaluable whenever facts and information must be recalled. Just like listening itself, careful note taking will reward you many times over throughout your life.

Empathic Listening

Empathic listening is more than just hearing another person, it means listening to what the person means. Empathic listening is the most effective means of listening to someone else because it allows the listener to attend to the entire content of the speaker's message. When we listen we must consider the role of the speaker, his or her respective relationship to us, and interpret his or her auxiliary messages via expressions, gestures, and movements. We even would interpret the lack of a direct message, or silence, by carefully listening.

In order to have empathy we must suspend our judgments and emotions. Empathic listening, therefore, requires that we remove our personal feelings, moods, and emotions about the person and subject. Empathy means that we hear what is said, not what we think the speaker will say. When we use empathic listening we don't allow our perceptions to dictate the message, rather we allow the message to speak for itself. In this way the message creates its own sense of individual perspective based upon its own merits.

CHAPTER SUMMARY

Most people are poor listeners. Even when listening carefully we're only able to recall one-half of what we heard, and a few days later even less. This doesn't mean we haven't heard someone—it means we haven't listened.

Listening is important to all of us. We spend more time listening than reading, writing, or even speaking. Most experts agree that listening is vital in school, at work, and at home.

There are eight skills for becoming a better listener. These include being an active listener by working along with the person speaking; concentrating on what is being said by remembering that thought is faster than speech; resisting distractions by focusing on the message that is presented; being open-minded by listing with empathy; overlooking delivery and appearance by paying strict attention to content; holding your judgment by not mentally arguing with the speaker; showing an interest in the content by listening with reference points; and taking careful notes to help in remembering important details.

EXERCISES FOR REVIEW

1. Clock the time you spend listening each day. For one hour count the minutes you spend speaking, reading, writing, and listening. Report your findings to class.
2. Visit a class at college that is held in a large lecture hall and has one lecturer. Observe the listening behaviors of audience members. What percentage of the audience is listening attentively? What kinds of things are people doing who are not listening attentively? What kinds of distractions exist in the environment? Write a report on your observations and present it to class.
3. Listen to a news interview program such as *"Meet the Press"* or *"This Week with David Brinkley."* Judge the interview based on the eight skills for good listening we've discussed in this chapter. How much do you remember two hours after the show? Two days after the show? Report your findings to class.
4. Select an article of about 500 words from the newspaper or a magazine such as *Time* or *Newsweek.* Create five questions about information provided in the article. Then, break into a small group and read the article to your classmates. After you've read it, give each listener your quiz of five questions. Discuss with other members of the group what those who scored well on the test did for good listening, and what those who scored poorly on the test need to do for improved listening.
5. Listen to a segment of a national news magazine program, such as *"20/20"* or *"60 Minutes."* Using the Cornell System of note taking, record information about the program.

NOTES

1. This study was reported to the American Psychological Association by Paul Cameron of Wayne State University. A summary of these findings can be found in Ronald B. Adler and George Rodman, *Understanding Human Communication*, Holt, Rinehart and Winston, New York, 1988, p. 78.
2. This finding has been supported in numerous studies over the past thirty years. For instance see Lyman Steil, Larry Barker, and Kittie Watson, *Effective Lis-*

tening, Addison-Wesley, Reading, Mass., 1983, pp. 38, 51.

3. Sperry Corporation, "Your Listening Profile," p. 7.

4. The recognition of the importance of listening cuts across all boundaries in business. For instance, notice the diversity of industries represented by the following sample of trade journals discussing listening: Anthony Alessandra and Jim Cathcart, "Good Listening Equals Better Management," *Fueloil & Oil Heat Solar Systems* (October, 1985), p. 48; R. Maidment, "Listening—the Overlooked and Underdeveloped Other Half of Talking," *Supervisory Management* (August, 1985), pp. 10–12; Lyman Steil, "How to Communicate by Listening," *Credit & Financial Management* (October, 1983), p. 17; and "Communication (Listening)," *American Salesman* (March, 1985), pp. 31–33. Not surprisingly, the time spent listening depends on job expectations and performance; but the 60 to 80 percent figure seems pretty accurate as a gage of time spent. See Leland Brown, *Communicating Facts and Ideas in Business,* Prentice-Hall, Englewood Cliffs, N.J., 1982, p. 380.

5. The actual figures based on a 1975 study are: listening, 54.93 percent; speaking, 23.19 percent; reading, 13.27 percent; and writing, 8.4 percent. See James J. Floyd, *Listening: A Practical Approach,* Scott, Foresman, Glenview, Illinois, 1985, p. 3.

6. These findings are based on twenty years of research by Dr. James Lynch of the University of Maryland Psychophysiology Center. Lynch and his associates charted human blood pressure during three activities: reading out loud, staring at a wall, and watching fish in a tank. Blood pressure was highest when people spoke and lowest when watching fish. They also found that hypertensives blood pressure dropped dramatically when they listened; thus concluding that listening is helpful for one's overall health. James J. Lynch, *The Language of the Heart: The Body's Response to Human Dialogue,* Basic Books, New York, 1983.

7. Robert T. Oliver, *History of Public Speaking in America,* Allyn and Bacon, Boston, 1965, p. 298.

8. For an interesting article on how appearance can affect listening see Jill Scott, "What Did You Say? I Was Listening to Your Tie," *English Journal* 73 (1986), p. 177.

9. Enid S. Waldhart and Robert N. Bostrom, "Notetaking, Listening and Modes of Retention," (paper presented to the International Listening Association, Washington, D.C., 1981); and Andrew D. Wolvin and Carolyn Coakley, *Listening,* Brown, Dubuque, Iowa, 1985, pp. 184–190.

Rumors

A professor, Jean-Noel Kapferer at the School for Advanced Business Studies in Paris has established the Foundation for Study and Information about Rumors, to learn more about rumors and how they occur. Kapferer states that it is time to start taking rumors seriously. The purpose of the study is to examine rumors in order to better understand and control them, detect and follow the evolution of rumors, and to alert public opinion to the danger of rumors.

Kapferer states, "In spite of what anyone says, people will still believe rumors." Kapferer went on to say that "psychologically people believe that reality is not that which is apparent. That the truth is hidden. People believe more in rumors than in official information." Kapferer suggests that rumors respond to an individual's need for intrigue or mystery. He calls rumors "the other side of reality."

The first rumor that Professor Kapferer is studying is the "rumor of villejuif." The "rumor of villejuif" has raged in France since 1976 and it states that dozens of food additives currently used in France contain cancer-causing agents. Despite repeated denials by hospitals, medical authorities, government ministers, and consumer groups the rumor persists. Kapferer has discovered that at least one-third of the households in France have heard the rumor and that 68% of those who have heard it actually believe it.

Another researcher who has examined the phenomenon of rumors predicts that out of every 100 people who hear a rumor, only about 40% can be swayed by the facts. Also suggested is that in order for rumors to succeed, there must be an element of believability.

In France, researchers state that most rumors revolve around French presidents. Those stories usually take three forms: the president is taking payoffs, he is dying, or he has an extraordinary sex life on the side. The only president to have escaped the rumor mill was former president Charles de Gaulle. Researchers suggest de Gaulle escaped such rumors since he was just "too credible." The only rumor that surfaced concerning de Gaulle was that he was not a general at all, but really gave himself two stars.

Most rumors today concern food. These rumors result from people's fears that in present day industrial society much of the commerically produced food is unsafe. The rumors concerning food have been around since the old poisoned well rumors of the 1600's.

Rumors have been around as long as people have been communicating. Who can forget such prevalent rumors as the one that former President John F. Kennedy was really alive and living in a sanatorium, that UFO's frequently land and mutilate animals, and the most common in the 1960's, that then Beatle Paul McCartney was killed in a car accident and was really dead! Heard any good rumors lately?

Name _____   Course _____

Listening Worksheet

This sheet can be used to keep a log of the time you spend communicating in various ways during a typical day. Pick three "blocks" of fifteen minutes during the morning, afternoon, and evening. For each block count the minutes and seconds you spend engaged in one of the five forms of communication listed in each column heading. Then total up the minutes and seconds when you have logged in all three blocks of time. How much of your day was spent in some form of communication? Which method of communication did you use the most? How much of this communication activity are you normally unaware of? Be prepared to discuss your findings with the rest of the class.

Time of Day	Own Thoughts	Speaking	Listening	Reading	Writing
Morning 15 Minutes					
Total Morning Time					
Afternoon 15 Minutes					
Total Afternoon Time					
Evening 15 Minutes					
Total Evening Time					
Total Time Spent for Entire Day					

Name _____   Course _____

Listening Worksheet

This sheet can be used to keep a log of the time you spend communicating in various ways during a typical day. Pick three "blocks" of fifteen minutes during the morning, afternoon, and evening. For each block count the minutes and seconds you spend engaged in one of the five forms of communication listed in each column heading. Then total up the minutes and seconds when you have logged in all three blocks of time. How much of your day was spent in some form of communication? Which method of communication did you use the most? How much of this communication activity are you normally unaware of? Be prepared to discuss your findings with the rest of the class.

Time of Day	Own Thoughts	Speaking	Listening	Reading	Writing
Morning 15 Minutes					
Total Morning Time					
Afternoon 15 Minutes					
Total Afternoon Time					
Evening 15 Minutes					
Total Evening Time					
Total Time Spent for Entire Day					

COMMUNICATION FACTS

Silence as Commrnciation

As we have read, "You cannot not communicate," and that statement includes the communicative value of silence. When people are silent in a transaction or conversation it communicates a great deal to the other member. The person could be saying that he doesn't wish to interact with the other party, is angry with the person, or is just not giving importance to the relationship. People often use silence as a method of abrogating responsibility, "Listen, I didn't say anything so I'm not responsible!". In addition silence can be used to show anger, "I'm angry with you so I will not speak to you any longer."

People grow very uncomfortable when the other party remains very silent throughout a conversation. A female student recently complained about the worst "blind date" she ever had where the fellow remained silent the entire evening and made her carry on the entire conversation. She told how she felt herself answering herself, and how he would give an occasional yes or no answer to a direct question. Certainly, most of us can sympathize with the poor woman in this situation. Silence must be interpreted in the context in which it takes place, the appropriateness of it as a response, and the type of verbal interactions that we have had with the silent party previously. Silence is significant and has definite communicative and message value.

5 Putting Your Ideas Into Words

Language plays a part in all our social interactions.

Before reading this chapter, ask yourself the following questions:

1. Why is language important?
2. How can I use language to effectively get across my ideas?
3. How can I use language to create vivid images for my listeners?

The power of language is amazing. Even the changing of a single word can prove of major consequence. As Mark Twain once observed, *"The difference between the right word and the almost right word, is the difference between lightening and the lightening bug."*

Good communicators know how the proper turn of a word can give a simple message a special wallop.[1] Consider Winston Churchill. In preparing a speech to announce Italy's invasion of France during the Second World War, he carefully sifted over every word. Should he characterize it as a *"spineless deed?"* Or, would it be better to describe it as a *"cowardly deed?"* He finally settled on calling it a *"dastardly deed,"* which means *"cowardly"* but sounds far worse. Franklin Roosevelt also knew how to turn a phrase.[2] Upon learning of the attack on Pearl Harbor, he asked an assistant to prepare an address declaring war on Japan. The assistant wrote the line: *"December 7, 1941: A date which will live in world history."* But before the speech Roosevelt replaced *"world history"* with *"infamy,"* saying instead: *"December 7, 1941: A date which will live in infamy."* While *"world history"* sounded bland and unemotional, *"infamy"* had a certain fiery appeal— lightening and the lightening bug.

The words you select give you the hammer to drive home your ideas. When searching for just the right word, ask yourself: What emotional impact do I want to have on my listeners? How do I want them to feel? How do I want them to react? What do I really want to get across?

Answering these questions will help you to find those sometimes elusive right words. And how can you be sure you've found those "right words?" By using language that is **appropriate, accurate, vivid,** and **effective.** The balance of this chapter will explore each in turn.

HOW TO USE LANGUAGE APPROPRIATELY

Your words need not be the most colorful, nor the most expressive, but they should be the most suitable. Your language should be appropriate for the situation, your subject, the communicator, and your listeners.

Appropriate for the Situation

Our words and expressions change as we travel from one speaking arena to the next. What works in the street would flop in the office; what sounds great in the classroom would sound artificial in the dorm; what is in on Saturday night would be out on Monday morning.

Most good communicators learn to gear their language for each occasion. *"There is a time for dialect, a place for slang, an occasion for literary form,"* writes William Safire, *"what is correct on the sports page is out of place on the op-ed page; what is with-it on the street may well be without it in the classroom."*[3] This was quickly discovered by Geraldine Ferraro when she became the first woman to run for the Vice Presidency in 1984. In her autobiography she writes: *"At a rally, the speaker is not supposed to talk at the people but with them, to interact with the crowd. I needed to have short, punchy lines and to know how to deliver them."*[4]

Just like Ms. Ferraro make your language fit the occasion. Situations change, so must your language.

Appropriate for the Subject

Appropriate language also fits the topic. Complex subjects require more frequent use of repetition, explanation, and definition. A simpler subject can be discussed in a more straightforward manner, without unneeded detail.

Choose language that will explain your subject in the most lucid, direct, and specific way. The operas of Richard Wagner or the miracle of the artificial heart might call for a more thorough explanation, while the process of performing CPR could be explained with considerably less detail.

Appropriate for the Communicator

Different communicators use different words in different ways. For instance, examine the following statement:

"We are called to a perfect mission: our mission, to feed the hungry, to clothe the naked, to house the homeless, to teach the illiterate, to provide jobs for the jobless, and to choose the human race over the nuclear race."[5]

Who do you think made this remark? Abraham Lincoln? Mike Tyson? Goldie Hawn? Jesse Jackson?

You probably were able to correctly guess Jesse Jackson. This is not surprising, since most people leave a stylistic imprint on their message. In the example of Reverend Jackson, the language was clearly distinguishable as his own because he typically uses words that lend a rhythmical cadence to his delivery.

Likewise work at perfecting your own style. While your use of language should always conform to the parameters of good taste and appropriateness, no one style exists for everyone. Pick up speaking tips from accomplished communicators like George Bush, Bill Cosby, or Barbara Walters, and incorporate their usable strengths into your use of language. Experiment; explore; through trial and error use language that seems most fitting for you. When it comes to style never seek to imitate, but always seek to initiate.

Appropriate for Your Listeners

What's perfectly understandable to one person, could be totally confusing to another. Using language that listeners can understand is especially important when technical, scientific, or recreational subjects are discussed. While you may be a *"wiz"* on baseball and understand all its nuances and terminologies, don't assume your listeners are. A *"can of corn,"* meaning a high fly ball to an avid baseball fan, would just be a container of vegetables to someone else.

Lee Iacocca, as head of the Chrysler Corporation, delivers countless speeches each year. In his autobiography he tells why he uses language that fits his audience: *"It's important to talk to people in their own language. If you do it well, they'll say, 'God, he said exactly what I was thinking.'"*[6]

Like Lee Iacocca, target your words to your listeners. Good communicators use words that stick in the minds of their listeners.

Be careful about using language that might irritate or turn off listeners. If you were doing a night club routine obscenities or ethnic jokes might get a laugh, but otherwise they're more likely to get a frown. Stay away from making racial, religious, political, ethnic, or sexual references that might alienate or offend.

Especially avoid using **sexist language.** Sexist language involves much more than obvious derogatory words like *"babe,"* *"sweet heart,"* or *"stud."* Making assumptions about one's profession by their gender is also sexist—all construction workers are not men and all nurses are not women. So is the use of job titles like *"firemen"* for *"firefighter,"* *"mailman"* for *"mailcarrier,"* or *"policeman"* for *"police officer."* Sexist language is at best inconsiderate, and at worst downright detrimental.

Always refer to adult females as women, not girls. Likewise, when a woman's marital status is unknown, refer to her as Ms.—unless she specifies that she prefers Miss or Mrs. But above all else, become sensitive to the use of "he" as an indefinite pronoun. This is still difficult for some people to grasp, since traditional teaching emphasized use of the generic he or him when the subject of the sentence could be either male or female. You can overcome this he/him problem in four ways. First, whenever possible, use the plural form:

Poor: *Before graduating, each student should make sure that **he** has **his** transcript.*
Better: *Before graduating, students should make sure that **they** have **their** transcripts.*

Second, use the pronoun *"you"* rather than *"he"* or *"she"*—this also helps to bring people into your message:

Poor: *Before studying, a student should have all **his** notes in order.*
Better: *Before studying, **you** should have **your** notes in order.*

Third, you can use the masculine and feminine pronouns in tandem:

Poor: *A good student gets **his** work done on time.*
Better: *A good student gets **his** or **her** work done on time.*

Rather than using pronouns in tandem, some communicators prefer to alternate their usage of he and she. For one paragraph, or example, the person might use she and for the next he. This is especially effective if traditional sexual stereotypes are violated—so that an executive is referred to as *"she"* and secretary as *"he."* Here's an example:

Poor: *Interviewers are quick to point out that **he** doesn't have any experience, or **he's** not the right **man** for the job.*
Better: *Interviewers are quick to point out that **he** doesn't have any experience, or **she's** not the right **person** for the job.*

Try analyzing your listeners to learn as much about them as you can. Suggestions for doing this are presented in Chapter 11.

The Language of Hawaii

For one thousand years the people of Hawaii had no written language. Information was passed down from one generation to the next through a series of dances—most particularly the hula dance.

In this dance each movement and position imparted information about the history of the Hawaiian culture and history. Subsequent generations of young Hawaiians learned about past rulers, battles, and events which formed their rich and varied history. With the arrival of the white missionaries and the English language, this dance carried less meaning. Many anthropologists fear that someday the hula dance will become a thing of the past in conveying information to succeeding generations.

HOW TO USE LANGUAGE ACCURATELY

When a communicator fails to use language with a cutting precision, confusion and even embarrassment can occur. Student speaker Jennifer Gordon learned this the hard way. Delivering a speech on the need for euthanasia, Jennifer kept referring to her terminally ill grandmother as *"inconsequent."* What she meant to say, of course, was that her grandmother was *"incontinent"*—which means unable to control bodily discharges. As a classmate later commented, *"I thought Jennifer was recommending mercy killing for her grandmother because she thought she was irrelevant, not because she was unable to contain natural discharges."* Because of the misuse of this one word, Jennifer was unable to convince many of her listeners.

The moral to this story is readily apparent. Never use a word unless you're sure of its meaning. If unsure, look in a dictionary—experienced communicators do this all the time. Consult a thesaurus. Consider the different shades of meaning you can paint by trying a different word. Instead of Jennifer saying her grandmother was *"incapacitated,"* for example, she could have said she was: *"debilitated,"* *"helpless,"* *"disabled,"* or *"weakened"*—each of these words would have given a slightly different slant to her grandmother's condition.

It's also worthwhile to expand your vocabulary by taking on new, challenging words. Malcolm X, the famous Black Muslim minister, amazingly copied down every word in the dictionary to enlarge his vocabulary! While this probably seems a bit too time consuming for most of us, make every effort to expand your vocabulary. Try learning one new word a day. A rich vocabulary will help you to put the proper word in the proper place.

The words that you use can have two types of meaning: denotative and connotative. We'll take a look at each, as well as the importance of using correct grammar.

Use Specific Denotations

Denotative meaning is exact, literal, and capable of simple interpretation. It conveys no passionate appeals, no emotional twists, no moral renderings. It simply describes a person, place, thing, event, or idea in direct, straightforward language. It's helpful to think of a word's denotative meaning as its dictionary definition. The denotative meaning of the noun *"house,"* for example, would *"be a place that provides shelter and living space."*

Sometimes people confuse the denotative meaning of a word. Does the speaker mean *"uninterested"* or *"disinterested;"* *"allusion"* or *"illusion;"* *"affect"* or *"effect?"* One way to help sort out these difficulties is to refer to a good English handbook.

Another problem with denotations is that meanings sometimes change according to time or location. If someone was described as *"gay"* thirty years ago, it would mean that they were happy; today it would probably mean they were homosexual. Language also changes by region. A sack, meaning a paper bag in the midwest, is a cloth laundry bag in the east. That's why it's advisable to consider what a word might mean to someone who has a different background than your own.

Use Clear Connotations

Connotative meaning is more emotional, interpretive, and subjective. Basically, the connotative meaning of a word is what the word implies rather than what it

Figure 5.1 When language is used accurately, people will pay attention.

actually means. Connotations suggest feelings, desires, opinions, and attitudes. When a man named Bernard Goetz shot four alleged 19 year old muggers on a New York subway in 1984, for example, the victims were described at various times as being: *"youths," "teenagers," "men," "boys,"* or *"children."* Clearly, each description conjured up a somewhat different image.

Research has consistently shown that the words used to describe an event have a noticeable effect on the way it's perceived by others.[7] With our language we show our feelings of love and hate, fear and security, hope and despair. Good communicators, like writers and poets, use connotation to enrich their meaning and give image to their visions.

Which should you use, denotative or connotative language? It depends on your purpose, subject, situation, and listeners. Do you want to sound totally objective and impartial? Then use more denotative words. Do you want to stir up your listeners, impelling them to take some action? Then more connotative words will do. Part of being a good communicator is being able to decide on the best, most accurate way to express an idea.

Use Proper Grammar

While most of us would never devalue a person's ideas because of grammatical faults, many listeners would find such blunders quite objectionable. That's why you should make a concerted effort to catch all grammatical errors. Speakers who constantly refer to *"you's"* or *"we's"* may end up turning the *"you's"* and *"we's"* in their audience off.

While the grammatical habits of a lifetime are difficult to break in a single semester, start now. Your instructor will help you, catching grammatical slips as they occur. Visit your college's learning laboratory, tutoring service, and workshops on grammar. Read a helpful book on grammar and usage. For, unlike some things, proper grammar can be learned and through practice perfected.

HOW TO USE LANGUAGE VIVIDLY

Just as your ideas need to be expressed with accuracy, they need to be brushed with a creative stroke. Vivid descriptions make a message more interesting to listen to, more absorbing to recall. Read, for example, this excerpt from a speech by United States Treasurer Katherine Davalos Ortega on what it means to be an American:

> *"Millions of our forebearers came to this country through the portal where the Statue of Liberty stands. Millions came through other portals—Latin America, Asia, and Africa.*
>
> > *Most of these succeeding generations of new Americans came to escape tyranny and to live their lives in freedom.*
> >
> > *Others came not of their free will, but their descendants would in time find freedom and equality in a land that never ceases to change— grow in spirit—to offer new vistas of hope and opportunity for each new generation."*[8]

Stirring, isn't it? Such an animated use of language livens up listeners and sparks their interest. Dull, bland words, on the other hand, leave listeners unmoved, the message unmemorable. Although there are several techniques for using language vividly, we'll explore two of the most effective: **imagery** and **rhythm**.

Create Imagery

There's an Arabian proverb that says "The one who is the best orator is the one who can turn another's ears into eyes." Turning ears into eyes is the result of putting vivid language to work. By painting imaginative and colorful descriptions you can turn the driest of subjects into the most stunning of messages. Expressive words have the almost magical power to make beautiful, striking images dance in the minds of listeners.

Here student speaker Kim Fields colorfully describes her first impression at meeting a new horse:

> *"He first spots you like a nervous boxer. His hooves dance forward and back, nostrils snorting like a firing engine. He is huge. His rump looks like a brown mountain, divided by a meadow of snow. His eyes reflect your image, and as you approach him you sense the potent odor of his power."*

But what if Kim had said instead:

> *"He moves a bit as he first spots you. He is huge and seems nervous. He is brown with white markings, and as you approach him you get a strong whiff of his horsey smell."*

The first version is more stimulating isn't it? By using vivid imagery Kim is able to magnetically capture our interest with her description of the horse. She is able to "turn our ears into eyes" by likening him to a nervous boxer; his nostrils to a firing engine; his markings to a brown mountain divided by a meadow of snow; and his odor to the awesome sense of his power.

One way to create powerful images is to appeal to the senses—touch, taste, sight, smell, and sound. Sensory images let listeners hear the roar of a mountain stream, feel the bite of a morning chill, or smell the aroma of a campfire breakfast. Here student speaker Rich Garcia appeals to sensory imagery in describing fighting a forest fire:

> *"At first the mountain of flame looks almost peaceful. Then as you get closer it hits you. The thick, acrid smoke embraces you with a chokehold, forcing down your throat the bitter taste of charred cotton. The heat is intense—you feel sunburned right down to the bone. But worst of all are the sounds. Trees explode as if a thousand cannons firing at once, and huge oaks snap as if toothpicks; you think you're trapped in a giant popcorn maker. Birds and animals give off piercing, desperate screams until drowned out by the advancing flame. Finally when the fire is out there's only silence; dead silence."*

With Rich's portrayal we taste the fire, likened to charred cotton; we feel the intense heat compared to being sunburned right down to the bone; and we hear its deadly sound as if trapped in a giant popcorn maker. We've not just heard about a fire—we've witnessed its terror firsthand.

How do you paint your descriptions with such a fresh stroke? By using **metaphors, personification, irony, hyperbole,** and **understatement.** Let's review each in turn.

Metaphors

Most accomplished communicators know how to evoke a colorful image through the use of a metaphor: a statement that points out striking similarities between two otherwise dissimilar things. A good metaphor not only enlivens, it renders an idea clear. When George Bush likens *"Iraq to a time-bomb waiting to go off"* we get the graphic image of a nation gone out of control. And when Jesse Jackson compares America's multi-racial makeup to a *"rainbow of many colors"* we vividly get the picture of what he means.

Sports writers are masters at turning a clever metaphor. Sports journalist Bugs Baer once wrote of hard throwing pitcher Lefty Grove: *"He could throw a lamb chop past a wolf."* And a writer for a New York paper described a game where the football Giants were decimated by the Chicago Bears with this metaphorical quip: *"Watching the Giants try to run against the Bears was like watching a stack of phone books dive into a shredder!"* Metaphors like these paint past events with a brilliant hue.

And how do you create a good metaphor? One way is to vary the verb that carries the metaphorical sense of the statement. For example:

"My car screamed under my army of baggage."

People scream, cars sag. Yet the verb *"screamed"* makes the weight of the baggage seem even more leaden.

A second way is to change an adjective. Here's one:

"The dead amusement park echoed my thoughts."

By making the amusement park *"dead"* rather than silent, the speaker demonstrates a greater sense of isolation.

A final way is to play with an adverb. For example:

"The snow stealthily fell; suffocating all my hope."

Cats can be stealthy. People can be stealthy. But snow can only fall. *"Stealthy"* snow sharply illustrates the silent power of the storm.

One type of metaphor you can use is a **simile.** Similes are usually introduced by *"like"* or *"as;"* for example, *"The man flew as if a bird"* or *"The teacher was like a dusty book that never had been opened."* Nancy Reagan creatively used one when she said, *"A woman is like a tea bag. You don't really know what she's like until she gets into hot water."*

Here are a few others:

"The students of this college are like the lost pieces of a puzzle."
"Lincoln embraced the Constitution as if it were a frightened child."

When communicators wish to have a dramatic impact they often use **archetypal metaphors.** These are metaphors with a universal appeal which are drawn from sources such as light and dark, victory and defeat, life and death, storm and calm and the like. One speaker who often used archetypal metaphors was Martin Luther King, Jr. Here he refers to the seasons of the year:

"This sweltering summer of the Negro's legitimate discontent will not pass until there is an invigorating autumn of freedom and equality."[9]

With this metaphor we learn much about Reverend King's vision of the future. He ties discontent with a sweltering summer and freedom with an invigorating autumn. Since autumn always follows summer, his message suggests that freedom and equality will eventually come.

Want to use archetypes? Link a problem with a disease (pornography is a cancer) and its solution with the cure (stiffer laws are an anecdote); compare rough times to a storm (homesickness is like a never-ending rain) and good times to a calm (getting over it was like looking at a peaceful sky); or tie a conflict to a war (we waged a tough battle) and its being resolved to a peace (but we earned a placid victory). Archetypes like these let you draw sharp contrasts in expressing an idea.

Implied metaphors let you describe something with a surgeon's precision rather than with an artist's flair. With an implied metaphor you don't merely say one thing is like something else; instead you speak it as if it actually were. This type of metaphor can be extremely suggestive. If you say *"my roommate is a pill"* you suggest someone hard to live with. Say *"my roommate is a snake"* and we get the impression of someone sneaky and dishonest. Winston Churchill knew how to imply with a metaphor. Hitler was compared to *"a boa constrictor devouring its prey,"* Mussolini to *"a jackal living off the dead,"* and the British Commonwealth to *"an old Lion protecting her cubs."* Here are some examples of implied metaphors—note the powerful image each conjures up:

"My opponent slithered into office."
"Los Angeles is one long freeway."

A good metaphor should spark a brilliant *"flash of recognition"* that strikes listeners with *"surprise or fascination."*[10] As long as the brilliance of the flash is familiar, the metaphor will work. But trouble occurs when the comparison seems too remote, the image too hard to digest. When a metaphor likens two things that don't have enough in common to justify the comparison, it becomes a *strained metaphor.* For example, take Shakespeare's famous *"All the world's a stage."* This metaphor works because it compares two easily visualized things. Likewise the metaphor "A camel is a horse designed by committee" makes sense because it colorfully describes the functionary purpose of a camel, while blaming its awkward appearance on the noted inefficiency of committees. But saying "A camel is a dog designed by committee" strains the suggestion. How is a camel like a dog? And why would it be designed by a committee? Revise all metaphors that make such distant comparisons. Here are some examples:

> **Strained:** *"The ship sank like a wounded bird."*
> **Strained:** *"The snow covered us as if a giant wave."*

How does a wounded bird sink? And how can the snow cover as if a wave? Here are the revised versions. See how much clearer they are to visualize:

> **Revised:** *"The ship sank like a barrel of lead."*
> **Revised:** *"The snow covered us as if a gentle, white blanket."*

Sometimes a metaphor seems to needlessly quarrel. When two or more incompatible images are tossed together in the same metaphor you've breed such confusion. These are called *mixed metaphors* and often leave listeners wondering, laughing, or both. For instance, say someone says the following:

> "In order to keep our nation afloat we must break down the wall of free trade."

This image is impossible to visualize. How can a nation float and break down a wall at the same time? Obviously one or the other must go. This metaphor makes more sense if it says instead:

> *"In order to keep our nation afloat we must not drown free trade."*

Now it becomes easier to imagine. Here are some others:

Mixed: *"The crowd attacked viciously, drowning itself with its fury."*
Mixed: *"The wind of the cold war is cutting at the fabric of society."*

The crowd was vicious and drowning? A wind can cut? In the revised versions we replace these with two comparisons that logically go together:

Revised: *"The crowd attacked viciously, destroying itself with its fury."*
Revised: *"The wind of the cold war is tearing at the fabric of society."*

Metaphors are so basic to speaking that we often use them without careful thought. Sometimes

this leads us to use **dead metaphors:** words once new and alive that have been so overused, they have lost all their bite and freshness. Such words no longer call to mind vivid images, instead they have become pat, meaningless cliches.

Here are some **cliches** still in circulation. If you spot a favorite of yours try replacing it with something more original:

high as a kite	*mad as a wet hen*
old as the hills	*blind as a bat*
dead as a doornail	*slept like a dog*
hard as a rock	*with a ten-foot pole*
fit to be tied	*a crying shame*
strong as an ox	*flat as a pancake*
tip of the iceberg	*nice as pie*
cool as a cucumber	*bored to tears*

Occasionally two cliches can be combined to give a simple phrase an imaginative spark. When this happens what sounds trite, suddenly becomes inventive. At the 1988 Democratic National Convention keynote speaker Ann Richards wished to make light of Republican opponent George Bush's wealthy background and habit of making verbal slips. She gave birth to a memorable metaphor when she said, *"Poor George—he was born with a silver foot in his mouth."* Needless to say, she brought the house down. By blending two well-known cliches, Ann Richards coined a new phrase with a catchy appeal.

Personification

"The waves *shouted* back at me" or "The cold hit me like a *fist*" are examples of personification. Personification is when an intimate object is given human qualities. This is often used to make an abstract idea seem more concrete and familiar. Personification not only makes complex ideas easier to grasp, it gives them a more interesting appeal. For example:

> *"The engine **coughed** to life."*
> *"The leaves **danced** as they fell to earth."*

Irony

Irony is an inventive form of sarcasm. It's a way of brushing an idea with an opposite and sour note. In expressing her displeasure at being vaccinated before going overseas, one traveler said: *"I just love being stuck with a half dozen four-inch needles."* Irony gives a creative twist to a message. Use it to show a wry form of contrast. Notice these examples:

> *"If the water gets any more polluted, we'll have to come out of the shower to get clean."*
> *"Being stung all night by mosquitos is my favorite pastime."*

Hyperbole

Hyperbole is a way of overstating an issue. It's a form of stylistic exaggeration designed to stress a point, like: *"I'm so hungry I could eat a horse."* Hyperbole is more used to demonstrate a strong feeling, than to give a realistic appraisal.

Approach hyperbole with a cautionary step. If you exaggerate too much you're likely to appear as more manipulative than creative. It's okay to say *"My talk on safe driving can save your life,"* but it's probably stretching it too far to say, *"My talk on safe driving is guaranteed to save every life in this audience."*

Understatement

Understatement is just the opposite of hyperbole. Instead of exaggerating something, understatement does just what the name implies—downplays an idea, making it seem less than it really is. Someone could understate the devastation of vehicular deaths by saying, *"Not a year goes by that not a few people are killed in automobile accidents."* "Not a few" means a lot, but sounds less dramatic. Understating an issue dresses it with a subtle flair—and the broader the gap of truth, the more intense the effect. For instance:

> *"The chances are that one or two of you want to pass this course."*
> *"Smoking isn't so bad; what's so terrible about cutting ten years off your life?"*

Watch Out for Overblown Imagery

Using imagery is like sharpening a knife—a little bit is fine, but too much can ruin the point. Excess imagery calls so much attention to itself that it takes listeners away from the real intent of the message. In the following example student speaker Carl Harkins allows himself to get carried away with his imagery:

> *"The federal bureaucracy is like an overgrown forest. Organizations and departments spring up like scrub pine. And once a program really starts to work, it's too soon felled like valuable timber. We need to creatively trim this forest. Cut out those programs that don't work, and plant in their place programs that will last like Redwood."*

Carl starts out fine—comparing the federal bureaucracy to an overgrown forest seems reasonable enough; but soon his imagery starts to grow like one. Carl needs to slash his imaginary forest with a machete. Here's a trimmed down version:

> *"The federal bureaucracy is like an overgrown forest. Organizations and departments spring up with abandon. And once a program really starts to work, it's too soon eliminated. We need to revitalize this bureaucracy. Cut out those programs that don't work, and put in their place those that will."*

Now Carl's point is crisply made. His imagery enhances his argument, but doesn't diminish his message.

While imagery gives a message its texture, rhythm gives it its glow. Let's see what this means.

Establish Rhythm

Like the tempo of the tide, or the beat of a lead guitar, rhythm refers to the magical pattern of a recurrent sound. When language has such a rhythmical charm it takes on an almost musical flavor. A good example of rhythm can be found in children's nursery rhymes—the blend and mix of words leads to a methodical, striking cadence. Here's a popular rhyme modified to eliminate sexual bias:

Jill and Jack Be Nimble
Jack be nimble, Jack be Quick,
Jack, jump over the candlestick.
Jill be nimble, jump it too,
If Jack can do it, so can you![11]

Notice the finely-tuned da-DUM da-DUM beat conveyed through even a simple reading? Many forms of music and literature are similarly capable of creating such a pleasant beat of sound.

Like artful writers, accomplished speakers dress their language with a rhythmical grace. Martin Luther King and Winston Churchill especially provided a rhythmical quality with their arresting use of the language. Observe the following passage from Dr. King's famous *"I Had A Dream"* speech:

> *"I have a dream that one day every valley shall be exalted;*
>> *every hill and mountain shall be made low,*
>> *the rough places will be made plain,*
>> *the crooked places will be made straight*
>> *and the glory of the Lord shall be revealed*
>> *and all flesh shall see it together."* [12]

You can almost hear the rhymed quality of Dr. King's words. Notice too that his rhythmical beat is not completely predictable; rather it comes and goes as if a boxer throwing in an occasional left jab.

There are many ways to establish rhythm in a message. We'll discuss six of the most important.

Parallelism

Parallelism is where words, phrases, or sentences are arranged in similar form. This gives a statement a certain harmonious appeal. Here is an example from a speech by Richard Nixon:

> *"Where peace is unknown, make it welcome; where peace is fragile, make it strong; where peace is temporary, make it permanent."*

Why does this statement have a rhythmical ring? Because it has balance. Nixon couples *"where peace"* with *"make it"* in three perfectly balanced clauses. This gives this passage its graceful strength. Here are a few more: [13]

> *"Let us follow our conscience, let us follow our dreams."*
>> *"The future belongs to the young, the strong, the brave."*

Antithesis

A second form of parallelism is antithesis or contrast, which uses a similar construction of words, phrases, or sentences to show opposed or sharply contrasting ideas. Remember this line from John F. Kennedy's Inaugural Address?

> *"Let us never negotiate out of fear. But let us never fear to negotiate."*

With this statement Kennedy effectively argues that fearful negotiations and negotiating out of fear are two opposing things that we shouldn't do. How does antithesis forcefully polish such an argument? By laying two issues side by side it brings greater attention to both. Examine the following:

> *"Let us accept all challenges; let us reject all defeats."*
>> *"One who thinks too much about the past, thinks too little about the future."*

Repetition

While in writing prose repetition is considered a vice, in speech communication it's more viewed as a device. This is because listeners don't have access to instant replay. They have no notes, no tapes, no aids for recall. But by artfully repeating a phrase listeners are given a magic marker to underline a key idea.

How does repetition work? Generally the same word or set of words is repeated at the beginning or end of successive clauses or sentences. Repetition not only gives a statement a stylistic appeal, it smoothly unifies a sequence of ideas. Student speaker Bob Morris accomplishes this by repeating the phrase "I saw:"

> *"I saw the hungry; I saw the homeless; I saw the needy; and I saw the future."*

Alliteration

One way to polish a line is to repeat a sound until it takes on an harmonious beat. This is called alliteration and is a favorite technique of poets and storytellers alike. Alliteration occurs when a consonant is repeated at the beginnings of words. Here's an example from a speech by Henry Kissinger:

> *"First, a world community requires the curbing of conflict."*

When sounds are repeated inside words it's an example of internal alliteration. For instance notice the *"K"* sounds in: "Peter Piper picked a peck of pickled peppers."

Repeating a vowel sound is called **assonance** and has a similarly enforcing effect. For example: "An *o*dd and *o*minous act." or "an *a*wful and *a*ugust bill."

The Power of Words

How powerful are words? George Smathers won a Senate race in Florida in part by his colorful description of his opponent Claude Pepper. Pepper, a sixty-year-old bachelor, had a sister who was an actress in New York, and a niece who worked on the Senator's Public Works Committee. Here is Smather's attack:

"My friends, the Good Book tells us that, "Ye shall know the truth, and the truth shall make you free." Well it's incumbent on me to tell you the truth about Claude Pepper. My friends, he is a sexagenarian. Why, my friends, after years of matriculating at Harvard, he now practices celibacy all by himself.

It's matter of public record that he commits nepotism with his own niece. And his sister is a well-known thespian in wicked Greenwich Village. Yes, my friends, Claude Pepper has heterosexual proclivities and is known for his notorious extroversion."

A final way to make an idea memorable is to use **rhyme.** For instance:

> *"Those families who pray together, stay together."*
> *(Billy Graham)*

A simple way to create rhyme is to use two words that end in *"tion."* For example:

> *"To tax or to cut taxes—that is the choice between stagnation or stimulation of our economy." (Jack Kemp)*

Climax

Want to heighten an idea's import? Want to make something easier to remember? Try climax. Climax is when words, phrases, or sentences are arranged in a desired order. You can go from least to most important; you can follow the alphabet; you can follow some logical sequence. Often this includes three things. Here's one from Franklin Roosevelt:

> *"I see one-third of a nation ill-housed, ill-clad, and ill-nourished."*

Work with a Verb

Verbs are powerful words. Verbs *"get," "give," "make,"* and *"hold."* Spin the proper verb with the proper preposition and you've got a dazzling line. Say *"We should resist crime"* and we get one meaning. But say *"We should stand up to crime"* and we get quite another. Here's one from Mike Dukakis:

> *"Everybody wants to bring down the deficit but no one wants to bring up taxes."*

Want to strike listeners with a catchy verb mixed with a challenging preposition? Here are some combinations:

Verb	Preposition	Verb	Preposition
bring	*up*	*do*	*for*
hold	*down*	*push*	*through*
work	*over*	*turn*	*out*

Try enlivening your language with imagery and rhythm. Imagery makes your language crisp and alive; rhythm makes it fluid and persistent. Used together they'll make your ideas clearer to understand, your descriptions more exciting to recall.

HOW TO USE LANGUAGE EFFECTIVELY

When language is used effectively it expresses an idea with the sharpness of a razor's edge. There are five techniques for being effective, which we can call the five "C's" of communicating. They are to be **clear, concrete, concise, colorful,** and **conversational.** Let's discuss each.

Be Clear

Being clear means punctuating your thoughts with simple, easy to understand words. It also means avoiding words that needlessly confuse—namely **jargon** and **euphemisms.**

Jargon is the specialized language of a group or profession. Sometimes jargon makes sense. As when Daryl Strawberry says to another baseball player, *"I hammered a heater into the seats"* (Translation: *"I hit a fastball for a homerun,"*) or when one trucker tells another over a CB, *"There's a smokey up on 29"* (Translation: *"There's a trooper on top of a hill at milepost 29."*) But most times jargon confuses, rather than clarifies. While you may understand what is meant by a *"prevent defense"* or a *"dot matrix printer,"* don't assume everyone else does. Explain an unfamiliar term; define a key abbreviation; and spell out a specialized term. Bear in mind Lincoln's advice when he said, *"Speak so the most lowly can understand you, and the rest will have no difficulty."*

A euphemism is a pleasant or neutral word that replaces one that's direct or unpleasant. Sometimes this seems harmless enough. Saying someone *"passed away"* rather than *"died,"* or is a *"senior citizen"* rather than *"old"* is a way of painting a description with a sensitive stroke. The problem with euphemisms is that they often make hazy that what should be clear. When a tax hike is called a *"revenue enhancement,"* or a patient's death is described as a *"negative patient care outcome,"* we have needlessly confused.

Be Concrete

Concrete words describe things that can be seen, heard, tasted, smelled, or touched. Abstract words, on the other hand, refer to qualities or concepts that cannot be perceived by the senses. Concrete words are specific and get a point across. Examples of concrete language include words like *"stick,"* *"cat,"* *"apple,"* and *"door"*—we can easily visualize each of these things. *"Politics,"* *"love,"* *"justice,"* and *"party"* are more abstract—it's hard to form a firm

mental picture of what each of these things mean. Some words, however, are neither completely concrete or abstract. *"Lemon"* is concrete, yet it can also mean an inefficient car or a bitter experience.

The problem with abstract language is that it often is too general to effectively make clear. Concrete words, however, make your descriptions specific, your meanings precise. Hammer down your point by saying directly what you mean. Say *"Chemistry 101,"* not *"a course in science;"* say *"a Honda Civic,"* not *"a small foreign car;"* say *"Highway 295,"* not *"a major interstate highway."* When describing something with an abstract quality—beauty, art, truth and so on—back it up with concrete detail. Don't say *"the forest was beautiful,"* say *"the Aspen pines and tall peaks seemed to reach for the sky."* Don't say *"the girl looked happy,"* say *"the girl's eyes lit up and her mouth broke into a wide grin."* Concrete words let you carve vivid descriptions which are worthy of recall.[14]

Be Concise

As a young writer Mark Twain was often paid by the word. He once observed: *"By hard, honest labor, I've dug all the large words out of my vocabulary. I never write metropolis for seven cents because I can get the same price for city. I never write policeman because I can get the same price for cop."*

That's pretty good advice—even if you're not getting paid by the word. For there's no message that can't be improved by cutting, chopping, excluding. Prune away the deadwood; cut words that clog rather than clarify. Instead use words with economy, so your message is direct, sharp, and straight to the point.

Good communicators know how to cut out clutter. Consider Lincoln's Gettysburg Address—probably the model of succinct English.[15] It consisted of ten superbly chiseled sentences, 269 words, only eighteen of three or more syllables.

And how can you cut like a Lincoln? Eliminate fanfare and equivocation. Don't say, *"On the subject of appearance Brooke Shields is more or less attractive,"* say, *"Brooke Shields is attractive."* Omit phrases like *"There is"* or *"There are."* Rather than saying *"There are people who are afraid of guns,"* say, *"Many people are afraid of guns."* Replace *"to be"* by an active verb. This not only enlivens, it sharpens the verb. Rather than saying *"The speech was a disappointment to the audience,"* say, *"The speech disappointed the audience,"* or just *"The speech disappointed."* Exclude clauses that start with who, what, or that. Don't say, *"Off-road vehicles, which are four-wheelers, are unsafe at any speed,"* say, *"Off-road four-wheelers are unsafe at any speed.*" Whittle away adverbs and adjectives. Rather than saying *"Eddie Murphy's brilliantly executed routine was funny,"* say *"Eddie Murphy's routine was funny."* Eliminate vague modifiers such as *"very,"* *"slightly,"* or *"especially."* Instead of saying *"This is very important,"* simply say, *"This is important."* Finally, never use a long word when a short one will do. It's clearer to say *"Cut all words that are unfamiliar or unnecessary"* than *"Obviate all words that are highfalutin or supererogatory!"*

Be Colorful

Besides adding color through imagery and rhythm, you can brighten your ideas with **variety.** What's the best way to add variety? Try sprucing up your sentences. Make all sentences long and your message will sound confusing; make all of them short, and it will sound monotonous. Create color by following or preceding a long sentence with one that's short and lively.

Here Ronald Reagan hits listeners with a brisk variety of sentence length. Notice his alternating pattern:

> *"Everyone is against protectionism in the abstract. That is easy. It is another matter to make the hard, courageous choices when it is your industry or your business that appears to be hurt by foreign competition. I know. We in the United States deal with the problem of protectionism every day of the year."*

What does he do? He starts with seven words in the first sentence, followed by three in the next; then he uses twenty-six, followed by two; then closes with sixteen. Average length? About eleven words per sentence. Try pacing yourself the same way. Here's another example:

> *"Elderly abuse? Last year over 100,000 elderly Americans were attacked, beaten, or otherwise abused in the United States. This must be stopped."*

Be Conversational

A cartoon in *The New Yorker* showed a speaker standing in front of an audience saying, *"And now I should like to depart from my prepared text and speak as a human being."* Speaking as a human being means conversing, not lecturing at your listeners. Conversational words are natural and relaxed—overly formal words are stiff and awkward.

In order to be conversational speak like you talk, not like you write. Cut stilted adverbs like *"therefore,"* *"nevertheless,"* and *"moreover."* In a conversation you wouldn't say *"Therefore this idea works,"* instead you'd say *"This idea works."* Use the active rather than the passive voice. Say *"I think,"* not *"It is thought."* Active language sounds alive, passive words seem dead. Stick with contractions—*"isn't,"* *"can't,"* *"won't"*—they sound more natural. Use lots of *"you,"* *"your,"* *"we,"* and *"ours"*—this makes a message sound more personal. And eliminate modifying expressions like *"I think."* *"I believe,"* and *"In my opinion"*—these weaken a sentence. Say *"We must stop pollution,"* not *"In my opinion we must stop pollution."* In short, keep your sentences short, keep your words plain, and keep your ideas simple.

CHAPTER SUMMARY

Language has incredible power. Even the changing of a single word can have tremendous impact. That's why it's important to find just the right word. Finding that right word means using language that is appropriate, accurate, vivid, and effective.

Language should be appropriate for the situation, subject, communicator, and listener. Being appropriate for the situation means fitting words for the event. Appropriate for the subject means expressing yourself in a lucid, direct, and specific way. Being appropriate for the communicator means fitting language to mesh with your personal style. And being appropriate for your listeners means using words that are clear and don't offend.

Language should be accurate so listeners can follow what was said. The meaning of words can be denotative or connotative. Denotative meaning is exact, literal, and capable of simple interpretation. Connotative meaning is more emotional, interpretive, and subjective. Of course, accuracy requires that every effort should be made to catch grammatical faults.

Using language vividly means brushing descriptions with a creative stroke. This can be done through imagery and rhythm. Imagery means describing something so it takes on a striking pose. This can be accomplished by using metaphors, personification, irony, hyperbole, and understatement. Beware of overblown imagery. Rhythm refers to the magical pattern of a recurrent sound. Rhythm can be established through parallelism, antithesis, repetition, alliteration, climax, and by working with a verb.

Using language effectively means being clear, concrete, concise, colorful, and conversational. Using language clearly means eliminating jargon and euphemisms. When language is concrete it paints specific descriptions. Concisely using the language means eliminating unnecessary words. Language can be used colorfully by showing variety in sentences. And language can be conversational when it sounds natural and personal.

EXERCISES FOR REVIEW

1. Write a short paper describing the importance of using language effectively. Why is this especially necessary when speaking? Give examples from personal experience.
2. Write a list detailing some of the more common ways sexist language is used. Be prepared to discuss some of the ways we can eliminate sexist language from our spoken vocabulary.
3. Make a list of some of the ways people use language ineffectively. What types of words tend to confuse the most? Be prepared to discuss with a small group of classmates.
4. What are some of the ways language can be used more vividly? Write one sentence using each technique.
5. Write one sentence using each of the following: metaphor, personification, irony, hyperbole, and understatement.

NOTES

1. English offers the richest, most varied selection of words of any language ever known. For example, the *Oxford English Dictionary* lists about half a million words, while comparable French and German dictionaries contain no more than 35,000. English is used for half the world's 10,000 newspapers, 75 percent of all the telexes and telegraphs, and 80 percent of all the output generated from computers. But English allows eloquence even with few words. William Shakespeare's vocabulary is estimated to have been no more than 15,000 words.
2. Roosevelt was not the only president to dramatically change a word at the last moment. On the morning of his inaugural address John Kennedy crossed out *"will"* in the line, "Ask not what your country will do for you; ask what you will do for your country," replacing it with *"can."* The *"can"* gave the line its strength and is the best remembered line of the address. The success of Kennedy's address was no accident either. He carefully studied 33 inaugural addresses before preparing his own.
3. William Safire, *On Language* (New York: Times Books, 1980), p. xiv.
4. Geraldine A. Ferraro and Linda Bird Francke, *Ferraro, My Story* (New York: Bantam Books, 1985).
5. Jesse Jackson, "The Rainbow Coalition," *Vital Speeches of the Day,* 51, November 15, 1984, p. 77.
6. Lee Iacocca and William Novak, *Iacocca: An Autobiography* (New York: Bantam Books, 1984).
7. For a thorough review of this research particularly as it relates to persuasion, see Erwin P. Bettinghaus and Michael J. Cody, *Persuasive Communication* 4th ed. (New York: Holt, Rinehart and Winston, 1987), pp. 110–112.
8. Katherine Davalos Ortega, "Keynote Address," *Vital Speeches of the Day,* 50, September 15, 1984, pp. 712–713.
9. King frequently appealed to the lightness or darkness of the day or the seasons of the year. Martin Luther King, "I Have A Dream," in Houston Peterson, *A Treasury of the World's Great Speeches* (New York: Simon and Schuster, 1965), p. 838.
10. Michael Osborn, *Orientations to Rhetorical Style* (Chicago: Science Research Associates, 1976), p. 10.
11. Douglas W. Larche, *Mother Goose and Father Gander: Equal Rhymes for Girls and Boys* (Indianola, Iowa: Father Gander Press, 1979).
12. Houston Peterson, p. 839.
13. Using the same initial wording in a sequence of phrases is a type of parallelism called anaphora. For instance, "Peace now, peace tomorrow, peace forever," is an example of anaphora.
14. A message using more concrete words is found to be clearer, more interesting, and better remembered. See J. Kisielius and B. Sternthal, "Examining the Vividness Controversy: An Availability-Valence Interpretation," *Journal of Consumer Research,* 12, 1986, pp. 418–431; C. C. Jorgensen and W. Kintsch, "The Role of Imagery in the Evaluation of Sentences," *Cognitive Psychology,* 4, 1973, pp. 110–116.
15. Seventy-six percent of the words in the Gettysburg Address were five letters or less. Contrary to popular opinion, Lincoln did not write his address on the back of an envelope; it was written on White House stationary. He added the final nine lines in the Gettysburg home of David Wills, where he was staying. The morning of the speech he added about 30 more words.

Name _____   Course _____

Language Worksheet

1. Below is a list of words. Label them according to whether they are more concrete or abstract.

brick ____   fulfilled ____   happy ____   hat ____
house ____   desk ____   education ____   car ____
hurricane ____   important ____   meaningful ____ girl ____

2. In each of the following sentences, choose the best word to complete the statement.
   speeding, rushing, moving, zooming

   a. The car went _____ by.

   b. When the plane took off it was really _____ .

   c. The rocket went _____ toward the Moon.

   d. He was always _____ about.

3. Examine the following sentences. Then rewrite them correcting instances of jargon, and euphemisms.

   a. A state of the art computer will network your home with your office.

   a. _____

   b. People on public assistance are socially stigmatized into thinking they are street people.

   b. _____

   c. The full court press caused the new wave to go around the arena.

   c. _____

4. Arrange the following sequences of words from the most abstract to the most concrete.

   a. boat, recreation, engine, Chris Craft

   a. _____   _____   _____   _____
      most concrete   concrete   abstract   most abstract

   b. Denver, United States, Earth, Colorado

   b. _____   _____   _____   _____
      most concrete   concrete   abstract   most abstract

   c. Congress, Senate, sub-committee, committee

   c. _____   _____   _____   _____
      most concrete   concrete   abstract   most abstract

d. tree, limb, leaf, branch

d. _____ _____ _____ _____
     most concrete   concrete   abstract   most abstract

5. Identify the following statements as *similes, metaphors, hyperbole, understatement, personification,* or *irony.*

    a. If I become any colder I'll simply melt away.
    b. Cars are so dangerous the chances are before their through they'll kill every American.
    c. The boat rocked like a gentle swing.
    d. The mountain smiled back at me.
    e. This is the winter of despair.

    a. _____   b. _____   c. _____

    d. _____   e. _____

6. Identify the device employed in the following statements as *parallelism, antithesis, repetition, alliteration,* or *climax*

    a. "Are women persons? I hardly believe any of our opponents will have the hardihood to say that."
    b. First we were shot at. Then we were imprisoned. And finally we were set free.
    c. Let the truth make you free! Come with us.
        Let the truth make you free! Work with us.
        Let the truth make you free! Vote with us.
    d. We will overcome any obstacle. We will accept any challenge. We will defeat any enemy.
    e. Be what you can; not what you can't.

    a. _____   b. _____   c. _____

    d. _____   e. _____

Table 5.1
Some Common Regionalisms in the United States

Description	General American	Regional Term
paper bag	bag	sack
bottled soda	soda	pop
sugared roll	sweet roll	sugar bun
frankfurter	hot dog, frank	weiner, dog
candy on a stick	lollypop	sucker
denim pants	dungarees	jeans
canvas shoes	sneakers	tennis shoes
man's dress tie	tie	cravat
small roadside restaurant	diner	truckstop
small fried potatoes	french fries	shoes, shoe strings
circular amusement ride	merry-go-round	carousel
major high way	express way	free way
small house	bungalow	cottage
reddish potatoe	sweet potatoe	yam
the cinema	the movies	picture show
blend drink of milk	milk shake	frappe
coast line along ocean	beach	the shore
hard breadish roll	hard roll	water roll
front steps to a house	front steps	stoop
dough with cheese and tomato paste	pizza pie	tomato pie
small suit case	carry case	gym bag
to bring something	carry	fetch
small narrow body of water	stream or creek	crick

6 Verbal and Nonverbal Communication

76

The way we sound to others has a great deal to do with the way they will interpret our messages.

QUESTIONS FOR RETENTION

1. How can I most effectively use my voice?
2. How do I send messages with my nonverbal behavior?
3. What are the nonverbal elements of communication?

Human beings are amazing sensing instruments. We use our senses to see, hear, touch, taste, and smell. All that we know in the world, all that we learn, is communicated through our senses. Our senses, therefore, provide us with a tremendous amount of information. The editors of *Scientific American* magazine, for instance, estimate that our visual system alone consists of more than one million channels, capable of instantly transmitting ten million bits of information to the brain. But since our brain only has the capacity for receiving twenty-seven bits of information per second from any or all of our five senses, we must be very selective as to what we accept or reject, respond to or ignore.

In this chapter we'll explore the ways that we communicate through our senses. The ways that we use distance and space. What movement and expression communicate. How we send signals using nonverbal channels of communication. And how our verbal messages tell so much about us. We will begin with one of the most remarkable instruments of all—the human voice.

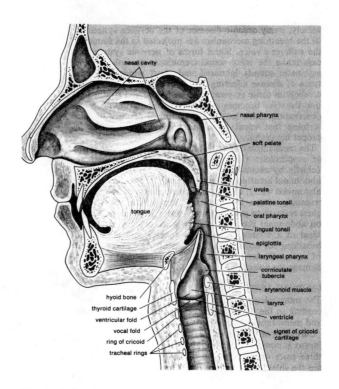

Figure 6.1
How We Produce Sounds.

VERBAL COMMUNICATION

Our voice is the instrument of our thoughts. How we use it, the way it sounds, the images it paints for our listeners all tells a great deal about us and our feelings.[1] Research shows that from the tone of our voice listeners can accurately detect anger two-thirds of the time; nervousness over half the time; and sadness nearly half the time. Not only does our voice reveal a great deal about our feelings, it also tells a great deal about us. No one sounds exactly like we do. Our voice is as unique—as well, we are. Think of how we associate people by the sound of their voice: Howard Cosell sounds harsh and raspy; Bill Cosby as shrill and strident; Tina Turner as modulated and soothing; Johnny Cash as deep and moving; Michael Jackson as high-pitched and squeaky. Now think of these same personalities with someone else's voice—these people wouldn't seem quite the same would they?

The human voice is produced as air is passed from the lungs through the larynx, or voice box. As it passes, the vocal folds vibrate to produce sound. This sound is given character and quality as it is resonated from the surfaces of the pharynx, mouth, and nasal cavities. Finally, this resonated sound is shaped into specific consonant and vowel sounds by the movement of the tongue, teeth, lips, and roof of the mouth. The ultimate sound is released in the form of words and sentences. Many factors contribute to the sound of your voice. For instance, the length and thickness

of your vocal folds helps to determine its deepness—that's why big, husky men often have deep voices. Likewise, the tension of your vocal folds determines its pitch—that's why when you're tense and nervous your voice becomes higher pitched and may occasionally squeak.

In an ideal world each of us would have a beautiful, golden voice. But in the real world we know that isn't true. While people blessed with a rich, resonant voice have advantages as communicators, it certainly isn't a necessity. Many of the world's greatest communicators spoke with weak, undistinguished, and even unpleasant voices. Teddy Roosevelt had a husky voice that frequently broke into shrillness under excitement; Winston Churchill spoke with a frequent stammer and slight lisp; Abraham Lincoln's voice was considered harsh and unpleasant; Elenor Roosevelt had a squeaky voice which frequently sounded strained. Even current day news reporters like Tom Brokaw, Barbara Walters, and John Stossel cover slight speech imperfections, yet each of them are excellent communicators.

To be an effective speaker you don't have to have a great voice, you just need to properly use the one that you have. Like a Roosevelt, Churchill, or Lincoln learn to control your voice, making it the very best that it can be. To help you better understand your voice, let's review those aspects you'll need to learn to control. They are: volume, pitch, rate, pauses, articulation, pronunciation, and variety.

Volume

There are few things as distressing to a listener as not being able to hear what someone is saying. Therefore, you need to project your voice so that your message can get across to everyone. Adjust your volume to take into account the size and acoustics of the room, the number of listeners, and any distracting background noises. When speaking to a large group look at someone seated near the rear of the room—if they seem to be straining to hear, you'll know you need to turn up the volume.

Speaking loudly enough doesn't mean shouting. If you bellow so loud that people's ears begin to ring, you're not likely to have very pleased nor informed listeners. Remember, you want people to listen to your ideas, not just hear your shouts. Sometimes even otherwise good speakers forget their volume. In 1980 Senator Ted Kennedy was frequently criticized for speaking too loudly while campaigning for the nomination for President. At one stop in Iowa, as he sensed his audience was unmoved by his speech, he began to shout louder and louder until he turned his entire audience off.[2] Don't fall into the same trap as Senator Kennedy; constantly try modulating your voice—an effective volume is always pleasing to the ear, but never overpowering to the senses.

Pitch

Pitch is the highness or lowness of your voice. It is caused by the frequency at which your vocal folds vibrate—the more taut your vocal folds, the more rapidly they vibrate, which in turn causes a higher pitch to your voice. Pitch will also follow your rate and volume. As you speak faster or become louder, your pitch will tend to rise.

The ups and downs of pitch are called **intonation patterns.** These vocal inflections give our voices their variety and color. By changing your pitch, for example, you can make the sentence, "The large green lady's purse was lost" either sound like the lady lost a large green purse, or that a purse was lost by a large green lady! By varying your pitch, much like a pianist would play different keys while performing a concerto, you can make your voice seem more interesting and pleasing to the ear. Your pitch will clue your listeners as to whether you're asking a question, telling a joke, or striking a dramatic point.

People who speak in a monotone use one constant pitch, hardly changing an octave. Speakers who

do this have a hard time keeping even the most dedicated listeners awake. To avoid speaking in a monotone, try gliding through a range of pitches. Identify the pitch that you use for normal conversation—this is called your **optimum pitch.** Then, when speaking to a group, range from your normal pitch no more than two octaves. If you try to speak in a pitch too high you'll sound shrill; if too low, forced. You can check your pitch by occasionally tape-recording yourself. If you find you constantly end sentences on the same inflection—either too high or two low—try to show greater flexibility, experimenting with a workable range of sound.

Rate

Rate refers to the speed that you speak. Typically Americans range from 120 to 190 words per minute, with the average falling around 145. However, as long as you sound interesting and understandable, there is no set rate for speaking. Daniel Webster

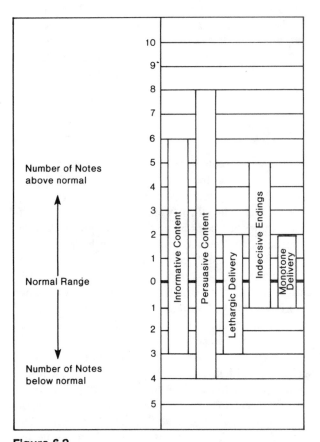

Figure 6.2
Vocal Ranges in Normal Conversation. A good range will consist of both high and low range variations within the context of the message.

spoke at a slow 90 words per minute, Franklin Roosevelt at 110, and John F. Kennedy breezed along at 180. Yet each of these speakers was extremely effective. A good rate doesn't roll along at one speed either, but starts and sputters, slows and speeds. When Martin Luther King began his famous *"I Had A Dream"* speech, for example, he started at 92 words per minute, and ended at a brisk 145. In contrast, radio announcers buzz along at a rate seldom falling below 140, often going along as fast as 190.[3] What's your best rate? To determine this you should measure what seems natural to your personality and fits the needs of your listeners.

Try to make your rate fit the subject. If describing the excitement of a basketball game, a faster rate will do. A faster rate keeps listeners actively involved, and is best suited for energetic or persuasive messages. Research shows that when being convinced listeners prefer a rate about 50 percent faster than their own. Use a slower tempo when explaining complex material. Not surprisingly, studies show that listeners remember a lot more when difficult subjects are presented in a slower way.[4]

Two things should be remembered about rate. First, don't speak so fast that listeners have a difficult time keeping up with your ideas. And second, don't go so slow that you put people to sleep. Rather utilize a brisk rate that is easily understandable. Check your rate with a friend or tape-recorder. Ask your teacher how you sound. Work on variety. When all this is considered, you should have a rate that feels natural and sounds appropriate.

Pauses

Good communicators never speak in a steady stream of words; rather they use a combination of phrases blended with timely moments of silence. Using pauses, and using them well, is one of the most difficult things for beginning speakers to grasp. At first, a second of silence will seem like an hour of emptiness. But as you become more proficient at communicating with others, you'll learn that a properly spaced pause can be a helpful way to enforce your ideas. As Mark Twain once said, *"The right word may be effective, but no word was ever as effective as a rightly timed pause."*

Experienced communicators use pausing with great skill. Johnny Carson's monologue is not just a series of one-liners. Instead, he expertly sets up a situation, and then by pausing at just the right spot, delivers the punch line at the perfect moment. The key to Carson's rhythm is timing. Take away the timing and the line falls dead.

How do you develop timing like a Carson? Part through practice and part through observation. As you work on your delivery see where a slight pause will naturally fit. Recognize that pauses logically occur after a rhetorical question, before an important point, or prior to a dramatic statement. As you practice, test-out your timing with trusted friends or family. Through trial and error you'll learn when and where to pause. Next observe polished speakers. Good communicators time their pauses so they sound perfectly natural. By watching them you'll be able to pick up invaluable tips that you can use to enhance your own speaking.

A negative type of delay is the **vocalized pause.** A vocalized pause is where someone fills in spaces with repetitive sounds like *"ah,"* *"um,"* or *"you know."* Not only are these nonfluencies annoying, but they also make a speaker seem less competent and dynamic to listeners. Your instructor will catch these and bring them to your attention. Once you know your favorite *"ah's"* and *"um's"* you'll be able to concentrate on removing them from your delivery. By replacing vocalized pauses with moments of silence, you can turn an annoying weakness into an effective strength.

Articulation

Articulation is the production of speech sounds using your lips, teeth, tongue, and soft and hard palate. Oftentimes people confuse pronunciation with articulation. Simply put, pronunciation is the act of saying a speech sound, while articulation is the actual production of the sound. In other words, if you mispronounce a word because of your accent it is an error of pronunciation—if you can't produce a certain speech sound because you wear braces or have a misaligned jaw, it is an error of articulation.[5] Most students confuse the two, and when they're really not pronouncing something correctly, they think they're not articulating it properly.

If you have difficulty articulating certain sounds it may be due to the fact that you thrust your tongue, have a cleft palate, wear a poorly fitting dental plate, or have some similar speech difficulty. Most of these problems need to be addressed by a trained speech pathologist. If you think you have such a problem, or your teacher diagnoses one, make an appointment with a speech lab. Many colleges offer free or low cost speech labs to deal with just such difficulties. If you don't know of one, ask your teacher to recommend one for you.

A far more common cause of poor articulation is laziness. Because we fall into bad habits of not manipulating our tongues, jaw, or soft palate properly,

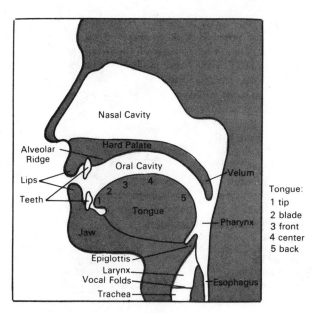

Figure 6.3
How Tongue Position Effects Articulation.

we end up misarticulating sounds. An even more common problem is the tendency to mumble and slur our words and sounds. Whenever this happens we've inhibited our effectiveness.

If you have the tendency to use poor articulation you can work to correct this difficulty. Practice pronouncing all speech sounds when saying a word or phrase: say *"go-ing,"* not *"goin;" "how are you,"* not *"how ah ya;"* or *"them,"* not *"dem."* By identifying and eliminating your most common errors, you'll be able to overcome them. Many students even find it helpful to keep a log of their most frequent sound errors. By practice and hard work these problems can be defeated one by one. To get you started, work through the worksheet at the end of the chapter.

Pronunciation

Do you say *"ideaer"* instead of *"idea;" "Illinois's"* rather than *"Illinois;"* or *"liberry"* when you mean *"library?"* If you do, you've made errors of pronunciation. Pronunciation is the expression of sounds and stresses to say a word correctly. If you consistently mispronounce words listeners might not understand you, become distracted paying more attention to your pronunciation than your content, or might even think you less intelligent.[6]

We mispronounce words in five general ways: by adding sounds, omitting sounds, substituting sounds, improperly accenting stress, or using connected speech. When we add sounds we put a sound

where it really doesn't belong. Thus, pneumonia becomes *p*-neumonia or arthritis is pronounced ar*thur*itis. Omitting a sound is just the opposite—we leave a sound out where it should be. So Mississippi becomes Mis*sip*pi or aluminum becomes alu*m*num. Substituting a sound is replacing a proper sound with an improper one. As a result America becomes Amer*e*ca or February is said as Feb*yu*ary. When we put stress on the wrong syllable we are improperly accenting a sound. Mu*se*um becomes *mu*seum or I*tal*ian becomes *I*talian. Connected speech is where we place so much emphasis on enunciating every sound that our words sound too studied. If Atlantic becomes *At lan tic* or because is said as *be* cause we are drawing too much attention to the way a word is said, and not enough to the idea it's supposed to convey.

The key is to get your ideas across to others. Therefore, when you think of correct pronunciation, imagine that which is spoken by the majority of better educated persons in your general area or ethnic community. Your chief concern with pronunciation should always be effectiveness. Only to the extent that your pronunciation gets in the way of your effectiveness is it a problem. Some people are "regional culturists" and wish to retain the accent of the part of the country in which they live. Others cherish their pronunciation from an ethnic viewpoint and don't want to see it changed. In either case the real question is your purpose as a communicator. If you wish to become a national news person, a standard form of pronunciation will need to be used. If, on the other hand, your designs are to work in your community, such a standard form wouldn't be necessary. The best technique is to *"switch codes."* Use your regional or ethnic dialect when appropriate, but practice the standard form for when it will work best. We'll now take a look at a particular form of pronunciation, and this is called dialect.

Dialect

A dialect is the general language used by a group of people from a particular region or ethnic background.[7] A dialect includes much more than just pronouncing sounds—it also involves grammar, syntax, and vocabulary. Consequently, your pronunciation along with the words that you use and the way you arrange them, all determines your dialect. Many times dialects are carry-overs from other languages. For instance, New York's Brooklyn had many Italian immigrants and based upon the Italian pronunciation of certain sound patterns the word theatre became *"thee-taa."* In old Milwaukee it was typically pronounced as *"the-ay-ter"* being a carry-over from

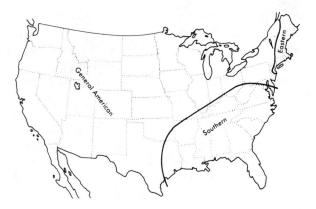

Figure 6.4
The Three Major Regions of Dialectal Pronunciation in the United States as Observed before 1940.

Figure 6.5
The Ten Major Regions of Dialectal Pronunciation in the United States: A. Eastern New England, B: New York City, C: Middle Atlantic, D: Southern, E: Western Pennsylvania, F: Southern Mountain, G: Central Midland, H: Northwest, I: Southwest, J: North Central.

the many German immigrants in that city and their pronunciation of *"das Theater."*

In the United States there are four general regional dialects: New England, New York City, Southern, and General American—which prevails in the Midwest, West, and Northwest. A New England dialect has some sound omissions and several substitutions. The most noticeable is the ignored *"r."* Thus, John Kennedy said, *"vigah"* not *"vigor."* New York City's dialect contains mostly sound distortions, so that speakers like Joan Rivers say *"caw-fee"* instead of *"coffee."* A Southern dialect varies pitch so that when Jimmy Carter addressed the 1976 Democratic Convention he said *"Italian,"* rather than *"Italian."* General American adds and distorts some sounds, but is considered the standard form. Speakers like Hugh Downs and Ronald Reagan practice this.[8]

Whether you speak with the nasal twang of a New Englander or the lilting pitch of the South, your dialect can cause some difficulties if speaking to people outside of your region. Studies show that oftentimes listeners make negative judgments about a speaker's credibility, reliability, leadership, responsibility, and education because of a dialect.[9] Unfortunately, this often occurs because of what linguists call **vocal stereotypes**—all people from one region or ethnic background are seen as being the same. The only place where a dialect seems to help is when someone is speaking to people who use the same dialect—then listeners seem to react favorably.

Try and keep your speech pattern flexible. This allows you the freedom to maintain your down South drawl or New York staccato when needed; but also to practice a standard dialect when it would prove most helpful. The more you can perfect your pronunciation,

the greater flexibility you'll have. Work through the exercises on pronunciation on the worksheet at the end of this chapter, study polished speakers, tape-record your own speech and analyze the way you pronounce words, consult a dictionary if not sure of a pronunciation. Above all else, be an observant listener. Respect everyone's individuality when they speak—a dialect does not make someone dumb, naive, or provincial. Be open-minded and listen to the words people say, not just the dialectal package their words come in.

Besides the four regional dialects, there are three other areas of dialect that we should be aware of. The first is Black English. The second concerns non-native bilingual speakers whose first language was Spanish. And the third is that of non-native bilingual speakers whose first language was rooted in Asia—be it Chinese, Vietnamese, or Japanese.[10] Here's a brief review of each.[11]

Black English

What is generally classified as black English is spoken at least some of the time by about 80 percent of black Americans. Black English is similar to white Southern English and traces its origins back to the "pidgin" that slaves developed during the time they were warehoused in African ports.

The essential differences between standard English and black English are in syntax and phonology. Black English follows a variation in the way thoughts are put together. In black English the *"r"* and *"l"* are frequently left off (mo for more, foo for fool); uses a non redundant plural (four thousand dollar); leaves out the pronoun (my mother sick) and drops final consonants (mend is men, rest is res). Additionally, black English leaves off *"ed"* endings so that *"talked last week"* becomes *"talk last week."* Finally, the *"th"* is changed so initial *"th"* becomes *"d"* (dat for that); medial *"th"* becomes *"v"* (favvor for father); and terminal *"th"* becomes *"f"* (wif for with).

Much of black English can be explained. African languages have no *"th"* sound—which explains the *"dat," "favvor," "wif"* difference. Also black English uses a richer to be verb, so while in standard English it can only be said, *"he is running,"* in black English it can also be said, *"he running,"* *"he be running,"* and *"he bes running."* As you can see, black English is a rich and varied dialect that should be respected—in many ways it's a language in its own right. For standard speech these differences can be overcome once each sound distortion is isolated. But for the community environment, black English is simply different, not wrong.

Spanish Speakers

Non-native English speakers whose first language is Spanish represent the fastest growing group of Americans. People from Mexico, Central and Latin America, and the Caribbean often have a difficult time pronouncing certain sounds in English. This is because English, unlike Spanish, is not phonetic. What this means is that English is not pronounced the way it is written. The word *"read"* can mean to read a book or that someone has read a book—same spellings but quite different meanings and pronunciation. Such an instance would be a rare case in the Spanish language, since most written sounds are also pronounced. Additionally, in Spanish there are five vowel sounds while in English there are fifteen.

Standard English prolongs vowel sounds, while in Spanish they are rapid and clipped. One way to help pronounce English sounds is to take longer to say an English word than you would a Spanish word—in other words, draw out the vowel sound. Another difference is that English has a stress-timed rhythm where certain syllables are heavily stressed while others are destressed or even reduced. In Spanish, on the other hand, all syllables are pronounced almost equally. Finally, Spanish speakers use more upward inflections than English speakers. By practicing proper vocal rhythm which is used in English, many of these dialectal differences can be reduced.

Typical difficulties for Spanish speakers are words that end in consonants, since most Spanish words end in vowels (plate or played becomes *play,* lost becomes *loss,* world becomes *whirl*). The *"th"*

sound doesn't exist either, so *"they"* sounds like *"day"* or *"think"* becomes *"tank."* Other common distortions are *"it"* for *"eat," "bet"* for *"bait," "pool"* for *"pull,"* and *"hot"* for *"hat."* These are all due to sounds that either don't exist in Spanish, or are easily confused with similar sounds. The best method for overcoming these difficulties is to practice the unique sounds of English while treasuring one's cultural heritage at the same time. Remember, pronunciation errors of native Spanish speakers are perfectly logical.[12]

Asian Speakers

Recently more and more people have emigrated to this country from the nations of Asia—Viet Nam, Cambodia, Taiwan, China, Japan, and Korea. The languages of these nations vary significantly, finding four general classifications: Tai (Southeast Asia); Ainu (western China); Altaic (Korean and Japanese); and Sino-Tibetan (China and Russia). These languages are so dissimilar that they are mutually unintelligible; for instance, Vietnamese requires hard glottal stops which is totally different from Mandarin Chinese. However, for our purposes here we'll try to draw some helpful general observations.

If you came from China, Taiwan, Cambodia, or Viet Nam you're likely to have particular difficulties with certain sounds. The most significant are the *"r"* and *"l."* This is because in Asian languages there is not a sound like either the English *"r"* or *"l."* Thus, *"comfort"* becomes *"comfot," "rest"* becomes *"est,"* and *"lily"* becomes *"iye."* Other sounds that pose difficulties are the *"th"* (thin becomes sin) and the *"ing,"* (going becomes go-en). Because Chinese is monosyllabic, words end in a vowel sound and therefore it's easy to omit final syllables—especially consonants. Thus, *"boat"* becomes *"bo," "side"*— *"si," "night"*—*"ni," "time"*—*"ti,"* and *"ten"*— *"tie."* Additionally, the present tense is used with the omission of linking verbs. So instead of *"he is sick"* it becomes *"he sick," "he was sick yesterday"* becomes *"he sick yesterday,"* and *"he will be sick tomorrow"* turns into *"he tomorrow sick."* Articles like *"the"* and *"a"* are frequently omitted so phrases like *"Sun very hot"* are typical. Finally Suffixes *"ed,"* and *"s,"* are all left off so we have *"he pick her up,"* and *"he see two cat."*

Japanese and Korean speakers have a slightly different problem. Japanese is a consonant-vowel language in which a consonant sound is always followed by a vowel. Therefore, there is a tendency to add an extra vowel sound after a word ending in a consonant. This is magnified by the fact that no Japanese words end with a consonant, as a result *"big"* becomes *"biga,"* *"them"*—*"theme,"* *"come"*—*"coma,"* and *"and"*—*"anda."* Both the *"r"* and *"l"* are not distinguishable as two separate sounds so *"read"* becomes *"ed,"* and *"lady"*—*"aedi."* Finally, the *"th"* poses problems so *"thank you"* becomes *"sank you"*.

It is difficult for an Asian speaker to learn to pronounce all the sounds of English. But through patience and practice many difficult sounds can be learned. As with all forms of dialect, difficulties are both natural and understandable.[13]

Establish Vocal Variety

When you use vocal variety your voice will play like a finely tuned instrument. It can make your listeners feel the pang of sadness or the delight of joy; the lightness of humor or the shadow of drama; the peace of the present or the rush of the new. All this is possible by the way you pace and time your delivery. Your skilled mix of volume, pitch, rate, and pausing gives your ideas a rich description beyond compare. By modulating and artistically using your voice you can give life to your ideas and feelings.

How do you develop a more expressive voice? Practice with a tape-recorder measuring your pacing as you go. Work on your delivery in front of classmates and friends. Ask your teacher for advice and guidance. Hone your articulation and pronunciation by completing the worksheet at the end of this chapter. And most of all, perfect your delivery day by day. When all this is accomplished, your voice will serve as the wings of your dreams; the echo of your beliefs.

NONVERBAL COMMUNICATION

Imagine you meet somebody for the first time. They seem pleasant enough, saying hello and carrying on a polite conversation. But you notice that they seldom look at you, never smile, and position themselves as far from you as they can comfortably get. You pick up these nonverbal cues and soon realize that despite the words used in the conversation, the person really isn't very friendly at all.

How did you reach this conclusion? By the person's nonverbal actions. In fact, we gain 90 percent of our information about someone based upon their nonverbal behavior alone.[14] Likewise, we believe nonverbal messages far more than those sent in words.[15] Greek historian Herodotus recognized this 2400 years ago when he wrote, *"Men trust their ears less than their eyes."*

We "trust our eyes" in many ways. We judge people by their appearance, facial expressions, eye contact, posture, movement, and gestures. All of this lets us determine if someone seems friendly or hostile, confident or insecure, knowledgeable or uninformed. The way that people communicate through movements, or body language, is called **kinesics.** Amazingly, it's estimated that a typical communicator can send more than 700,000 kinesic signals through the use of bodily movements alone. The focus of this section will be to discuss this language without words.

Appearance

Usually people see you before they hear you. That's why it's important to consider how you look. Most of us do this naturally. We dress up for an interview, down for a party, inbetween for a class. Research shows that listeners respond most favorably to speakers who dress similarly to them, but more on the conservative than flashy side.[16]

How do you decide on what to wear for a presentation? First, realize that you don't want your attire to draw away from your performance. If the way you're dressed gets more attention than the content of your message, it's a problem. Second, determine the image you want to convey. When Robert Kennedy ran for President in 1968, he frequently would speak without a suit jacket and with his sleeves rolled up—this conveyed a hard working image. A union leader talking to factory workers would best wear an open shirt or casual blouse and slacks; a person addressing the board of directors would need much more formal attire. Always wear clothes that meet the expectations of the occasion. For a class, neat but not overly formal attire is best. Finally, dress so you feel comfortable and most at ease. If you don't feel right, you won't sound right. In short, be neat, be well groomed, dress naturally, and always fall on the side of being a bit more formal than casual. For without a doubt, your personal appearance has a lot to do with the success of your message.

Facial Expressions

Facial expressions communicate a tremendous amount of useful information. Researcher Albert Mehrabian has developed a formula to account for the emotional impact of a communicator's message. He says words account for 7 percent, vocal elements 38 percent, and facial expressions an extraordinary 55 percent.[17] This is all the more amazing when we realize that the

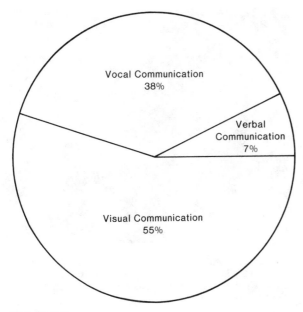

Figure 6.6
Time Spent Communicating.

appeared. Therefore, based on current findings, you should look at listeners 70 to 90 percent of the time.

Also measure how you look at listeners. A blank stare will do more harm than good. Some speakers just look at the floor, others at the ceiling, and some dart their eyes back and forth like a scared rabbit—all these methods are equally bad. To be effective you should look at all your listeners—ignoring no one. When speaking to a large group it's a good idea to establish contact with one person for several seconds, and then move on to someone else in another part of the room—this makes everyone feel like a part of the speech. As professional speaker Jack Valenti characterizes it, this gives everyone a *"figurative handshake."* With a larger audience, say in an auditorium, it's best to scan the whole group rather than pick out individuals. When speaking to one person, as in an interview, look at the person showing openness, sincerity, and confidence. As Ralph Waldo Emerson so aptly put it, *"The alleged power to charm down is a power behind the eye."*

Movement and Posture

People who rock back and forth, lean, move their hands in and out of their pockets, and fidget around are bound to look uneasy. How can you present a calm and confident image? When speaking in public use the lectern only to rest your notes—then take a half step back, don't lean and don't grab it. Secondly, don't slouch or shift aimlessly from foot to foot—be comfortable, but remember you are standing before a group. Third, don't lean against the blackboard or sit on the edge of the desk—short speeches generally require a formal stand-up delivery. Fourth, don't pace back and forth as if an absent minded professor. A few steps taken with precision will have a far more positive effect. A step and lean forward will evoke importance; a step back a less important point. Finally, use your hands and arms in creative gestures or place them in a consistent comfortable pose—this will help your listeners and make your job easier at the same time. If being interviewed, sit upright—don't slouch down, appear comfortable, and avoid moving back and forth. In short the more natural you look, the more natural you'll feel.

Gestures

Different people use different gestures with equal effectiveness. Woodrow Wilson spoke with power in reserve using his index finger to point at his listeners like an angry schoolmaster; Teddy Roosevelt used sweeping, emphatic gestures that seemed to draw in

human face is capable of a quarter of a million different expressions!

How do you use facial expressiveness to help communicate information? First, use your face to help transmit your intent—are you being funny or serious? Clever or cute? Positive or negative? By using your face expressively you can make your true meaning clear. Second, use your face to project a positive image. If you look defeated before you start—your listeners will quickly pick that up. Finally, use your face as an effective gesture—smile, frown, grimace, show surprise, look quizzical. Let your face be a tool to show listeners how you feel about them, the subject, and yourself.

Eye Contact

We've all heard the expression, *"the eyes are the mirrors of the soul"* or that someone will be given the *"evil eye."* All this serves to remind us just how important eye contact is in communication. Eye contact has been linked to perceived sincerity, trustworthiness, friendliness, and dynamism. No wonder good speakers make an extra effort to look at their listeners.

Just how often should you look at your listeners? As a general rule, the more the better. One study found that communicators who averaged 63 percent eye contact rates were judged as more sincere than those who averaged just 20 percent. Another researcher varied eye contact rates into three groups of 0 percent, 50 percent, and 90 percent—not surprisingly, the higher the rate the more credible the person everyone in one fluid motion; Martin Luther King used both hands to drive home especially telling points; John F. Kennedy used the diagonal side of his hand to make frequent jabs in the air; and Susan B. Anthony spoke in a deliberate manner barely using a gesture at all. None of these speakers were wrong in the way they approached the use of gestures, for gesturing is a very individualized art.[18]

What looks fluid and natural for one person may look awkward and canned for another. The key with gesturing is that you don't want it to draw from the content of your message. Avoid distracting gestures such as playing with a paper clip or rubber band, wringing your hands together, toying with a ring, or swinging your arms around like a windmill. Good gestures should look natural, be appropriate for your listeners and occasion, and help to reinforce the content of your message.

Just how do you gesture effectively? One way is to keep your arms free and loose at your sides. Don't lock them tightly against your body. Another is to keep your hands in front of you—you may even rest one or both lightly on the podium or desk. Try and use your arms, hands, head, and body to punctuate your ideas. Good gestures can include a push of the hands away from the body to show rejection, an open palm to show caution, a finger or two held up to show organization, a vertical movement of the hand to show division, and a bringing of the palms together to show unity. There are literally thousands of gestures that you can use. Pick the gestures that best suit you and your purpose, practice in front of a mirror, and let your gestures become one with your message.

NONVERBAL ELEMENTS OF COMMUNICATION

In order to fully grasp those things which influence our nonverbal behavior, we must understand several key elements. These include the study of proxemics, time, touch, smell, taste, image, and environment. Here's a review of each.

Proxemics

Proxemics is the study of the way we structure distance and space. The distances that we place between ourselves and others reveals a great deal about the type of messages we send, the type of reactions we receive, and the level of comfort we feel. Anthropologist Edward Hall has categorized the four zones of distance people place between themselves and others as intimate, personal, social, and public. Let's look at each.

Figure 6.7 When people ride together in an elevator there is very little communication. Most people avoid looking at one another and instead focus on the floor numbers above the door.

Intimate Distance

When people communicate at a distance of eighteen inches or less, they are exchanging messages at an intimate distance. In this close phase the presence of another person is unmistakable, and nonverbal behavior is easily recognized. Oftentimes intimate distance is used to discuss confidential matters and is usually reserved for people with whom we feel very comfortable.

Personal Distance

Personal distance extends from 1 1/2 to 4 feet. This is the general distance used for normal conversation. At this range two people can converse without involving other individuals outside their immediate sphere.

Social Distance

Communicating at a range from 4 to 12 feet is an exchange of information at a social distance. This is reserved for people we meet in formal situations such as in interviews, business meetings, party conversations and the like.

Public Distance

The most expansive zone is public distance which extends from 12 feet and beyond. This zone encompasses public speeches, formal group presentations, class instructions and such similar formal presentations. At

Table 6.1
Table of Proxemics

Distance	Description	Vocal Characteristics	Disclosure of Information
0–6 inches	Intimate (close phase)	soft whisper	confidential
6–18 inches	Intimate (far phase)	audible whisper	private
1 1/2 to 2 1/2 feet	Personal (close phase)	soft voice	personal
2 1/2 to 4 feet	Personal (far phase)	lowered voice	individual
4 to 7 feet	Social (close phase)	full voice	non-personal
7 to 12 feet	Social (far phase)	louder full voice	public
12 to 25 feet	Public (close phase)	public speaking voice	open to all
25 or more feet	Public (far phase)	shouting	open to all

Chart adapted from Chapter X of THE HIDDEN DIMENSION by Edward T. Hall. Copyright © 1966 by Edward T. Hall. Reprinted by permission of Doubleday & Company, Inc.

this range there is little opportunity for close physical observation or contact.

What does proxemics tell us about communicative behavior? Look at the way your classmates arrange their seats in class. Notice that each arranges his or her seat a comfortable distance from nearby students—generally two to three feet. We all feel the need to surround ourselves in such a protective bubble. This is often referred to as the **"body buffer zone."** Interestingly, studies show that women need less space than men, and that men will sit closer to females than other males. It's also been found that criminals who have committed violent crimes need far more space than less violent criminals.

Our need for space changes with the situation. On a crowded subway car, for instance, we tolerate people sitting so close to us that we can actually feel their presence. On a relatively empty subway car, however, we would expect other passengers to distance themselves from us by several feet. Observe how two strangers react in an otherwise empty elevator. Chances are each will automatically move to a separate corner—allowing as much distance between themselves as possible. Our need for space, the way we use space, the way we expect others to respect our personal space, greatly influences all our communicative interactions.

Time

What does time communicate? Imagine two people interviewing for the same job. One arrives on time, the other shows up two hours late. Who do you think will get the job? Or think of your attitude toward two friends calling you for a missed assignment. One calls at three in the afternoon, the other at three in the morning. You'd give each quite a different reaction, wouldn't you? We are greatly influenced by time. We act one way in the morning, another at night; we measure a conversation with a professor in minutes, we talk to a friend for hours; we don't worry if we meet a date a few minutes late, we arrive at work exactly on time.

Time can be divided into three categories: **technical, formal,** and **informal.** Technical time is used to measure distance, such as *"light years away."* Formal time represents the units we use to mark the passing of events—seconds, minutes, hours, days, and so on. Informal time represents the importance we place on a situation based on the time it occurs. A phone call in the morning seems normal, a call in the middle of the night gives us a scare.

Likewise, different cultures view time in considerably different ways. In North America we structure time much more precisely than in South America. A meeting in New York will be scheduled to end at a set time, in Rio de Janeiro it seldom matters. Most

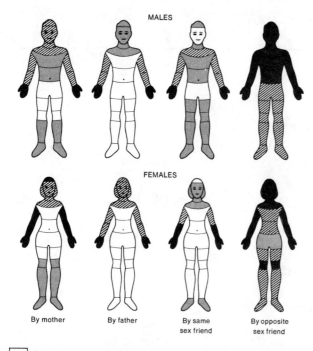

MALES

FEMALES

By mother   By father   By same sex friend   By opposite sex friend

Indicates 0-25% *reported being touched in that area by the relevant person.*
Indicates 26-50% *reported being touched in that area by the relevant person.*
Indicates 51-75% *reported being touched in that area by the relevant person.*
Indicates 76-100% *reported being touched in that area by the relevant person.*

Figure 6.8
Haptic Communication of the Human Body. Sidney Jourard has reported in the *New Society* that certain areas of the body are touched more frequently than others. The type and amount of tactile communication is also affected by the sex and relationship of the person doing the touching. (See: Sidney Jourard, "Out of Touch: The Body Tatoo," *New Society*, 9, November 1967, p. 660–62.)

Americans invite a guest for dinner at a precise time. In India, however, it is up to the guest to arrive whenever he or she pleases. The Sioux Indians have no word for *"late."* Visitors arrive when they can, leave when they want. Therefore, the way we use time—be it to a nation, a group, or a friend—communicates more than most people would ever imagine.

Touch

From earliest childhood we place great import on touch. Research shows that babies who are held regularly grow up to be more affectionate, while sadly, infants who are seldom touched soon grow apathetic. As we mature we continue to communicate through touching. We shake hands, kiss, and embrace. A pat on the back or sweep of the head provides positive reinforcement. For example, patients who were touched by their nurses improved in both attitude and verbal output. On the other hand, negative messages can also be communicated. A point in the chest, slap, or punch indicates aggression and dislike.

How do we use touch differently? Men touch less than women, and girls more than adult females. Girls are more likely to hold hands or hug their parents. Boys resist touching with the exception of contact during sports activities where things like the high-five are acceptable. In America two men seldom embrace, yet in much of the world this is a normal occurrence. And often two women will dance, while this rarely occurs between two heterosexual men.

Use touch wisely to help communicate your ideas. Give a warm handshake, supportive pat, or gentle nudge. If in a disagreement, avoid physical contact—it only increases hostility. In conclusion, use touch as one more weapon in your communication arsenal.

Smell

Think of what each of the following odors communicates: the aroma of a freshly baked pie; someone with alcohol on his breath; the odor of a raging fire. Each of these smells tells us something—something tastes good; someone has had too much to drink; a threatening fire is nearby. Indeed, we gain a lot of information from our sense of smell. Advertisers recognize this, bombarding us with commercials for colognes, mouth wash, fresheners, and deodorants. Sometimes a smell communicates a positive image, as the fragrance of an expensive perfume. At other times it conjures up a negative image, as the heavy odor of tobacco.

People have different abilities when it comes to smell. Research conducted at the University of Pennsylvania found that women have a keener sense of smell than men, and that our ability to pick out odors declines after age forty. People over age 65 have a difficult time picking out certain odors, like lemon, soap, and natural gas. The researcher concluded that this helps to explain why so many elderly people die from accidental gas poisonings each year. Whether it be the pleasantness of perfume, or the danger of gas, smell is another important element of nonverbal communication.

Taste

What tastes better, Pepsi or Coke? Each company has spent millions of dollars trying to convince us there's a difference. Whether it be cola or crackers, advertisers spend a lot of time getting us to think about taste. Just as with the elements of touch and smell, taste helps us make decisions about whether something is good or bad, worthwhile or a waste of time.

Image

What image do you have of Pee Wee Herman? How about John Candy? Chances are you think of one as skinny, the other as fat. Image plays a major role in the way we judge people. Experts categorize physical bodies into three separate groups. The **endomorph** is soft, round, and fat; the **mesomorph** is bony, muscular, and athletic; the **ectomorph** is tall, thin, and fragile. Studies show that people think endomorphs are friendly, generous, and complacent. Mesomorphs are considered cheerful, argumentative, and confident. Ectomorphs are seen as serious, sensitive, and shy. Research suggests that endomorphs receive fewer job offers, and that a taller man has a better chance of being hired than one who is shorter.[19]

We also judge image by what people wear. This is called **object language,** and is a major subject of research. People who wear glasses, for example, are seen as being intelligent, industrious, and religious. On the other hand, women who smoke little cigars and men who carry shoulder bags are seen in a more negative light. One aspect of object language concerns jewelry. Trappings such as rings, bracelets and the like are called **artifacts.** People who wear a great deal of jewelry are viewed less favorably than those who wear less.

Many people in our society wear uniforms—police officers, military personal, nurses and so on. Uniforms are called **status symbols,** and allow us to make numerous judgments about someone. For example, we'd probably allow a woman wearing a nurses' uniform to give us a hypodermic needle, while we'd resist someone else. Similarly, if given a choice, we're more likely to ask directions of a police officer dressed in blue, than of someone not in uniform. As a result, the image people present tells a great deal, whether they intend it to or not.

Environment

Our environment consists of thousands of nonverbal messages. Flags, bumper stickers, buttons, and signs all tell us something. For instance, imagine two cars each with a different bumper sticker, one saying "ROCK AND SEX LIVES," the other "GO TO CHURCH—TODAY," consider the different judgements you'd make about each driver based on the bumper sticker alone.

There are four factors which help us to categorize nonverbal messages in our environment—**signals, signs, symbols,** and **icons.** A signal represents a message sent in another form. Smoke signals or dots and dashes of Morse code are examples of this. Signs give greater information. These would in-

clude such things as barber poles or traffic lights. Symbols are a bit more abstract. These are things which represent a belief like totem poles or crosses. Icons include numerous trappings, and are the most complex. Examples of icons would be a funeral, with all the paraphernalia surrounding it.

Whatever we learn, however we observe it, everything in our environment tells us something. Indeed the world of nonverbal communication is one which has unlimited value.

CHAPTER SUMMARY

We communicate using all our senses. How we arrange space, how we move, how we look, and how we use our voice all says a great deal. One way to look at communication is through our verbal and nonverbal behavior.

The study of verbal communication includes how we use our voice. In order to use our voices properly we need to control volume, raise and lower pitch, vary rate, use pausing, and be alert to articulation and pronunciation. One aspect of pronunciation is dialect, which includes black English and non-native Spanish and Asian-American vocal patterns.

Nonverbal behavior includes our appearance, facial expressions, eye contact, movement and posture, and gestures. Other elements of nonverbal communication includes the study of proxemics, time, touch, smell, taste, image, and environment.

EXERCISES FOR REVIEW

1. Meet with a group of 4 or 5 classmates. Then have each person recite the alphabet showing one of the emotions listed below and have the group guess which emotion was being expressed. Discuss the inflection and vocal variety used by each classmate.
   emotions, anger, happiness, puzzlement, confidence, affection, sadness, authoritativeness, weakness, fear, love, friendliness, ambition, excitement, tiredness.
2. Observe the following sentences. Then see through vocal inflection how many different meanings you can give to each sentence.
   a. *"Father," said Pete, "I want to talk to you."*
   b. *"Look out!" "Look Out!" the police officer told the crowd.*
   c. *The small plain child's toy was lost.*
   d. *The great big happy elephant's trainer smiled.*
3. Determine your own rate of pitch by doing the following: go to a piano and find your optimum pitch in relation to the middle C and the highest

and lowest note that you can sing without a noticeable loss of quality. The interval of this range is your singing voice; your most effective speaking voice will be two octaves above and below your optimum pitch. Practice reciting the alphabet or a passage from a book by varying your pitch above and below your optimum pitch.

4. Review the way people communicate nonverbally, as discussed in this chapter. Then write a few sentences discussing how you will improve in your ability to use appearance, facial expressions, eye contact, movement and posture, and gestures. Give specifics that you intend to work on.

5. Write a 200 word essay discussing one of the nonverbal elements discussed in the chapter. Describe how people communicate using this element, and what generalizations you can draw from its observation.

NOTES

1. This is just one study of several which has measured listener perception based on voice. See, J. R. Davitz and L. J. Davitz, "The Communication of Feelings by Content-Free Speech," *Journal of Communication,* 9, 1959, pp. 6–13.
2. L. Patrick Devlin, "An Analysis of Kennedy's Communication in the 1980 Campaign," *Quarterly Journal of Speech,* 68, November 1982, pp. 397–417.
3. For a thorough discussion of speaking rate see, Richard L. Street Jr., and Robert M. Brady, "Speech Rate Acceptance Ranges as a Function of Evaluative Domain, Listeners Speech Rate, and Communication Context," *Communication Monographs,* 49, 1982, pp. 290–308.
4. Robert N. Bostrom and Carol L. Bryant, "Factors in the Retention of Information Presented Orally: The Role of Short-Term Listening," *Western Journal of Speech Communication,* 44, 1980, pp. 137–145.
5. The relationship between articulation and pronunciation is open to debate among experts. The determination made here is my own with the intent on making this information as clear to the reader as possible. For related readings, see, Kenneth C. Crannell, *Voice and Articulation* (Belmont, Ca.: Wadsworth, 1987).
6. Anthony MuLac and Mary Jo Rudd, "Effects of Selected American Regional Dialects Upon Regional Audience Members," *Communication Monographs,* 44, 1977, pp. 185–195.
7. I have used dialect here to represent three speech patterns—dialect, accent, and regionalism. Traditionally, a dialect is the ethnocultural variety of language; an accent is the prominence of a particular syllable native to region or social background; and a regionalism is directly identifiable to a geographical area.
8. For practical exercises to help you overcome any of these four dialects, see, Kenneth C. Crannell, *Voice and Articulation* (Belmont, Ca.: Wadsworth, 1987), pp. 257–331.
9. Numerous studies have supported this phenomenon. For instance, see, David W. Addington, "The Relationship of Selected Vocal Characteristics to Personality Perception," *Speech Monographs,* 35, November 1968, pp. 493–499.
10. These languages are lumped together recognizing there are substantial differences between them well beyond the scope of this book. However, there are certain generalities that can be drawn and they are discussed here. My gratitude to Professor's Ann Seidler and Doris Bianchi from Montclair State College for their assistance.
11. I would like to thank Professor Tommie Ems of the College of Lake County and Professor Paulette Dale of Miami Dade Community College for so generously sharing their materials and insight on this subject with me.
12. There are several good books providing exercises for Spanish speakers. For instance, see, A. Compton, *Pronouncing ESL: For Spanish Speakers* (San Francisco: Carousel House, 1983); P. Dale and L. Poms, *English Pronunciation for Spanish Speakers* (Englewood Cliffs, N.J.: Prentice-Hall, 1985).
13. For some useful books providing exercises for students from Asia, see, Harvey Taylor, *Say It Right: Pronunciation Practice for Japanese Students* (New York: Regents Publishing Co., 1983); Lewis Herman and Marguerite Herman, *Foreign Dialect* (New York: Theatre Arts Books, 1943); Jerry Blunt, *Stage Dialects* (Scranton, Pa.: Chandler Publishers, 1967).
14. The 90 figure includes vocal characteristics as well. See, A. Mehrabian, *Silent Messages* (Belmont, Ca.: Wadsworth, 1971); Mark Knapp, *Nonverbal Communication in Human Interaction* (New York: Holt, Rinehart and Winston, 1972).
15. Interestingly, when someone's nonverbal behavior is inconsistent with their words respondents tend to believe the body language rather than the words. See, Dale G. Leathers, "The Impact of Multichannel Message Inconsistency on Verbal and Nonverbal Decoding Behavior," *Communication Monographs,* 46, 1979, pp. 88–100.
16. A number of studies have confirmed this. For a review see, Lawrence R. Rosenfeld and Jean M. Civikly, *With Words Unspoken* (New York: Holt, Rinehart and Winston, 1976).
17. Albert Mehrabian, "Communication Without Words," *Psychology Today,* 11, September 1968, p. 53.
18. This view may differ with some. Traditionally gesturing followed a very catalogued, structured form, but current practice has moved away from this standard. For more on gestures see, Desmond Morris, Peter Collett, Peter Marsh, and Marie O'Shaughnessy, *Gestures* (New York: Stein and Day, 1979).
19. This is also found to be true in presidential elections. Throughout American history the taller candidate has always won the election. The lone exception to this phenomenon occurred in 1976, when 5'10 Jimmy Carter defeated 6'1 Gerald Ford.

Name _____ Course _____

Pronunciation & Articulation Worksheet

1. Practice the following lists of words to improve your pronunciation. Work to identify each sound in the word. You may wish to do this with a group of classmates.

run	*lady*	*bat*	*stop*	*her*
ring	*lily*	*bet*	*stay*	*harm*
rule	*love*	*bit*	*slay*	*heard*
river	*lolly*	*beat*	*slang*	*hurt*
race	*lace*	*bent*	*song*	*hit*
shape	*wet*	*free*	*cat*	*play*
shame	*went*	*freed*	*catch*	*pray*
shin	*want*	*frog*	*can't*	*prom*
share	*won't*	*fog*	*carp*	*probe*
shoe	*wilt*	*fried*	*cob*	*pang*

2. Below are two lists of words which are commonly mispronounced; in the first column the correct pronunciation is shown, in the second how the word is often mispronounced. Can you think of words people often have problems pronouncing? List them in the two columns on the right, in the first column the way the word should be pronounced, in the second the way it is often mistakenly mispronounced.

Correct	Incorrect	Correct	Incorrect
ask	*ax*	_____	_____
want to go	*wanna go*	_____	_____
what are you doing	*whach ya doin*	_____	_____
thinking	*thinkin*	_____	_____
call you	*call ya*	_____	_____
bet you	*betcha*	_____	_____
don't know	*dunno*	_____	_____

3. Announcers on radio and television realize the need for precise articulation. One way they sharpen their articulation skills is to practice tongue twisters like those listed below. Try these yourself—begin slowly, then speed up to your normal rate as they become more familiar. You may want to work with a group of classmates on these.

   a. *The big boy batted the ball back to the backstop.*
   b. *Richard, Ron, Rita and Rochelle ran rapidly in Rochester.*
   c. *Sally saw several sea shells at the sea shore, said Sam.*
   d. *Little Lora loved to lap lemon-lime ice lots of the time.*
   e. *"Tell time," said Tim, "or you will be one sad, mad, lad Tony, and that's no baloney."*
   f. *Peter picked a peck of pickled peppers. How many peppers did Peter pick?*
   g. *Friendly Frank frowned frequently, Fred Freeman found.*

4. What words are the hardest to pronounce? List them below, then discuss with the rest of class.

_____	_____	_____
_____	_____	_____
_____	_____	_____
_____	_____	_____
_____	_____	_____

5. Work at pronouncing the following sounds, then write two words which use that sound.

Sound	Word Using Sound	Word Using Sound
th	_____	_____
ng	_____	_____
wh	_____	_____
sh	_____	_____
fa	_____	_____
kn	_____	_____
ith	_____	_____

Eye Gestures

Of all the organs of the human body, the eyes are the most communicative. Eyes communicate information through eye contact, staring, gazing, and blinking. Since facial expressions communicate about 55% of all our nonverbal messages, when they are used in conjunction with the eyes we communicate about three-fourths of all our nonverbal information.

Oftentimes, a parent will look directly into the eyes of a child to determine whether the child is telling the truth or lying. Folklore persists in the continuance of such notions as "The eyes are the windows of the soul," which indicates how people have always relied on the eyes for information. Ancient kings are reported to have looked at the eyes of messengers before accepting their messages; if the messenger was disbelieved he might be put to death! Thus, throughout history people have always placed a great reliance on the eyes to gain information and to determine truth.

When we originally initiate a relationship with someone else we inevitably look at the person's eyes; this is particularly apparent in social relationships. Panhandlers use the eyes of prospective donors as a gage to determine if the person is likely to donate money to them or refuse their request. Muggers have reported that they use the eyes of potential victims as an important factor to ascertain fear or a lack of confidence. In social encounters it is virtually impossible to maintain a conversation with someone who does not respond with at least a semblance of eye contact. Psychiatrists generally use eye contact to gain an initial form of communication with prospective patients; this has been noted as being particularly effective in the treatment of schizophrenics. Studies have shown that when demonstrators and protestors achieve eye contact with the police they are less likely to be treated violently.

Should we choose to ignore someone we cannot achieve eye contact with that person. Research has shown that once two people achieve some form of eye contact the person must be dealt with. Eye contact forces the recognition of another human being. Animals have also been observed to use eye contact to "size up" another threatening creature. Waiters, waitresses, and butlers have been trained to disdain from direct eye contact with those they are serving to maintain a social distance from the person. Job interviewers also use eye contact to indicate interest or a lack of interest in the candidate.

In society, gazes are used to inform other people of our interest, or concern for them. Social rules dictate whom we can look at, for how long, and when we can look at them. Most individuals are very sensitive about being stared at and will react in some way if the look continues. Many people feel as if they have a "sixth sense" which gives them a feeling if someone is gazing at them without their knowledge.

Staring is often used to show concern or displeasure with someone else. Elementary school teachers perfectly use the stare as a method to quiet a disruptive student. Many people discuss how they "look someone else down," as a way to show how staring can indicate their mood and feelings. People who are considered inferior in general society can often be stared at with little response; thus, such people as beggars, children, or the homeless are looked at but do not look back.

When we blink at someone we show a feeling of flirting or interest. Thus, the precocious female will repeatedly blink at the male to whom she is flirting. People who are truly in love for the first time find it difficult to take their eyes from one another. People also blink or close their eyes to show displeasure with someone else. Thus, when a person closes his eyes while addressing someone he is telling the person that he considers his opinions of little merit.

7 Communicating in Social Encounters

CHAPTER OUTLINE

By nature, human beings like to communicate with one another.

QUESTIONS FOR RETENTION

Before reading this chapter, ask yourself the following questions:

1. What do I naturally do every time I have a conversation?
2. What is meant by perception?
3. How can I improve in the way I interact with others?

Before you came to class today you undoubtedly engaged in countless social interactions. Perhaps you visited with a family member, spoke to the cashier in the cafeteria, or reviewed today's assignment with a classmate. Just think of it, all these conversations and perhaps several more, in just the space of a few hours. Imagine how many more social interactions you'll participate in through the course of the entire day.

We engage in social interactions in many ways. We interact with people at home, at work, in school, at parties, and on the street. The focus of this chapter will be to examine these everyday social encounters. We'll review how we interact, the reasons for our interactions, and the factors which influence the success or failure of our conversational exchanges. Let's start by looking at the nature of conversation itself.

THE NATURE OF CONVERSATION

You've been a conversationalist most of your life. As an intelligent person you recognized that there was a need to interact with others and express your thoughts and feelings about a whole host of subjects. Whether you realize it or not, many of the skills you use in normal day-to-day conversation follow a logical and realistic pattern. Let's see what they are:

Figure 7.1 When we relate to one other person, or a small group of people, we are engaging in interpersonal communication.

You Analyze Your Listeners

You arrive at work and see your employer's young son Jeff and his friend Tony. You stop and visit with them about the world series. As your boss walks in, you ask her if the company has completed networking all their computers.

What you've naturally done is a prerequisite for any conversation—to gear the content of your message to the interest of your listeners. Jeff and Tony would probably not understand networking and your boss might have more important things on her mind than the world series.

You Understand Your Purpose

During semester break you go to visit your Aunt Mary who just lost her husband in a tragic car accident. You tell her how much you care for her, that your Uncle Fred was a wonderful man, and that if she needs anything to let you know.

Every conversation, just like any interaction, has a purpose. In this case your purpose was informative: to express your feelings for your aunt; sadness over your uncle's death; and of your willingness to help if needed.

You Create An Organized Message

One day a young woman stops you on campus and asks how to reach Stone Hall. You tell her to walk to the end of the quad until she reaches the administration building, to make a right turn, and then walk past two buildings until she sees Science Hall on her left, to then make a left turn at the big oak tree and Stone Hall will be the third building on her right.

Your directions were only clear to the young woman because they were put forth in a logical and orderly manner. In every conversation we take great care to present all information in an organized fashion so that it can be easily followed and understood by our listeners.

You're Alert to the Response of Your Listeners

One day your classmate, Michelle, asks to show you her new car she just purchased from a used car dealer. You quickly notice that the car has been in a rather bad accident and has been roughly patched up. As you start to tell her this she gets a pained expression on her face and says, "But it was a great buy, wasn't it?" You adjust your comments and answer, "Sure, no used car is perfect."

As an effective conversationalist you're constantly aware of the changing response of the person you're talking to. Looks of confusion, discomfort, or anger are all warning signs for you to adjust or modify your comments. Likewise, looks of delight and agreement encourage you to continue in the same vein.

You Make Your Message as Effective as Possible

At a recent party you're joking with several friends about some of your professors. As you start to imitate the accent and walk of Dr. Wolfsen, your biology professor, your friends break into fits of laughter. You then proceed to imitate the particular mannerisms of several other professors.

When you converse you use whatever method will best allow you to communicate your ideas. In the case of the party conversation, imitations were successful in helping you accomplish this purpose.

Do all these situations sound familiar? The chances are they do—for you probably do them every day without even thinking about it. But what other factors influence our interactions? We'll start with one of the most important of all—perception.

PERCEPTION

What is perception? It's the conscious awareness of events and occurrences in our environment. Of course each of us bases our perceptions on our needs and experiences. When walking down the street we might notice the scenery; a traffic officer expired parking meters; a panhandler a likely target to hit for change. We all witnessed the same things, but placed a sig-

nificantly different importance on each of these observations. Show a hungry child a bakery and all she'll think about is a loaf of bread; let a child who's just eaten visit the same bakery and he'll think of cookies and cake. What does this mean? It means that perception is a very **subjective phenomenon**—the value we place on our observations changes with our needs and interests. Just as people are different, so are their perceptions.

How can we tell that our perceptions are different? Observe the two figure-ground relationships pictured on the next page. In the first figure do you see two facial profiles, a vase, or both? Take a quick look at the second figure. Some people see a young woman, others an old woman, and a few people both. Which did you see? Now study it more carefully—do you see both women? Why is there a difference? Because of selective perception. Let's see what this means.

Selective Perception

We choose to perceive only that information which seems most pertinent. We do this both intentionally and unintentionally. Intentional perception occurs when we purposely pay attention to one message, blocking out all others. An example of this would be a classroom lecture. We would focus on the words of the professor, ignoring outside traffic, coughing, or the ringing of a bell. Unintentional perception is more difficult to recognize. We perceive things which seem important, even if our observations tell us otherwise. For instance, a mother may hear a crying infant, even while engrossed in an exciting movie; her instincts of motherhood predominate over her desire for joy.

In order to selectively perceive we need to observe stimuli. A **stimulus** is any agent or action which causes us to pay it heed. If you stay up all night to study for a test, the stimulus would be the need to pass the test. Sometimes we utilize **stimulus correction.** This is where we fill in blanks, round out rough figures, or group the unknown into known categories. If we notice tire tracks while walking across a field, for example, we would assume a car was once in that location. We have selectively perceived that which we know—cars make tracks—and placed it into a known category—therefore a car was previously here. Once a conclusion is drawn we have closure, and are mentally satisfied that we have perceived the event correctly.

Why do we perceive events differently? Because we are all shaped by different experiences, interests, fears, prejudices, likes, and dislikes. An attractive woman walking a dog may conjure up different thoughts in three different observers. A man

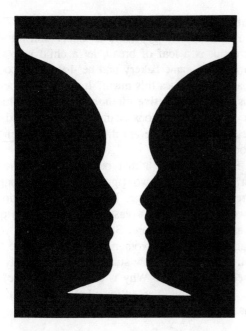

Figure 7.2
Figure-Ground Relationship 1. Do you see a vase, profiles, or both?

Figure 7.3
Figure-Ground Relationship 2. Do you see an old woman, a young woman, or both?

might notice her sexual appeal, a woman her cute poodle, and a clothes designer her fashionable dress. All three observers selected that information which seemed most important to them.

What other factors influence perception? One is organization, and we'll examine that now.

Organization

People like things to make sense. Once we have observed an event, we need to understand it according to our own frame of reference. This is the process of organization. Usually we organize observations according to our past experiences. A person who nearly drowned as a child might view the ocean with an overwhelming sense of fear; while a surfer might observe the same scene with an excited delight.

What happens when we can't organize information according to past experience? When this happens we behave cautiously, being careful to withhold judgment. Ever tasted a new food? You probably took a small bite, testing to see if it tasted right. Once we feel secure, like a child after the first day of school, we organize our impressions according to experience rather than being unsure. Sometimes, however, we allow a past experience to color an otherwise uncertain event. If we learn, for example, that the unknown food happens to be rattlesnake. Then we fall back on experience—*"I don't care how it tastes, I'm not eating a snake!"*

Can we change the way we organize information? Certainly, by undergoing an experience. Once we learn that a previous impression was wrong—snake doesn't taste so bad afterall—we move on, organizing information according to a new sense of enlightenment. Just as we grow with experience, we organize perceived events with a renewed sense of strength.

One thing which affects our inner strength is our sense of self-concept, and this is the next area we'll discuss.

SELF-CONCEPT

How do you feel about yourself? Are you a stud or a fox, a fighter or a lover, a thinker or a doer, a mover or a shaker? At an early age each of us forms judgments about our appearance, intellect, likability, athletic ability, friendliness and the like. These conceptions about our own identity are learned from the way others treat us. The little girl who is constantly told she's pretty, soon learns to accept that fact; likewise, the boy who's told he's no good, all too often sets out to prove that true.

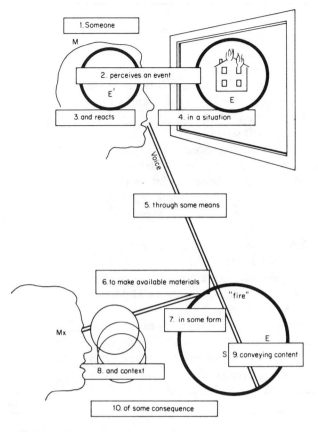

1. Someone

M

2. perceives an event

E'

3. and reacts

4. in a situation

E

Voice

5. through some means

6. to make available materials

"fire"

Mx

7. in some form

E

S   9. conveying content

8. and context

10. of some consequence

Figure 7.4
Gerbner Model. Observe the Gerbner model of
communication above and notice how a person's awareness
of seeing a fire and their response of sounding an alarm are
determined by their perception of the event. (Source:
George Gerbner, "Toward a General Model of
Communication," *Audio-Visual Communication Review*, 34
[Summer, 1956], pp. 172–73.)

Figure 7.5 How we communicate with others is largely
determined by how we feel about ourselves.

Sometimes our self-concept changes. The student who just scraped by in high school, but who now packs an A average in college, will learn he's not so dumb after all. At other times we maintain a false sense of self-identity. The obese woman who diets and becomes a slender beauty may still think of herself as heavy rather than thin. The way we see the world and the way the world see us, is forever a picture without a clearly focused view.

How do we form our self-concept? Primarily through three factors—relationships, experience, and feedback. Early in our lives our primary relationships are with our parents. The girl who's told she's pretty, or the boy who's told he's bad, probably first heard that at home. As adolescents our primary relationships change from those of the home to those of our peer group. What friends think or don't think of us, tell or don't tell us, gives us the material to form a self-view. Later, as our world enlarges, we have personal relationships with many others—friends, teachers, strangers and so on. Experiences come at us with every turn. If we succeed in school at an early age, it confirms that we can succeed later on. The boy or girl who is a hit in a school play, may turn that experience into a lifetime career. Feedback represents the response we receive from others, be it based on our looks, actions, or personality. If people tend to laugh at our jokes and tell us we're funny, we soon begin to believe we have a pretty clever sense of humor after all.

We should view self-concept really as self-concepts, since we have multiple images of ourselves and the world. The ogre at home may be the backslapper at work, the genius in math may be the dunce in history, and the smash in tennis may be the slouch in golf. Our self-concept changes with every exchange, with every person, with every day. We see ourselves one way in front of our parents, another in front of friends. A plant foreman who sees himself as smart in front of coworkers, may feel dumb in front of executives; a junior high big shot may feel like a senior high small fry. For without doubt, with every encounter our self-image fluctuates like the ever changing tide.

Can our self-image be influenced by a false belief? Indeed it can, and this is known as the self-fulfilling prophecy.

The Self-Fulfilling Prophecy

The self-fulfilling prophecy (SFP) means that when someone acts upon a false belief, they've turned a false concept into a real truth.[1] If a person is told they can't do something because they're not big enough, smart enough, or good enough, they soon

HOMOPHILY AND HETEROPHILY

Social interactions can be significantly affected by the homophily and heterophily of the participants. Homophily is the degree of similarity between the parties engaged in an interpersonal exchange. Heterophily refers to the degree of difference between the two parties. The difference can exist in any category: age, religion, economic status, education, political views, and so on.

As we might expect, more effective communication occurs when the participants are homophilous. People like relating to others who are similar to themselves; thus, students like communicating with other students, professors with professors, clerical workers with clerical workers. We like communicating to others who are like us for several reasons. When we give positive ratings to people who are like ourselves we are, in a sense, giving high ratings to ourselves. In a homophilous situation we are more at ease in the communication and can assume a common field of experience. Two car salesmen do not need to define the difference between wholesale and retail book value of automobiles. Finally, we enjoy communicating with others with whom we feel equal. When we are homophilous we generally are in an equal relationship with the other member of the interaction.

Several communicologists have suggested that when two members of the transaction are optimally heterophilous, change can best be brought about by the communication. When two people are homophilous they are both presumed to be equally competent with the material. However, when one member of the exchange is more competent, he or she can best persuade the other and therefore suggest change.

begin to accept this view. On the other hand, if someone is told they can do something, they quickly begin to believe they really can. This was demonstrated in George Bernard Shaw's play, *Pygmalion*. In the play a professor bets a colleague that he can make a polished aristocrat out of a simple country girl. He teaches the girl proper English, behavior, and manners—and sure enough, by the end of the play the *"girl"* has become a *"lady."* This is why the self-fulfilling prophecy is also known as *"the pygmalion effect."*

Research supports the conclusions drawn in *Pygmalion*. One study has been repeated thirty times and always reaches the same conclusion. In it teachers are told that certain students in their classes are intellectually gifted and should do exceptionally well. These students, however, are no more gifted than any others, being picked just at random. But at the end of the year results show that the "gifted" group of students get better grades, learn more, and improve in their I.Q. The same conclusions are reached in studies with adults. One researcher told a welding instructor that some students in his class had test scores which indicated they had a superior ability to learn welding—of course, in reality they were no different than the rest of the class. What happened? The so-called "special group" learned the material in half the time, were absent less, and scored an average of ten points higher on the final exam.

What does this research tell us? That most people behave as they're expected to. If someone is told they can learn something, they believe that they can. If told they can't, they tend not to. How do we explain this? Some experts suggest that we manage our lives by a series of scripts furnished by others, such as parents, friends, and coworkers.[2] If shown confidence, we react positively; if viewed with doubt, we tend to fail.

We react to our environment with a variety of social behaviors. This is our next area of discussion.

SOCIAL BEHAVIORS

The way we interact with others gives numerous clues about the way we feel about them and ourselves. These *"clues"* of social behavior include our language, tone, expression, and self-portrayal. Here's how this occurs.

Language

How do you handle words? Do you describe things with a positive light? Or do you discuss them with a negative jab? If two people were describing the same job one might say *"The job's difficult, but presents many challenges."* While the other might argue, *"It's demanding, with no reward."* Same job, different reactions. Why is this so? Because in our language we reveal the true way we feel about ourselves. People who feel good about themselves generally feel good about the things around them; people who are unhappy see the world in a far less pleasant way.

Our choice of words also tells a great deal. Someone using slang, interspersed with obscenities, is really saying a lot about him or herself. If a woman describes every man she meets as a *"hunk"* or a *"nerd,"* what's she really saying about herself? While our words reveal a lot, our tone tells even more.

Tone

Do you sound upbeat, giving your words an excited spark? Or do you sound down, painting your ideas with a darkened gloom? The sentence *"What are you doing?"* can be said with a questioning twist, a sarcastic turn, or a hostile slash. Same words—different meanings. Why do we use tone so dramatically? Because tone shows how we really feel, not how we want others to think we feel. The worried mother asking her child about his cough doesn't just listen to the words, *"I'm okay."* Instead she keeps her pulse close to the tone. Is he really saying he's fine, or is he telling me something else?

Expression

We not only listen to the words someone uses, we also pay attention to the package they come in. Pleasant words wrapped in a frown, grimace, or smirk tell us just the opposite of what they're supposed to say. Nasty words, said with a smile, leave us confused as to what really was meant. Ever notice a really happy person? Someone who feels completely at ease with the way she is? Chances are you based your conclusions from the person's expression. People with a poor self-concept tend to look defeated before they start. As one experienced interviewer phrased it, "I can always tell when an applicant is burned out—it's written all over his face."

Language, tone, and expression tell a lot. But we learn even more when we combine all these factors in a self-portrait.

Self-Portrayal

Every time we communicate we paint a self-portrait of ourselves. Observe how three people might respond differently to the question, *"What do you do?"* "I go to school." "I attend college." "I am a pre-med major at state college."* Three replies, and three revealing responses. The first person is content to say she's a student. The second wants to report that he attends college. And the third wants to enhance her image by saying she goes to a competitive college and plans to become a doctor.

Do self-portraits reveal the way we really feel about ourselves? Probably, but not necessarily. After you know someone for awhile you generally learn how they really feel about themselves. But people we meet in brief encounters sometimes give us a false view. The cocky athlete might really be a timid bench warmer. Often we present untrue self-portraits by wearing a *mask.* Masks allow us to present the image we think others want to see, not the image we really feel. The pushy salesman might really be a novice working on her first sale. Masks allow us to play a role, and that's what we'll next discuss.

ROLE PLAYING

We play different roles with different people. We might be bold at home, timid at work; nice to the guys, fresh to the girls; deep with a professor, light with a friend. The role we choose to play, therefore, reveals the way we feel about ourselves, the other person, and the relationship between us.

How can we examine the roles we play? One way is through role-coordinates—a method of diagraming a communicative interaction between two people. Two of the most familiar are *OK/NOT OK* and *ADULT/PARENT/CHILD*.[3] Both of these schemes are transactional—they reflect behaviors in-

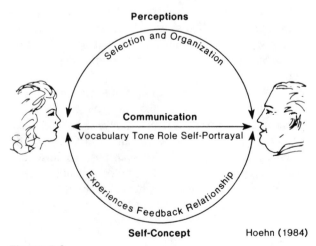

Figure 7.6
Model of Social Communication. (Hoehn, 1984).

dicating that both the sender and the receiver are sending messages. Let's see how they work.

OK/Not OK

There are four possible interactions with this scheme:

I'm not Ok	You're not OK
I'm not OK	You're OK
I'm OK	You're not OK
I'm OK	You're OK

Each pair reflects the feelings and behavior of one communicator toward another. The first indicates the role of the sender, the second the receiver. As an example, let's imagine Tom just bought a new jacket and asks his friend Sue for her reaction. If Sue says, *"I really like your jacket, Tom,"* this interaction can be described as *OK/OK,* since Sue feels okay about Tom and okay about admiring his jacket. But if Sue says, *"That's the worst looking thing I ever saw, only someone like me would buy a jacket like that,"* the interaction can be described as **NOT OK/NOT OK.** Here Sue feels not okay about her own taste in clothes, nor Toms. If Sue says instead, *"That's a nice jacket Tom, I wish mine were like that,"* it would be **NOT OK/OK.** She'd have assigned herself a not okay role, Tom one that is. However if she says, *"The jacket is awful. You sure don't have my taste in clothes,"* it would be **OK/NOT OK.** Here her role is okay, Tom's is not.

What role does Tom see for himself and Sue? If he responds to Sue's complement about his jacket by saying, *"Only someone like you would like a cheap thing like this,"* he has assigned a **NOT OK/NOT OK** role for each. While Sue initiated an **OK/OK** relationship, Tom rejected it with just the opposite response. But if Tom replies, *"Yeah, it's nice, too bad yours isn't,"* he has assigned **OK/NOT OK.** His jacket is good, Sue's isn't. The simplest **OK/OK** response to Sue's complement would be, *"Thanks."* Here Sue feels okay about the relationship, and so does Tom.

What does it mean to be **OK**? It means to give yourself permission to be the way you are. You feel good about yourself, and not guilty, tired, confused, or attacked. When you assign others an **OK** role you likewise give them credit for such positive attributes. You haven't assigned guilt, nor been made to feel guilty by others. Your exchange is built upon an honest, open, and understanding relationship.

Adult/Parent/Child

Another set of role-coordinates is the **ADULT/ PARENT/CHILD** scheme. This scheme provides nine possible combinations. They are:

Adult	Child
Adult	Parent
Adult	Adult
Parent	Child
Parent	Parent
Parent	Adult
Child	Child
Child	Parent
Child	Adult

What does each role mean? An adult is the voice of reason; the adult deals with facts. The parent is the voice of authority; the parent deals with punishments and warnings. The child is the voice of emotion; the child deals with wants. These roles have nothing to do with age, rather they interpret behavior—someone acting as a parent could be six, someone as a child sixty-six.

Let's imagine that an employee has written a report for his supervisor. The supervisor is not satisfied with the report and returns it to the employee with one of the following reactions:

	Supervisor	Employee
"This makes me sick."	*Child*	*Child*
"You're fired."	*Parent*	*Child*
"I can't understand why you did this."	*Adult*	*Child*
"Rewrite this or you're fired."	*Parent*	*Adult*
"Let's work together to improve this."	*Adult*	*Adult*

Each of these reactions indicates that the supervisor has assigned a role to herself and the employee. The first response, *"This makes me sick,"* is purely emotional and leaves the employee little choice but to respond in a similar way—thus the coordinates are **CHILD/CHILD.** The *"You're fired"* response communicates punishment. The supervisor is the voice of authority, the employee is left with that of emotion; consequently this becomes **PARENT/CHILD.** The third response, *"I can't understand why you did this,"* shows more reason, therefore the supervisor is acting like an adult. But it infers that the employee willfully wrote a poor report, making him feel like a child. It becomes **ADULT/CHILD.** The fourth response is clearly authoritative—*"Rewrite this or you're fired"*—but does allow the employee a choice; so this is **PARENT/ADULT.** The last reaction,

Table 7.1
Communicative Behaviors with Others

	Negative	*Passive*	*Aggressive*	*Assertive*
Public and social relationships with others	I'm not OK, you're not OK.	I'm not OK, you're OK.	I'm OK, you're not OK.	I'm OK, you're OK.
Level of personal confidence	Low	Low	Looks high but is low.	High
Intimate relationships with others	Child to Child	Child to Parent	Parent to Child	Adult to Adult
Decision making	Very difficult. Frequently, no decision.	Lets others decide.	Decides for others.	Agreement; mutually cooperative.
Responsiveness to others	Hostility; frequent signs of anger.	Defensive; shows humility.	Manipulative; demanding.	Mutual respect; openness.
Behavior in complex situations	Flees; avoids issue.	Allows others to dominate.	Attacks; dominates others.	Mutual friendliness.
Level of success	Seldom achieved.	Allows others to win.	Tries to defeat others; only one winner.	Success of issue is shared objective.
Practical adaptation and use	Look for positives in others.	Be more open; less defensive.	Be more open; less condescending.	Optimum; ultimate objective of all relationships.

"Let's work together to improve this," is clearly the most rational, offering a solution in a non-attacking way. It's reflected as **ADULT/ADULT**.

Let's now review four possible responses of the employee to the supervisor's "You're fired" comment:

	Employee	Supervisor
"Please don't, I couldn't help it."	Child	Parent
"You know I did the best I could."	Child	Adult
"You fire me and I'll get you fired."	Parent	Parent
"Firing me won't get the report done."	Adult	Parent

In the first response, *"Please don't, I couldn't help it,"* the employee has given himself the role of child, the supervisor the role of authority—this becomes **CHILD/PARENT**. The second *"You know I did the best I could,"* still represents the voice of want, but credits the supervisor with the chance to reason. So it is **CHILD/ADULT**. In the third statement the employee threatens the supervisor with the statement, *"You fire me and I'll get you fired."* This is the voice of authority reacting to another voice of authority, so it becomes **PARENT/PARENT**. In the fourth statement the employee tries to appear the most reasonable by mentioning that firing him won't get the report written. But the supervisor still has the final authority. Thus this becomes **ADULT/PARENT**.

Which role-coordinates are the most successful? **ADULT/ADULT** clearly is the best. It allows both parties to look at an issue out of reason, rather than out of emotion, threats, or need. It's true that sometimes we must play the role of parent, after all a child must be warned not to touch a hot stove. Likewise we all occasionally become children, asking another to fill an emotional need. But generally communication works best when two people interact as adults, mutually ignoring factors like intimidation, stress, and fear.

SKILLS FOR IMPROVING OUR SOCIAL INTERACTIONS

How do we become more sensitive communicators? By becoming aware of the feelings and needs of others. When we put this awareness to work everyone benefits. These skills include openness, empathy, supportiveness, positiveness, and equality. We'll review each in turn.

Openness

What does openness mean? It means being honest with others, willing to disclose our true feelings and emotions. Of course, some inner-thoughts will remain guarded; but those ideas we do express will be presented without fear or concern. Openness also permits us the right to express our feelings as our own. Information that is disclosed, whether it be factual, emotional, or judgmental, belongs to us and us alone.

Empathy

Empathizing with another person means understanding their feelings and emotions. Empathy shouldn't be confused with sympathy, which is feeling sorry for someone else. Rather, empathizing means being sensitive to someone else's moods, thoughts, and emotions. It lets us see *"where they're coming from."* Empathy is sometimes difficult to master—but it's essential for true interpersonal dialogue to occur.

Supportiveness

When we're open and empathetic with someone, we're naturally supportive. Supportiveness is nearly impossible to sustain when we feel threatened or under attack. But when people are open with us, it's natural to be supportive back. How do we practice supportiveness? By being a good listener, avoiding criticisms, and providing a sense of compassionate understanding. Such is the fabric of all meaningful relationships.

Positiveness

Being positive means feeling good about ourselves. If we aren't upbeat, our attitudes toward others won't be either. How do we manifest positiveness? By sending pleasant signals to others. Smiles, nods, grins, agreements, and similar supportive actions all tell the other person that we feel good about them and the relationship.

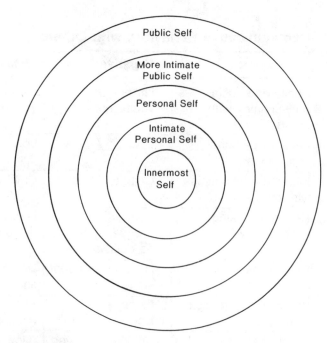

Figure 7.7
Self-Disclosure. Self-disclosure signifies the amount or degrees of our "true selves" that we are willing to show to others. The level of our self-disclosure is depicted through five concentric circles. *Public self* is the self that we show to acquaintances and to people with whom we have casual relationships; *more intimate public self* is what we show to people we know quite well in business or formal settings; *personal self* is the self that we show to close friends; *intimate personal self* is what we show to intimate personal friends and our relatives; and *innermost self* is what we seldom show to anyone—if it is shown at all is will be disclosed to a spouse or parent.

Equality

Perfect equality never really exists. One communicator is always smarter, richer, more powerful, more attractive, or more relaxed. How do we bring equality to such a relationship? By being ourselves and allotting others that same privilege. Bear in mind that while people may be unequal, they never need to communicate unequally.

How do we put the building blocks of openness, empathy, supportiveness, positiveness, and equality to work? By striving to include each of them in all our social interactions. Try to be open, show concerned empathy, work at supportiveness, reflect positiveness, and practice equality. When all this happens everybody benefits, allowing a true interpersonal exchange to take place.

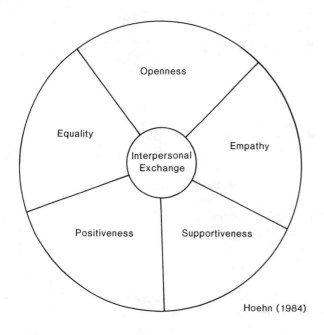

Figure 7.8
Skills for Effective Social Interaction (Hoehn, 1984).

CHAPTER SUMMARY

We've worked at conversation for most of our lives. As skilled conversationalists we've learned to analyze our listeners, understand our purpose, create an organized message, be alert to the response of our listeners, and make our messages as effective as possible.

Perception means being consciously aware of events and occurrences in our environment. We choose that information which seems most pertinent by practicing selective perception. This necessitates the organizing of data so it makes sense according to our past experiences.

The way we feel about ourselves is our self-concept. We acquire our self-concept through relationships, experience, and feedback. One important factor of self-concept is the self-fulfilling prophecy, or SFP. The SFP occurs when we turn a false concept into a true reality.

Our social behavior provides clues about the way we feel about ourselves and others. This can be gaged by our use of language, tone, expression, and self-portrayal. We play different roles with different people. Two of the most common coordinates to study roles are **OK/NOT OK** and **ADULT/PARENT/CHILD.**

The five skills for improving our social interactions are openness, empathy, supportiveness, positiveness, and equality. When all of this occurs everybody benefits.

EXERCISES FOR REVIEW

1. On a sheet of paper draw five columns, one for each of the five things people do naturally in conversation. Then observe people in other classes, in the cafeteria, or in similar public places engaged in conversations. Put a check in the appropriate column every time they reflect one of the five skills. Be prepared to discuss this in class.
2. Write a 200 word paper describing perception and how it applies in your daily life. Be sure to include selective perception and organization in your discussion.
3. Meet with a small group of classmates and discuss self-concept. Particularly consider the self-fulfilling prophecy and how it may have impacted on your life.
4. Review the four social behaviors discussed in the chapter. Then write a short paragraph on each describing how it influences our social interactions. Be prepared to discuss this in class.
5. Meet with a small group of classmates and act out each of the coordinate possibilities in **OK/NOT OK** and **ADULT/PARENT/CHILD.** Then discuss what types of behaviors dictated each coordinate response.

NOTES

1. The self-fulfilling prophecy was first suggested by sociologist Robert Merton of Columbia University.
2. The concept of scripting is suggested by Eric Berne in his book, *Games People Play.*
3. Both of these coordinates are discussed in Thomas A. Harris, *I'm OK—You're OK: A Practical Guide to Transactional Analysis,* (New York: Harper & Row, 1969).

Prosody

Every human being uses sound to manipulate the message in his or her communication. Whenever we send a verbal message we are using two components: the symbols that we choose to use (linguistic factor) and paralanguage (prosody) which is the gestural component of the spoken message. Prosody consists of rate, tone, volume, pitch, and every other qualitative factor of the verbal message.

When we are infants we use prosody as a first form of communication by babbling or uttering cries. All infants babble in the same pattern regardless of the language of that culture; thus, the sounds used in babbling are the basic sounds used in every language. Once the infant reaches six months of age the idle babbling stops and the infant's sound patterns begin to imitate the language of the culture in which they live. Therefore, babbles at six months follow the language of the parents as to pitch, quality, rate, and tone.

As adults we use prosody as an element in our communicated messages to connote anger, sarcasm, sorrow, happiness, and so forth. Even when the symbolic or linguistic pattern of the message is the same, through prosody the person can change the meaning of the communication. For instance, the word stop can be said in at least ten different ways—each communicating something entirely different. The prosodic component is also used to show rank, importance, or role when we communicate with other people. In simple essence, it's not what we say but how we say it that really matters.

Perception Checklist

Rank in order of priority your top ten concerns concerning the way others react to your messages. Put 1 for your top concern, 2 for your second greatest concern, and so on.

_____ Listeners take what I say too seriously.

_____ Listeners don't take what I say seriously enough.

_____ People tend to treat me with a lack of respect.

_____ A lot of people interrupt me while I'm speaking.

_____ If I'm one of two people speaking, I'm usually the one ignored.

_____ Store clerks frequently treat me in a rude fashion.

_____ People often appear bored when I'm speaking.

_____ Listeners often refuse to look me in the eye when I'm talking to them.

_____ Many people act like they're not listening to me.

_____ Members of the opposite sex often misinterpret what I mean.

_____ Members of my own sex often think I'm joking around when I'm really serious.

_____ When I'm a member of a large group people prefer to listen to someone else.

_____ Older people show me less respect than people my own age.

_____ Sometimes listeners act like my comments are confusing.

_____ People often ask me to repeat what I just said.

_____ I notice that a lot of people cut me off in mid-sentence.

_____ Often people seem to just disagree with me just to start an argument.

_____ A lot of my friends will never let me get in the last word.

_____ I feel people treat me with less respect because of some part of my appearance I can't control.

_____ People often ask me to speak up.

_____ Sometimes people tell me I'm shouting when I don't even realize it.

_____ I notice a lot of people touch me when they're talking to me.

_____ Some people I know have to top everything I say.

_____ Often listeners will confer with someone else to check on something I just said.

8 Communicating in Your Career

CHAPTER OUTLINE

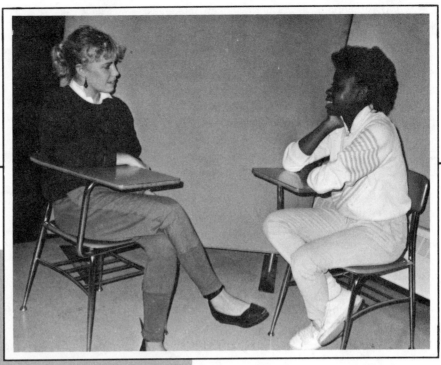

Being a good interviewer means listening to the other person.

QUESTIONS FOR RETENTION

Before reading this chapter, ask yourself the following questions:

1. What guidelines should I follow when going to an employment interview?
2. How can I present an oral report?
3. How can I effectively speak over the telephone?

The world of work is a world of spoken messages. No matter what your career goal is—business or banking, sales or social work, medicine or marketing—communication is going to play a very big part in your life's work. The three most common forms of career communications are interviews, oral reports, and speaking over the telephone. The focus of this chapter will be to examine each in turn.

THE INTERVIEW

An interview is an interesting thing. It isn't a speech or a conversation or a discussion, although it's much like all three. Yet, the interaction between two people—the dyad—is one of the most important ways individuals communicate in their careers. An interview with an employer, a meeting with a coworker, a talk with a subordinate, are just some of the ways that two people exchange information in a professional setting. In the course of this section we'll discuss some of the ways you can be successful in the strange world of the interview.[1]

Features of Interviews

Whether you're interviewing someone else, or being interviewed yourself, every interview has some common features. These features help to distinguish an interview from a typically more casual day-to-day conversation.

First, all interviews have a purpose. People meet in interviews with a particular reason in mind—to get a job, to discuss a problem, to evaluate a performance and the like. Just as every conversation has a purpose, so does every interview.

Second, all interviews are highly structured—they have a beginning, a middle, and an end. During the beginning both participants establish a rapport, determine the formality or informality of the exchange, and clarify their purpose. In the middle both parties exchange information, opinions, and points of view. At the end there is a summary, a few closing remarks, and perhaps a promise to meet again or reestablish contact in the near future. Interviews also follow a structure in the sense that often both parties have some prearranged questions or lines of thought that they wish to pursue.

Third, all interviews are by nature interactive. This means that an interview is not a monologue whereby one person only talks and the other just listens. An interview is more like a conversation, where both parties take turns speaking and listening. While one participant may be more an information seeker and the other an information dispenser, both parties

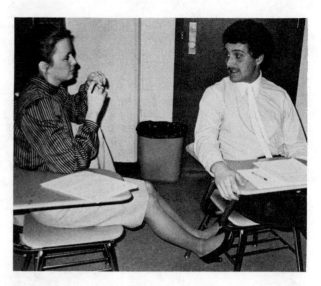

Figure 8.1
One-on-one communication can comprise some of the most influential, satisfying, and rewarding experiences of all communication activity.

must be careful listeners and astute observers. A good interactive interview is not just a along series of questions and answers, but rather a shared exchange whereby one response prompts the next question so that a real dialogue can occur.

Communicating In An Interview

In many ways successfully communicating in an interview is like effectively preparing any other message. You should prepare all your materials in advance and carefully go over potential questions and responses. In other words, rehearse for the interview just as you would for any upcoming presentation. During the interview expressively use your voice, occasionally pause, speak clearly, establish eye contact, exhibit positive facial expressions, and practice good posture. But in addition, there are some other skills which are even more essential.

To begin, communicating in an interview means being a good listener. Both questions and answers must be understood and remembered. Many times responses may need further elaboration and detail which always requires concentration. Or, if being questioned, you may need to clarify a question so as to present an accurate response. In order to perfect your listening during an interview, practice the skills of good listening discussed in Chapter Four.

Second, nonverbal behavior is very important in interviews. When being interviewed dress appropriately and exert a relaxed, confident manner. If interviewing someone else, make sure they're comfortably seated and exhibit toward them a pose and behavior that signals interest and support. Throughout the interaction both interviewer and interviewee should demonstrate energy and mutual support.

Third, show openness. This means being honest with the other person. Don't fabricate answers or cloak tricky questions under the guise of innocent inquiries. Neither interviewer nor interviewee should have a **"hidden agenda"**—unmentioned motives or purposes—during the interview. Be forthright, precise and sincere in having an honest, open dialogue.

Last, build a mutual feeling of trust and respect. Show sympathy, understanding, and interest in the other person. Let your interactive partner express him or herself fully and completely. At all times show integrity and create a positive communicative environment.

Conducting An Interview

There are many types of questions which can be asked in an interview. We'll review the six most frequent: primary questions, follow-up questions, direct questions, indirect questions, open questions and closed questions. It's not only important to be aware of these types of questions if conducting an interview, but also to recognize them if being interviewed yourself.

Primary questions introduce a new topic or area of exploration. Typical primary questions in an employment interview, for example, would be: *"What qualifies you for this job"* or *"Tell me about your college program"*. **Follow-up questions** probe more deeply and are born from the information provided from a primary question. *"Elaborate on that experience"* **or** *"Tell me a little more about your major in college"* would be follow-up's.

Direct questions are specific and get information quickly. Usually direct questions generate very short answers and sometimes can be answered with only one or two words, *"How many computer courses did you take"* or *"How many years did you work*

at your last job" are examples of these. **Indirect questions** are less specific and more free-wheeling. These seek to encourage an interviewee to respond while thinking on his or her feet. Needless to say, answers to indirect questions tend to be much longer than those which are direct. Typical indirect questions would include: *"What is your greatest weakness"* or *"Where do you expect to be in five years?"*

Good interviewers use both open and closed questions. **Closed questions** set the categories and limit the range of possible responses. For instance, *"Will you graduate with one or two majors"* or *"Have you ever worked in sales or marketing"* are these types of inquiries. These questions are easy to code and record since potential answers are already prescribed. **Open questions** allow the interviewee to control the response. Thus, *"What salary do you expect to earn"* or *"Why do you want this job"* are typical of these. With this kind of question the person being questioned can go into as much detail as he or she sees fit.

Primary, direct, and closed questions produce a great deal of concrete, substantial information in a relatively short period of time. On the other hand, follow-up, indirect, and open questions produce more thought provoking responses that are open to greater interpretation.

You'll notice that all six types of questions somewhat overlap. Either a direct, indirect, open, or closed question could be your primary question. Also, a closed question could be direct, *"Did you do better in math or science"* or indirect, *"Do you think math or science is more important for this job?"* Consequently, your mix of questions, the way you ask them, and the order in which they're asked all help to set the climate and tone of the interview.

By carefully blending questions you can build an **interview schedule**. An interview schedule is a prearranged framework of questions that you intend to ask during an interview session. In using such a schedule, you can gain the most relevant information while avoiding repetition, becoming side-tracked, or neglecting to find out essential information that otherwise you might forget to ask. Interview schedules can be either traditional or branching. Here's an example of each:

Traditional Schedule of Questions

I. *Are you a junior or senior in college?*
(primary, direct, closed question)

    A. *What's your major?*
(secondary, direct, open question)

        1. *Why did you select this major?*
(secondary, indirect, open question)

        2. *Is this major difficult?*
(secondary, indirect, open question)

    B. *What kind of work experiences have you had while in college?*
(secondary, direct, open question)

        1. *What did you learn from this experience?*
(secondary, indirect, open question)

        2. *Based on this experience, do you think you're best suited for sales, marketing, or customer relations?*
(secondary, direct, closed question)

Branching Schedule of Questions

1. *Did you take computer courses while at college?*

If Yes	*If No*
2. *Will these courses help in performing this job?*	2. *What courses did you take instead?*
If Yes	*If No*
3. *Are you interested in taking more computer courses?*	3. *Would you be interested in taking computer courses on your own time?*

Observe that the traditional schedule of questions moves in an organizational pattern that starts with a general subject (college) and moves into more specific probing questions about courses in college and related work experience. By blending questions in this manner, the interviewer is able to logically lead the interviewee through each progression of the session. This almost always leads the person being questioned to provide more self-reflective and revealing answers. Notice, too, that a variety of question types are used to keep the interaction fresh and moving. When this is done, interviews take on a controlled spontaneity all their own. Normally a branching schedule is used when the interviewer has a clear focus of what information s/he wishes to learn. This type of organizational pattern is particularly useful when seeking specific information. Accordingly, this style is often used for surveys and polls. In the example just cited, notice that the interviewer is particularly trying to focus in on the interviewee's experience and background with computers. With a more elaborate schedule, the interviewer could also have branches under *"no"* responses. A branch schedule allows the questioner to set a rather structured agenda which elicits the most information.

Regardless of what types of questions you use, you should plan your questions in advance, have a clear organizational pattern in mind, and show flexibility during the course of the actual interview. An interviewer who holds rigidly to a set of prearranged questions without variation or fluctuation, is unable to elicit the most from the session. A good interviewer is organized yet versatile; guiding yet conversational; and observant yet responsive. By carefully preparing for the interview and thinking through a proper strategy, you'll let all interviewees present themselves in their best light.

Types of Interviews

There are many types of interviews. There are counseling interviews often used for advisement and therapy, exit interviews designed to elicit information when someone is leaving a position, and appraisal interviews which assess a person's performance. But, the three types of interviews that you're most likely to use are the informational, persuasive, and employment interview. We'll review each in turn.

Informational Interviews

Informational interviews are used to gather information about a person, subject, idea, or event. These are used in market research when people are asked about a particular commercial product. Survey organizations like Gallup and Harris also use these to poll the public on their views concerning a political candidate or social situation. Oftentimes, speakers use informational interviews to generate ideas for a speech or to learn more about an audience. In a work environment, informational interviews are frequently used by teachers, doctors, lawyers, executives, and scientists to learn as much as possible about a person's needs or subject under review. The design of this type of interview is always to learn as much as possible while injecting a minimum of personal input and commentary.

Persuasive Interviews

Often one person tries to persuade another to do something. Someone plying a sales pitch is a typical example of this. Other examples include political workers trying to get someone to vote for a candidate, cause volunteers trying to convince someone to support an issue, or fund raisers trying to get someone to contribute to a charity. If conducting a persuasive interview, create interest in your subject, show the interviewee where they can directly benefit, build a trusting rapport, keep your message focused on the situation at hand, and reiterate your most important point toward the close of the session.

Employment Interviews

Employment interviews are the punctuation marks of a person's career, the high points that distinguish someone's opportunities and accomplishments. Perhaps in no other type of one-on-one interaction are the stakes so high, the promises so great, as in an employment interview. The impact of this type of interview is amazing: careers have been determined; futures have been decided; lives have been changed. Think of it in terms of your own future—the chances are that in your professional lifetime you'll have between three and eight different jobs. This means that you'll have to undergo numerous career-oriented interviews. Your success or failure in these interviews will largely determine whether your future plans are fulfilled or neglected.

The purpose of the employment interview is always clear and straightforward—it's to fit the right person with the right job. If doing the interviewing, you have to pick that *"right"* person out of the entire universe of potential workers.[2] This is no easy task, and a lot rides on your decision. Your company will invest significant time and resources in the person you choose. Therefore, your choice must be based on a firm foundation of logic and reason. In short, you must plan for the interview as if it were a presidential address.

How do you plan to conduct an employment interview? As an interviewer your task is threefold: First, you must gain sufficient information about the applicant to see if s/he meets the specific requirements of the job; second, you must assess the person's skills and proficiencies; and third, you must

determine if they'll fit in with the job and company. Basically, practice the techniques presented thus far in this chapter: adhere to the features of an interview, plan well-ahead, communicate effectively, and ask a well-ordered schedule of questions. When all this is realized, you, your company, and the person your interviewing will all benefit.

The greater likelihood is, however, that you'll be more an interviewee than an interviewer. Coming across effectively in an employment interview will test all your skills as a communicator. If you don't understand a question while being interviewed, say so; if you want to tell more about your training and experience, do so; if you feel that something has been left out that you want to mention, tell so. Be prepared, show motivation, be energetic. Before the interview carefully prepare a readable, up-to-date resume and specific cover letter—remember, a written resume and cover letter are vehicles of communication and will influence the interaction. During the session practice all the techniques discussed in this chapter. Particularly pay attention to answering all questions completely and fully. Near the close of the interview, have a few relevant questions that are brief and restricted to information you couldn't find out in any other way. And after the interview drop a note to the interviewer thanking him or her for their time and courtesy. The following guidelines should prove helpful in preparing for a job interview.

Guidelines for Employment Interviews

Rehearse and prepare

Plan ahead for your interview. Spend some time researching the company and job. Anticipate likely questions and areas that you'll need to bring out. It's always a good idea to rehearse the interview with a friend or roommate and condition yourself for the actual event. Make the situation as realistic as possible and run through the interview several times until you feel fairly comfortable with it. One good technique to lessen nervousness is to write out the ten questions you'd least like being asked. Then prepare answers for each and have your practicing partner ask those most feared questions. You'll find this will lessen tension and increase confidence.

Make a Good First Impression

Most people are astounded to learn that most interviewers make up their minds about an applicant in the first 30 seconds of an interview. This 30-second hurdle is termed the *"Halo Effect"* by psychologists.[3]

In order to make your first impression a good one, you need to do several things. First, dress appropriately; if undecided about what's proper for the interview, remember that it's better to fall on the side of being a bit too formal rather than being a bit too casual. The day before check yourself out in a full-length mirror. Smile and act as if you were greeting the interviewer. Then ask: Do I like the way I look? If not, choose something else—in order to be comfortable you must feel comfortable. Second, upon entering the room hold your head high, smile, and maintain good eye contact. Exude confidence and competence. Finally, have a few opening comments in mind. These can be general remarks that will serve to break the ice and create a positive first image.

Let the Interviewer Set the Tone

Remember you're on the interviewer's turf. Therefore let him or her set the tone. Have a few comments prepared—reference to a topical business item is always good as it shows you're prepared and knowledgeable. Follow the lead of the interviewer; don't enter into unrelated subjects unless s/he opens the door. And keep in mind that the average interviewer sees dozens of applicants; consequently, don't assume the interviewer knows all the details on your resume and cover letter—be prepared to refresh his or her memory and cover the same ground once again.

Help Yourself with A Handshake

Generally you should offer a handshake, but remember the interviewer sets the tone. If s/he motions you to sit down, it would be awkward to present your hand. Also cold, clammy handshakes can create a negative first impression in nothing flat. An effective way to avoid this is to arrive early enough for your appointment to visit the restroom and run hot water over your hands until they're warm. Dry them thoroughly and keep your hands clasped. Then when the time comes to offer your hand, it should convey a sense of confidence and self-assurance.

Choose the Best Seat

The interviewer may offer you a seat in front of or beside the desk. If you have a choice, always take the one next to the desk. This way you reduce barriers and start on a more equal footing. If the choice is on the left of the interviewer, so much the better. Studies show that people pay more attention to what's on their left. Should your chair be facing the desk, shift it slightly so that it's a bit more to the left side.

Use Positive Nonverbal Language

We already know of the importance of nonverbal language. To create a positive image sit straight, with your hands and feet relaxed. Keep good eye contact, but don't stare. Be conscious of nervous habits like foot tapping, hand wringing, or playing with jewelry. Some people even find it helpful to play calming music before an interview.

Recognize Time Limits

Most interviews take about half an hour. Of course this varies, but it's a good barometer. Most interviewers know in rather short order if you're the right person for the job. If you see the interviewer is pressed for time or looks at his or her watch, don't drag out the session by asking detailed, long-winded questions.

What to Do If the Interviewer Gets Off Track

Sometimes interviewers get off topic—after all, they're human too! If the questioner gets off track for more than five minutes, don't hesitate to diplomatically pose a question about the company or position. Also, always have a list of prepared questions in case the interviewer only asks one or two things and then falls silent. If this happens be prepared to discuss things that will show you in the best light. And if the interviewer shares personal problems with you, never give advice. Politely plead a lack of expertise and instead make reference to a question about the job.

What to Do If Asked an Illegal Question

Questions about your race, religion, marital status and the like are all illegal. If asked one of these questions, never accuse the interviewer of wrongdoing. If it's a question you have no objection to answering and believe it's asked innocently, answer it straight out. If you have objections, however, it's your right under the law to decline and politely explain to the interviewer you have no objection to answering the question, but understand that you're not supposed to.

Prepare for Three Typical Questions

In most interviews at least one of these three questions are likely to be raised. Your answers to these may spell the difference between getting the job or being passed over.

The Most Frequent Complaints of Bosses About Employees

The Burke Marketing Research Company asked executives in 100 of the nation's 1,000 largest companies, "What employee behavior disturbs you the most?". The result provided a list of behaviors that often blinded employers to the good qualities of their employees. The survey listed the 8 most critical complaints in order:

1. *Dishonesty and lying*—If a company believed that an employee lacked integrity, all other positive attributes became meaningless. Bosses considered all forms of dishonesty, from direct stealing to "intellectual dishonesty." For instance, one employer complained about an employee who took a job with a November 16th deadline even though he knew he would be on vacation that week.

2. *Irresponsibility*—This encompassed an employee not doing his job or using company time for personal business. Particular annoyance was shown by employers when employees ran second businesses, using company phones and time.

3. *Arrogance*—Employers disliked an employee who showed arrogant and excessively aggressive behavior. Many bosses felt that this led to problems with other employees and general disharmony within the office.

4. *Absenteeism and lateness*—Many employers felt that certain employees would be late no matter when the day started. Being late or excessively absent made for an employee who was irresponsible and unreliable.

5. *Not following instructions*—When employees ignored company policies and procedures it was considered to be a breach of discipline and respect for the job. Such behavior was particularly a problem in larger and more conservative companies.

6. *Whining and complaining*—These types of employees are never content or satisfied. Bosses found them to be a constantly disruptive influence.

7. *Absence of commitment*—When an employee showed a lack of concern or dedication for his job. Such behavior usually resulted in a failure to receive promotions or raises.

8. *Laziness and lack of motivation*—This behavior indicated to employers that the employee did not care about the company or the job. The reaction of bosses was, "Then why should we care about him or her?"

Why do you want this job? Don't give trite answers like *"I like working with people"* or *"This job will be interesting."* Instead, give some concrete reasons about the position, your expectations, and aspirations.

Tell me about yourself? Don't give your life history. Instead relate some common thread that winds its way back to explaining why you're the right person for the job.

What is your greatest weakness? Never say you don't have any! State a rather innocent weakness and then tell how you're overcoming it. In other words, build a weakness into a strength.

These guidelines should help prepare you for upcoming job interviews. Remember to prepare thoroughly, exude positive communication, and above all else, be your natural self.

Interview Preparation Outline

Here's an outline to help make sure that all your interviews are successful ones.

I. *Pre-interview Preparation*
   A. *Establish purpose of interview*
      1. *Clearly understand objectives*
      2. *Determine what's to be accomplished*
   B. *Determine what to wear*
   C. *Obtain and collect all materials and documents*
      1. *Have a resume*
      2. *Bring copies of diplomas, transcripts, and references*
   D. *Make an appointment and get directions*
   E. *Learn as much about the job and company as possible*
   F. *Find out who the interviewer is and his or her position*
   G. *Practice likely questions*
   H. *Prepare a brief introduction in case it's needed*
II. *The Interview Session*
   A. *Be on time*
   B. *Try to establish immediate rapport*
      1. *Present a pleasant greeting*
      2. *Allow interviewer to make opening comments*
   C. *Practice comfortable, yet not overly relaxed posture*
   D. *Think before answering questions*
   E. *Keep answers to the point, and avoid overly long or brief responses*
   F. *Maintain direct eye contact when speaking*
   G. *Listen carefully to what's being said*
   H. *Be sure to mention all your strong points*
   I. *Make sure to have a few questions to ask at end*
   J. *Speak in a clear, easy to understand voice*
III. *Closing the Interview*
   A. *Be alert to when the interviewer wants to conclude*
   B. *Don't introduce any new material during the closing*
   C. *Close with a handshake and a smile*
IV. *After the Interview*
   A. *Continue looking for a job, don't assume you've been chosen*
   B. *Call the interviewer in a week to see if a decision has been made*
   C. *Write a brief thank you note thanking the interviewer for his or her time and interest*

A good interview will help you get a job, but once you have it you'll still need to effectively communicate. One of the most frequent methods is the oral report, and this is our next subject of discussion.

ORAL REPORTS

The chances are that you'll need to give many oral reports during the course of your lifetime. You might talk about a study you've done, report on something you've read, or present conclusions you've drawn from a collection of research. Whatever the motivation, a good oral report is both enlightening and complete.

In a business setting people inform coworkers about a variety of subjects. They explain new procedures, interpret a series of statistical returns, suggest a proposed policy, or describe a new selling strategy. Regardless of the type, an oral report needs to be concise, thorough, and extremely well-organized.

When preparing an oral report make sure your remarks are short and balanced. Some professional reports are only five minutes long. If your report is brief, pack in as much as you can. How do you do this? Pick out the two or three main ideas that stand out. Then back each one with logic and information. Bear in mind that you're probably speaking to a group of fellow experts—so weigh your evidence carefully. Begin your presentation with a reasoned, well—tested rationale—this helps to make your case right at the start. At the end restate your rationale, and summarize your major findings and conclusions.

How can you enhance an oral report? One way to spark up an otherwise mundane report is to bring in visual aids. Flip charts, transparencies, handouts, and slides prove particularly successful. Have a series of year by year accounts to report? Use a line graph. What to show proportions? Try a pie graph. Decide to show a comparison? Present a bar graph. Wish to describe something firsthand? Bring in some slides. Want listeners to follow you step-by-step? Give them each a handout. Hope to point out your most important ideas? A chart works great. Make all visuals large, neat, and easy to read. Follow the suggestions detailed in Chapter 13 on visual aids. You'll find that an effective visual aid lets listeners not only hear what you're saying, but see what you mean.[4]

While oral reports mean speaking to many, conversing on the phone means talking to one. Let's see how we can make our *"phone impression"* a good impression.

Facial Expressions

Are our facial expressions inborn or are they learned? Darwin claimed that they are inborn citing for example, head shaking to indicate "no." He suggests that this may have developed from a baby's sideways turn of the head as a gesture of refusing the mother's breast when satisfied.

Recent researchers have found that in studies of children born deaf and blind, they exhibited the same facial expressions as sighted children. Other researchers have concluded that similar facial expressions exist in all cultures, such as: fear, surprise, anger, happiness, contempt, interest, and sadness. Birdwhistell suggests that the raising and lowering of the eyebrow occurs across all cultures as a method of greeting. However, he also suggests that many facial expressions vary from country to country and can be somewhat different within a country.

The next time you see someone from a different culture notice his or her facial expressions. Which expressions are similar to yours and which are different?

SPEAKING OVER THE TELEPHONE

What could sound more basic than talking on the telephone? After all you've probably done it thousands of times. But what seems natural at home, becomes special at work. People make all sorts of judgements based on your voice and demeanor over the phone. People you may never meet, who may never see your face, but who create an image of you based on your sound alone. Are you believable? Do you sound knowledgeable? Are you someone they wish to do business with? All of these signals are communicated in the space of a few minutes. How do we put those few minutes to good use? By following some reasonable guidelines. Let's see what they are.

Guidelines for Speaking Over the Telephone

Introduce Yourself First

Don't assume the person on the other end knows who you are. State your full name, position, and company that you represent.

Check If It's Convenient to Talk

Before launching into a conversation, find out if it's a good time to call. If not, arrange to call at another, more suitable time. This not only shows good manners, but also assures that the other party will give you time to hear you out.

Don't Interrupt the Call

Constant interruptions with comments to coworkers or chatter with a passerby, will seriously disrupt any conversation. Stay focused on the conversation underway, and not on any outside interactions.

Be A Good Listener

We already know about the importance of listening. Obviously, listening is particularly crucial in a telephone conversation as one party cannot see the other. Hear what the other person is saying, pay attention to their tone, and pick up on subtle hesitations.

Find Out the Names of Assistants and Secretaries

Seek to establish a rapport with the people who are associated with the individual you want to talk to. Remember their names and how to pronounce them, and exert a positive, upbeat sound. Humanizing a relationship can make a difference of how quickly or in what priority you're able to speak to their boss.

Promptly Return Calls

Being hard to reach doesn't necessarily mean you're important—it just means you're isolated from developing a conversation. Be as available as possible, and return calls quickly—even if to report that you're still working on the answer.

These guidelines should prove helpful when talking over the phone. But remember that the most important ingredient of all is your sincerity. If you sound likeable, remain polite, and utilize a clear tone all your calls should be successful ones.

CHAPTER SUMMARY

Interviews are particularly important in the world of work. The features of all interviews are that they have a purpose, are highly structured, and are interactive. When communicating in an interview we should practice careful listening, effectively use nonverbal behavior, be open, and show trust. If conducting an interview we should use a variety of questions, combining and mixing as we go. Either a traditional or branching schedule of questions helps. The three major types of interviews are those that are informational, persuasive, and for employment. If going to an employment interview we should rehearse, make a good first impression, let the interviewer set the tone, use a handshake, choose the best seat, include positive nonverbal language, recognize time limits, keep the interviewer on track, and appropriately handle illegal questions.

Frequently we must give oral reports. Oral reports should be informative and concise. Each report should begin with a rationale, have a few main ideas, and close with a rationale and summary. Visual aids such as charts, slides, and handouts prove particularly helpful.

Speaking over the telephone seems basic, but really is a skill in need of polish. When talking on the phone we should introduce ourselves, check if it's the best time to call, not interrupt the call, be a good listener, find out the names of assistants, and promptly return calls. By doing this we can present our best image over the phone.

EXERCISES FOR REVIEW

1. Based on the discussion in this chapter, identify what type of interview question each of the following questions are. Are they a primary question, follow-up question, direct question, indirect question, open question, or closed question?
   a. *What do you think of his company?*
   b. *What is your grade point average?*
   c. *To begin, have you ever had a communication course?*
   d. *Why did you say you thought speech training was important?*
   e. *Would you say you're a leader or a follower?*
   f. *Why should we hire you?*
2. Imagine you're being interviewed in an employment interview. Based on the material presented in this chapter, describe how you would handle each of the following circumstances should they occur during the interview:
   a. *You're asked the question: Are you a homosexual?*
   b. *You're offered a choice of a seat on the right of the desk, left of the desk, or facing the desk.*
   c. *Before the interview you notice your hands feel cold and clammy.*
   d. *The interviewer asks you: "Do you think I should get a divorce or stay married?"*
   e. *You stumble over a chair as you enter the room.*
   f. *The interviewer begins by asking if there's anything you want to say.*
   g. *The interviewer asks you to tell of your greatest failure so far in your life.*
3. Prepare to interview a classmate in an employment interview. Prepare a vast array of questions, create a question schedule, and follow the communicative technique discussed in this chapter. If playing the role of employee, follow the guidelines suggested in this chapter and come across as effectively as possible. Prepare for it as if it were a real job interview and make the situation as realistic as possible.
4. Prepare an oral report to be delivered in class. It can be on any subject—a book you've read, a movie you've seen, a place you've visited. Make it about five minutes long and follow the suggestions made in this chapter.
5. Write a 200 word paper on the way you'll utilize each of the methods of communication discussed in this chapter in your career-choice. Be sure to specifically mention the interview, oral reports, and the telephone.

NOTES

1. For an excellent account of interviewing, see Charles J. Stewart and William B. Cash, Jr., *Interviewing: Principles and Practices,* 3rd ed. (Dubuque, Iowa: Brown, 1982).
2. This theory is expound in H. Maslow, "Measurement in the Selection and Development Process," in *Behavioral Science Research in Industrial Relations,* Industrial Relations Monographs, 21 (New York: Industrial Relations Counsellors, 1962), pp. 121–148.
3. For a discussion of the Halo Effect see Joyce Brothers, "How to Get the Job You Want," *Parade Magazine,* November 16, 1986, pp. 4–6.
4. For helpful guides on how to present a visual program, see, Richard Wiegand, "It Doesn't Need to be Dull to be Good: How to Improve Staff Presentations," *Business Horizons,* 28, July/August 1985, pp. 35–42 and Paul LeRoux, "The Fine Art of Show-and-Tell," *Working Woman,* September 1985, pp. 126–131.

INTERVIEW CHECKLIST

(check each item as you complete it for your interview)

____ Established the purpose of the interview

____ Determined the requirements of the position and basic qualifications needed

____ Set a definite time and date for the interview

____ Received a location and know the way to get there, including the room location

____ Determined the appropriate dress requirements for the session

____ Gathered necessary materials and documents that may be required during the interview

____ Rehearsed possible questions and answers

____ Learned as much about the interviewer as possible

____ Prepared a brief introduction

____ Prepared a current resume

____ Acquired reference letters from former employers and teachers

____ Confirmed the appointment before the scheduled meeting time

____ Practiced correct posture

____ Practiced correct demeanor and manners

____ Made a mental list of all relevant experience and education in case it's not discussed during the question and answer phase

____ Created several well thought out questions about the position and company

____ Practiced effective eye contact

____ Practiced speaking in a clear and understandable fashion

____ Arranged to leave early enough to arrive at the interview session with some time to spare

____ After the interview written a thank you note to the interviewer

____ After a week has gone by called the interviewer to see if a decision has been made

____ Continued to examine possible leads for other positions

Name _____ Interviewer _____ Interviewee _____

INTERVIEW EVALUATION

Interview Content:	Superior	Excellent	Good	Fair	Needs Work
Opening well handled					
Rapport established					
Purpose established					
Effective transition to interview body					
Specific questions utilized					
Specific, clear answers presented					
Systematic organization of interview					
Effective adaptation to interview partner					
Conclusion well handled?					
Interview Presentation:					
Effective vocal skills					
Effective bodily action					
Sympathetic, critical listening					
Appropriate language					
General Effectiveness:					

GRADE _____

Electronic Recruiting for Jobs

The traditional job search of recent college graduates may be taking a radical change. In the past, college graduates would meet with prospective employers at the campus or visit them at the location of the business; however, this is rapidly being replaced with electronic recruiting.

Electronic recruiting involves the applicant placing his or her resume in a database by filling out a career information form. The resume is then an electronic resource that is transmitted to prospective employers at terminals located at personal offices around the country. Job requirements are matched against education, experience, skills, salary requirements, career objectives, and other factors contained in the resume. The resumes are scanned on a computer screen to determine the most desired by the hiring employers. The computer can then be instructed to invite candidates to call the company to discuss the opportunity in detail.

In south Florida a series of electronic interviews were conducted for a series of job openings. Letters were sent to 297 candidates, and 85 responded, six were hired and 20 more received immediate offers. The whole process, from start to finish, took less than six weeks. Were such a search conducted in the traditional method, the entire process would have taken several months.

Such companies as General Database Technology conduct the electronic resume service. Dale H. Learn, who founded the company, predicts that by the end of the decade as many as one million men and women will be searching for jobs using this method. The advantages to the applicant are that it eliminates, or at least reduces, the leg work necessary to find a job. It also saves companies thousands of dollars in travel expenses and in the interviewing of uninteresting or unqualified candidates.

This service is expected to be used by thousands of companies in the next several years. The cost usually runs as a free service for the first 90 days and then increases to $25 a year to maintain the resume. Most companies are expected to pick up the cost from newly hired candidates. This service is certain to change the picture of job hunting for aspiring young professionals. This service does not do away with the need for the personal interview, but it does quicken the entire recruiting process.

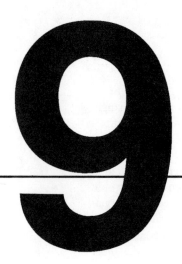

Communicating in Small Groups

When each group member follows a set agenda an orderly and beneficial discussion will take place.

QUESTIONS FOR RETENTION

Before reading this chapter, ask yourself the following questions:

1. What is a small group?
2. How can I effectively lead a small group?
3. How can I successfully participate in a small group?

Communicating in a small group is a special experience. Groups make decisions, study ideas, formulate plans, and present results. But working in a group is no easy task. It takes patience, understanding, and cooperation. When such a "collaborative spirit" is harnessed, however, the results can be astonishing. Consider the Manhattan Project. During World War II the United States began work on an atomic bomb to end the war. How did they do it? By pulling together a group of scientists dedicated to this single task. Within two years the scientists accomplished their mission and ended the war. Many found the results nothing short of miraculous. For without a doubt, groups let us reach places together that we could never could have reached alone.

In this chapter we'll examine what the small group can mean to you. Let's begin by learning what a group is.

UNDERSTANDING GROUPS

Figure 9.1
A gathering of people is not a group unless they share some commality of purpose.

People are constantly forming groups. We form a group called a nation to protect our mutual interests. We produce and raise children in a group called a family. And we join a group called a union to protect our rights as workers, to learn and call it a class, to worship and call it a congregation. Some groups, such as a family, are permanent, while others like a class are temporary and disband once their work is completed. We belong to some groups by choice—a congregation—while we belong to others out of necessity—a nation. Regardless of the reasons for the group, or the way it came about, all groups fulfill a need. They build an individual weakness into a collective strength.

So what is a group? By assimilating much of the research done on group behavior we can explain groups in four basic ways.

First, a small group usually consists of around five people. Some groups can have as few as three people, others as many as eleven—generally odd numbers are preferable to even.[1] Two people—**a dyad**—couldn't be a group because they can't create the unique environment peculiar to groups. As we know from our study of interviews, the interaction between two people is quite different than that shared between several.[2] One important factor is that the group must be a size where everyone can fully participate. When a group is a manageable size people can comfortably shift between speaking and listening.

Second, all members need to be interdependent. This means that everyone must share in the interaction and group effort. A small group is not a collection of individuals each pulling their own way. Instead, a group needs a cooperative spirit to propel it towards its ultimate goal. This doesn't mean people sacrificing their individuality either. Rather, it's the recognition that each person has a collective stake in the results. The group is incomplete unless everyone is involved.

Third, members need to mutually influence one another. Each person must share ideas, express viewpoints, respond to questions, and listen to opposing thoughts. The art of being a good discussant is a bit persuasive, a little informative, and a lot open-minded. Small groups are a mixture of thoughts, feelings, and facts all mutually contributed. If someone either dominates or remains uninvolved, the entire process is thwarted.[3]

Fourth, groups need to share a common purpose. A collection of seven people who live in the same apartment house is not a group. But if they form a tenant right's organization, they soon become one. Effective groups clearly establish a fixed purpose. They ask: What are we striving for? What do we want to accomplish? Why does this group exist? When this is understood the entire group benefits.[4]

Just as there are different purposes, there are different types of groups. This is our next subject of discussion.

TYPES OF SMALL GROUPS

The six most popular types of groups are experimental groups, mediating groups, learning groups, information-gathering groups, work groups, and problem-solving groups. Let's look at each in turn.[5]

Experimental Groups

The purpose of experimental groups is to foster personal growth. Frequently people meet in these groups to broaden personal insights, overcome personality problems, or make adjustments to changes in their living environment. These groups encourage feedback and openness. Examples include counseling seminars, drug or alcohol rehabilitation programs, and committees for people contemplating a change in career.

Mediating Groups

Some groups are created to coordinate the activities of other groups, reconcile differences, or distribute resources. Often these groups are composed of representatives from different departments who come together to better understand the concerns of the overall organization. By talking out differences major problems are often avoided. Mediating groups include neighborhood committees, arbitration boards, and management interactive sessions.

Learning Groups

Organizations often create learning groups to open up new ideas and insights for members. These frequently take place at seminars where people are placed in specific groups to learn about new technological developments, innovative strategies, or changing procedures.

Information-Gathering Groups

The purpose of an information-gathering group is to come up with information about an agreed upon topic. If a community is concerned about the environment, for example, such a group might be formed to look into recycling, auto emissions, industrial waste and the like. Typically each member gathers information independently and then brings it to the group for all to share. The function of information-gathering groups is not to reach a conclusion, but rather to discuss all possible solutions so someone else can make an informed ultimate decision. In the case just cited, the mayor might initiate a policy on environmental control.

Work Groups

The purpose of a work group is to perform some task more efficiently by pooling and coordinating everyone's efforts. For nearly one-hundred years studies have supported the view that groups are more efficient in performing tasks than any one person working alone.[6] In colleges, work groups are formed to develop new courses, set standards, increase enrollment and so on.

Problem-Solving Groups

These are groups designed to solve a particular problem. Businesses form research teams, task forces, and committees to do this all the time. The rationale is that a solution will be found quicker, implemented sooner, and applied faster when a group of people are making the decision. This is supported by much research which shows that groups generally make better decisions and find more workable solutions than one person working alone.[7] In your life you're almost certain to be a member of many problem-solving groups. Because this type of group is the most popular, it will be the main focus of this chapter.

As we've already begun to recognize, groups have many advantages. In this next section we'll focus on some other factors which make the small group so useful.

ADVANTAGES OF SMALL GROUPS

Major American corporations have long recognized the advantages of the small group. Texas Instruments, for example, has over 9,000 "small teams" which specialize in finding productivity improvements. 3M Corporation has several hundred four to ten person "venture teams" that design, develop, and implement new product lines. And companies like General Electric, IBM, and General Motors frequently use task forces composed of particularly creative employees to come up with new ideas and concepts.[8] Each of these companies, and thousands more like them, have realized that small groups can serve as building blocks for creativity and organization.

There are several reasons why groups are frequently preferred. First, groups pool their resources in terms of time, labor, and energy. People working together can gather more information, offer more viewpoints, and accomplish more tasks. Second, groups are quicker to catch errors. It's fairly easy for one person working alone to make a mistake; but a group of people, all working together, have a built in error-correction mechanism that can promptly catch such oversights. And last, groups are able to more clearly understand a problem. Group thinking lets every person function as part of a well-tuned engine. People working in groups show greater creativity, flexibility, and productivity.[9] Often this isn't the result of more people being involved, rather it's be-

DYADS AND TRIADS IN GROUP DISCUSSION

Often in group discussion two or three members of the group form a social system and a collective within the overall group. These members primarily interact with each other and not with the other members. When two discussants link together it is called a dyad and when three link it is called a triad. Below, are listed several comparisons of dyads and triads:

Dyads

1. More competitive in a win-lose context and there is a greater feeling of pressure to be accepted in the early stages of the relationship.
2. A greater likelihood for closeness and direct interaction with the other member. Difficulty arises in the case of a tie or deadlock.
3. When there is difficulty in the interaction a power struggle may develop between both parties. Because there is less anonymity, there is a greater power struggle than in a triad.
4. Both dyads and triads seek open and compatible conditions.

Triads

1. Oftentimes, tend to divide into a coalition. When a coalition is formed two equals will pair against the stronger.
2. Once the power struggle emerges the pair forms a closer relationship with each other than with the third member.
3. Within the triad arbitrators, stabilizers, monitors and social maintainers may be formed to continue the relationship.
4. Triads permit greater anonymity and are less predictable because they are more complex.

---

cause someone in the group will know the answer or come up with the perfect idea. Members of a productive, well-functioning group are like a collection of musicians playing separate instruments. Collectively they produce a melody, separately they just make sound.

DISADVANTAGES OF SMALL GROUPS

Just as there's an upside to groups, there's likewise a side that's down. If you've ever been part of a committee that got little done, you probably thought at the time, *"I could have done this better myself."* As a result, when many people think of groups they're reminded of the old saying, *"A camel is a horse designed by committee."* While this skepticism is understandable, it doesn't mean that groups have to be inefficient or ineffective. The disadvantages of a group can almost always be avoided by a highly motivated, clear-thinking body of members. Therefore, look at these disadvantages as warning signs to watch out for when part of a group interaction.

One disadvantage is that groups usually take more time. By their very nature, problem-solving groups must explore every aspect of an issue. If a group is asked to come up with a plan to clean up the environment, for example, they're likely to examine every side of the question. Where an individual might come up with a solution in a few days, a committee might take several weeks. What the group produces in quality, it pays for in time.

Another disadvantage is the potential for conflict. Conflict is not necessarily negative; in fact, some conflict productively gives the group exposure to a broad range of ideas. The problem isn't with the conflict, rather it's with how it's handled. If members become bogged down with petty differences and personal conflicts, the group is bound to be less efficient. Consequently, group members must always handle conflict with a cushioned glove.

Finally, groups must avoid the dangerous side of the *"group think"* phenomenon. When people work together they often get a false sense of security in their collective decision. Research shows that this often leads groups to make overly hazardous decisions. Because everyone shares in the decision, no one member feels individually responsible. This is known as the **risky-shift phenomenon,** and is a constant concern of people who work with groups. When engaged in a group be aware of this tendency and carefully weigh all moral and ethical considerations before agreeing to any decision.[10]

One way groups can avoid these potential disadvantages is to have effective leadership. We turn, therefore, to examining leadership in the small group.

LEADERSHIP IN SMALL GROUPS

Leadership is very important in a group discussion. You might be the leader because you were appointed, volunteered, or emerged during the course of the discussion. Regardless of how you got there, true leadership is usually earned rather than rewarded. According to research, people perceived as leaders tend to be energetic, self-confident, extroverted, dependable, persistent, intelligent, and well spoken.[11]

People tend to lead groups in different ways. An **autocratic leader** tells the group what to do, attempting to dictate or control. **Democratic leaders** are more open to suggestion, and work for consensus, agreement, and mutual support. **Laissez-faire leaders** have a *"hands off"* policy allowing a group to find its own way with little or no guidance. Sometimes leaders exemplify a bit of all three. On some issues they might be demanding, on others open to suggestion, and on some free to let the group pave the way.

And just what style of leadership is best? When practiced appropriately, democratic leadership offers the efficiency of the authoritarian, while stimulating the spontaneity of the laissez-faire. However, each style has its place and purpose. A formal organization like the military finds that the authoritarian style works best. Research shows that authoritarian leaders are more successful in getting certain tasks accomplished. Laissez-faire leaders, on the other hand, work best when the entire group is equally committed and responsible. This style is preferred for therapy groups where members are encouraged to *"open up."* Probably for most situations the most effective style is the one that adapts to the group's purpose, needs, and situation. A good leader remains one who is steady, yet flexible.

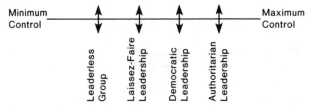

Figure 9.2
Types of Leaders.

While some groups might not have an assigned leader, all groups are thirsty for leadership. And leadership brings with it responsibilities. Just what kind of leader should you be? Here are some suggestions to help.

Formulate Some Ideas in Advance

Before your discussion think about what needs to be discussed. Pick out those issues which are most crucial, in what order they should be covered, and how much time should be spent on each. Then present your *"game plan"* to other members before the meeting.

Meet with the Group in Advance to Make Assignments

Choose a mutually convenient time and place for the group to meet. Present your game plan and arrange for each person to work on a specific part of the group's subject. This way you'll ensure that the group won't overlook an important aspect of your topic.

Prepare Handouts in Advance

Your group might want to refer to handouts—charts, graphs, articles, and the like—during the discussion. If you intend to use handouts make sure you have an adequate number for everyone in the audience. Then see that they're distributed at the appropriate time.

Start the Discussion on Time

Be sure to start the discussion at the agreed upon time. If some members straggle in late, don't stop and repeat all that's been said. This only causes unnecessary repetition, which may encourage the group to discuss things already covered.

Introduce the Group Members and Topic

Present a brief introduction of your topic. Be sure to keep it objxective and nonjudgmental. Then provide a personal introduction of each member of the group.

Clarify the Purpose of the Discussion

Even though you've already discussed this with members, it's important to repeat the focus of the discussion to refresh everyone's mind. Explain what the group's mission is and what you hope to accomplish.

Encourage Everyone to Participate

Don't let a few people dominate, leaving the rest in the wake of their volume. Encourage everyone to be a part of the process and decision. Stimulate the free flow of conversation—people are most committed to decisions they helped to create.

Control the Flow and Direction of the Discussion

Direct the discussion so that every voice is heard and listened to. Stick to your plan and guide the discussion from point to point. If the group gets off track, pull them back; if members fall silent, pick them up; if the discussion hits a roadblock, push it forward. To get everyone involved try open-ended questions. Manage the group, but don't stifle the conversation.

Resolve Conflicts between Members

Serve as the arbitrator between squabbling members. Intervene when two people engage in side conversations or refer to unrelated items. Don't allow hostility between several members to disrupt the work of the group. Keep the purpose of the discussion firmly fixed in everyone's mind.

Summarize throughout the Discussion

A good leader is like an observant guide: s/he tells the group where they've been, and reminds them where they have to go. Keep your summaries short and to the point, updating only when necessary.

At the Proper Time Bring the Discussion to a Close

Present a final summary stating the group's findings and conclusions. Be sure to express your appreciation to everyone in the group as well as to the audience.

Let People in the Audience Ask Questions

Often a group report will be followed by questions from the audience. If your group takes questions, call on people as they raise their hands. Don't let one questioner dominate, but try and give everyone a chance. Likewise give all group members an opportunity to respond.

Whether you lead or not, you're certain to participate. This is our next subject of discussion.

PARTICIPATING IN SMALL GROUPS

All participants have an obligation to be equally committed to the goals of the group. Participants should never think, *"Let the leader do it."* Instead they need to become an integral part of the group's effort—after all, a good group is everyone's responsibility. Participants should help to keep the group on track, maintain a congenial group atmosphere, and see that the group reaches its ultimate goal.

How do we do this? By following some basic procedures. Here are some suggestions.

Be Prepared

Determine in advance what's going to be discussed, what research needs to be done, and what materials need to brought in. Do appropriate background reading and thinking about the topic, assess your position, and firm up your thinking. Jot down important ideas and report a few minutes early, never late to the discussion.

Stay Open-Minded

We all have strong views on certain subjects. But come to a discussion with an open mind, willing to listen to new ideas and viewpoints. A closed-minded person ends up contributing very little to a group discussion.

Bring Supportive Materials

Back up your ideas with facts and evidence. For most discussions it's allowable to bring documents, books, articles, clippings, handouts and the like. You may even read short excerpts to support an idea.

Quickly Become Involved in the Discussion

When you speak up early it tends to break the ice and make everyone feel more at ease. Also, by mentioning important ideas early, you're more likely to get the full attention and consideration of the rest of the group.

Fulfill Group Assignments

We know that one of the advantages of the small group is that work can easily be divided. Assignments could include gathering material, interviewing key people, running a poll, picking up brochures and the like. When everyone works together the entire group benefits.

Be Group-Oriented

Groups are successful when people link personal goals with group responsibilities. Sometimes members place personal considerations ahead of those of the group. People might have hidden agendas, pet concerns, or selfish motives that influence their comments and contributions. Always be conscious of such hidden motives and contribute a positive group-centered effort.

Encourage Full Participation

In order for a fruitful discussion to take place, everyone must play an active role in the process. This means encouraging members to contribute their views, ideas, and thoughts. If there are one or two quiet members, draw them out by asking their opinions, concerns, and thoughts. Listen carefully and build a supportive group environment whereby everyone feels an important part of the process.

Don't Take Criticisms Personally

Some people act as if a criticism of an idea is a criticism of them. Remember that the purpose of a discussion is to explore all possible solutions—this means some ideas will be rejected, others compromised, and a few changed. Present each subject as an open idea, removed from your personal sense of reputation or ego.

Don't Make Attacking Statements

Try to avoid personality clashes with other members. While it's fine to clash on ideas, never clash over personalities. Always center the nature of objections on the issue at hand, offering alternative suggestions and compromises. In keeping disagreements idea-centered, focus on the subject rather than on the person, and if necessary move away from the conflict—don't hit it head-on.[12]

Stay on the Subject

Sometimes a group moves in such a pattern that a member is likely to broach any topic at any moment. A group doing this is likely to discuss many subjects, discovering few results. It's everyone's responsibility to keep the group firmly focused on a single topic. Don't rush to judgments—practice caution—but move the group along at a reasonable pace. It's fine to change subjects, but point out when such a shift is being made. Research shows that every third statement, or about every fifty seconds, a group shifts into a new area of discussion.[13] This works best if shifts are gradual and the group keeps steadily moving toward its ultimate goal.

Work at a Conclusion

Hopefully your group will agree on a conclusion. But be sincere. If you really don't agree with the rest of the group, say so. It's nice when a group reaches consensus, but it's never necessary.

Openly Respond to Questions

If questions are asked try to frame your answers in a clear, straightforward manner. Refrain from giving jabs to someone in the group who took a different view. Instead make your answers objective and to the point. Additionally, give other members an equal chance to respond.

How can we measure participation? One way is through the **Interaction Process Analysis (IPA)** prepared by Robert F. Bales.[14] The IPA is a scale that lets an observer record the type of comments being made by each person in a group. Comments range from a 1, the most positive, to a 12, the most negative. People with many high scores tend to be more argumentative, those with lower scores more suppor-

| A. Positive Reactions | 1. *Shows solidarity,* raises other's status, gives help, reward
2. *Shows tension release,* jokes, laughs, shows satisfaction
3. *Agrees,* shows passive acceptance, understands, concurs, complies |

| B. Attempted Answers | 4. *Gives suggestions,* direction, implying autonomy for other
5. *Gives opinion,* evaluation, analysis, expresses feeling, wish
6. *Gives orientation,* information, repeats, clarifies, confirms |

| C. Questions | 7. *Asks for orientation,* information, repetition, confirmation
8. *Asks for opinion,* evaluation, analysis, expression of feeling
9. *Asks for suggestion,* direction, possible ways of action |

| D. Negative Reactions | 10. *Disagrees,* shows passive rejection, formality, withholds help
11. *Shows tension,* asks for help, withdraws out of field
12. *Shows antagonism,* deflates other's status, defends or asserts self |

Figure 9.3
Interaction Process Analysis. (Source: Robert F. Bales, INTERACTION PROCESS ANALYSIS, Cambridge, Mass.: Addison-Wesley, 1950, Chart 1, p. 9. Copyright 1950 by The University of Chicago. All Rights Reserved.)

supportive. Look at the chart. Try and mirror those positive attributes represented in blocks A and B. In this way your participation will benefit you and the group.

Fortunately, there are systematic ways to help groups work in a positive direction, without getting off track. By following six logical steps, your group can proceed with an orderly, clearly focused discussion. We turn, therefore, to examining one such time-tested method of organizing a group discussion.[15]

ORGANIZING A DISCUSSION

There are many ways to organize the interaction that occurs within a group. One of the most successful is *the reflective-thinking method* developed by American philosopher, John Dewey.[16] This scheme lets groups organize a discussion in six progressive steps. They are: (1) define and delimit the problem; (2) analyze the background of the problem; (3) establish the goals of the group; (4) evaluate all possible solutions; (5) choose the best solution; and (6) implement the chosen solution. Here they are in outline form.

Step 1 Define and Delimit the Problem
    A. Define all key terms
    B. Limit the topic by narrowing the group's focus
Step 2 Analyze the Background of the Problem
    A. Present a brief history of the subject
    B. State recent developments concerning the topic
Step 3 Establish the Goals of the Group
    A. Agree on what the group wants to accomplish
    B. Review possible ways of looking at the problem
Step 4 Evaluate All Possible Solutions
    A. Hear-out all possible suggestions
    B. Set the conditions for an acceptable solution
Step 5 Choose the Best Solution
    A. Evaluate all solutions
    B. Agree on a solution that meets with the approval the group
Step 6 Implement the Chosen Solution
    A. Discuss how the solution can be put into action
    B. Determine how each member can individually contribute to the implementation

Let's examine each of these steps in actual practice. For our imaginary discussion we'll pretend a group is discussing the question, *"What should we do about the increasing number of runaway youths in our society?"* Here's what this group needs to do.

Step 1 Define and Delimit the Problem

The group must first understand the question it's meeting to discuss. Sometimes the problem is fairly obvious, at other times it may be a bit more obscure. Unless the group defines exactly what the problem is, however, they're likely to fail meeting the issue head-on.

Our test group would need to first define all key terms. What is meant by a *"youth."* Is it anyone under twenty-one? Eighteen? Or is it someone still younger? And what about *"runaway?"* Does that include someone missing for twelve hours or twelve days? What does the group mean by *"society."* Does it mean America? Or is it their local community? Such terms are bound to cause confusions later on, unless clarified right from the start.

The group would also need to limit the problem. Do they wish to talk about children who are kidnapped? What about children who are disowned by their parents, called throwaways? Should the group get into what often happens to runaways—things like drugs, crime, and prostitution? Or should it strictly talk about why children runaway? By limiting a topic a group sets the boundaries of the discussion. Bear in mind that most groups usually have less than an hour to discuss their topic. Therefore, a group needs to narrow the focus of their discussion early on.

Step 2 Analyze the Background of the Problem

After the problem has been limited and defined, it needs to be analyzed. This means presenting some background material so key issues can clearly be understood. Did this problem exist in earlier times? How was it treated then? Why does this problem seem more severe today? Often the history of a problem sheds great light on the status of the current day. Our group on runaways, for example, could look at some of these questions. How were runaways viewed at the turn of the century? Would apprentices be considered runaways? What about young men who "ran away to sea?" More recent historical developments likewise need to be discussed. What was done about runaways twenty years ago? Are there more children leaving home today than a decade ago? How has the situation changed? Once questions like these are answered a problem takes on new dimensions.

Properly analyzing a question requires sufficient research. Gather materials from the library. Check out books, encyclopedias, magazines, and newspapers. Our test group found several books and articles that proved of great help. Use your own knowledge and experience, talk to informed people, get the ideas of friends. One member of our group talked to a woman who ran a runaway shelter. Another got insight from a friend who had been a runaway several years before. Ask people for their opinions, conduct a poll, and listen to the news.

When you've gathered supportive material you've bolstered your group. Feel free to bring a variety of materials with you—books, articles, clippings, and the like. One woman handed everyone in the audience a brochure she got from a shelter for runaways. Another group member displayed a *"Talk, Don't Run"* poster he picked up at a local school. As many groups have found, the foundation of a productive discussion is built on material and information.

Step 3 Establish the Goals of the Group

Sometimes people start proposing solutions before the group's even had a chance to agree on what they want to talk about. When this happens a group's sure to go off course. Goals let us focus on the problem at hand as most people in the group see it. It doesn't mean one person going off on a personal tangent. How do we establish goals? One way is for everyone to present a plan on what they'd like to see the group accomplish. For example. in our test group one member suggested they concentrate on ways to prevent youths from running away. Another thought they should concentrate on helping kids currently on the street. A clearly established set of goals lays the groundwork for looking at solutions.

Step 4 Evaluate All Possible Solutions

In many ways the discussion of a discussion is in step four. Most groups spend one-half to two-thirds of their time discussing possible solutions. Why? Because this is where people get to suggest their ideas and suggestions. What kind of solutions work? Almost any are acceptable, as long as they conform to your limitations and goals. An open discussion means putting forward solutions without concern for their logic, practicality, or workability.

Brainstorming is one way of getting ideas on the table. It opens the group up to a whole spectrum of solutions and encourages members to build one suggestion on top of another. This type of open-creativity often "piggybacks" a group toward the best solution. Using this method, our test group came up with six possible solutions: (1) create a federal agency to deal with runaways; (2) begin a massive education program in the schools on the dangers of running away; (3) provide counseling services for parents and children to head-off problems; (4) establish halfway houses for children who want to leave home; (5) increase criminal penalties for people who prey on runaways; and (6) establish houses where children having a problem at home can go to "cool off." Half a dozen possible solutions gives the group a good range of ideas to work on. Notice that a few of these might be combined into the group's ultimate decision.

Step 5 Choose the Best Solution

What's the best solution? This is where the fun of a discussion really takes place. Step five lets groups get to the meat of the matter. What will work? What won't? Which solution really deals with the problem? Which solutions don't quite get to the point? These are difficult questions, and ones that have to be carefully addressed.

How can a group pick that best solution? One way is to measure all solutions against the goals already set. Consider one, and then move on to the next. Don't skip any, being sure to give each an honest review. Sometimes two or three suggestions can be combined into a final agreement. Our test group elected to go with three: (1) create a federal agency to deal with this problem; (2) provide free counseling to head-off problems; and (3) establish halfway houses for children who have left home.

Sometimes agreement is hard to reach. Ideally groups should seek to achieve **consensus.** Consensus means that everyone in the group can at least partially agree with the solution. This is preferable to going by a majority vote, polling, or trading off one idea for another. Occasionally, however, one or two members just refuse to go along. When this occurs a group should report its findings as: *"Four people in our group agree on solution one, two on solution three."* This gives listeners an honest reflection of the group's feelings. Luckily this didn't occur in our test group. As with most successful groups, everyone gave in on some ideas, listened to others, and thought about the rest. The solution truly represented a group, and not an individual effort.

Step 6 Implement the Chosen Solution

Once a solution is accepted, it needs to be implemented. This may involve notifying a higher authority, presenting a report to a committee, or taking a direct action. In the case of our test group, they decided to encourage people to write their elected officials encouraging adoption of the group's solution. Likewise, the group agreed they had a new awareness and concern about this important issue.

Oftentimes a panel discussion is held in front of a group of people. When this happens the group is usually expected to present a final report and take questions. The report should be brief, encapsulating the group's findings and solution. Questions should be taken seriously, affording all panel members the opportunity to participate. Remember that members of the group are considered the experts. They are the ones who researched, analyzed, and discussed the subject in great depth. Therefore make a final report that does justice to the group's effort and work.

How important are these six steps? They probably make the difference between a group that succeeds and one that falls short. A group that jumps around from step to step is begging for trouble. For instance, if the topic isn't clearly defined all the following steps become impossible. What do you do if someone jumps ahead to a solution? Pull them back, reminding them the group needs to understand a few other things first. Once in a while a group will ignore a step entirely. When this happens it is a blueprint for disaster. One student told of a group she was in that failed to define *"education"* during a discussion on sex education. What happened? When the group got to step four—possible solutions—one person was discussing elementary school, another high school, and still another nursery school! Needless to say, this group had an impossible job trying to agree on anything.

Avoid these potential pitfalls by going through each step as you would the doors to a maze. Once one is completed, don't go back, and move on to the next. If someone wishes to move back rather than forward, resist, reminding them that point has already been covered. A good group is everyone's responsibility—a bad group is everyone's fault. Work with other group members to make your group the best that it can be. Few things are as satisfying as a productive group discussion that makes everyone feel better.

SEATING IN SMALL GROUPS

No where is seating more important than in the small group. Seating influences interaction, leadership, friendliness, and participation. Matching the right seat with the right person often makes a tremendous difference. How you pick that certain *"right seat"* is the subject of this discussion.

Do you want to be seen as a leader? If sitting at a rectangular table pick a seat at either end. One re-

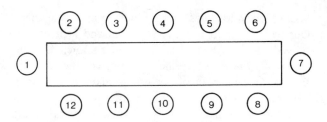

Figure 9.4
Jurist Seating Arrangement.

searcher observed juries seated at such a table who were asked to select a spokesperson. Ninety-eight percent of the time they picked the person at the head. So if seated at a table like the one above, pick seats one or seven.

What do you do if the chairs are arranged in a semicircle, as usually occurs in a panel discussion? Then go for the middle seat. Research shows that over ninety percent of the time the person in the middle is seen as the leader, makes the first remark, talks the most, and is seen as the most supportive. Do you tend to be reserved and quiet in a group? Then avoid the seats at the end. People who made the second and third most remarks sat on either side of the leader; those who made the least sat on the ends. Sometimes groups even end up a discussion with their seats turned in a four-person semicircle, completely isolating a quiet person on the end.

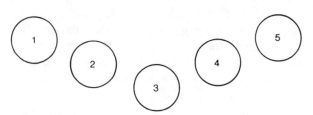

Figure 9.5
Panel Discussion Seating.

Seating also affects the degree of hostility generated between two people. If approaching a discussion where there's likely to be a confrontation, as seen in Figure 9.6, avoid putting barriers or distance between you and the other person. For example, if you feel you're likely to have differences with a Ms. Y, choose your seat carefully. Avoid seats two, three, and four—each places the table and distance between you. Instead pick seats five or one—they pose no barrier and have limited distance. Ms. Y is much less likely to initiate an argument with someone right next to her.

How can you use seating to your advantage? If you want to be seen as a leader pick a seat in the middle or at the head—if you don't avoid those seats.

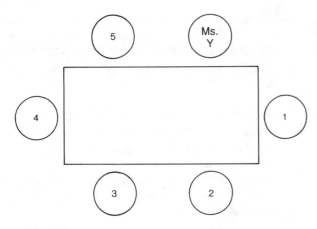

Figure 9.6
Spatial Group Seating.

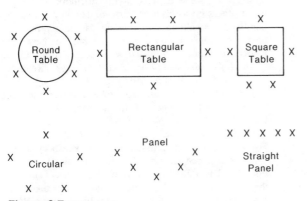

Figure 9.7
Common Seating Arrangements Utilized in Group Discussion.

If you tend to be shy, avoid sitting on the end of a panel. Do you sometimes talk too much? Then stay away from the middle, rather move to one of the ends. And cut down on hostility by reducing distance between you and the other person. Figure 9.7 shows some of the more common seating patterns used for small groups. Make a mental note of the seats that would best fit your needs and personality.

SELECTING A TOPIC FOR DISCUSSION

Chances are you'll soon have the opportunity to pick a topic for a group report. Whether you select one from the list at the end of this chapter, or make one up, you'll need to keep certain things in mind. A good topic is usually phrased as a question—that's why most use the word *"should."* A topic shouldn't be so broad that it could never be settled in a short discussion, or so narrow that there's little to discuss. Finally, a topic shouldn't reflect a built in bias—rather a topic should open up a world of exploration.

If picking a topic with fellow group members, try to select something where everyone doesn't automatically agree. A few differences of opinion are good for a group, livening up the discussion. Next, pick something that's easily researchable. If your subject is so unique that there's little written about it, you'll have a tough time finding information. And last, pick a subject that sounds interesting. Timely topics that spark an immediate curiosity usually work best.

A good topic will help to make for a good discussion. But the most important element is the group itself. When each person works hard, keeps an open mind, and struggles to reach a collective decision a real group effort has been realized. For in the final analysis, groups are nothing more than a collection of many working as one.

CHAPTER SUMMARY

People often communicate in small groups. A small group consists of between three and eleven people, allows each participant to be interdependent, opens up each person to mutual influence, and shares a common purpose. The six types of groups most frequently used include experimental groups, mediating groups, learning groups, information-gathering groups, work groups, and problem-solving groups. The focus of this chapter is on the problem-solving group.

Groups have advantages and disadvantages. Advantages include being able to pool resources, to more easily catch errors, and to more clearly see a problem. Disadvantages are that groups take more time, experience conflict, and make riskier decisions.

Leadership is important in the small group. A good leader should formulate ideas in advance, meet with the group early on, prepare handouts, start the discussion on time, introduce the discussants and topic, clarify the purpose of the discussion, encourage participation, control the flow of interaction, resolve conflicts, summarize frequently, close the discussion, and allow listeners to ask questions.

At some point almost everyone participates in a small group. Participants should be prepared, stay open-minded, bring supportive materials, quickly get involved in the discussion, fulfill all group assignments, be group-oriented, encourage full participation, don't take criticisms personally, avoid making attacking statements, stay on the subject, work at a conclusion, and openly respond to questions. One way to measure participation is through the Interaction Process Analysis.

The reflective-thinking method is an excellent way to organize a discussion. A group should work through six progressive steps which include defining and delimiting a problem, analyzing the background of the problem, establishing the goals of the group, evaluating all possible solutions, choosing the best solution, and implementing the chosen solution.

Seating affects interaction, leadership, friendliness, and participation. People who sit at the head of a table or in the middle of a group are seen as the leader. Usually those people who sit at the end of a group are less likely to actively engage in the discussion. Hostility increases if people sit far apart or have a table between them.

A good topic for discussion should be phrased as a question, not be too broad, not be too narrow, and not have a built in bias. Pick a topic that offers a difference of opinion, is easily researchable, and sounds interesting. When all this is realized you should enjoy a productive discussion.

EXERCISES FOR REVIEW

1. Attend a city council meeting, school board, social or club meeting, or some other function where a small group is at work. Observe the group to see if it follows the criteria presented in this chapter. What type of group is it? What kind of leadership is there? What style of leadership is used? How many participants are there? Does the group follow six progressive steps? How does the group report its findings? Report back to class with your conclusions.

2. Listen to a group of classmates discussing an agreed upon topic in a small group. Pick one person and using the Interaction Process Analysis "score" their comments. How positive were they? How negative? Did they tend to ask questions? Or did they seem more inclined to produce answers? After the discussion share your analysis with the person.

3. Imagine you're the leader of a small group. Based on the material presented in this chapter, describe how you would handle each of the following circumstances should they occur in the group you're leading:

   a. *One person never seems to talk.*
   b. *One person never stops talking.*
   c. *One person constantly gets off topic.*
   d. *One person keeps making negative personal remarks.*
   e. *The group seems to be repeating itself.*
   f. *Two people can't seem to agree on anything.*
   g. *The group can't reach a conclusion.*

4. Form three experimental groups and have the leader of each group practice one of the forms of leadership discussed in the chapter. Have one be autocratic, one democratic, and one laissez-faire. Then compare the results. Which group was most productive? Which accomplished the least? In which group were the participants most satisfied? In which least satisfied? Discuss this in class.

5. Form a group with four or five classmates to discuss one of the topics listed at the end of this chapter. Meet with the group to pick a topic, decide if a leader is wanted, and split up assignments. Research your topic and then discuss it in front of the class. Answer questions from listeners at the end.

NOTES

1. While all agree that the small group must have at least three members, there is some difference as to its maximum size—some experts saying no more than eight while others go as high as thirteen. The key is that the number be small enough that all can freely interact; thus eleven is used as a maximum number here. See Robert F. Bales, *Interaction Process Analysis: A Method for the Study of Small Groups* (Reading, Mass.: Addison-Wesley, 1950), p. 33.

2. For an interesting discussion of the differences between these two types of interactions, see A. Paul Hare, *Handbook of Small Group Research*, 2nd ed. (New York: Free Press, 1976), pp. 226–227.

3. For a review of the material on this aspect of the small group see, Dennis S. Gouran and B. Aubrey Fisher, "The Functions of Human Communication in the Formation, Maintenance, and Performance of Small Groups," in Carroll C. Arnold and John Waite Bowers, eds., *Handbook of Rhetorical and Communication Theory* (Boston: Allyn and Bacon, 1984), pp. 622–658.

4. For some collected research on the purpose of groups and an interesting debate on their value see, Christian J. Buys, "Humans Would Do Better Without Groups," *Personality and Social Psychology Bulletin*, 4, 1978, pp. 123–125; Lynn R. Anderson, "Groups Would Do Better Without Humans," *Personality and Social Psychology Bulletin*, 4, 1978, pp. 557–558.

5. For a discussion of the types of groups, see Dorwin Cartwright and Alvin Zander, *Group Dynamics: Research and Theory*, 3rd ed. (New York: Harper & Row, 1968), pp. 411–415, 461–464.

6. The first study measuring task accomplishment of groups and individuals was by N. Triplett, "The Dynamogenic Factors in Peacemaking and Competition," *American Journal of Psychology*, p. 1897, pp. 507–533. For a more recent review of the studies showing this, see M. Shaw, *Group Dynamics: The Psychology of Small Group Behavior* (New York: McGraw-Hill, 1976).

7. The superiority of groups in solving problems over individuals has plagued social scientists for years. The predominant view is that generally groups do generate better solutions. For instance, see Carl Larson, "Speech Communication Research on Small Groups," *Speech Teacher*, 20, 1971, pp. 89–107. It has also been suggested that the better the communication within the group, the higher the quality of

the solution. For instance, see Dale G. Leathers, "Process Description and Movement in Small Group Communication," *Quarterly Journal of Speech,* 55, 1969, p. 287.

8. For examples of how groups are used in business organizations, see Thomas J. Peters and Robert H. Waterman, Jr., *In Search of Excellence* (New York: Warner Books, 1982), p. 127.

9. Dorothy I. Marquart, "Group Problem-Solving," *Journal of Social Psychology,* 41, 1955, pp. 103–113.

10. The risky-shift in group discussion has been researched with countless variables and conditions. The most thorough scholarship of this phenomenon, including a test of risk-type questions appears in N. Kogan and M. Wallach, *Risk-Taking: A Study in Cognition and Personality* (New York: Holt, Rinehart and Winston, 1964).

11. See R. D. Mann, "A Review of the Relationship Between Personality and Performance in Small Groups," *Psychological Bulletin,* 56, 1959, pp. 241–270.

12. Thomas J. Knutson, "An Experimental Study of the Effects of Orientation Behavior on Small Group Consensus," *Speech Monographs,* 39, 1972, pp. 159–165.

13. See Dennis S. Gouran and John E. Baird, Jr., "An Analysis of Distributional and Sequential Structure in Problem-Solving and Informal Group Discussions," *Speech Monographs,* 39, 1972, pp. 16–22.

14. Robert F. Bales, *Interaction Process Analysis* (Reading, Mass.: Addison-Wesley Press, 1950).

15. There are many organization formats. This procedure has proven to be most successful in problem-solving groups.

16. John Dewey, *How We Think* (Boston: Heath, 1933). For a discussion of other organizational patterns for reaching a decision see John Cragan and David Wright, *Communication in Small Group Discussions: A Case Study Approach* (St. Paul, Minn., West, 1980).

Name _____   Course _____

Exercise _____

Reactions to Group Experience

Complete this "reaction to group experience" and give it to your instructor at the completion of your groups exercise.

Directions: Check the point on each scale which best represents your true opinion. Be objective in answering 7, 8, 9.

1. How satisified are you with the conclusions or decisions reached? (If none reached, evaluate discussion as far as it got.)

    /_____/_____/
    Very satisfied   Moderately satisfied   Very dissatisfied

2. How productive was this discussion in terms of new ideas and information?

    /_____/_____/
    Very valuable   Moderately valuable   Waste of time

3. How orderly and systematic was the group in its overall approach?

    /_____/_____/
    Too regulated   About right   Chaotic

4. Was the atmosphere of the group conductive to effective communication?

    /_____/_____/
    Too cooperative   About right   Too competitive

5. Was the responsibility for leadership properly distributed?

    /_____/_____/
    Too concentrated   About right   Too diffused

6. How do you feel about the nature of your leadership?

    /_____/_____/
    Too autocratic   About right   Too laissez faire

7. Who contributed most to the substance? _____

    least? _____

8. Who was the best listener? _____

    the poorest? _____

9. Who did the most to build good group atmosphere? _____

10. My overall feeling with regard to my experiences in the group is . . .

    /_____/_____/
    Highly positive   Indifferent   Highly negative

11. The one thing I couldn't stand was _____

12. The one thing I really liked was _____

Discussion Topics

Here are fifty ideas for a group discussion. Meet with your group and pick a topic. Then prepare to discuss it in front of the rest of the class.

1. Should the United States have capital punishment?

2. Should the United States permit abortions?

3. What should be done to clean-up our environment?

4. Should every American be required to serve two years of community service before his or her 21st birthday?

5. Should juvenile murderers be executed?

6. What can be done to conserve energy?

7. Should nuclear power plants be banned?

8. Should drugs be legalized?

9. What should be done about teenage runaways?

10. Should handguns be banned?

11. Should women be drafted into the military?

12. Should we reinstitute the military draft?

13. Should people who sell drugs near a school be executed?

14. Is there too much violence on television?

15. Should prostitution be legalized?

16. Should art depicting sex or violence be censored?

17. Should the government fund art that many people consider obscene?

18. Should the United States have a national health program?

19. Should sex education be taught in the public schools?

20. Should professional sports limit athlete's salaries?

21. Should decency ratings be placed on all record albums?

22. Should homosexuals be permitted to teach in public schools?

23. Should condoms be given to high school students to help prevent A.I.D.S.?

24. Should children with A.I.D.S. be permitted to attend regular classes in public school?

25. Should immigration to the United States be reduced?

26. Should sports gambling be legalized?

27. Should rapists be offered castration instead of prison?

28. Should prisons be made more severe?

29. Should people be informed if someone working with them has A.I.D.S.?

30. Should air bags be required in all new cars?

31. Should police be allowed to set up roadblocks to catch drunken drivers?

32. Should people buy American made products?

33. Should the United States do more to stop terrorism?

34. What changes have occurred in the American family in the last fifty years?

35. Is marriage obsolete?

36. Should medical experiments on animals be banned?

37. Is it right to criticize people who wear fur coats?

38. Should English become the official language of the United States?

39. Should Washington D. C. and Puerto Rico become states?

40. Should more money be spent on A.I.D.S. research?

41. Is college necessary in today's economy?

42. Are women treated equally in our society?

43. Should adopted children have the right to locate their natural parents?

44. Should the President be permitted to serve more than two terms?

45. Can video games be harmful to children?

46. Should juvenile criminals be treated as adults?

47. Why are there so many serial murders in our country?

48. What will America be like in 100 years?

49. Should marijuana be legalized?

50. Should smoking be banned in all public places?

Exercise, Bomb Shelter

This exercise has two phases. First answer the problem individually and secondly meet with your group and by consensus decide on a group response.

The problem is as follows: You own a bomb shelter which has sufficient food, water, and space to accommodate 5 people. A nuclear attack takes place and you have 20 minutes to decide which five people you will admit to the bomb shelter. The rest will surely die. After your group makes its decision discuss your criteria with the rest of the class. (rank each choice 1 first to come in, 2 second to come in, etc. through 5 the last to be admitted).

Individual Answer	*Group Answer*
____ you	____ you
____ 12 year old paperboy	____ 12 year old paperboy
____ 65 year old lady living next door	____ 65 year old lady living next door
____ 28 year old police woman	____ 28 year old police woman
____ 42 year old minister	____ 42 year old minister
____ 50 year old nurse	____ 50 year old nurse
____ 23 year old football player	____ 23 year old football player
____ 19 year old beauty queen	____ 19 year old beauty queen
____ 15 year old deaf boy	____ 15 year old deaf boy
____ 48 year old builder	____ 48 year old builder
____ 30 year old Army captain	____ 30 year old Army captain
____ 16 year old retarded girl	____ 16 year old retarded girl

It is suggested that on individual responses you rank 1 through 12 (first to last to be admitted) as it will assist group with discussion.

COMMUNICATION FACTS

Estimated Number of Cases of Speech Defects in the United States

Type of Speech Problem	Ages 5 to 21 Years		All Ages	
	percent	*number*	*percent*	*number*
Functional Articulatory	3%	1,500,000	3%	6,000,000
Stuttering	.7%	350,000	.7%	1,400,000
Voice	.2%	100,000	.2%	400,000
Cleft Palate Speech	.1%	50,000	.1%	200,000
Cerebral Palsy Speech	.2%	100,000	.2%	400,000
Retarded Speech Development	.3%	150,000	.5%	1,000,000
Impaired Hearing with Speech Defect	.5%	250,000	5%	1,000,000
Totals	5.0%	2,500,000	5.0%	10,000,000

Name _____

NASA Moon Survival Task
Individual Worksheet
(complete this worksheet alone)

INSTRUCTIONS: You are a member of a space crew originally scheduled to rendezvous with a mother ship on the lighted surface of the moon. Due to mechanical difficulties, however, your ship was forced to land at a spot some 200 miles from the rendezvous point. During the landing, much of the equipment aboard was damaged and since survival depends on reaching the mother ship, the most critical items available must be chosen for the 200 mile trip. Below are listed the 15 items left intact and undamaged after landing. Your task is to rank them in terms of their importance for your crew in allowing them to reach the rendezvous point. Place the number 1 by the most important item, the number 2 by the second most important, and so on, through number 15, the least important. You have 15 minutes to complete this phase of the exercise.

____ Box of matches

____ Food concentrate

____ 50 feet of nylon rope

____ Parachute silk

____ Portable heating unit

____ Two .45 caliber pistols

____ One case of dehydrated Pet milk

____ Stellar map (of the moon's constellation)

____ Two 100 lb. tanks of oxygen

____ Life raft

____ Magnetic compass

____ 5 gallons of water

____ Signal flares

____ First aid kit containing injection needles

____ Solar-powered FM receiver transmitter

Correct answers in appendix.

NASA Moon Survival Task
Group Worksheet
(complete this worksheet with your group)

INSTRUCTIONS: This is an exercise in group decision-making. Your group is to employ the method of Group Consensus in reaching its decision. This means that the prediction for each of the 15 survival items must be agreed upon by each group member before it becomes a part of the group decision. Consensus is difficult to reach. Therefore, not all ranking will meet with everyone's complete approval. Try as a group, to make each ranking one with which all group members can at least partially agree. Here are some guides to use in reaching consensus:

1. Avoid arguing for your own individual judgments.
2. Approach the task on the basis of logic.
3. Avoid changing your mind only in order to reach agreement and avoid conflict. Support only solutions with which you are able to agree somewhat, at least.
4. Avoid "conflict-reducing" techniques such as majority vote, averaging, or trading, in reaching your decision.
5. View differences of opinion as helpful rather than as a hindrance in decision-making.
6. Individuals should not change answers on their own sheets.

_____ Box of matches

_____ Food concentrate

_____ 50 feet of nylon rope

_____ Parachute silk

_____ Portable heating unit

_____ Two .45 caliber pistols

_____ One case dehydrated Pet milk

_____ Two 100 lb. tanks of oxygen

_____ Stellar map (of moon's constellation)

_____ Life raft

_____ Magnetic compass

_____ 5 gallons of water

_____ Signal flares

_____ First aid kit containing injection needles

_____ Solar-powered FM receiver-transmitter

Correct answers are provided in the appendix. Don't look before completing work!

Group Exercise: Parole Board

Compose a group of five people to form a parole board. The purpose of the parole board is to interview five individuals who are presently serving 30 year sentences for murder. Each person should be interviewed for five minutes for the board to determine the following information: who would benefit the most by being released from jail; who has been the most rehabilitated while serving their sentence; who would be least likely to commit another crime; and who is the most repentent.

The people to play the role of the convicts should be sincere and try to be as persuasive as possible to earn their early release. The parole board will have to decide which of the five convicts will receive a change in their present sentence in the following manner:

1. One person is to have their sentence changed to death and is to be executed;
2. One person is to have their 30 year sentence changed to life imprisonment without parole;
3. One person is to continue their present 30 year sentence;
4. One person is to have their 30 year sentence reduced to 10 years and;
5. One person is to be immediately released from prison.

After the interviews the parole board should leave the room, and by consensus, make their decision for each person; remember, only one change can be given to each person, for instance, all the convicts could not be executed or released. The group should return to the class and give their decisions to the convicts as they are escorted to the front of the parole board. After the decisions are given the board should give their rationale for each decision to the rest of the class and the specific criteria that they used. The biographies of the five convicts are as follows.

Convict #1

Eric is 26 and is in the third year of his 30 year sentence. Eric worked as a busboy in a restaurant and had an argument with his boss. That night Eric returned to the restaurant and poured gasoline in the kerosene heater. The next morning when the boss turned the heater on it exploded and he and five other people were killed. Eric regrets the action and is especially upset that five innocent people were killed. This was Eric's first criminal conviction.

Convict #2

Mary is 37 and is in the fourth year of her thirty year sentence. Mary worked as a call girl in a run down massage parlor in the downtown area of the city. Mary was robbing the wallet of a 65 year old customer and when the man saw her; she struggled with him and stabbed him in the heart. The man died instantly and Mary claims she is sorry and would like to reclaim her life. Mary had been convicted four other times of charges of prostitution.

Convict #3

Joe is 45 and is in the first year of his 30 year sentence. Joe is a millionaire and owns numerous run down apartment buildings in the poor parts of the city. In order to collect on a $900,000 insurance policy Joe burned down one of his apartment buildings that he thought was empty; however, a family of ''squatters'' were in the building and as a result were burned to death. Joe was convicted of arson in the deaths of six people; four of them children. Joe is sorry for the family and has no prior convictions.

Convict #4

Pam is 19 and is in the first year of her 30 year sentence. When Pam was 18 she was upset about not being invited to her senior prom, so she took her father's rifle and went to the prom shooting nine students to death. Pam claims that she was temporarily insane and regrets the deaths of her former classmates. Pam was arrested once before, when she was 16, for shoplifting.

Convict #5

Mike is 31 and is in the third year of his 30 year sentence. Mike drinks heavily and on a recent Friday he learned that his wife of 2 years was leaving him because of his drinking. Mike showed up at his construction job in a drunken state and was fired, whereupon Mike went to a local bar to have more drinks. Mike then drove his car down a sidewalk running over and killing 12 people. Since he has been in jail Mike has stopped drinking and believes he would never hurt anyone again. Mike was convicted of burglary when he was 21 and assault and battery when he was 27.

Group Exercise: The Kidney Machine

Thousands of Americans suffer from various kidney disfunctions which requires that their blood be cleansed by the use of a kidney machine. The use of the apparatus demands that patients use the machine once or twice a week and remain connected to the device for over 20 hours per week. Because of the price of the machine there are many more people needing the use of the apparatus than there are machines available.

You and your group are members of a hospital board which has access to two of these machines. Your group will interview six candidates who need to use the machine; those that don't will surely die within six months. Cost and availability to pay for the machine should not be a factor in your decision since all costs will be paid for by an independent foundation. Each of the candidates coming before the panel have been judged as physically able to use the machine and survive for at least another 20 years with this treatment.

The group will consider six candidates for the two machines and should use the following criteria:

1. Determine who is most deserving of being saved;
2. Agree as a group which people will benefit society the most:
3. Determine which person is most needed by family or friends.

The group must agree by consensus (all must agree) on the two people to receive the treatment and therefore be saved; the rest will perish. A spokesperson for the group should then report to the entire class the group's decision and their rationale for their decision. A profile of each of the seven candidates is listed as follows;

Candidate 1

Dr. Albert Riverra an M.D. who is 57 years old. Dr. Riverra is married and has a daughter who is 17 and a son in college who is 22. Dr. Riverra operates a general practice from his home and is upper-middle class. He asks that he be saved so that he can continue his work as a doctor and see that his son and daughter become established in life.

Candidate 2

Mary Albertson a housewife who is 39. Mrs. Albertson has no children but supports two foster children who live overseas. Her husband is a salesman for a food company and the family is middle class. Mary asks that she be saved as her husband needs her and she donates many hours a week to various charity organizations.

Candidate 3

Barbara Adams is 29 and has two children aged 6 and 9. Barbara has never been married and had the children with two different men whom she has no idea where they are or even what their real names were. Since Barbara receives no child support she depends on welfare for her's and the children's livelihood. Barbara has never worked and readily admits that she frequently uses drugs and alcohol. Barbara asks that she be saved because her children mean a great deal to her.

Candidate 4

Rich Carlson a construction worker who is 42. Rich is divorced form his wife and has two children aged 10 and 12 who live with his wife. Rich pays child support of $100 per week but has twice been charged by the court for failure to make these payments. Rich drinks heavily but now claims that he is on "the wagon" since he discovered his kidney problem. Rich asks that he be saved so that he can see his two sons grow up.

Candidate 5

Sara Carpone is a famous author and cook who is 65. Sara is world famous as the host of the popular television show, "Cooking with Carpone" and has authored over 25 cook books. Sara has never married and therefore has no children of her own. She has, however, supported two nephews who are now 25 and 33; both are unskilled and have never been able to hold a job and depend on Sara's assistance. Sara asks that she be saved as she has the ultimate cook book that she is now working on and she points out that her television show is enjoyed by over 10 million housewives every day.

Candidate 6

Todd Frammel is 35 and is a recently released convict from state prison. Todd was twice convicted of robbery and just completed his second five year term. Todd learned how to be a sheet metal worker while in jail and is presently seeking a job in that area. Todd has promised that he will never steal again and asks to be saved so that he can get married and settle down.

Sources of Information

Name:_____ Course: _____

General Topic of Group: _____

Specific Purpose of Group: _____

_____

Printed Sources:

Author: _____ Date: _____

Title: _____

Article Title: _____

Number of Pages Used; _____ Publisher: _____

Author: _____ Date: _____

Title: _____

Article Title: _____

Number of Pages Used: _____ Publisher: _____

Author: _____ Date: _____

Title: _____

Article Title: _____

Number of Pages Used: _____ Publisher: _____

Author: _____ Date: _____

Title: _____

Article Title: _____

Number of Pages Used: _____ Publisher: _____

Interview Sources:

Name of Person Interviewed: _____ Date: _____

Position of Title: _____

Reason for Expertise on Subject: _____

Name _____ Course _____

Group Subject _____

Name _____   Course _____

Group Subject _____

Group Discussion Evaluation Form

Seat: ⃝ ⃝ ⃝ ⃝ ⃝ ⃝   Place X where person is sitting

Overall Group Effectiveness:	Needs Work	Fair	Good	Very Good	Excellent
Analysis: Clear definition and knowledge of the problem. Testing information and reasoning.					
Evidence: Factual and authoritative evidence on various aspects of the problem.					
Logical Reasoning: Ability to think logically and to stay on the significant issues of the agenda.					
Adaptation: An understanding and assistance toward other members of the group and to the entire discussion situation.					
Cooperation: Willingness to see the value of other discussant's viewpoints and to modify one's own opinions.					
Contributions to the Group: Interaction. Not dominating the group but participating and sharing in the group discussion.					
Language and Delivery: Effective use of words and a clear fourthright delivery for ease of understanding and listening.					
Response to Questions: Answering questions in a clear and open manner. Well thought out answers.					

Overall Comments:

Individual Grade _____

Group Grade _____

Exercise Task Assignments

Form a group of five people and discuss each of the three problems listed below. Agree on a solution for each and then compare your results with those of other groups.

Relatively Speaking

When Johnny Smith was drafted, he filled out an army form and listed one "J. Smith" as next of kin. Shortly thereafter, this J. Smith received an official letter inquiring into the exact relationship. Never a man of few words, J. Smith replied as follows: "Brothers and sisters I have none, Johnny's father is my fathers son."

How was J. Smith related to the soldier?

Truth and Falsehood

In a faraway land there were two races. The Ananias were inveterate liars, while the Diogenes were unfailingly voracious. Once upon a time a stranger visited the land, and on meeting a party of three inhabitants inquired as to what race they belonged.

The first murmured something that the Stranger did not catch. The second remarked, "He said he was an Anania." The third said to the second, "You are a liar."

Now the question is, of what race was the third man?

Scrambled Box Tops

Three boxes—one containing two black marbles, one containing two white marbles, and the third containing one black marble and one white marble—are put before you. The boxes are labeled to indicate their contents—BB, WW, BW—but you are told that the tops have been switched so that every box is now incorrectly labeled. You are asked to take one marble at a time out of any box, without looking inside, and using this sampling process, to determine the contents of all three boxes.

What is the smallest number of drawings you will need to determine the contents of each box?

10 Researching Your Ideas

Digging for information takes time and effort.

QUESTIONS FOR RETENTION

Before reading this chapter, ask yourself the following questions:

1. How do I gather information from the library?
2. How can I send away for information?
3. What's the best way to copy down information?

Chances are the thought of spending several hours researching your next assignment doesn't seem particularly appealing to you. In fact, few things can seem as downright painful as the thought of spending a Saturday afternoon in the library. But while digging for facts whispers boredom, it shouts importance. It's only through research that you give substance to your ideas, provide support for your convictions, and add impact to your message.

There are lots of ways you can gather information for an upcoming assignment. You can look up written resources, write to special interest organizations, interview someone in the know, or poll a group of people to get a global view. Sometimes you can use yourself as a resource. Let's turn first, therefore, to the resource of your own experience.

USING YOUR OWN OBSERVATIONS AND EXPERIENCE

Your lifetime observations and experiences provide a gold mine of useful information.[1] Look within yourself. What do you know? What have you seen? What

have you done? Listeners delight in hearing about personal experiences. A personal touch adds credibility to your ideas, and gives freshness to your message. Of course you never want to rely entirely on personal experience. If you do your ideas will sound shallow and unsupported. Rather use experiences and observations along with other forms of support—magazines, books, interviews, and the like. Here's how this worked for one student:

Brad Reeves talked about small boat safety. He presented information gathered from boating magazines, books on maritime law, and interviews with representatives of the Coast Guard. As a boat owner himself, Brad was also able to supplement his presentation with firsthand knowledge. He told of the many near misses he'd had with out of control boats; of the number of boat operators he'd seen who were intoxicated or under age; and how a friend was nearly hit while water skiing.

Figure 10.1
All public communication requires some type of research.

Brad's presentation made a lot of sense to his listeners. Why? Because he blended research with personal experience. Sometimes observation can be just as effective. The following student had no experience with her subject, but was able to use personal observation to graphically illustrate her point:

Mary Curtis was in a group discussing coronary bypass surgery. Besides presenting information from medical journals, Mary told of the bypass operation she observed with other nursing students. She told how she had a perfect view of the operation from a glass dome just four feet above the surgeon's head. How two doctors worked simultaneously, one cutting a vein in the patient's leg, while the other stood at the chest and ripped open the sternum with a saw. Of ribs being cracked with giant clamps. And how once the damaged artery was removed, it was held up was squeezed so that cholesterol came out like toothpaste.

Mixed with facts and details Mary's observations gave her presentation that all-important human touch. That's why many professional communicators recommend that the first place to start researching an idea is "in your own head."[2]

What if you have no firsthand knowledge of your topic? Can you still include yourself in your content? Indeed you can. Many people do this by conducting a personal investigation. Discussing animal overpopulation? Visit an animal shelter. Talking about water pollution? Take water samples from a nearby river. Speaking about worker safety? Get permission to visit an assembly line. Not only will investigating a subject give your ideas a personal flavor, it will also give them a believable taste.

Once you've searched within yourself, you'll next need to visit a library. We'll now turn our attention to this resource.

USING THE LIBRARY

Libraries are fascinating places. Located within its walls is a wealth of information. Books, magazines, newspapers, computer searches, videotapes, recordings, software, musical scores, and even works of art are readily available. Don't limit yourself to your college library either. Your local library may be less busy and have as much, or even more material for you to examine. Sometimes it's also helpful to research in specialized libraries found in museums or historical societies.

How can you learn more about using the library? Visit your college or community library and familiarize yourself with its surroundings. If you have a question ask the librarian—you'll find s/he is very willing to help. Take an orientation tour. After the tour pick up handouts and brochures mapping the library's rooms and explaining its services. You'll find that learning how to use the library will not only prove valuable in this class, but in other classes as well.

Perhaps you're already quite knowledgeable about using a library. In that case, this section will only serve as a review. But whether novice or expert, you'll find the following discussion provides some helpful guidelines for doing library research.

We'll begin by traveling with a classmate on her search for information. This student's search was successful; let's see why.

As the mother of three young children, Martha Wong was very concerned about child abductions. She decided this would make a good topic for an upcoming speech.

At the library Martha first visited the card catalogue. Since she didn't know the specific titles of any books on this subject, nor the names of any authors, she looked under the subject heading. Martha started under "children," saw the subheading "abductions and kidnappings," and sure enough found a couple of books that by their description on the catalogue card, sounded just perfect.

Martha checked out the books and went to the reference section. There she located statistical information on the number of abductions in the *World Almanac and Book of Facts.* She searched further, looking in the *Statistical Abstract of the United States,* and in *Facts on File.* Finally, she wanted a legal definition of abduction, so she consulted *Black's Law Dictionary.*

Martha's next stop was the *Readers' Guide to Periodical Literature.* Starting with the most recent edition and working her way back, she located several promising magazine articles. The *New York Times Index* also supplied a few useful articles on her subject under the listing, *"kidnapping."* While looking at one article, Martha found the name of a national organization for missing and exploited children; she decided she'd later write them for information.

Martha's final step was to visit with a staff librarian and ask her to search the topic through the computerized data service. Using DIALOG the operator asked for the key words. Remembering that she'd need to narrow her search or she'd be overwhelmed with output, Martha phrased, *"child abductions."* She was amazed when many of the sources that were recommended were one's she'd already discovered after many hours of research. The librarian reminded Martha that once she knew her precise topic, the computer research service should be the place to start, not finish a search. Regardless, Martha was pleased as she found several promising sources from the computer search.

Martha's speech was a success. By her careful, organized search she presented an informed message to all her listeners.

What worked for this student can work for you too. Start like Martha did with one resource at a time. Don't be overwhelmed by the size of the job ahead of you; instead, take it step by step and the solution will unfold in the matter of a few hours. Here's a good place to start—the card catalogue.

The Card Catalogue

The card catalogue lists the general collection of books in the library. Books are listed alphabetically under author, title, and subject (one book may be listed under several different subjects). Unless you're looking for a specific book or author, your best bet is to proceed, as Martha did, to the subject listing.

The traditional card file is familiar to practically every library. Books are described on 3 × 5 cards. There is quite a bit of useful information included on each card. By carefully reading the card first, you can save yourself quite a bit of research time later on. The single most important piece of information on the card is the call number, which is always located in the upper left corner. Once you have the call number, you can simply track down the book in the stacks. For the book in the illustration below, you would proceed to section P, look for number 90, and finally under P90 locate book .H59. This is the Library of Congress catalog format, which is by far the most common. However, a few libraries still use the Dewey Decimal System, which catalogs books into ten categories rather than twenty. Regardless of which system your library uses, the procedure for locating a book is the same.

In many libraries the card catalogue is becoming a relic of the past, as out of date as yesteryear's icebox. Card catalogs take too much time and space to maintain. Basically, the card catalogue may have been replaced in your library by a printed catalogue containing small reproductions of cards; a catalogue on microfilm or microfiche that is read with a special reader; or a computerized listing of all registered

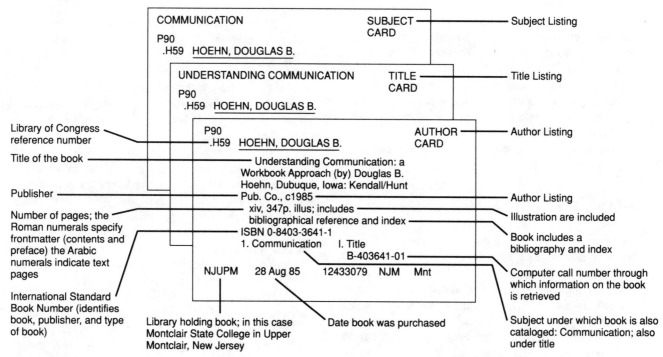

Figure 10.2
Three Sample Catalog Cards. All books are listed in the card catalog by author, title, and subject. There is a great deal of information included on each card. A proper understanding of this information can allow you to pick the best book possible, without having to first examine several.

```
000–099   General Works
100–199   Philosophy
200–299   Religion
300–399   Social Sciences
400–499   Language
500–599   Pure Science
600–699   Technology
700–799   The Arts
800–899   Literature
900–999   History
```

Figure 10.3
Dewey Decimal System.

```
A   General Works—Polygraphy
B   Philosophy—Religion—Psychology
C   Archeology—General Biography
D   History and Topography (except America)
E   America—American History
F   Local History—Latin American History
G   Geography—Anthropology—Sports
H   Social Sciences—Business
I   Political Science
K   Law
L   Education
M   Music
N   Art—Architecture
P   Language and Literature—Drama
Q   Science
R   Medicine
S   Agriculture—Plant and Animal Husbandry
T   Technology
U   Military Science
V   Naval Science
Z   Bibliography and Library Science
```

Figure 10.4
Library of Congress System.

books. If the catalogue is computerized, you gain access by simply typing in a request. In the long run this method is superior, because it enables you to conduct a customized search through all your library's holdings.

If you want to review a book's relevance before searching it out, examine the *Book Review Index* or *Book Review Digest* located in the reference section. Both these resources provide short reviews of current books. If another borrower has a book out that you wish to examine, ask the librarian to hold it for you when it's returned. And if the library doesn't have a particular book you need, ask if you can order it on interlibrary loan.

Lastly, be conscious of the time-factor when considering a book for an upcoming assignment. It's unrealistic to expect that you'll be able to read several complete books for each assignment; instead, pick out the most relevant sections or chapters and

read just those. When Martha reviewed her books, for example, she read chapters on child abductions, not those on child abuse, runaways, or child prostitution.

The Reference Section

Martha found the reference section particularly useful. The chances are you will too. The reference section includes encyclopedias, dictionaries, indexes, bibliographies, atlases, gazetteers, almanacs, yearbooks, and biographical reference works. Each of these sources can supply you with a rich assortment of facts, statistics, and general information. Reference works also can provide a thumbnail sketch of your issue, presented in an accurate, objective manner. Let's review some of the books you might find helpful in this section.

Encyclopedias

A good place to start investigating a topic is in a standard encyclopedia. General encyclopedias provide brief overviews of most issues and also give succinct bibliographies for further reading. Consequently, they're a very convenient resource. Keep in mind, however, that these are secondary sources, and it's always necessary to get some original source material from books and articles after you've reviewed the subject in the encyclopedia. Here are several of the major encyclopedias; always use the most recent edition:

Collier's Encyclopedia, 24 volumes
Encyclopedia Americana, 30 volumes
Encyclopedia International, 20 volumes
The New Encyclopedia Britannica, 30 volumes

There are also specialized encyclopedias. These give more specific, detailed, and technical information than a general encyclopedia. Specialized encyclopedias are devoted to a broad range of subjects, including: music, art, business, economics, literature, philosophy, and science. For a detailed list look through the reference section of the library. Some of the most useful are listed below:

International Cyclopedia of Music and Musicians
Encyclopedia of World Art, 15 volumes
Encyclopedia of Advertising
Encyclopedia of Psychology
The Encyclopedia of Philosophy, 4 volumes
Encyclopedia of Computer Science and Technology,
    14 volumes
An Encyclopedia of Religion
The Encyclopedia of Management

Dictionaries

There are many types of dictionaries. Basically, standard English dictionaries fall into one of two types: abridged or unabridged. Unabridged dictionaries are more comprehensive and complete than abridged or college dictionaries. Two of the best standard dictionaries are *Webster's Third New International Dictionary of the English Language* and *The Random House Dictionary of the English Language*. For a more historical view of the language, the best is *The Oxford English Dictionary* which consists of 13 volumes, plus supplements. Sometimes the history of a word can be enlightening. One student speaking about the environment, looked up pollution and found it's historical definition was of shame or sin. He was able to drive home his contemporary message with that classical definition.

Special dictionaries give coverage to specific usages of the language. Martha found *Black's Law Dictionary* of particular use. Another student wanted to find out what SEATO stood for and looked it up in the *Acronyms, Initialisms, and Abbreviations Dictionary*. If you want to find the proper name of something—people, places, works of art and the like, look it up in the *New Century Cyclopedia of Names*. Other useful dictionaries include the *Dictionary of American Slang*, *Webster's New Dictionary of Synonyms* and the *Dictionary of Modern English Usage*.

Indexes and Bibliographies

There are many special indexes and bibliographies that lead to articles and books in specific areas. These books exist for just about all fields—there are even bibliographies of bibliographies! Does your topic have to do with sociology? Look it up in the *International Bibliography of Sociology*. Not sure if there's a bibliography in your area of interest? Consult the most recent *Bibliographic Index: A cumulative Bibliography of Bibliographies*. A sampling of some others includes the *Bibliographical Index, Art Index, Business Periodicals Index, The Education Index*, and *General Sciences Index*. Probably the best, however, is the *Essay and General Literature Index*, published since 1900, and now semiannually. It lists tens of thousands of articles appearing in books that otherwise would be next to impossible to find. If you're exploring a particular subject, ask the librarian for the index or bibliography that covers that area. We'll discuss the most frequently used indexes for magazines and newspapers in the section under that heading.

snap-shot, *sb.* Add: **1. b.** (Earlier example.)
1845 F. TOLFREY *Sportsman in Canada* II. v. 131 It is capital practice is this snipe-shooting for a youngster; at least it makes a man a good snap-shot.
2. a. (Later examples.) Also *fig.*
1903 'O. HENRY' in *Everybody's Mag.* Aug. 194/1 You see a man doing nothing but loafing around making snapshots. **1928** *Observer* 17 June 10/2, I asked President Masaryk..if he could give me a snapshot of the difference between what he found when he came to Prague in 1918, and what he has the satisfaction of seeing now. **1930** [see *HUSTLE v.* 5]. **1950** G. B. SHAW *Farfetched Fables* iii. 109 What are you doing here?..Only hiking round the island. May I take a snapshot? **1962** M. MCLUHAN *Gutenberg Galaxy* 241 He [*sc.* Montaigne] bred up a great race of self-portrayers by means of the mental snapshot. **1975** P. FUSSELL *Gt. War & Mod. Memory* i. 10 British and German soldiers..meeting in No Man's Land to exchange cigarets and to take snapshots. **1978** P. O'DONNELL *Dragon's Claw* iii. 47 Snapshots of sight and sound, of touch, taste, and smell.
b. *Computers.* A record of the contents of some or all of the storage locations in a computer at a particular stage in the execution of a program (see quot. 1963). Freq. *attrib.*
1963 GREGORY & VAN HORN *Automatic Data-Processing Systems* (ed. 2) xii. 473 Some simplified forms of postmortem routines give only a storage snapshot, which is a complete copy of all storage locations at the time the processor stopped. A snapshot routine may also list the instruction that caused the program to stop, the current contents of arithmetic units and indexes, and perhaps, several of the most-recently executed jumps thus indicating the path of program control. A differential snapshot lists the contents of storage locations that have changed from their initial value or from their value in a prior snapshot. **1966** *IFIP-ICC Vocab. Information Processing* 85 When a trace program gives output only on selected instructions, or for selected conditions, it is called a snapshot program. **1973** C. W. GEAR *Introd. Computer Sci.* vi. 244 An alternative is to take a series of snapshots at points in the program section.
2*. In various sports, a quick shot (of the ball, etc.) at goal.
1961 *Times* 29 May 4/3 [In Polo.] After Hanut had scored with a lovely snapshot to make it 3–2. **1963** *Globe & Mail* (Toronto) 21 Jan. 16/3 [In Hockey.] Hull responded by taking a quick pass from Balfour and scoring on a quick snap-shot. **1976** *Oadby & Wigston* (Leics.) *Advertiser* 26 Nov. 15/4 [In Football.] Saints hit back and a snapshot by Jim White hit the crossbar.
3. (Further examples.)
1894 [see *ENLARGER* 1 b]. **1901** MERWIN & WEBSTER *Calumet 'K'* xv. 288 Young men with snap-shot cameras waylaid Bannon. **1967** J. PHILIP et al. *Best of Granta* I. 17 The winning photo in *The Granta* Holiday Snapshot Competition shows a couple kissing on a beach. **1977** R. E. HARRINGTON *Quintain* iii. 24 He searched the terrain, storing quick snapshot impressions. **1977** *N.Y. Rev. Bks.* 23 June 25/3 The crudely chronological order of snapshot-sequences pasted in family albums.

Figure 10.5
Entry from *A Supplement to the Oxford English Dictionary.*

Atlases and Gazetteers

Atlases are bound collections of maps. In addition, most atlases contain charts and graphs that furnish information about the geography of countries, states, and regions. Gazetteers are geographical dictionaries. In alphabetical fashion these reference books provide detail about a location's climate, population, natural resources, and so on. You can also learn how to pronounce the name of an unfamiliar place by looking in a Gazetteer. Here are a few:

Cosmopolitan World Atlas
National Geographic Atlas of the World
The Times Atlas of the World
Webster's New Geographical Dictionary

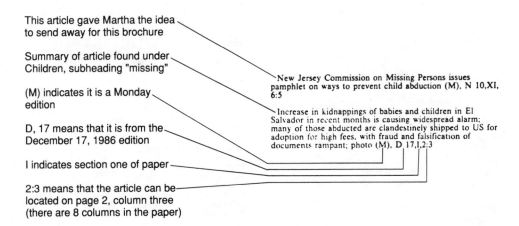

This article gave Martha the idea to send away for this brochure

Summary of article found under Children, subheading "missing"

(M) indicates it is a Monday edition

D, 17 means that it is from the December 17, 1986 edition

I indicates section one of paper

2:3 means that the article can be located on page 2, column three (there are 8 columns in the paper)

New Jersey Commission on Missing Persons issues pamphlet on ways to prevent child abduction (M), N 10,XI, 6:5

Increase in kidnappings of babies and children in El Salvador in recent months is causing widespread alarm; many of those abducted are clandestinely shipped to US for adoption for high fees, with fraud and falsification of documents rampant; photo (M), D 17,I,2:3

Figure 10.6
Use of the *New York Times Index.* In this article, Martha Wong found some useful information for her speech on child abductions.

Almanacs and Yearbooks

Almanacs report facts and statistics about a variety of subjects. Martha found some compelling figures on child abductions by looking in such a book. Yearbooks, as the name implies, come out annually and record information about the previous year. Both these books are excellent sources for providing complex material in a simple, straightforward manner. Here are five of the best:

World Almanac and Book of Facts (annually)
Statistical Abstract of the United States (annually)
Facts on File Yearbook (annually)
Americana Annual (annually)
Britannica Book of the Year (annually)

Biographical Reference Works

If you want to learn about a person, living or dead, check a biographical reference. These works outline a person's life, accomplishments, and credentials. Some of the most helpful are:

American Men and Women of Science, 7 volumes (1982)
Current Biography (annually)
Webster's Biographical Dictionary (1972)
Who's Who in America, 2 volumes (biannually)
International Who's Who (annually)
Notable American Women, 3 volumes (biannually)

Newspapers and Magazines

You'll probably use magazines and newspapers for a lot of your research. These resources range from scholarly journals to everyday tabloids. Newspapers and magazines have the advantage of being concise and current. Martha was able to find several recent articles on child abductions. Let's begin by locating an article in the newspaper.

No printed resource can be more up-to-the-minute than the newspaper. By using newspaper indexes, you can easily access this timely information. The most thoroughly indexed newspaper is the *New York Times.* The *New York Times Index* is a cumulative annual index published since 1913. Indexes come out twice a month for issues in the current year. The index has listings arranged by subject; that's why Martha was able to quickly locate articles on missing children. Each listing also includes a brief synopsis of the article. One advantage of this index is that almost every library has every back issue of the *New York Times* stored on microfilm. Magazine articles may be missing because the issue was lost or not subscribed to in the first place; but, you're always likely to find the *New York Times.*

Other newspapers are also indexed. *The Wall Street Journal Index,* published since 1958, contains useful sources for financial and business topics. The *Newspaper Index,* published since 1972, indexes several papers including the *Chicago Tribune, Los Angeles Times,* and *Washington Post.* Another useful index is that for the *Christian Science Monitor,* which has been indexed since 1960. There's also an excellent possibility that some leading papers in your region, such as the *Detroit News* or *Philadelphia Inquirer,* may be indexed in your library. Speaking about a campus issue? Look for back issues of your college newspaper. If you're not sure which newspapers your library subscribes to, ask the librarian.

Magazines are the mainstay of most research. The most important resource of all is the *Readers' Guide to Periodical Literature.* The *Readers' Guide* is

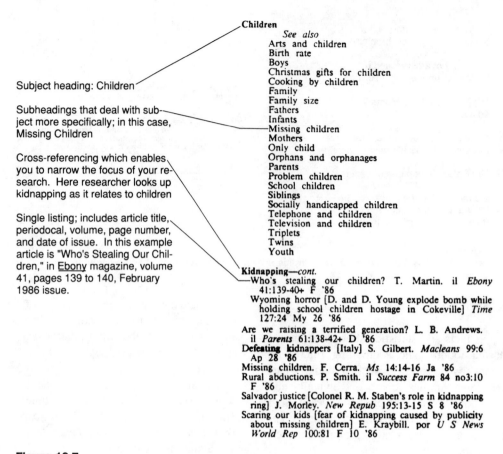

Subject heading: Children

Subheadings that deal with subject more specifically; in this case, Missing Children

Cross-referencing which enables you to narrow the focus of your research. Here researcher looks up kidnapping as it relates to children

Single listing; includes article title, periodocal, volume, page number, and date of issue. In this example article is "Who's Stealing Our Children," in Ebony magazine, volume 41, pages 139 to 140, February 1986 issue.

Children
    See also
    Arts and children
    Birth rate
    Boys
    Christmas gifts for children
    Cooking by children
    Family
    Family size
    Fathers
    Infants
    Missing children
    Mothers
    Only child
    Orphans and orphanages
    Parents
    Problem children
    School children
    Siblings
    Socially handicapped children
    Telephone and children
    Television and children
    Triplets
    Twins
    Youth

Kidnapping—*cont.*
    Who's stealing our children? T. Martin. il *Ebony* 41:139-40+ F '86
    Wyoming horror [D. and D. Young explode bomb while holding school children hostage in Cokeville] *Time* 127:24 My 26 '86
    Are we raising a terrified generation? L. B. Andrews. il *Parents* 61:138-42+ D '86
    Defeating kidnappers [Italy] S. Gilbert. *Macleans* 99:6 Ap 28 '86
    Missing children. F. Cerra. *Ms* 14:14-16 Ja '86
    Rural abductions. P. Smith. il *Success Farm* 84 no3:10 F '86
    Salvador justice [Colonel R. M. Staben's role in kidnapping ring] J. Morley. *New Repub* 195:13-15 S 8 '86
    Scaring our kids [fear of kidnapping caused by publicity about missing children] E. Kraybill. por *U S News World Rep* 100:81 F 10 '86

Figure 10.7
Use of the *Reader's Guide to Periodical Literature*. This example is taken from the *Reader's Guide to Periodical Literature*, 1986 edition, page 1068.

the general-purpose catalogue of over 180 popular magazines. Dating back to 1900, and updated semimonthly, it lists by author, title, and subject, articles published during that particular year. Magazines that are listed in this index include *Time, Newsweek, U. S. News and World Report, Psychology Today, Esquire, and Rolling Stone.* You name the subject, and you can probably find it in the *Readers' Guide.*

Using the *Readers' Guide* is very easy. Look up your subject, check under the subheading, and you're likely to find several articles of immediate interest. When Martha used the *Readers' Guide* she looked under *"children,"* subheading *"missing."* She also cross-referenced by looking under *"kidnapping."* As the figure above illustrates, all the information needed—article title, magazine, volume, page number, and date of the issue is included. All you need do is copy down this information and go to the periodicals room and get that particular issue.

Several recommendations are in order when using the *Readers' Guide.* First, start with the most recent index and work back in time. This is what Martha did for her speech. An exception would be if your topic was about a particular period in history; in that case you'd start with the year of the event.

Second, copy down the citations for several promising articles—there's a good chance not all the magazines you need will be available. Last, be creative when researching your subject. Different topics are listed under many different headings; for instance, Martha found some articles under kidnapping, not under children or abductions.

There are also many specialized indexes. Since the *Readers' Guide* covers magazines of general interest, these specialized indexes catalog more specific areas. For example:

Art Index. Published quarterly since 1929.

Poole's Index to Periodical Literature. An index of 19th century American and British periodicals, 1802–1907.

Popular Periodicals Index. Index to 25 contemporary periodicals not otherwise indexed, annually since 1973.

Applied Science and Technology Index. Monthly since 1958.

Business Periodicals Index. Annually since 1958.

Psychological Abstracts. Monthly since 1927.

The Education Index. Monthly since 1929.

You also can access articles in magazines by using a laserdisc periodical index called **InfoTrac**.[3] Libraries increasingly are employing this system, and there's a good chance yours might have it available. InfoTrac is simple to operate. Type in your search topic, say *"child abductions,"* and the system will supply you with a printout of all relevant articles. The index database consists of more than half a million references to articles published since 1982, located in one thousand general interest, business, and technical periodicals. The system also indexes both the *New York Times* and *Wall Street Journal.* If available, use of this system can save you vast amounts of valuable research time.

Vertical File

The vertical file, sometimes referred to as the information file, is one of the library's best kept secrets: students are just unaware that it exists. Basically, the vertical file contains clippings, pamphlets, and brochures located in folders arranged by subject. Had Martha known of the vertical file, she would have discovered that several brochures she was sending away for were sitting in a file, less than ten feet away. Usually this file is located near the reference section. If you can't find it, check with the librarian.

Computerized Research Services

The musty shelves of the library are gradually being replaced by the electrical impulses of computerized databases. As a researcher, you live on the threshold of an exciting time, where the technology of library research is changing and being expanded day by day. The likelihood is that your library has access to a database—if not, they soon will. The promise of computerized research services is virtually limitless, and you need to be aware of its potential and application.

A computerized research service is a computer-based information retrieval system which searches indexes and abstracts on-line. There are several major retrieval services, and more are likely to come. The three major subscriber services are: BRS (Bibliographical Retrieval Service); DIALOG (developed by Lockheed Corporation); and ORBIT (developed by System Development Corporation). A typical computerized reference service will provide on-line access to approximately 300 databases. Databases cover practically every subject from abortion to zoology. A typical database will index articles in periodicals, government documents, scholarly journals, unpublished materials, books, conference papers, and countless other resources. For example, DIALOG

alone contains over 80 million records from such sources. Probably the two most useful databases are *ERIC* (Educational Resources Information Center) which covers all aspects of education, and the *Social Science Citation Index,* which, as the name suggests, provides references for the social sciences. Your librarian will be able to suggest which is the best database for you to search.

You needn't be a computer wiz to use these services. The procedure is simple enough so that in some libraries students can search on their own, while in most a trained librarian is there to lend a hand. Searches can be made by author, title, or subject; however, the most common approach is to use key words (called *descriptors*) stored within each database thesaurus. Your librarian can help with your key words, or you can determine them for yourself. Appropriate key words can be found in the multivolume *Library of Congress Subject Headings.* This resource lists the various headings under which the Library of Congress catalogs books. By following its system of cross-references and subheadings, the most fruitful key words for your search can be determined.

The key words you pick for your search are very important. This is why it's suggested that you know exactly what your topic is before using a retrieval service. A student researching athletic scholarships wasn't sure if he should search under athletics, colleges, or scholarships; thus, he needed to do some preliminary research. Martha, however, knew her exact topic from the word go; therefore, she could have immediately begun a search under *"child abductions."* If your key words are too general, you'll receive a long list of sources with very few that really target your issue. If Martha searched under *"children,"* for example, she'd get such a long, off-topic list that it would take her hours to isolate the most useful articles. On the other hand, your key words shouldn't be too specific. If they are, you're likely to receive a short list containing very few citations. For instance if Martha searched under *"child abductions by strangers in rural America,"* she'd only get three articles. Accordingly, phrase your key words carefully; understand your topic fully. At the moment you do, start your search.

There are tremendous advantages to using a computer retrieval service. The first is the element of time. An on-line search inquires into weekly, monthly, and annual indexes simultaneously. Within a matter of minutes you receive a useful list of citations that would take endless hours to acquire otherwise. A second advantage is thoroughness. Databases are updated sooner and more frequently than are printed indexes: if an article exists a search is sure to find it. Many resources that are located through a database would be impossible to find through traditional research methods. Third, your citations are delivered in a neat itemized list. You then have the opportunity to review the list and pick the most promising articles. Lastly, searches are economical. Many colleges provide this service free of charge. Others charge a nominal fee, ranging from $10 to $30. However, even if you library charges for a search, considering the time and effort saved, it's probably a worthwhile expenditure.

Database research isn't appropriate for all types of searches. The technology is recent, and indexed material only goes back about fifteen years; if you're researching an historical event, a computerized search probably won't do much good. Also, some topics might be so localized—say a topic about an immediate campus concern—that a detailed search would prove fruitless. When considering a search, ask yourself if it will prove beneficial; if you're not sure ask the librarian, s/he can offer some helpful suggestions.

If you don't want to go to the library, you can access computer research services right from your home work station. All you need is a modem (telephone hookup) and telecommunications software. Some database services are free; while others charge a fee ranging from modest to exorbitant. Most services charge a lower rate if you access them at night or on weekends.

Once you start doing research on a computer you'll soon become addicted. Many students are amazed at how quickly a computer search sifts through information while thoroughly exploring their subject. Start experimenting with this technology now; once you do, library research will never seem the same again.

Sometimes you can't find the information you need in the library. When this happens you might want to write away for it. Let's see how this is done.

SENDING FOR INFORMATION

If your topic is at all current, there's an excellent possibility that there's some organization for the idea and another against it. Organizations abound on all sides of controversial issues. Abortion? Pro Life is against it; Free Choice is for it. Gun Control? The National Rifle Association is against it; the American Alliance Against Violence is for it. Euthanasia? Americans United for Life are against it; the Hemlock Society is for it. Whatever your issue, somebody, somewhere, probably has something to say about it.

Getting this information isn't very difficult. Check the phone book. You might find the organization you're looking for right around the corner. Visit the library and consult the *Encyclopedia of Associa-*

tions. This three volume book, located in the reference section, furnishes the listings and addresses of thousands of organizations.

The beauty of sending for information is that it's almost always free. The express purpose of these organizations is to get their point of view out to the public; consequently, they're very willing to send you pamphlets, handouts, and booklets galore. However, bear in mind that this information probably isn't totally objective. Most organized groups admittedly only care about one side of an issue. Their views are subjective and biased. As a result, this information may be prejudiced, slanted, misleading, and even downright wrong. Tread with care, explore all sides of an issue, and consult a balance of other sources for a more objective and complete picture. It also can be dangerous to put too much emphasis on material ordered through the mail. One student didn't receive the material she ordered until three months after her discussion was over. Another student expected some brochures he ordered to give him lots of useful material, only to find it was totally off-track. He ended up rushing to the library at the last minute.

Don't overlook government sponsored agencies when writing away for information. Whether federal or state, these agencies cover a broad range of issues and concerns. For state agencies consult the phone book under the name of your state. For federal, look under the United States. A complete listing of the 25,000 booklets available from the federal government can be obtained by writing the U. S. Government Printing Office, Washington, D.C., 20402. You may also find that your college library has a listing for your examination. If researching a consumer issue, write the U. S. Consumer Information Center, Pueblo, Colorado, 81002.

Explore all possible sources when writing for information. One student speaking about robotics wrote to several computer companies and received hundreds of pages of up-to-date information. Speaking about drunk driving? Call MADD or SADD (Mothers or Students Against Drunk Driving). On sickle cell anemia? Write the National Association for Sickle Cell Disease. Discussing smoking? Write the American Cancer Society and the American Tobacco Institute. Also feel free to contact the congressional representative for your home or college district; the local office will be glad to help. Reach out and examine all the information that's available. The chances are it's only a phone call or postage stamp away.

Having gathered some written materials, you might want to gain an insight from someone in the know. You accomplish this with an interview.

INTERVIEWING

As discussed in Chapter Eight, few things are as informative as a face-to-face interview. The interview is a particularly useful way of doing research. Search out the views of others: classmates, professors, administrators, or experts off campus. Of course never start with an interview first—rather use it as a follow-up to other research. Next, make certain the person being interviewed has something to offer based on their position, expertise, reputation, or experience. Never interview someone just for the sake of doing so. Finally, use the interview to give an added touch—another viewpoint—to your knowledge of an issue.

Sometimes it's helpful to interview someone who can furnish firsthand knowledge about your topic. This will help to shape your own thinking, while giving your ideas that all-important personal touch. For example:

- *A woman interviewed a farmer whose small family farm was about to be foreclosed.*
- *A man interviewed a high school math teacher who was about to quit teaching to take a higher paying job in industry.*
- *A woman interviewed a classmate who had taken a year off college to hitchhike across country.*
- *A man interviewed a mother and her three children living in one room in a welfare hotel.*

Why are interviews valuable? First, an interview can shed light on a topic where there's not a lot of other coverage. Often this includes topics that are localized to the college community. Second, interviews can supply up-to-the-minute information. Reporters have "broken" many a story because of an interview. Third, an interview can give a sense of reality to facts and statistics by sharing the observations of people directly affected by the issue. And last, an interview can lend the insight of an expert. By being on a college campus you're probably surrounded by people worth interviewing—historians, mathematicians, scientists, and student hobbyists to name a few. For example, observe how Martha used an interview to research child abductions:

When she was done in the library Martha had a lot of background material. But she wanted some further information from an expert. In the phone book she located a local chapter of Child Find (an organization committed to finding missing children). She visited their office and made an appointment to interview the director. Martha then went home and prepared a list of questions.

Meeting with the director Martha began by reminding her of the reason for the interview. She then asked a series of questions about abductions. While answering one question, the director mentioned the National Commission on Missing and Exploited Children. Martha intended on asking about this organization later, but since it was brought up, probed deeper with questions about the national commission.

After the interview Martha wrote the director a thank you note. She then began compiling her notes. She was pleased with what she'd learned in her half hour interview.

Deciding on who to interview takes a little thought. Discussing campus security? Talk to someone from law enforcement. Speaking about hospital care? Interview a health professional. Addressing the issue of women's athletics? See the head of the athletic department.

As you cast about for a subject, base your decision on what the person can add to your presentation. In other words, what can they tell you about your topic that you don't already know? Here are some things to keep in mind when selecting a subject for an interview:

Who is most knowledgeable about your topic? Base your decision on the person's reputation, experience, qualifications, or responsibilities.

Who will be easy to talk to? Try and select someone who is open and willing to express his or her viewpoint.

Who has a unique perspective about your topic? Try and pick someone whose experiences and knowledge are different from your own.

Once you've selected your interviewee, follow these guidelines:

Ask for the Interview in Advance

Don't expect to walk in and start questioning someone on the spur of the moment. Someone worth interviewing is probably quite busy, so agree to meet with them at their convenience.

If Possible, Ask for the Interview in Person

It's harder to brush someone off in person than by mail or over the phone. This is why Martha went personally to request her interview with Child Find.

State the Reason for the Interview

People appreciate knowing why they're being questioned. Tell them in advance the purpose and expected length of the interview. Keep the anticipated time requirement realistic—usually half an hour or less is sufficient.

Request to Interview the Most Qualified Person

Start at the top by asking to interview the head of an organization first, and then work your way down. Martha requested an interview with the director, not an assistant. In dealing with administrative organizations, it's best to start with the leaders first.[4]

Be Courteous When Asking for the Interview

The person agreeing to an interview is doing you a favor. Use flattery and tell them how they're helping you. Use your communication skills to sell the idea of your interview.

Martha added a lot to her presentation by using an interview. But while interviewing someone may seem easy, it's really a complicated process taking great skill. Successful interviewers like David Frost, Diane Sawyer, and Barbara Walters have spent years honing their craft. In addition, they spend hours before every interview preparing questions and perfecting their technique. Before going out and questioning someone, carefully review the techniques discussed in Chapter Eight.

Sometimes it's desirable to get the views of many, rather than the thoughts of one. When you want a wide-range of opinion try survey research.

SURVEY RESEARCH

Following are two statements Martha could make in her speech on child abductions. The first is based on opinion, the second on survey research.

1. *I'm sure most students feel that more needs to be done to find missing children.*

2. *Of 50 students polled, 90% feel that more needs to be done to find missing children.*

Doesn't the second statement sound more compelling? This is why survey research is a time-tested way of gathering information. In order to conduct a survey, you'll need to prepare a questionnaire (ways to do this are discussed in the next chapter). You'll then need to decide on how you want to collect your responses. You can use telephone surveys, survey interviews, or printed surveys.[5] Here's a description of each:

Telephone Surveys

Surveys over the phone are actually very easy to do. Simply pick a name, say the next to last on each page of the directory, and make the call. If there's no answer, try the next number and so on. State the purpose of the survey, and read each question off your list while carefully noting the response.

Survey Interviews

Survey interviews are similar to phone surveys, except that you ask your questions in person. Pick people at random, explain your purpose, and read off your list of questions.

Printed Surveys

With this method you distribute a questionnaire to a person and ask them to fill it out. Many speakers prefer this method because respondents feel less inhibited when privately filling out a questionnaire. It also lets people go into more detail in their answers. Finally, with a printed survey your vocal inflection or manner of questioning will not bias your results.

Regardless of the method used, try to see that your questionnaire is standardized and your survey is random. A standardized questionnaire is one where the questions are identical for each respondent. A printed questionnaire does this automatically—every form is identical to every other form; but if you read your questions rather than hand them out, be sure to work off a master list—reading your questions in the same order and manner. Second, try and distribute all questionnaires randomly to get a good cross section of the pool of people you wish to study. When a random method is used, every member of a group, at least theoretically, has an equal chance of being questioned. Martha might stand in the middle of campus and question every tenth person that passes.[6] Or, if using the phone, might call every twentieth name with a campus number.

Figure 10.8
Sample Bibliography Card for a Book.

Sometimes you don't want a random sample, however. You might want people who are older, younger, fat, or thin. For instance, Martha might want to interview students who look like they're partners, or students who are education majors. Survey those people which will give you the most helpful information, and skip the rest. And bear in mind that generally the more people you interview, the more valid your results.

Once you've collected your information, you'll need to put it in some order. Let's see how this is done.

TAKING NOTES

It's best to store your information on index cards. Roomy 4 × 6 inch or 5 × 8 inch cards are preferable for jotting down facts and ideas. Use one card per idea. Putting two or more details on the same card only complicates your task when you come to preparing your presentation. It's especially important to be thorough and accurate when copying down information. If you fail to note a book or article correctly, you may end up going back and trying to find it a second time. If an article looks particularly useful, it's a good idea to photocopy it noting where you found it on the back of the copy. This way you'll have the complete text to review at your leisure. However never use photocopying in place of note taking. The process of taking notes lets you digest and evaluate material as you transcribe it by hand. Once you paraphrase and nutshell something on a card, it's yours for the keeping.

It's advisable to start your research by reviewing one or two sources that will give you an overview of the subject. This early stage of research is important, because it helps establish the parameters for

your presentation, while narrowing the focus of your search. Sometimes these overview articles provide you with a new angle or another idea to explore. Bear in mind that the first stage of research is to shape your thinking rather than to collect specific information.

It's usually advantageous to allow a few days between your general reading and actual collection of information. Digest the general information and let it percolate in your mind for a while before rushing into more specific research.

When you locate a source be sure to fill out a bibliography card. For books include the author, title, publisher, publisher's location, date of publication, and call number. On the bottom of the card you also may want to state the relevance of the book to your topic. See the illustration above of a book Martha used. For a magazine or newspaper, include the author, article title, title of periodical, volume number, date of publication, and page numbers for the entire article (newspapers also will include section and column number). Just as with a book, jot down any commentary. The illustration on the next page shows how this should look. Also fill out a bibliography card for an interview. Note the name of the interviewee, his or her position, the date and time it occurred, and its location.

Observe in both illustrations that there's a large circled letter printed on the top of each card. This is very important and will save you a great deal of time later on. For her first source (in this case the book) Martha wrote an A on top; for the next source (the magazine) a B; for her third she would write a C, and so on working her way through the alphabet. How is this time saving? As she starts to collect information from each source, Martha will need to identify where

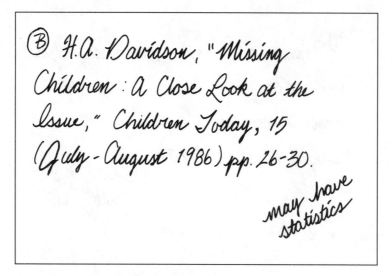

Figure 10.9
Sample Bibliography Card for a Magazine.

she found that material. Rather than writing the title and author all she will note is Al for the first fact taken from the book, A2 for the second, and so on. All information taken from the magazine article will be marked B1, B2, etc. Writing an A or a B is a lot easier than writing the entire name of the author or article title on each card.

Once you locate a useful looking source you're ready to start taking notes. You want to make your notes thorough enough so they make you totally independent of the source from which they came. Don't rely on your trusty memory or a sketchy excerpt to fill in the blanks. While you're taking notes keep evaluating the strength of the material. Does it appear very useful, fairly useful, are only slightly useful? Some note takers put a star or check on a note that looks especially promising, and a question mark on one that doesn't. Of course never be too harsh in prejudging material—sometimes the simplest statement or fact can end up driving home an important point.

Here are the three things that you should mark on each card:

- *An identifier, usually the letter that correlates with the bibliography card (A, B, C, etc.); also jot down the page number where the information appeared.*
- *A category heading, some key word or subject listing that helps you organize your material.*
- *The example, statistics, or fact you plan to use in your presentation.*

If copying down a particularly long passage it's wise to *summarize* or *paraphrase*. Summarizing means condensing a long statement into one or two sentences. Paraphrasing means restating the author's idea, but phrasing those ideas in your own words. For most presentations summarizing is preferable.

Fill out as many cards as necessary for each source. The time and care you spend in note taking will pay dividends when it comes time to present your report. The more complete, your notes, the more effective your message.

GUIDELINES FOR DOING RESEARCH

The task of research can be greatly simplified by following an orderly, methodical approach. Here are some suggestions.

Start Early

Research takes time and patience. A rushed research job leads to a poor performance. Gage how much time you'll need and arrange your schedule accordingly.

Develop a Research Strategy

Some people research by a strategy of hit or miss. They either find information, or pick up and start looking somewhere else. It's much better to plan a schedule—plotting out your quest for information. Here was Martha's schedule for her speech due March 12th:

March 1 Do some background reading in library
March 2 Write National Commission on Missing Children
March 3 Visit Child Find and set up interview
March 4 Visit library—run a computer search
March 5 Survey students on campus
March 7 Interview director of Child Find

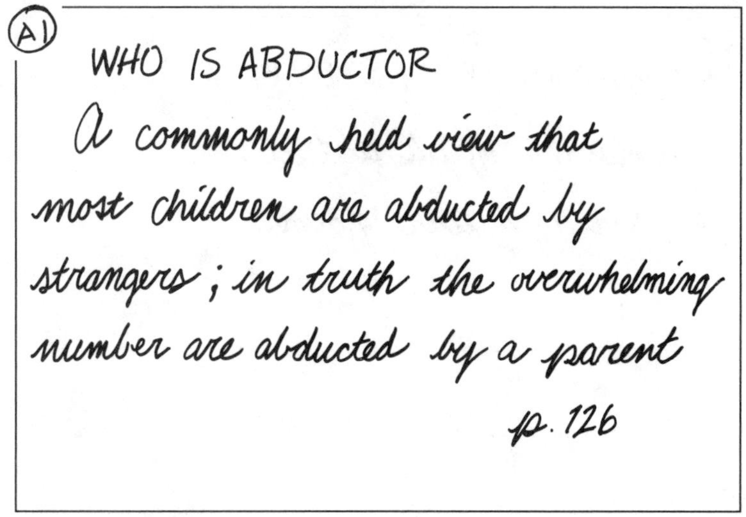

WHO IS ABDUCTOR

A commonly held view that most children are abducted by strangers; in truth the overwhelming number are abducted by a parent

p. 126

Figure 10.10
Note Card Using an Example.

March 8 Visit library—get recommended sources from computer search
March 9 Visit library—check vertical file and tie up loose ends

Post this schedule in a visible place. This way you won't get overwhelmed at the last minute.

Back Your Ideas with Useful Information

There are three types of information that prove most useful. Here's a description of each:

Examples

Examples include facts that are believed to be true, but aren't reported as a number or quote. For instance, Martha could use the following examples: *"Most children are abducted by an estranged parent,"* or *"More girls than boys are abducted."*

Statistics

Statistics point out comparisons and contrasts with mathematical detail. For example, Martha could use the following: *"90% of all children are abducted by a parent."* Statistical support can also take the form of ratios, *"There is a 1 in 10,000 chance of your child being abducted,"* or a number, *"Every year 50,000 children are abducted."*

Testimony

Testimony includes words of another that are quoted or paraphrased. Testimonial evidence is as powerful as the person it comes from. Always note the name and position of the person making the remark. Here's a quote Martha used:

> *"Sally Glass, a critic of the panic caused over reported child abductions said, 'The typical child has a greater chance of being struck by lightning than of being abducted by a stranger.'"*

Observe Martha's use of examples, statistics, and testimony in figures 10.10, 10.11, and 10.12. Notice that A1 comes from the book by Newman, and that cards B1 and B2 come from the magazine article by Davidson.

Evaluate Your Material

How sound is your information? Suppose, for example, Martha locates twelve books on missing children. Should she read all twelve? Certainly not—she wouldn't have enough time. Selecting the best sources is sometimes difficult; here are some questions to help decide.

Is the Source Relevant?

Don't waste your time reviewing material that isn't directly related to your topic. Once you know the precise subject you're researching, restrict yourself to information that directly targets that issue. Martha ignored articles on child abuse, adoptions, and runaways.

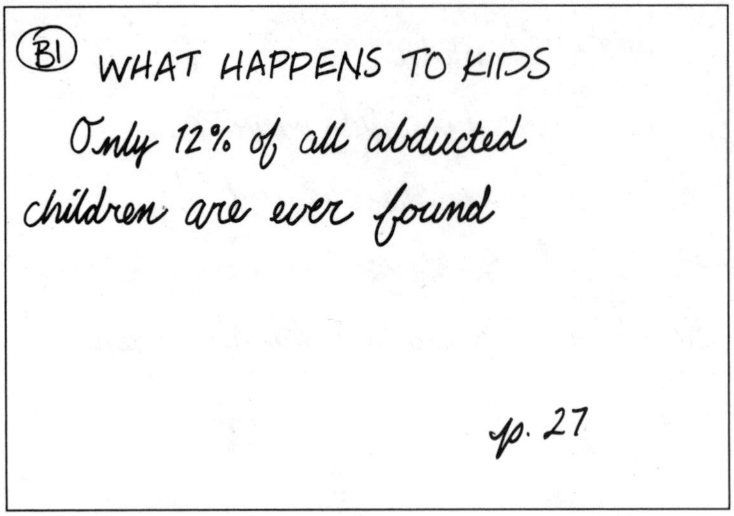

Figure 10.11
Note Card Using a Statistic.

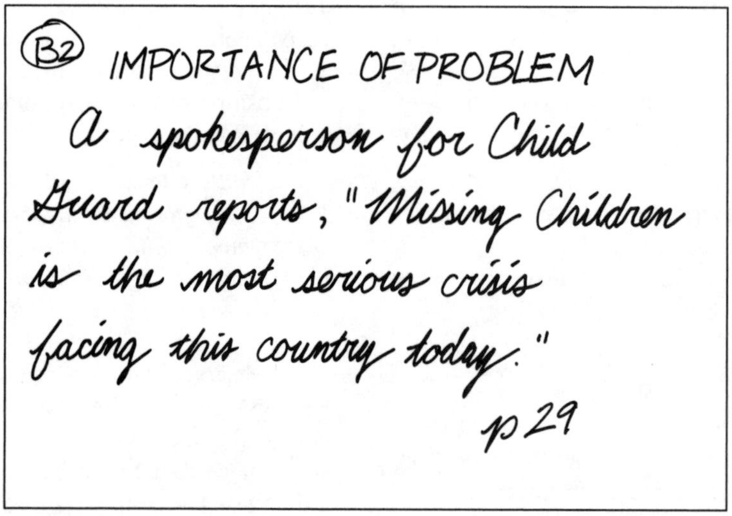

Figure 10.12
Note Card Using Testimony.

Is the Source Current?

As a general rule, start with the most recent information and work your way back. Up-to-date material will not only provide the latest information, but will also lead you to other sources in the bibliography. Even if researching an historical topic, review the newest publications first—you can always go back and look at older sources later.

Is the Source Credible?

Determine what will seem most believable to your listeners. Will they be more impressed with the opinion of an expert, or a report from a sensational tabloid sold at the supermarket? Look for material in professional journals and main stream publications. And if using a biased source, balance it with information from one with an opposing viewpoint.

Is the Source Comprehensive?

Suppose Martha locates seven articles, five consist of three pages or more, while two are only one page long. Which should she review? Clearly her time would be better spent examining the longer articles. One good article that covers a subject in depth is more valuable than several that only deal with it superficially.

Doing research means digging for information in every possible place. Don't just remain glued to the library. Look within yourself, conduct an interview, try a survey, write away for some timely information. After all, a creative researcher becomes a challenging communicator.

CHAPTER SUMMARY

One of your more important tasks will be to gather information through research. A good place to begin is within yourself. Give a personal touch to your message by turning to your own observations and experiences.

Most research will take place in the library. The card catalogue should be used to locate a book. The reference section is a ripe resource. Here you can find encyclopedias, dictionaries, indexes and bibliographies, atlases and gazetteers, almanacs and yearbooks, biographical reference works, and newspapers and magazines. If looking for a newspaper the most useful index is for the *New York Times*. Magazines can be located by looking in the *Readers' Guide to Periodical Literature* or by using InfoTrac. The vertical file includes collections of clippings and brochures. Computerized research services offer great promise, providing access to millions of sources.

Many students like to send for information. You can locate the names and addresses of thousands of organizations by consulting the *Encyclopedia of Associations*. Another valuable resource is the U.S. Government.

The face-to-face investigative interview is a valued tool for gathering information. You can interview classmates, teachers, or people off campus. If questioning someone you should carefully arrange and conduct your interview.

Survey research can be used to get the ideas of a group. The three best ways to survey people are to use the telephone, interview them in person, or hand them a written questionnaire.

Once you've collected your material, you'll need to put it in some order. You do this by taking notes. You should put one idea per card, and thoroughly list all the information you need.

Guidelines for conducting research includes starting early, developing a research strategy, backing your ideas with useful information, evaluating your material, and by using a variety of resources.

EXERCISES FOR REVIEW

1. Write one sentence describing the kind of information you can expect to locate in each of the following sources:

general encyclopedias	*magazine indexes*
special dictionaries	*atlases and gazetteers*
indexes and bibliographies	*almanacs and*
biographical	*yearbooks*
reference works	*newspaper indexes*

2. Pick an imaginary subject for a group discussion from the list below. For the topic you've chosen, do research in the library finding at least one citation from any nine of the following fourteen sources: card catalogue, *Readers' Guide, New York Times Index*, encyclopedia, specialized encyclopedia, atlas, gazetteer, dictionary, almanac, yearbook, index, bibliographical reference, vertical file, or biographical reference. Copy down the citation for each of the nine sources and hand it in to your *instructor*.

Mayan Indians	*foreign imports*
cancer therapy	*Carolina Islands*
air pollution	*Grover Cleveland*
highway safety	*college tuition*
data processing	*Viet Nam War*

3. Visit the library on campus. Find out which computerized retrieval service is available and what the procedure is for conducting a database search. Write up this information and submit it to your instructor.

4. Pick a subject for a future oral report. Using the *Readers' Guide* and *New York Times Index* find 3 articles from each index that would be useful for this report. Following the format discussed in the chapter, prepare a bibliography card for each article.

5. Following are listed several questions. Using the appropriate reference, provide the correct answer for each. Note with the answer the resource where you located the information to answer each question.
   a. *The height of Mount Everest.*
   b. *Birth date of Thomas Jefferson.*
   c. *The old English definition of the word, "fag."*
   d. *The worst plane crash in 1974.*
   e. *The date of the issue of the New York Times in 1915 that announced the sinking of the British steamship, Lusitania.*
   f. *The address of the headquarters of the National Council on Alcoholism.*
   g. *Time magazine's "Man of the Year" in 1939.*
   h. *The names of all the oceans surrounding Australia.*
   i. *A title of a book authored by Joseph Conrad.*

NOTES

1. For a thorough discussion of how personal observation and experience can be used in preparation, see, William L. Rivers, *Finding Facts,* Prentice-Hall, Englewood Cliffs, New Jersey, 1975, pp. 56–75.

2. Joan Detz, *How to Write & Give A Speech,* St. Martin, New York, 1984, p. 17.

3. Kent Stephen, "Laserdisc Technology Enters Mainstream," *American Libraries* (April 1986), p. 252.

4. This is a view shared by many interviewing experts. See, Charles J. Stewart and William B. Cash, *Interviewing: Principles and Practices.* 5th edition William C. Brown, Dubuque, Iowa, 1988 and William C. Donaghy, *The Interview: Skills and Applications,* Scott, Foresman, Glenview, Illinois, 1984.

5. You also can survey a group through the mail. However, when considering time and cost this method is not practicable for class research.

6. In actual practice, true random samples are difficult to obtain. Martha's sampling procedure is not truly random, since it's designed to survey college students, not the general population. Additionally, if Martha just handed out questionnaires during the daylight hours, her sample would not be random since evening students would not have an equal chance of being surveyed. Being that random samples are so difficult to obtain, compromises must be made. For the purpose of this class, it is the concept of trying to obtain a random sample that is more important than its actual implementation.

Name _____   Course _____

Sources of Information Worksheet

General Purpose: _____

Specific Purpose of Presentation: _____

_____

Printed Sources:

Author: _____   Date: _____

Title: _____

Article Title: _____

Number of Pages Used: _____   Publisher: _____

Author: _____   Date: _____

Title: _____

Article Title: _____

Number of Pages Used: _____   Publisher: _____

Author: _____   Date: _____

Title: _____

Article Title: _____

Number of Pages Used: _____   Publisher: _____

Author: _____   Date: _____

Title: _____

Article Title: _____

Number of Pages Used: _____   Publisher: _____

Author: _____   Date: _____

Title: _____

Article Title: _____

Number of Pages Used: _____   Publisher: _____

Interview Sources:

Name of Person Interviewed: _____   Date: _____

Position or Title: _____

Reason for Expertise on Subject: _____

Name _____   Course _____

Sources of Information Worksheet

General Purpose: _____

Specific Purpose of Presentation: _____

_____

Printed Sources:

Author: _____   Date: _____

Title: _____

Article Title: _____

Number of Pages Used: _____   Publisher: _____

Author: _____   Date: _____

Title: _____

Article Title: _____

Number of Pages Used: _____   Publisher: _____

Author: _____   Date: _____

Title: _____

Article Title: _____

Number of Pages Used: _____   Publisher: _____

Author: _____   Date: _____

Title: _____

Article Title: _____

Number of Pages Used: _____   Publisher: _____

Author: _____   Date: _____

Title: _____

Article Title: _____

Number of Pages Used: _____   Publisher: _____

Interview Sources:

Name of Person Interviewed: _____   Date: _____

Position or Title: _____

Reason for Expertise on Subject: _____

COMMUNICATION FACTS

How Often Do You Use These Words

Five Lists of the 20 Most Common English Words Used in Speaking and Writing

Rank	Written Vocabulary		Spoken Vocabulary		
1	the	the	the	the	I
2	of	of	and	of	you
3	and	and	of	and	the
4	to	to	to	to	a
5	a	a	a	a	on
6	in	in	in	in	to
7	that	that	that	is	that
8	it	is	is	that	it
9	is	I	it	could	is
10	I	it	they	it	and
11	for	for	you	you	get
12	be	as	this	this	will
13	was	with	we	for	of
14	as	was	have	have	in
15	you	his	are	are	he
16	with	he	was	be	we
17	he	be	be	they	they
18	on	not	he	he	see
19	have	by	for	we	have
20	by	but	on	as	for

Words are listed in order, from the most used to the twentieth used.

11 Understanding Your Listeners

172

Any group of people can be an audience.

QUESTIONS FOR RETENTION

Before reading this chapter, ask yourself the following questions:

1. Why do I need to understand my listeners?
2. What do I need to learn about my listeners?
3. How can I collect information about my listeners?

When it comes to speaking about drugs, few people are more convincing than David Toma. A big city narcotics officer for twenty-one years, he's seen the pain and tragedy of drug abuse many times. His unorthodox methods for catching drug pushers were so successful that the television shows "Toma" and "Baretta" were based on his career. David Toma also knows the darker side of drugs. As a former addict, he's experienced the horrors of drug abuse firsthand.

Since 1971 David Toma has spoken in thousands of high schools to over one million students, teachers, and parents. When he visits a school Toma addresses two separate audiences—in the morning he speaks to students, at night to parents.

When talking to students Toma pulls no punches. His message is packed with graphic examples and grisly illustrations. He tells of the chemicals in marijuana and the numbness and memory loss it brings to smokers; of the youthful drug user who gouged his eyes out during withdrawal; of the young girl locked away in a psychiatric ward. He uses harsh language and street terms that students understand. Charged with emotion and drama, Toma's message is electric. After a recent appearance one seventeen year old senior observed, *"It was the most powerful thing I ever listened to."* Another senior commented, *"It really hit home."* And a junior said, *"He spoke our language. He was a realist. He knew what we were thinking."*

When addressing parents Toma's technique is quite different. He uses no harsh language, doesn't scream, doesn't threaten. He stays away from grisly stories and graphic examples. Instead he talks about the importance of love, honesty, respect, and discipline in the home. As one parent commented, *"He talked about what it's like to be a parent. I understood his message."* Another said, *"He spoke as one adult to another adult. I really appreciated that."* And one mother responded, *"He was right on target; his speech hit me right between my eyes."*[1]

How did David Toma "hit his listeners right between their eyes?" He linked his message with his audience. Good communicators do this all the time. Consider someone running for president. To farmers s/he might talk about farm price supports, to factory workers a program to rejuvenate industry, and to city residents the need for more police on the street. Does this mean that people who fit their message with their listeners are being unethical or deceptive? Not so long as they're being sincere and truthful. Telling listeners things they can easily understand isn't only legitimate, it's necessary. Imagine the result if David

Toma spoke to parents in street language, and lectured students about honesty, respect, and discipline in the home? Would his speech have been so positively received? Probably not. That's why analyzing listeners is one of the most important tasks confronting any communicator.[2]

Effective communicators are **listener-minded.** They realize that the primary purpose of any message is to get a desired response; it's not to sound impressive or blow off steam. A helpful analogy is to think of an oral presentation as a gift. When you buy someone a present you want it to be something they'll enjoy. A great gift for one person could be an embarrassing disaster for another. Presentations are much the same way. The better you know your listeners, the closer you can match their needs and interests with your content.[3] This means you should make some educated guesses about your listeners. You do this by asking yourself a few simple questions:

1. *Who will be my listeners?*
2. *What do they know and care about?*
3. *How can I get them to understand my message?*

Sometimes people don't analyze their listeners as carefully as they should. This oversight can have serious consequences:

In May of 1813 Napoleon Bonaparte was master of Europe. In concluding an armistice with Austrian statesman, Prince Metternich, Napoleon said: "The French cannot complain much of me. To spare them, I have sacrificed the Germans and the Poles. I have lost in the campaign of Moscow 300,000 men, and there were not more than 30,000 Frenchmen among them.

Shocked beyond belief, Metternich replied, "You forget, Sire, you're speaking to a German!"[4]

As a result of this meeting an armistice wasn't signed and Austria declared war on France. Within a year allied armies marched on Paris and Napoleon was exiled to Elba.

Analyzing listeners takes time and planning. While a failure to do so won't cost you an empire, it can jeopardize your success.[5] That's why it's important to plan your messages like a Toma, not a Napoleon.

The aim of this chapter is to review the ways you can come to understand your listeners. Whether speaking to one or a thousand, properly analyzing listeners is a key to effective communication.

Figure 11.1
Abraham Lincoln. *"Fourscore and seven years ago our fathers brought forth on this continent a new nation conceived in liberty and dedicated to the proposition that all men are created equal. Now we are engaged in a great civil war, testing whether that nation, or any nation so conceived and so dedicated, can long endure."*

Lincoln's "Gettysburg Address" has become a classic in the oratory of the world. In fact, it is very doubtful if any other speech as compact as this has received greater study.

Unlike most modern followers of Lincoln, who deliver the "Gettysburg Address" in a deep bass, Lincoln had a thin, squeaky voice. Lincoln, however, had great personal dignity and dignity would be an outstanding characteristic in a speech of this kind. The artist, Ferris, has pictured Lincoln in the midst of a gesture. (Courtesy, Bettman Archive)

LEARNING ABOUT YOUR LISTENERS

Types of Audiences

One way to start understanding an audience is to think about why people are listening to you in the first place. Is it because you've caught their passing curiosity? Did they come a distance just to hear what you have to say? Or are they there because they have to be? We can loosely categorize these audience types as "passerby," "voluntary," and "captive."[6]

"**Passerby**" are people who just happen to stop and catch someone speaking. They probably just have a temporary curiosity about the subject. Speakers standing on a soapbox in a park usually attract this type of listener. Passerby listeners need stimulating language and exciting examples to hold their interest.

"**Volunteers**" are people listening because they want to. They have an interest and frequently even some knowledge about the subject. Since you know they're listening by choice, you can explore a subject in greater depth and don't need to be overly sensational or dramatic.

"**Captives**," as the name implies, are people who are required to listen. Most classes are captive. Even if attendance isn't required, students feel obligated to attend. Since most of your speaking will be directed toward this type of audience, let's take a closer look at addressing your classmates.

Your Class As An Audience

Sometimes students think a speech class audience is somehow "artificial" and not an audience found in the *"real world."* This is a serious mistake. After all, each of your classmates is a real person with real thoughts, attitudes, and feelings. You may feel more comfortable when addressing your classmates because they're not total strangers, but imagine if you spoke to another speech class at a different time? The chances are you'd discover they're just as *"real"* as any other group of listeners.

Actually speaking to your class presents certain advantages. Speech classes are excellent testing grounds for trying out different strategies and techniques. When you talk to your classmates an important promotion, business decision, or election isn't hanging in the balance. Here you have the freedom to experiment and learn through trial and error. There are no bosses to impress, no committees to convince, no voters to persuade. Your mission is to practice and learn. As one student commented, *"In this class I wasn't expected to already be a great communicator; rather I was free to become better at what I do."*

Who are your classmates? Survey's tell us that most college students in the 1990's are optimistic about their future and the future of the nation. Nearly nine out of ten want to have children, and 85 percent expect to marry. Most want jobs that are challenging and pay well. While many are politically conservative, most students are liberal when it comes to racial issues, sexual equality, and sexual freedom. The average student age is increasingly becoming older, with more and more people attending classes part-time or in the evening.[7] These generalizations may or may not be true about your class. But it goes to show that the average classroom listener is a pretty interesting person.

Thinking about your classmates as an audience? Ask yourself three questions: (1) *What are their inter-*

ests? (2) *What do they know about my subject?* and (3) *What are their expectations?* Let's look at each in turn.

What are my listeners' interests?

A student named Steve Bell had an interesting hobby: collecting political campaign buttons. He had buttons from Andrew Jackson to Jesse Jackson. Steve talked to the class about his button collection. It was terribly boring. He discussed the difference between lithograph and celluloid buttons, between hinged back and open back buttons, between staff and mass distribution buttons. After he was done, Steve's listeners suddenly came alive with questions: Had he met any candidates? Where did he find buttons? Did collectors trade buttons? Were any worth a lot of money? One student finally said, *"This stuff is so interesting. Why didn't you tell us about it in your presentation?"*

Where did Steve go wrong? He failed to consider the interests of his audience. Most listeners don't like to hear the technical background of a topic. Rather they like to hear things that have general interest. Figure out what's most relevant and meaningful to your listeners and build your presentation around that. If Steve had, he'd realized people would find campaigns and candidates more interesting than details about manufacturing. When weighing the interests of your listeners, remember the lesson of *People* magazine. Why do you think Time-Life came out with *People several years ago?* Because they found that the "People" section of *Time* was the most widely read part of the magazine. In the same way, build interest by being "people" oriented.

What do my listeners' know about my topic?

Some people make the mistake of thinking their listeners know as much about their topic as they do. What they forget is that all people can't be knowledgeable about all things. A speaker expert at computers who throws in terms like mainframe, microcomputing, and modem is likely to confuse a lot of listeners. After all, some people don't know a cursor from a command key.

How do you find out what knowledge your listeners have about your subject? Check out their interests; see what hobbies they have; tabulate their majors of study. Once you've learned what your classmates know, you'll be able to gear your presen-

tation accordingly. Even if speaking about a difficult subject, paint it in simple terms. Albert Einstein was once asked to explain the theory of relativity. He described it with this simple analogy: *"Time is relative. If you sit on a park bench with your girl friend for an hour, it seems like a minute. But if you sit on a hot stove for a minute, it seems like an hour."* As a result, Einstein's audience easily got the idea that time is relative to other events.

What are my listeners' expectations?

What do your listeners expect to hear? Do they expect to be instructed, convinced, or amused? Failing to recognize the expectations of your audience can have serious repercussions. Several years ago Senator Daniel Patrick Moynihan was asked to deliver a short, entertaining after dinner speech. Instead he presented a forty minute civics lecture, packed with statistics and detail. By the time the speech ended half the audience had left, and the other half were restlessly bored. Don't make the same mistake as Senator Moynihan. Keep the expectations of your listeners foremost in mind. Remember, a little surprise is good, a lot is disaster.

How do you learn about your listener's interests, knowledge, and expectations? One way is to do a demographic analysis. Let's see how this is done.

DEMOGRAPHIC AUDIENCE ANALYSIS

Demographics are observable traits of your listeners such as age, gender, religion, sociocultural background, group membership and the like. We'll discuss demographics in two ways: first, how you identify traits, and second how you put those observations to use. Here are some major things to consider.[8]

Age

Few things affect a person's outlook more than age. Aristotle observed a long time ago that young listeners are optimistic, trusting, idealistic, and easily persuaded. He believed the young *"have strong passions"* and that *"their lives are spent not in memory but in expectation."* On the other hand, Aristotle suggested that elderly listeners are more cynical, practical, and harder to persuade. Indeed, some of Aristotle's predictions are quite accurate. Research reveals, for instance, that younger listeners are easier to persuade and more flexible in their thinking. Research also suggests that when addressing children and the elderly, speakers tend to be more redundant and use simpler explanations.[9]

Aristotle aside, there's little doubt that age plays an important role in a person's outlook and experience. The chances are that events experienced by your parents—Vietnam, Watergate, and the fabulous fifties are things you've only read about. Likewise things that seem important today—AIDS, Star Wars, and the winner of the 1993 Super Bowl will seem like ancient history to your children. For we all are but products of the time and world in which we live.

Estimating the age of your listeners is particularly important when planning a speech. If you're speaking to a younger audience and mention Roosevelt's Bank Holiday, you'd better be prepared to explain what it is. Similarly, when addressing an older audience don't assume they'll know a Nike from a Puma or that the Grateful Dead isn't a horror movie. Of course some listeners might know things you wouldn't expect them to. Some older listeners might prefer Madonna to Mozart and some younger listeners might be experts on Franklin Roosevelt. But analyzing an audience means making some overall general assumptions.

Probably most of your classmates are in their teens and twenties. There's a good chance, however, that you'll have some listeners who are decades older. Increasingly college classes are becoming multi-generational. It's not at all unusual for some students to be in their thirties, forties, fifties, and beyond. Therefore you may have to address several generations in one room. This will give you invaluable experience, since most audiences you'll address during your lifetime will include listeners of many ages.

Gender

Differences between men and women are becoming less pronounced every year. Today women head major corporations, purchase four out of every ten new cars, sit in both houses of Congress, and march as cadets at West Point. Likewise men now have careers as nurses, work as secretaries, raise children, and do needlepoint. Sexual stereotypes are breaking down at every turn. Speakers who fail to recognize these changes are likely to offend male and female listeners alike.

Nevertheless, certain topics are more likely of greater interest to one sex than the other. More men are probably interested in football or automotive mechanics and more women in cooking or makeup. Of course, these are generalizations. Some women can tear apart an engine and some men can cook a great souffle. The key is to avoid offending or ignoring any member of your audience. Make some general assumptions, but do it with a considerate grace.

In summary, men and women share a broad range of interests, knowledge, and experience. Appeal to those things men and women have in common and eliminate outmoded sexual stereotypes. Instead of talking about *"how to pick up women"* change it to *"how to meet members of the opposite sex;"* or rather than *"how to apply eye shadow"* discuss *"how to take care of your skin."* With a little common sense and sensitivity most topics can be made appealing for everyone.

Religion

Baptist or Buddhist? Morman or Methodist? Jewish or Jehovah Witness? The odds are you'll have people belonging to these religions and probably many more in your group of listeners. Today several million college students are born-again Christians and almost half a million are practicing Muslims. Similarly, listeners in your class could include atheists, agnostics, Catholics, and evangelical Christians just to name a few. Without question, few things fire listener's emotions and enthusiasm more than religious conviction.

If you choose to bring up religion do so with caution. For you can assume that your view on religion—regardless of what it is—probably won't be shared by everyone. Sometimes even topics which seem perfectly innocent can have religious overtones:

Pat Fischer worked part-time as a chef. He decided to deliver a speech where he'd demonstrate several new recipes for pork. Pat showed how pork could be cubed, broiled, barbecued, and roasted. He was shocked to notice that at the end of his speech several listeners were not only disinterested, but seemed almost annoyed with his presentation.

What went wrong? Pat failed to realize that ten members of his audience would not eat pork—three Orthodox Jews and seven Muslims. Obviously none of these listeners were interested in learning new pork recipes. Remember Pat's experience. When you think of an audience, think of their religion.

Sociocultural Background

The sociocultural background of an audience includes its racial, ethnic, and cultural makeup. People from different sociocultural backgrounds have varied interests, experiences, beliefs, and ways of looking at things. It's helpful to remember that you have many audiences within an audience. In a typical American audience, for example, you're likely to find people of European descent, Blacks, Asian-Americans, Chicanos, Latinos, Puerto Ricans, American Indians and many others. Try and find out the background of your listeners so you can adjust your speech accordingly.

College audiences frequently include students from many different countries. Here's how this factor impacted on one student's speech:

The topic of Rose Sanchez's speech was "How to make business meetings more efficient." Rose told of the time wasted in small talk and idle chatter during business negotiations. She gave solid recommendations concerning how executives could get right to specifics and save countless hours each week.

In Rose's audience were several students from Saudi Arabia. They were taken aback by her message and found it of little value. As one Saudi student commented, *"This is not the way we do business."*

What did the Saudi student mean? Saudi's place great value on family, friends, and relationships. As a result, in Saudi business dealings a significant amount of time is spent in "small talk" discussing family and friends before engaging in business. This is rooted in the belief that trust can only be established once both partners feel comfortable with one another. Unfortunately, Rose failed to take this into consideration, turning off many listeners.[10]

Group Membership

People belong to all sorts of clubs. Workers belong to unions, executives to country clubs, activists to political parties, shoppers to shopper's clubs. Students belong to organizations from Save the Whales to Save the Children; from the Sierra Club to the ski club. Sororities, fraternities, religious organizations, and athletic clubs abound on many campuses.

You can usually tell a lot about a person by the kind of group they belong to. Some of your listeners belong to the National Rifle Association? Most likely subjects such as gun control would be of interest. People belong to the Crusade for Christ? Prayer in school would be a good topic. Members of Green Peace? Environmental issues would be in order. People belong to the National Organization for Women? Feminist issues would be appealing. Whether speaking to this class, or an audience out-

side, club membership always provides a excellent clue of listener's interests and opinions.

Age, gender, religion, sociocultural background, and group membership all are important facts to consider. There are others as well—education, occupation, geographic residence, economic position, intelligence, and social status just to name a few. In fact all characteristics can be reviewed in a demographic analysis. For your classroom presentations you could also consider academic major, year in school, college living arrangements, co-curricular activities, and future educational plans.

A demographic analysis lets you know what listeners' are—but it doesn't tell you what they think. That's why your next step should be to examine the psychology of your audience.

HOW LISTENERS THINK

Many of the forces which shape your audience's behavior come from within listeners themselves. These psychological factors are especially important in persuasion. However, they're also of note when trying to arouse interest in presentations whose purpose is informative or entertaining. Let's begin by examining motivation.

Motivation

Motivation is the drive that makes people want to reach a certain goal. According to psychologist Abraham Maslow, there are five hierarchical needs which motivate behavior. Here we'll touch on each.[11]

1. What are your listeners' psychological needs?

These include the primary need for survival and satisfaction. When these needs are aroused, they can dominate behavior. Want to appeal to this basic need? Tell listeners how your content will improve their physical well-being or sexual attraction.

2. What are your listeners' safety and security needs?

These second level needs operate on fear. All listeners want protection and security. You appeal to this need by establishing a fear (*"Many drivers are killed because they don't wear seat belts"*) and then offering a solution (*"so buckle up"*).

3. What are your listeners' belongingness needs?

This need marks the beginning of the higher level needs on the hierarchy—moving beyond mere survival and safety. Want to appeal to this need? Tell listeners to get on the "bandwagon" and join everyone else. Most people don't like to be left out in the cold. An appeal like *"everyone else is saying 'no' to drugs, so why don't you"* works here.

4. What are your listeners' esteem needs?

Everyone wants to feel proud and successful. You can appeal to these needs by explaining how your content will advance people in their lives or career. Many times speakers begin with a positive comment (*"You live in a great neighborhood"*) and then deliver their appeal (*"so help clean up litter in the streets"*).

5. What are your listeners' self-actualization needs?

These are the highest needs on the hierarchy and appeal to achievement for its own sake. Tell listeners how they can expand their horizons or become more complete human beings by appealing to these needs. For instance: *"Take World Cultures so you can understand people from around the world"* would encourage listeners to strive for self-growth.

Attitudes, Values, and Beliefs

Listeners make judgments about what they hear based on what they already know and believe. That's because most people are egocentric and pay closer attention to messages that affect their own attitudes, their own beliefs, and their own values. And what are attitudes, beliefs, and values? They're characteristics in our human consciousness which dictate how we think and feel. Although closely related, they exist in the human mind like the layers of an onion. At the innermost level are values, with beliefs in the middle, and attitudes closest to the surface.

An **attitude** includes what you know or think about a subject, whether you like or dislike it, and how you act or intend to act toward it. Most people behave in a certain way because of an attitude. For example, if most of your listeners have an attitude that all laws must be obeyed, you'll have a tough time persuading them that people who smoke marijuana shouldn't be prosecuted. On the other hand,

if most listeners have an attitude that agrees with your position, all you need do is confirm that which they already believe. There are two things you should especially consider when weighing the attitude of your listeners: what's their attitude toward the speaker, and what's their attitude toward the topic. Here's a review of each:

Attitude Toward the Speaker

What do your listeners think of you? Do they see you as an expert or someone with only superficial knowledge about your subject? You can usually offset a negative audience attitude by establishing your credibility right at the start. Tell listeners why they can trust you and expect to get reliable information. This isn't bragging—it's a way of showing people your serious about your subject. When one student spoke about physical exercise, for example, he explained that he'd worked in a health club for three years. Thus, his audience knew he was somewhat knowledgeable about this topic. Even if you're not an expert, you can enhance your credibility by explaining how you got your information. A student accomplished this for a discussion on alcoholism. She mentioned that she'd read several articles and talked to two counselors to learn more about her subject.

Attitude Toward the Topic

What do listener's think about your subject? Do they find it interesting or a total bore? One speaker told students why they should invest in IRA's to plan for their retirement. Her audience remained unmoved. As one listener said, *"Retirement is a long time away for me."* Students want to hear about immediate benefits, not something forty years down the road. It's also important to find out if listeners agree or disagree with your position. A student named Ken, for instance, believed all highways in sparsely populated western states should have unlimited speed limits. Before his speech he found that only five listeners agreed with him, and eighteen people either were neutral or thought he was wrong. Ken realized he couldn't convince all his listeners, so he set out to modify their views. As one person commented, *"He made several good points, and got me thinking about the subject."* Of course if your listeners already agree with you, it's important to reinforce their views. That's why it's helpful to know what your listeners believe.

A **belief** is an underlying conviction about the truth or correctiveness of something. Oftentimes beliefs are based on cultural training. For instance, many listeners might believe that people shouldn't live together before marriage. If tackling this subject you'll have to first discuss how that belief can be changed or altered.

A **value** is a deeply rooted belief about a concept's inherent worth or worthiness. According to experts, our important social attitudes are anchored in values. This means when targeting listeners it's best to concentrate on values. This is because values are small in number and are more likely to be shared by many people. Politicians often focus on values. They'll talk about family, freedom, nationalism, and the like.[12]

How do you determine your listener's attitudes, beliefs, and values? Find out what opinions they have about controversial issues; see what organizations they belong to; listen to their comments in class. Normally you can make some pretty accurate inferences by keeping your ears and eyes open. Often by knowing one attitude you can make some safe assumptions about others. Do listeners support college sports? If they do the chances are they also support other co-curricular activities. Do they belong to environmental organizations? If so issues about the ecology or wildlife would be of interest. Lots of business majors in your audience? They probably believe in capitalism and free enterprise. Knowing your listener's belief system is not only helpful in choosing a topic, it's also useful when figuring out what to say.

If addressing an audience with a different belief system than your own, you'll need to do five things. Establish a positive first impression (*"I've thoroughly researched my topic"*); don't use threats (*"I think we all can benefit from this speech"*); use logic and rational appeals (*"Here's evidence to support my view"*); limit what you hope to accomplish (*"You may not agree with me, but hopefully you'll see there's another side"*); and provide opposing arguments (*"The other side of this issue is . . ."*).[13]

Here's how one student put this into practice:

Sarah Morgan discussed why she believed we should have prayer in school. She realized many listeners disagreed with her position, so Sarah first mentioned how everyone wanted what's best for children. Next she discussed how no one was suggesting students be forced to pray. Third, she cited surveys and quoted from educators and jurists to support her view. Fourth, she reminded her audience that they didn't have to agree, just think about the other side of this issue. And last, she mentioned that people opposed to prayer in school thought it mixed church and state, but this didn't have to be the case. While many listeners still disagreed with Sarah, most were impressed with her presentation.

Examining the thinking of your listeners completes the second step in audience analysis. The last step is to assess the communication environment.

ANALYSIS OF THE COMMUNICATION ENVIRONMENT

It's important to be sensitive to the environment of your message. These elements include the physical setting, size of your audience, and context of surrounding events.

Physical Setting

Karen Robinson was delighted when she was invited to tell a community club about her recent trip to Egypt. Karen carefully organized her slides and wrote down what she would read as each slide flashed on the screen. Arriving for the speech, Karen discovered the club met in an old grange hall. Looking to plug in her slide projector, she suddenly noticed there were no electrical outlets. Realizing she'd have to read her notes without slides, Karen was dismayed to find there was no podium. She ended up reading her notes to the audience while awkwardly shuffling papers from one hand to the other.

What happened to Karen? She failed to check out the physical setting of her speech beforehand. Don't make the same mistake. When invited to speak, be direct and ask questions of the person who booked the speech. If possible, visit the room yourself a few days in advance, or else arrive early on the day of your presentation and give it a quick inspection. Is the room too hot or too cold? See about adjusting the thermostat. How are the seats arranged? Move them so everyone has a good view. Is there a microphone? Test it out in advance. In short, do everything you can to make the environment of your presentation as comfortable as possible.

Sometimes there are things which are simply beyond your control. Maybe the temperature can't be adjusted, the room is too small, or the lights can't be dimmed. When this happens work harder to make your presentation even more exciting. The key is to be adaptable. If listeners see you're making every effort to be accommodating, they'll be more willing to overlook annoying discomforts.

Size of Your Audience

Most speech classes have relatively small audiences—probably from fifteen to twenty-five people. This is an ideal size for perfecting your skills as a communicator. In other situations, however, it's possible you'll have audiences in the hundreds, thousands, or—if appearing on radio or television—millions. Some speakers prefer larger audiences, while others like the informality of a smaller group.

When considering the environment of a presentation calculate the size of your audience. If not sure, ask someone in the know. The unfortunate speaker is recalled who brought handouts for 75 people, only to find he'd be addressing an audience of 300. It's good to adjust to the number of listeners. If faced with a small audience in a large room, ask listeners to move toward the front. This way you can sound more personal.

Context of Surrounding Events

Things that happened in the recent past can affect the outcome of a presentation. Frequently this involves previous speakers. Imagine, for example, that the speech preceding yours discusses a controversial subject which leaves the audience divided, and perhaps even hostile. Before presenting your speech you'll need to dissipate some of those negative feelings. At other times the speaker before you might present a convincing opposing argument on the very issue you intend to address. What can you do? Don't ignore the earlier speaker. Instead say, *"Many people feel that way, but here's the other side of the story."* This way you'll ease the audience into your content.

Other events can also have influence. What's the weather like? What's going on in the news? What happened earlier in the day? Listener's reactions and moods are shaped by things happening around them. Good speakers use this to their advantage. Arriving late for a campaign speech in 1988 due to a snowstorm, presidential candidate Michael Dukakis said, *"I'd heard of the blizzard of '88, but I thought it happened in 1888, not 1988."* His audience quickly got over his being late. Similar references to surrounding events gives a presentation a touch of the immediate.

COLLECTING INFORMATION ABOUT YOUR LISTENERS

You probably already know quite a bit about your classmates. How do you learn more? Through observation, interviews, and questionnaires. Here's how you can use each of these methods to learn about your listeners.[14]

Observation

Probably the easiest way to collect information is through personal observation. This is especially easy in a speech class, since most classmates reveal things about themselves in speeches and conversations. One student even integrated her observations into the content of her speech:

Tonya Green delivered a speech on study habits. In her speech she said, *"Before class today I observed ten people talking, five daydreaming, three looking out the window, and only two bothering to review their notes."*

Experienced communicators frequently use observation. Before a presentation they'll listen to conversations and comments among their listeners. There is, however, one danger of using observation—it's totally subjective. Your impressions could be 100 percent correct, or they could be 100 percent wrong. A more exact way of collecting information is to use an interview.

Interviewing

An information-gathering interview, discussed in Chapter 10, is an excellent way to learn about an audience. A carefully planned series of interviews can give you information that would be difficult to find any other way. In fact, interviewing each member of the class would be the most thorough way of doing an audience analysis. Such thorough interviewing is seldom done, however. It's simply unrealistic in terms of time and energy. But if you do decide to use the interview, prepare a few short questions and ask them of three or four people seated in different parts of the room. This way you'll get a good cross-section of opinion.

Questionnaires

A good questionnaire can elicit a great deal of useful information in a short space of time. While preparing and submitting a list of questions may seem easy, it's really a specialized skill beyond the scope of this class. By following these suggestions, however, you'll be able to develop a questionnaire that will be sufficient for the purpose of analyzing listeners.[15]

There are three types of questionnaire questions: forced-choice, scale items, and open-response questions.

Forced-choice questions require a respondent to select an answer from two or more alternatives. For example:

Do you believe in capital punishment?
____ Yes
____ No
____ Unsure

Would you be willing to execute someone?
____ Yes
____ No
____ Unsure

Forced-choice questions are easy to write and tabulate. Just add up the yes'es and no's, figure the percentage, and you have your statistic.

Scale items allow respondents a greater range for their responses. These items are especially useful for showing the in-depth commitment or conviction of listeners. For example:

Do you agree that capital punishment is legalized murder?

/	/	/	/	/
Strongly Agree	Somewhat Agree	Indifferent	Somewhat Disagree	Strongly Disagree

To what extent do you believe capital punishment is a deterrent to crime?

/	/	/	/	/
Definitely is a deterrent	Probably is a deterrent	Undecided	Probably is not a deterrent	Definitely is not a deterrent

When using scale items be careful not to show an obvious bias. If all your questions are worded so that capital punishment sounds wrong, you're likely to tilt your responses in one direction. You can reduce bias by balancing your questions—word half your questions favoring each side of an issue.

In some cases you might want to get more detail. **Open-response questions** give listeners maximum latitude for their answers. For example:

What's your view of capital punishment?
Do you think teenagers who commit murder should receive the death penalty?

One problem with open-response questions is that they invite off-topic and irrelevant answers. In order to keep answers relatively short you can leave a desired number of lines after each question.

Because each type of question has its own advantages and disadvantages, a well-designed questionnaire will include all three types. The illustration on the next page shows a questionnaire distributed before a classroom speech on the need for people to keep a vial of life in their refrigerators at home (a sealed tube containing a family's medical history in case of emergency). By using each type of question the student, Brenda Phillips, discovered what her listeners knew about the vial of life, if they'd be interested in hearing about it, and what their attitudes were toward the subject. Here's what Brenda learned from each question:

1. *Two-thirds of the class didn't know what a vial of life was. Brenda would need to explain the vial of life clearly at the start of her speech.*
2. *Five students knew someone who kept a vial of life in their home. Half the class wasn't sure. Indicated to Brenda that there was little personal involvement with issue.*
3. *Nearly half the class had experienced an ambulance being called to their homes. This signaled Brenda that listeners had some awareness of what happens in a medical emergency. Brenda can appeal to this in speech.*
4. *Audience was mixed concerning whether medical emergency workers had enough information about a patient. Half felt they had enough, and half felt they didn't. This indicated to Brenda that she'd have to consider both sides when discussing this point.*
5. *Almost 90 percent thought medical care workers would look for a vial of life in an emergency. This told Brenda that most listeners had a positive attitude toward her subject.*
6. *Every listener thought that having a medical history in the home was a good idea. But some doubted its practicality. Several people felt that people wouldn't keep it up to date. Two people suggested that people might make mistakes and put down incorrect information that could do them harm in an emergency. Brenda realized she'd have to deal with this question in speech.*

The questionnaire gave Brenda a lot of useful information that she wouldn't have been able to get any other way. Want to use a questionnaire? Review our discussion in Chapter 10, and keep the following things in mind:

1. Carefully prepare a questionnaire that will provide all the information you need.
2. Word your questions as clearly as you can.
3. Use all three types of questions—forced-choice, scale items, and open-response.
4. Keep you questionnaire short and to the point.
5. Don't reveal the names of individual respondents.

INTRODUCTION REASSURES
RESPONDENT

Please answer each question as honestly as possible. To protect your confidentiality, do not write your name on this form. Thank you for your participation.

FORCED-CHOICE QUESTIONS
ESTABLISH LISTENER'S
INTEREST IN ISSUE

1. Do you know what a Vial of Life is?

___ Yes
___ No
___ Not Sure

PINPOINTS LISTENER'S
DIRECT INVOLVEMENT WITH
SUBJECT

2. Do you know anyone who has a Vial of Life in their home?

___ Yes
___ No
___ Not Sure

3. Has an ambulance ever been called to your home in an emergency?

___ Yes
___ No
___ Not Sure

SCALE ITEMS PROVIDE
GREATER DETAIL ABOUT
LISTENER'S VIEW OF ISSUE;
REVEALS ATTITUDE TOWARD
SUBJECT

4. Do you agree that emergency medical care workers normally have enough information about a patient?

Strongly Agree	Somewhat Agree	Not Sure	Somewhat Disagree	Strongly Disagree

5. Do you believe most emergency medical care personnel would bother looking for a Vial of Life in an emergency?

Definitely Would	Probably Would	Not Sure	Probably Would Not	Definitely Would Not

OPEN-RESPONSE QUESTION
PROVIDES INFORMATION
AND DETAIL; WILL HELP IN
DEVELOPMENT OF SPEECH

6. Would having a thorough medical history in every home save lives? How practical an idea do you think it is?

_____

_____

_____

ADAPTING TO YOUR LISTENERS

A thorough audience analysis tells a lot. You'll know listener's characteristics, interests, knowledge, and attitudes. This information gives you a clear mental picture of your audience. But all this material is of little value unless you put it to work.

Often beginning communicators overlook this most basic point. They'll go through the motions of learning about their audience, only to fail to utilize that which they've learned. Good speakers don't make that mistake. Think back to David Toma. Whether speaking to students or parents he used examples, language, and appeals that were designed especially for that group of listeners. That's what effective communication is all about—adapting a message to fit an audience.

Sometimes this is hard to do. You might be so wrapped up in your subject that you forget everyone else isn't as into it as you are. How do you overcome this? By becoming one with your listeners. Think like them; feel like them; react like them. This means merging your thoughts and interests with those of your listeners. Anticipate how they'll respond to each point in your message. Will it be understandable? Will it be interesting? Will it be provocative? Will it run counter to their beliefs? By putting yourself in the place of your listeners you'll be able to see your presentation as they'll see it.

Here's how one student put this into practice:

As an agricultural major Judy Woods decided she'd present an informative speech on apples. By doing an audience analysis she learned that most of her listeners didn't know a Rome from a Jonathan and though a McIntosh was a computer, not something to eat.

Judy realized she'd have to use basic terms and examples to explain her subject. Judy concentrated on the nutritional value of apples telling how they provided energy, aided digestion, and helped the body to resist infections.

Judy rehearsed until she was satisfied her speech would meet the expectations and interests of her audience She then asked a couple of friends who were not agricultural majors to listen in. Every time she said something that wasn't clear she asked them to stop her. Judy was stopped three times, and each time clarified the point. By the time she was done practicing Judy was confident she had an interesting and understandable speech for her audience.

Judy did it, so can you. With effort and practice, you'll soon be able to successfully fit every message to every listener.

CHAPTER SUMMARY

Good communicators are listener-minded. Communicators address three types of audiences: passerby, voluntary, and captive. Speech classes are considered captive audiences. Classroom audiences are 'real' audiences and should be analyzed in terms of their interests, knowledge, and expectations.

Communicators should begin with a demographic analysis. Demographics are the observable traits of a group. These include things like age, gender, religion, sociocultural background, group membership and so on.

A second step is to examine the thinking of listeners. Many of the forces which shape listener's responses come from within listeners themselves. The first of these is motivation. Motivation is the drive that makes people want to reach a certain goal. The second is attitude. An attitude is what someone thinks, likes, and feels about a subject. The third are beliefs and values. While beliefs are rooted in cultural upbringing, most speakers concentrate on values because they're fewer in number and likely to be shared by many listeners.

A third step is to examine the environment of the message. Considerations include physical setting, size of the audience, surrounding events and the like.

You can collect information about an audience through observation, interviews, and questionnaires. When using questionnaires you can ask forced-choice, scale items, and open-response questions. Once you've collected all your information, you should adapt it to fit your listeners.

EXERCISES FOR REVIEW

1. Plan that you're going to present a five minute oral report on any topic of your choice. Fill out the blank audience analysis form at the end of this chapter for the presentation. Hand it in to your instructor.

2. Choose a magazine like *Glamour, Ms., Popular Photography, Sports Illustrated,* or *Seventeen.* Look through the pages of the magazine and examine the advertisements. Write a short paper considering the following: For whom are the ads intended? What would be the demographics of the average reader? Why would the advertised product choose to advertise in this particular periodical?

3. Examine this classroom. What are its advantages and disadvantages as a place for communicating? Write a 200 word paper outlining your observations.

4. Following are listed 4 sample speech topics, and 2 hypothetical types of audiences to whom the speech might be delivered. Pick any two of the examples and write a short paper on how you would present your message for each type of audience.

   A. Raising the maximum speed limit to 65 mph
      audience #1: 50% don't drive, 50% do drive
      audience #2: 10% don't drive, 90% do drive

   B. How to make a dress
      audience #1: 80% male, 20% female
      audience #2: 20% male, 80% female

   C. Buying a personal home computer
      audience #1: 30% data processing majors, 40% business majors, 20% engineering majors, 10% liberal arts majors
      audience #2: 30% art majors, 50% English majors, 20% education majors

   D. Disciplining your teenager
      audience #1: 80% 18 to 25 years old, 20% 25 and over
      audience #2: 20% 18 to 25 years old, 80% 25 and over

5. Meet with a group of 4 or 5 classmates. Prepare several typical questions for an interview and questionnaire that you might use for a future assignment. Discuss your questions with the group. How are the questions worded? Are they clear? Do they provide the information you need? Who would be the best people in class to use as interviewees to give you a barometer of the group's feelings, attitudes, and beliefs? How can your questions be improved? Revise your questions as needed.

NOTES

1. These observations and quotations are collected from several different articles written after David Toma addressed students and parents at Shawnee High School in Medford, New Jersey. They can be found in the *Courier Post*, Cherry Hill, N.J., February 10, 1988, pp.6–8.

2. How audience analysis is important in presidential debates is discussed in David L. Vancil and Sue D. Pendell, "Winning Presidential Debates: An Analysis of Criteria Influencing Audience Response," *Western Journal of Speech Communication* (Winter 1984), pp. 62–74.

3. Estimating what listeners think of you as a speaker tells you a lot about how you can most effectively communicate your message. See Martin J. Medhurst, "Resistance, Conservatism, and Theory Building: A Cautionary Note," *The Western Journal of Speech Communication* (Spring 1985), pp. 103–115. This essay focuses on resistance to a message based on political conservatism.

4. Nigel Nicolson, *Napoleon 1812*, Harper & Row, New York, 1985, p. 177.

5. Mary John Smith, "Contingency Rules Theory, Context, and Compliance Behaviors," *Human Communication Research* 10 (Summer 1984), pp. 489–512.

6. Theorists suggest many different types of audiences. Of course, all types somewhat overlap. For instance a listener could be "passerby" because they stop by chance, but "voluntary" because they elect to stay.

7. These generalizations are gleaned from a survey of 1,000 college students from 104 different campuses. See Anthony M. Casar and Philip Lerman, *USA Today*, "Tracking Tomorrow's Trends," Kansas City, Mo., Andrews, McMeel and Parker, 1986, pp. 150–183.

8. For two interesting discussions of demographics see Carl H. Botan and Lawrence R. Frey, "Do Workers Trust Labor Unions and Their Messages?" *Communication Monographs* 50 (September 1983), pp. 233–244 and James Atlas, "Beyond Demographics," *The Atlantic Monthly* (October 1984), pp. 49–58.

9. This research is gleaned from several sources. For instance see Gwen Asburn and Alice Gordon, "Features of Simplified Register in Speech to Elderly Conversationalists," *International Journal of Psycholinguistics* 8:3 (1981), pp. 7–31 and William J. McGuire, "Attitudes and Attitude Change," in *The Handbook of Social Psychology* 11, ed. Gardner Lindzey and Elliot Aronson, Random House, New York, 1985, pp. 287–288. Interestingly, people are most susceptible to persuasion between the ages of 9 and 12.

10. A helpful discussion of culture in relationship to communication can be found in Brent D. Ruben, *Communication and Human Behavior*, MacMillian, New York, 1988, pp. 381–416.

11. Abraham H. Maslow, "A Theory of Human Motivation," *Motivation and Personality*, 2nd ed., Harper, New York, 1970.

12. Randall K. Stutman and Sara E. Newell, "Beliefs Versus Values: Salient Beliefs in Designing a Persuasive Message," *Western Journal of Speech Communication* 48 (Fall 1984), pp. 362–372. For an interesting example of how values are used in the analysis of political speeches, see Steve Goldzwig, "James Watt's Subversion of Values: An Analysis of Rhetorical Failure," *Southern Speech Communication Journal* 50 (Summer 1985), pp. 305–326 and Henry Z. Scheele, "Ronald Reagan's 1980 Acceptance Address: A Focus on American Values," *Western Journal of Speech Communication* 48 (Fall 1984), pp. 51–61.

13. This is termed the co-active approach and can be found in Herbert W. Simons, *Persuasion: Understanding, Practice, and Analysis*, Addison-Wesley, Reading, Mass., 1976, pp. 134–138.

14. James W. Gibson and Michael S. Hanna, *Audience Analysis: A Programmed Approach to Receiver Behavior*, Prentice-Hall, Englewood Cliffs, N.J., 1976, pp. 25–26.

15. To learn more about surveying groups and preparing and using questionnaires, see Fred N. Kerlinger, *Scientific Behavioral Research: A Conceptual Primer*, Holt, Rinehart and Winston, New York, 1979.

Voice-prints as a Form of Identification

Most people have heard of fingerprints as a method of identifying someone, but, the majority of people have probably not heard of voice-prints as a form of identification. Since each person has a very distinctive vocal tone there is a method of classifying every individual's unique voice. Vocal differences are only able to be discerned when they are transformed from an audible to a visual form. Bell Laboratories has developed an instrument that records the human voice and prints out a spectrogram which reveals the individual identity of the vocal sound for each person.

Spectrograms show the frequency of sounds, the time of the sound, and the intensity of the voice. Through this method each person has a "print" of his or her particular voice which is unlike that of anyone else's. Several recent court cases have used voice-prints as a form of identification for people convicted of crimes. When this form of evidence has been challenged in the higher courts, the courts have upheld voice-prints as an admissible form of legal evidence for identification. For example, the United States v. Albert Raymond and Roland Addison and the United States District Court Criminal Number 800–71, February 2, 1972.

Name _____ Course _____

Audience Analysis

This is a typical audience analysis form filled out by one student:

General Purpose *TO INFORM*

Specific Purpose *TO INFORM MY AUDIENCE ABOUT PURCHASING A COMPUTER*

Central Idea *WHEN BUYING A COMPUTER SHOP AROUND AND LOOK AT KNOWN BRANDS*

Age Range *18-45* Gender *10 MALE 114 FEMALE* Religion *VARIED*

Grp. Membership *5 IN COMPUTER CLUB* Sociocultural Bkgd. *VARIED- SEVERAL ASIAN STUDENTS*

Interest in Subject *MOST WANT TO KNOW MORE ABOUT COMPUTERS*

Knowledge about Subject *MOSTLY LIMITED ; FEW KNOW A LOT*

Audience Expectation *TO BE INFORMED - CLASS SPEECH*

Attitude toward Speaker *MUST ESTABLISH CREDIBILITY*

Attitude toward Topic *NO STRONG ATTITUDES PRO OR CON*

Occasion *CLASS* Time *10 AM*

Time Limit *5 MIN.* Assignment *INFORM SPEECH*

Room Size *30 SEATS* Audience Size *24 STUDENTS*

AV Capabilities *WON'T NEED*

Seating *MOVABLE SEATS* Podium *YES*

Number of Other Speakers and topics *5 — VARIED TOPICS*

Other Considerations *MAY USE A CHART. NEED CLIPS TO ATTACH TO CHALKBOARD*

Audience Analysis Form

Fill this form out for an upcoming assignment.

Name _____ Course _____

Assignment _____

General Purpose _____

Specific Purpose _____

Central Idea _____

_____

Age Range _____ Gender _____ Religion _____

Group Membership _____ Sociocultural Background _____

Interest in Subject _____

Knowledge about Subject _____

Audience Expectation _____

Attitude toward Speaker _____

Attitude toward Topic _____

Occasion _____ Time of Presentation _____

Time Limit _____ Assignment _____

Room Size _____ Audience Size _____

AV Capabilities _____

Seating _____ Podium Available _____

Number of Other Speakers _____

Possible Other Topics _____

_____

Other Considerations _____

_____

Can clothes effect your chances of being convicted in court?

Courtroom fashion can influence your chances of being convicted in a court of law. Pittsburgh attorney John Doherty said, "There's a lot they don't teach you in law school. . . . I don't want my client dressed in a way that will offend anybody. I don't want my client to dress the part of that of which he or she is accused. The jury will stereotype him." Doherty mentioned the suspected narcotics salesman who arrived for a pretrial interview wearing boots with live goldfish in the clear plastic heels— "He never did get into court with those boots."

Attorney William Manifesto says, "They are not fooled by one's dress or by how glib one is, but you should try to take away any negative attitude that is visual." "Jurors make much of things I might consider totally inconsequential or irrelevant," says attorney Stanley Greenfield. "If you can get your clients to dress in a way that's acceptable to the norm, you can't go wrong." Former public defender Sallie Radick agrees, "Clothing is critical."

Radick recalls the time that she asked a rape suspect to show her what he planned to wear during his trial. He arrived at her office wearing a smartly dressed shirt open to the waist, skin-tight pants, and high-heeled shoes. On her advice, he wore a three-piece suit into court. "He was acquitted, but he could have been convicted just on what he was wearing."

Several attorneys advise that men wear a suit that is a conservative color, white shirt, and tie. Women should dress in soft-fitting outfits, dresses, pastel shades, and with a conservative look. As attorney Radick states, "You don't want to look too flashy or too pretty. You just want to pass muster." "I often thought Jean Harris might have been acquitted if she'd looked more remorseful during her trial." Radick says of the convicted diet doctor killer. "But she always looked just perfect. Had she toned it down, I really think there would have been a difference."

Lester G. Nauhaus represents many defendants as director of the Pittsburgh area public defender office. He advises clients to "wear a coat and tie, shave, get a haircut and don't chew gum." "Chewing gum to me shows a lack of seriousness." But still, there are those people who wear what they want to anyway. Nauhaus recalls one man who, charged with a violent crime, showed up in court wearing a T-shirt which, in bright, bold letters, declared to the world: "I'm a maniac." Needless to say, he was convicted.

12

Preparing
a Speech

When we have a clear, specific purpose we will have an interesting presentation for our audience.

QUESTIONS FOR RETENTION

Before reading this chapter, ask yourself the following questions:

1. How can I prepare a speech in ten simple steps?
2. How can I deliver a speech in five simple steps?
3. How can I organize a speech?

D Day's fast approaching! *"D day,"* you wonder, *"What's that?"* D day stands for Delivery Day—the day you'll be presenting your first speech. Maybe it's in two days, or maybe it's in two weeks, but sooner or later it's bound to happen. You might be asked to introduce yourself or someone else; to inform about something you know or to demonstrate how something works; to tell an entertaining story or to convince people to take a stand. But whatever type of speech you present, speaking in front of a group is as much a thrill as it is a challenge.

While you've probably only been in this class for a few weeks, you've been preparing for this speech for a very long time. Good speakers recognize that all their experiences help to shape every speech they'll ever deliver. This is demonstrated in the often told story about British statesman Disraeli. After giving a stirring address in the House of Commons a woman stopped him and said, *"I was entranced by your talk. It's been on my mind all day."* *"Madam,"* replied Disraeli, *"It's been on my mind all my life."* Just like Disraeli, you possess a wealth of experiences, knowledge, and common sense which has well prepared you for this and every other speech you'll ever present.[1]

"Fine," you say, *"I've had a lot of experiences, I know some things, and I'm loaded with common sense, but it's still not going to be easy speaking in front of a group of people!"* If you think your job might be difficult, consider what it was like for Helen Keller:

Helen Keller lost both her sight and hearing while just a baby. She knew no sounds; she knew no words. Being deaf and blind in the 1880's one would think she could never learn to effectively communicate with others. Yet, Helen Keller became a legend in her own time. With the help of a caring teacher she learned to see though blind; to hear though deaf.

Working year after year Helen learned each letter, each syllable, and each word only through the sense of touch. She learned speech by placing her finger on the speaker's lips. To form sounds she used her hand to follow the movement of her teacher's throat, lips, and tongue. Eventually Helen was not only able to speak English, but French and German as well.

After graduating from Radcliffe Helen began to speak on behalf of the handicapped. For the next 60 years Helen Keller spoke to thousands of audiences around the world, touching everyone with her message. She held her own with the likes of Oliver Wendell Holmes and Mark Twain. She met all the Presidents from Teddy Roosevelt to Lyndon Johnson. Though deaf and blind, Helen Keller overcame overwhelming handicaps to inspire audiences everywhere.

Imagine what it must have been like for Helen Keller to get up and deliver that very first speech? Yet she did, and has served as an inspiration to others ever since. Like Helen Keller, you too can become a successful speaker. This first speech is only a start—through effort and practice you'll feel your ease and confidence grow every day, every class, every speech.

Of course, this chapter serves as a first step in preparing and presenting a speech. As the course unfolds your instructor will offer additional tips and advice to help you along the way. But, by following the steps presented in this chapter, you'll find that preparing your first speech isn't that difficult after all. In fact, you may find it's a lot more fun than expected.

Figure 12.1
Patrick Henry. Patrick Henry was one of the most colorful and persuasive speakers during the American Revolution. This painting by Clyde O. Deland shows his address to the Virginia House of Burgesses. (Courtesy, Bettman Archive)

TEN STEPS FOR PREPARING A SPEECH

Presented are ten steps for preparing a speech. Bear in mind, however, that speeches are seldom prepared in such a progressive order. Building a speech is a continual process of revising and reworking, of rethinking, and reshaping, of reexamining and recasting. For instance, while Step 1 is to pick a topic, you might find that after Step 4 (analyzing your audience) you'll want to go back and trim or expand your subject. Therefore, feel free to evaluate your work every step of the way. But by following these ten steps, you'll easily accomplish your purpose of putting together a clear and organized speech.

Step 1: Select A Topic

There are two types of topics you can speak about: subjects you already know something about and subjects which you'd like to know more about. Usually it's best to pick a topic that's already somewhat familiar to you. It could be a hobby of yours, a job you've had, or a place you've visited. Sometimes it's best to make a list of several promising topics and then ask yourself three questions about each one. First, is it interesting? The chances are if it's interesting to you, it will be to other as well. Second, can it be easily discussed in a speech? Some things are just too complicated or difficult to talk about. And third, will it fit your purpose? If you're supposed to introduce yourself, don't end up talking about someone else. Likewise if you're to inform your audience, stay away from controversial issues.

Once you've decided on a topic, trim it down and narrow its focus. Remember, if your speech is to be 3 to 5 minutes long, you've only got about 500 words to cover your entire subject! Therefore, it's often best to pick one particularly interesting aspect of your topic. Maybe one facet of your hobby, one part of your job, or one thing you liked about a place you visited. Keep in mind that it's better to cover one thing well, than several things superficially.

Can't think of a subject? Try looking through the card catalogue in the library, an encyclopedia, or a current magazine. Get ideas from a friend, your teacher, or a classmate. Make a list of things you've done or things you find interesting. If you really work at it, the chances are you'll find more than enough to talk about. Having a topic, you'll need to determine a purpose.

Step 2: Decide On Your Purpose

As discussed in Chapter Two, every speech has one of three purposes: to inform, to persuade, or to entertain. You might inform about yourself or how something works; persuade about how something is wrong and ought to be changed; or entertain with interesting stories and experiences you've had. An important part of planning a speech is to write down your general purpose statement: *To inform; to persuade; to entertain. This gives you the reason for your speech.*

Once you've determined your **general purpose,** you'll have to decide on the **specific purpose**—this lets you state the concrete goals of your presentation. Let's say your speech is to introduce yourself. Your purpose statement would look like this:

General Purpose: *To inform*
Specific Purpose: *To inform my audience about myself.*

On the other hand, if your speech is persuasive and you decide to tell students they should donate blood, it would resemble this:

General Purpose: *To persuade*
Specific Purpose: *To persuade my audience that they should donate blood during the campus blood drive.*

Or, if your speech is entertaining and you want to relate your experiences as a summer camp counselor, it would look like this:

General Purpose: *To entertain*
Specific Purpose: *To entertain my audience with experiences I had while working as a counselor at Camp Tomahawk.*

It's important to clarify both your general and specific purpose by writing each down as you begin to plan your speech. Remember that your topic must fit your purpose—if your purpose is informative, your topic better be as well. Once you've created your purpose statements, it's easy to form the central idea.

Step 3: Form a Central Idea

Just like every play has a plot, and every composition has a theme, every speech needs a central idea. The central idea is a single sentence which clearly states what you want to say in your speech. In order to create a central idea you must first decide on how many main points you want—usually two or three is the norm, although for a first speech some teachers might

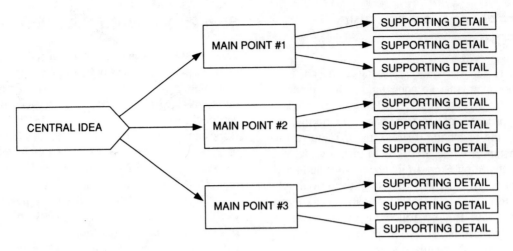

Figure 12.2
Supporting Your Main Points. A speech proceeds from the general to the specific; when supporting your main points, have enough information to back up your ideas, but not so much that your speech becomes complicated or repetitious.

ask for only one. Let's now form a central idea for each of our three examples:

General Purpose: *To inform*
Specific Purpose: *To inform my audience about myself.*
Central Idea: *I had an interesting childhood, have held many different types of jobs, and plan to be a teacher when I graduate.*

General Purpose: *To persuade*
Specific Purpose: *To persuade my audience that they should donate blood during the campus blood drive.*
Central Idea: *By donating blood students can help ease the blood shortage and save many lives.*

General Purpose: *To entertain*
Specific Purpose: *To entertain my audience with experiences I had while working as a counselor at Camp Tomahawk.*
Central Idea: *While a counselor at Camp Tomahawk I survived 3 overnight hikes, 8 parents weekends, and 129 food fights.*

See how much clearer the content of each speech is? We now know exactly what each speaker will be talking about. That's the value of writing out a central idea—it forces you to focus on precisely what it is you want to say. With some topics you won't be able to form a central idea until you've done some background reading. With others you might want to change a point here or there as you continue to develop your speech. And sometimes you'll want to reassess the central idea once you've taken a closer look at your audience.

Step 4: Analyze Your Audience

A few years ago John Glenn addressed a group of school children and described his orbital flight as America's first astronaut in space. To demonstrate how small these first efforts were, he stretched his hand over his head as far as it would go—about 80 inches—and asked the children to imagine the earth as being that big around. He then said that if the earth were that size his flight had barely scratched the surface, traveling less than one inch above ground. The children clearly got his message. But would John Glenn have spoken to a group of astronomers that way? Probably not. What he did was to gear his speech to his audience. Whenever you deliver a speech you need to do much the same thing.

Let's consider this class. Outside of knowing that everyone is in college, what else do you know about them? What are their interests? How old are they? What are their majors? What do they like to do? How many are men? How many are women? What do they know? What are their racial and ethnic backgrounds? By posing questions like these you can make your topic fit your audience.

And how can you collect such information? Talk with the person sitting next to you. Look at the rest of the people in the class. Bounce some ideas off a classmate. Then copy down as much information as you can. As you think about your classmates you'll be able to make a good guesstimate as to what they're interested in and what they'd like to hear. If your topic seems too complicated, simplify it; if it seems too basic, expand it; and if it seems too uninteresting, change it. Likewise deliver your speech with your listeners in mind. Make your examples meaningful, you vocabulary understandable, your comparisons reasonable. Audiences appreciate a speaker who has taken the time and trouble to think of them first; in other words, a speaker who's listener-centered. Once you've learned what your audience wants to hear, you're all set to begin doing some research.

Step 5: Research Your Topic

Almost any speech needs research. If you're speaking about yourself, you'll need to think back and search out important details and experiences. If you're introducing someone else, you'll need to get as much information about them as you can.

Most topics require research in the library. Look in the *Readers' Guide* for related magazine articles; check the card catalogue for a good book or two; consult a newspaper index for a helpful article; and refer to an encyclopedia or other reference book for general information. For some topics you might even want to consult people directly—professors, doctors, government representatives, or spokespersons for special interest organizations. The more information you collect, the easier it will be to support your ideas.[2]

Step 6: Support Your Ideas

Just as an artist weaves brush with oil to create beauty on canvas, a speaker weaves support with idea to create beauty of thought. Supporting ideas is one of your most important tasks as a speaker. After you've formed the central idea, you know exactly what the main thoughts of your speech are. Now your task is to support each one, making your speech come alive in the minds of listeners.

If your speech is informative you'll want to use lots of examples. Tell how one thing compares to another. Show how another thing contrasts with an idea. Illustrate your content with meaningful stories. Use statistics to support a point. Giving an introduction? Throw in some anecdotes and personal experiences. Relate a short story. Try a famous quote to tie a thought together. Build each point with enough support so it's bound to sound informative.

Persuading your audience? You'll need to use lots of proof. Use statistics to show that something is true, or that one thing is better than another. Quote or paraphrase expert testimony from people in the know. Describe a case history to give a human touch to your message. Perhaps even create an imaginary story to help sell an idea.

When entertaining your listeners stories and anecdotes work best. Include some humor—be able to laugh at yourself. Incorporate some personal experiences that everyone can relate to. Often it's helpful to think of at least one good short story for each one of your points. After all, the most entertaining speeches are those that are supported with a rich assortment of material.

Once you've determined how to support your ideas, you'll then need to put them in some workable order.

Step 7: Organize Your Speech

A speech that's logically ordered is easy for an audience to understand and follow. Basically all speeches are organized like this:

I. *Main Point number 1*
   A. *Supporting detail for point 1*
   B. *Supporting detail for point 1*
II. *Main Point number 2*
   A. *Supporting detail for point 2*
   B. *Supporting detail for point 2*
III. *Main Point number 3*
   A. *Supporting detail for point 3*
   B. *Supporting detail for point 3*

Notice that this speech has three main points—it just as easily could have two, four, or even one.

Begin organizing your speech by taking each of your main thoughts from your central idea statement and writing it out as a sentence. Try and word all points similarly, using parallel language whenever possible. For example, here's what we did for our speech about donating blood:

Central Idea: *By donating blood students can help ease the blood shortage and save many lives.*
Main Point 1: *A failure to donate blood has caused a serious blood shortage.*
Main Point 2: A commitment to donate blood will help save many lives.

Once you've got your main points worded, you'll next need to put them in some order. Do you want to use chronological order? This means organizing your speech by time. You might use this if introducing yourself, starting with your childhood and finishing with future plans. Do you want to use topical order? This means putting your ideas into categories—they could be your own, or categories that are already known. You might organize your experiences as a camp counselor this way. Or do you want to state a problem and then solve it? People giving persuasive speeches often do this.

Having determined the order, your final task is to add supporting details under each point. Let's do this for our speech on donating blood. Since it's a persuasive speech, we'll use problem-solution order.

I. *A failure to donate blood has caused a serious blood shortage.*
   A. *Blood bank reserves are at an all-time low.*
   B. *Many operations are being postponed because of the blood shortage.*
II. *A commitment to donate blood will help save many lives.*
   A. *Hospitals report that an adequate blood supply will protect people with rare types.*
   B. *By having blood on hand many serious accident victims can be saved.*

Of course, you could go into even further detail—adding more support in the form of examples, statistics, and testimony for each point.

Once you've organized your speech, the next step is to tie all your ideas together.

Step 8: Connect Your Ideas

One sure-fire way of turning off listeners is to have a speech that stutters and pauses. On the other hand, a speech that flows smoothly from one idea to the next is bound to impress everyone. By using connectives you can tie all your ideas neatly together. You'll want to use them when you go from the introduction to the body, from the body to the conclusion, and from one main point to the next. Sometimes you may even want to join two subpoints together by placing a connective between them.

There are lots of ways to connect ideas. One way is to use transitions—words, phrases, or sentences that link one point with the next. Observe in the transitional that follows how the speaker has taken one thought from each point and joined them together in one sentence:

Point #1: *Last year thousands of operations were delayed because of a shortage of blood.*
Transitional: *Not only did a blood shortage delay operations, it also may have cost some people their lives.*
Point #2: *For instance, one major hospital reported that several accident victims probably died because they had to wait too long to receive transfusions.*

See how casually this speaker shifts from one point to the next? This is what a good transition can do for you.

There are also other ways to connect your ideas in a speech. You can preview what you're about to say, preparing your audience for your next point. You can review what you've already said, giving a summary of what's been covered. You can use numbers to help signify each new idea: point 1 is , point 2 is, and so on. Or, you can highlight ideas by saying things like *"most of all"* or *"above all else."* Try and mix in several different types of connectives. Need help? Refer to the list of connectives on the next page. Once you've linked all the ideas of your speech together, you're ready to prepare its conclusion.[3]

Step 9: Prepare A Conclusion

Have you ever watched the Kentucky Derby? The winner often saves a little extra energy for the last turn, sprinting to the finish line with a final surge of power. That's what you want to do in a speech to — end with a surge, not a sputter.

When you prepare a conclusion you want to make sure it does three things: restates your central idea, summarizes your main points, and neatly wraps your speech up with a final thought. There are lots of ways to do this. One of the easiest is to refer back to the introduction—simply mirror the beginning in the end. If you open with a question, answer it in the end. If you start with a story, give its moral as you close. Another way is to end with a quotation or dramatic statement. If you're giving an entertaining speech, closing with a short story or humor is best. And if your speech is persuasive, leave your listeners on the edge of their seats with a call to action. Whatever you do, avoid ending with a bland *"that's all"* or *"that's the end."* Conclusions are far too useful to waste on obvious words.

When you've settled on a conclusion, you're finally ready to prepare the last part of your speech—the introduction.

Step 10: Prepare An Introduction

The introduction is the single most important part of your speech—that's why it pays to wait until the end to prepare it. Until you know exactly what it is you want to say, how can you possibly introduce it? A good introduction should do three things: it should gain the attention of your listeners; it should prepare them for the subject of the speech; and it should establish a relationship between you and your audience.

One way to open a speech is to make a startling statement. Saying something that shocks or surprises an audience grabs their attention right at the start. Sometimes a rhetorical question or touching quotation can do the same thing. Stories and humor are often used to introduce an entertaining speech—these tend

Table 12.1
Connectives. Connectives may be single words, phrases, sentences, or even short paragraphs. Here are some of those most frequently used.

Intent	Connectives		
To show addition	and moreover too in follows that	further again also likewise	furthermore in addition besides and then
To show cause-effect	as a result hence thereupon	accordingly otherwise thus	consequently therefore to this end
To show comparisons	similarly parallel to also	in comparison to in the same way in conjunction with	in like manner just as allied to
To show concessions	I admit it is true certainly	I concede it is evident none the less	granted no doubt but still
To draw conclusions	all in all in particular lastly as was said as was supported	as has been said in brief in simpler terms as is known the evidence says	in conclusion finally on the whole as was proven concerning
To show contrasts	in spite of nevertheless granted	on the other hand however notwithstanding	despite this none the less even so
To show location	adjacent to above nearby	elsewhere on the other side below	farther on opposite to nearly
Signposts	first finally previously anterior to this	second lastly during this time as just mentioned	third next the first stage following
Spotlights	more so moreover in particular most of all	consequently most importantly above all the top thing	accordingly especially even more so above all else
To summarize	therefore finally to say as we have seen in conclusion	to conclude on the whole up to this point let me restate	to sum up in summary in short last
Ancillary connectives	and or last thereby basically on the contrary	also nor besides primarily for example fundamentally	too but in addition for instance to be sure regardless of

to pull listeners right into your content. Whatever type of introduction you elect to use, make sure it previews your topic and gives the audience an incentive to listen to the rest of your content. But above all else, make sure your introduction is original. Stay away from trite comments like, *"It's a pleasure to speak to you today"* or *"To start, let me say."* Just as every speech should be special, so should every introduction.

How long should your introduction be? The rule is to keep it short, sweet, and to the point. No more than half a dozen sentences at most. One famous story tells of a man introducing his speech while speaking to the student body of Yale. The speaker painstakingly took every letter in the word Yale, and spent 15 minutes explaining what each one meant—Y stood for youth, A for ambition, L for loyalty, and E for enthusiasm. Finally, as he was about to get into the body of his speech, one student turned to another and said, *"I'm glad we don't go the Massachusetts Institute of Technology!"* Remember the lesson learned from the speaker at Yale; the best introduction, is one that gets straight to the point.

FIVE STEPS FOR DELIVERING A SPEECH

Having prepared your content, you'll need to get it delivered. Actually by carefully planning your speech, you've made your job of presenting it that much

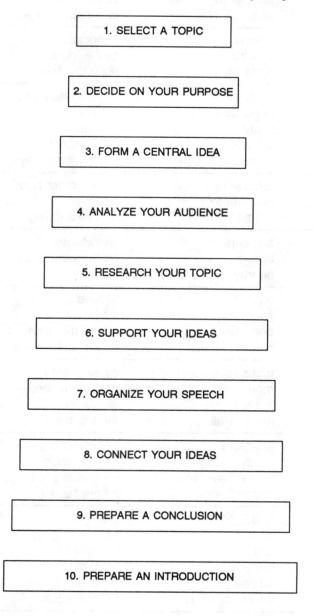

1. SELECT A TOPIC

2. DECIDE ON YOUR PURPOSE

3. FORM A CENTRAL IDEA

4. ANALYZE YOUR AUDIENCE

5. RESEARCH YOUR TOPIC

6. SUPPORT YOUR IDEAS

7. ORGANIZE YOUR SPEECH

8. CONNECT YOUR IDEAS

9. PREPARE A CONCLUSION

10. PREPARE AN INTRODUCTION

Figure 12.3
Ten Steps for Preparing a Speech.

easier. We'll now review the five steps which can take your speech from the drawing board to the podium.

Step 1: Create a Speaking Outline

Writer Eleanor Dienstag calls an outline a detailed road map to your original points. And in many ways that's exactly what it is—an outline forces you to examine the logic of your thinking and the content of your message. Do you have ample support for each idea? Does every point relate back to your central idea? Do you move smoothly from one point to the next? Do you give special attention to your most important ideas? And do you thoroughly cover your subject? By putting your speech in outline form, you'll be able to answer each of these questions—for an outline allows you to see your speech has a whole, rather than as a collection of parts.

The first thing you'll want to do is prepare a working outline. Write out your purpose statements and central idea, sketch in an introduction, write in each point with supporting detail, tie in all connecting devices, and put in a solid conclusion. Make sure to write all your ideas down as complete sentences. This helps to crystalize everything you want to say. It's also a good idea to label each part of your speech: introduction, body, connectives, conclusion.

Your next step is to prepare a speaking outline. Since you want this outline to be "speaker-friendly," use short phrases and key works that will jog your memory—if you use sentences you'll end up reading too much. The only sentences you'll want to write out are the introduction, conclusion, connectives, and—if used, quotations. As you practice with this outline add in some cues where appropriate. Cues are reminders to help as you're speaking—*"slow down," "pause," "speak up,"* and so forth. It's best to transfer this outline to a series of note cards—cards are easier to handle and refer to during a speech. Write on only one side of the card, use large letters, and double space.

Having put your ideas in order, you'll next need to think about how you'll get them across.

Step 2: Word Your Speech

Words in a speech do amazing things. They let listeners see your content, feel its emotion, and understand its compassion. Accomplished speakers let words paint colorful, vivid images in the minds of their listeners. In his 1961 Inaugural Address, President Kennedy wanted to make the point that the United States and Soviet Union could reduce suspicion through mutual cooperation. But he didn't phrase it that way. He said, *"If a beachhead of cooperation can push back the jungle of suspicion."* The result? Millions of people not only heard his words, they saw what he meant.

Creating a speech means thinking more with your tongue than your pen. Use short sentences that have a bite. Mark Twain once advised writers to strike out every third word. *"You have no idea what vigor adds to style,"* he said. Involve listeners by using pronouns like *"we," "you,"* and *"us."* Use an active voice—saying *"I think"* rather than *"It is thought."* Throw in contractions—*"isn't," "we're"* —they sound more personal. Stay away from complicated jargon that confuses. Be language-sensitive— avoid using sexist, ethnic, or racial slurs. Don't stereotype people—all construction workers are not men and all secretaries are not women, everyone doesn't want to be married, and disabled people aren't any different than anyone else. In short, word your speech with the three "B's" in mind: be clear; be sensitive; be conversational.

Step 3: Work On Your Voice

Your voice is a marvelous instrument. It can move people to happiness; it can bring them to despair; it can foster contentment; it can create unrest. Few people are blessed with melodic voices that are music to the ear. Most of us have to work with the ordinary. But through work and practice, any voice can be used to make even the simplest speech sound truly extraordinary.

Your first responsibility is to speak up. Nothing is worse than listening to a speaker you have to strain

Figure 12.4
Always use the proper volume when speaking to an audience.

to hear. Speak from the bottom half of your register—it sounds more forceful. You also want to speak at a rate that's brisk, yet easy to follow. Clock yourself while practicing so your rate is about 120 to 190 words per minute. Speak fast enough so your speech keeps moving, slow enough to be understood. Try to articulate all sounds, making sure you know how to pronounce something before you say it. Build in vocal variety—vary your rate and your volume; use a mix of pausing and pacing that gives an interesting mix to your delivery. Lastly, sound enthusiastic. An animated voice sparks everyone's attention.

Once you've worked on your voice, you're ready to start perfecting the rest of your delivery.

Step 4: Perfect Your Delivery

Don't make the same mistake as the new minister in a small town. Finding only two people at his first service, he delivered his sermon calmly, not putting any feeling or energy into his performance. When he was done, he asked an old farmer in the congregation what he thought: *"Wal, if I had a wagon-load of hay and went out to feed a herd of cattle and found only two cows. . . I sure wouldn't turn around and say they didn't need a full feedin."*

The old farmer reminds us of an important point: never deliver a speech halfheartedly—put every bit of energy you can muster into your performance. How do you speak with energy and confidence? First, use your face to express information. Don't be afraid to smile—research shows it takes a lot more energy to frown than to grin. Second, look at your audience. Ralph Waldo Emerson said that eyes *"Can threaten like a loaded pistol, insult like a hiss or kick, or by beams of kindness make the heart dance with joy."* Use your eyes to make listener's hearts dance with joy. Pick out someone in your audience, look at them for a few seconds, and then move on to someone else. How much should you look at listeners? The more the better—try to look at listeners 90 percent of the time. Third, practice good posture. Avoid leaning on the podium or nervously pacing back and forth. Use effective movement to help explain your content. And finally, try and bring in a few gestures—they can make the important seem even more so. The best kind of gestures are those that come naturally.

How do you improve delivery? One way is through practice.

Step 5: Practice Your Speech

There's a legend that tells how Demosthenes became the greatest orator in ancient Greece. It says that Demosthenes locked himself in an underground cave for three months where all he could do was practice public speaking. To make sure he didn't come out early, he shaved off all the hair on one side of his head. When the hair grew back, Demosthenes came out of the cave, an accomplished speechmaker.

Practice is important even if it's not done in a cave or with your head half-shaved. Rehearse first by running though your outline, saying your speech out loud each time. Experience shows that after four times phrases and key ideas start to stick in your mind.[4] Next start timing your performance: if it's too short, add material; too long, cut some. Work on all the things we discussed earlier—use an effective

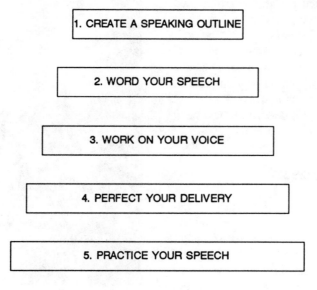

Figure 12.5
Five Steps For Delivering a Speech.

voice, practice eye contact, gestures, and movement. Some students like to rehearse in front of a mirror. Others in front of empty chairs. A few in the vacant classroom where the speech will be given. After you feel relatively comfortable with your delivery, try it on a friend, roommate, or spouse. See what they think. Don't try rehearsing it all in one night either; a good speech takes time to percolate until it sounds just right. Finally, don't commit your speech to memory, and don't read it. As an old speech adage reminds, *"familiarize, don't memorize."*

All experienced speakers recognize the value of practice. Before presenting his keynote address to the 1984 Democratic Convention, Mario Cuomo spent a total of 16 hours over the course of ten days preparing and practicing his address. That's why the three "P's" of speechmaking are: practice, practice, and practice. By rehearsing a carefully prepared speech you're bound to makes this and all your speech performances something worth remembering.

FOUR TYPICAL SPEECHES

For your next speech you might be asked to introduce yourself or to introduce someone else; to inform about an interesting subject or to demonstrate how something works. We'll now take a look at how you can prepare each of these typical speeches.

Speech to Introduce Yourself

Your first assignment might be to introduce yourself. One way to do this is to pick one event or interest in your life and tell how it helped to shape you as a person. A good way to organize this type of speech is to use causal order—describe the event and then tell how you were changed as a result. For example, this speaker tells what it's like having a younger brother who's autistic and how this made her want to work with autistic children in her career:

Central Idea: *Having a younger brother who's autistic has made me decide that I want to work with autistic children in my career.*
Main Point I: *Having a younger brother who's autistic posses many challenges.*
Main Point II: *Because of my experiences with my brother, I've decided to work with autistic children in my career.*

Chronological Order
1. Step one is to do some warm up exercises.
2. Step two is to do some vigorous exercises.
3. Step three is to do some cooling off exercises.

Spatial Order
1. Neck exercises help reduce stress.
2. Arm exercises help reduce tightness.
3. Leg exercises help reduce weariness.

Topical Order
1. Conditioning exercises strengthen muscles.
2. Firming exercises reduce flab.
3. Cardiovascular exercises improve circulation.

Causal Order
1. More Americans are taking up exercise every year.
2. More Americans are suffering injuries from exercising every year.

Problem-Solution Order
1. Many people who run long distances suffer from leg cramps.
2. Leg cramps can be eliminated by doing proper warm up exercises.

Climax Order
1. Many people exercise without warming up.
2. Many people exercise who are out of shape.
3. Many people die from over-exercising.

Figure 12.6
Organizational Patterns of Speech. Not sure how to organize your ideas? Here's how a speech on exercise could be presented using each organizational pattern.

Speech to Introduce Someone Else

You might be asked to introduce someone from history, a celebrity, or a classmate. When introducing someone try and tell things which make them sound like the special and unique person they are. Usually it's best to wait and say their name at the very end. You can organize this speech using topical order— classifying your speech into three or so categories. For instance, you could use topical order to introduce a classmate:

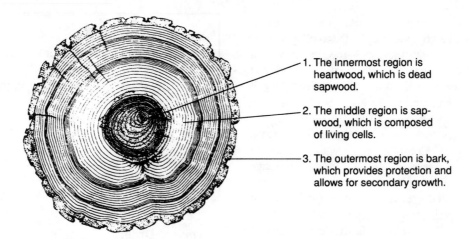

1. The innermost region is heartwood, which is dead sapwood.

2. The middle region is sapwood, which is composed of living cells.

3. The outermost region is bark, which provides protection and allows for secondary growth.

Figure 12.7
An Example of Spatial Order. This speaker described the growth regions of a tree by working from the inside out.

Central Idea: *The person I'm introducing comes from a large family, has received many awards, and plans to pursue a career in medicine.*
Main Point I: *He is the father of 5 children and has 6 brothers and 3 sisters.*
Main Point II: *He has won many community, athletic, and academic awards.*
Main Point III: *He plans to pursue a career in medicine.*

Speech to Inform Your Audience

When you inform an audience you want to teach them something. Try and pick a topic you know a lot about. It could be a hobby of yours, a job you've held, a trip you've taken, or something you'll be doing in your career. Remember to keep your speech simple and don't get hung up on detail or technicalities. One way to organize this speech is to use spatial order. This means discussing things as they relate to one another—left to right, inside to outside, high to low, etc. For example, this speaker described his trip across country from west to east:

Central Idea: *On my trip across country I stopped in Denver, Chicago, and Washington D.C.*
Main Point I: *The first city I visited was Denver.*
Main Point II: *The second city I visited was Chicago.*
Main Point III: The third city I visited was Washington D.C.

Speech to Demonstrate A Process

You might be asked to demonstrate how something works or how something can be done. Usually you'll show your listeners how they can do something so

they'll later be able to do it themselves. Often it's helpful to use a visual aid—posters, a model, an object—to help demonstrate your idea. If you use a visual aid, however, make sure it can be easily seen and that it's alright with your teacher to use one. One way to organize this speech is to use chronological order—arranging your speech by time from start to finish. For instance, after hearing of a student who became paralyzed after diving into a shallow pool, you decide it might be helpful to demonstrate safe diving techniques. You make up one poster for each step in the process and organize your speech this way:

Central Idea: *To avoid being seriously injured while diving always plan your dive, check your dive site, point your hands, carefully position your arms, and relax as you hit the water.*
Main Point I: *A first step for safe diving is to plan your dive by making sure you have secure footing.*
Main Point II: *A second step for safe diving is to check your dive site for obstacles and water depth.*
Main Point III: *A third step for safe diving is to point your hands so you don't hit the water flat.*
Main Point IV: *A fourth step for safe diving is to carefully position your arms over your head.*
Main Point V: *A fifth step for safe diving is to arch your back and tilt your head back as you follow your arms into the water.*

The patterns we've just discussed are only suggestions—you'll have to make the ultimate decision as to what's the best way to organize your ideas. But by recognizing the importance of organization, you're already well on your way toward presenting a message that's clear and responsible. Here's how one student collected his ideas and developed them into a clear and impressive message.

Table 12.2
Patterns of Organization

Pattern	Description	Most Frequent Purpose	Most Appropriate Use
Chronological Order	A pattern where ideas are arranged according to time.	Informative or Entertaining	Best for listing a series of events or describing a process.
Spatial Order	A pattern where ideas are arranged according to an area or direction.	Informative or Entertaining	Best for explaining or describing something; for showing how a series of things relate to one another.
Topical Order	A pattern where ideas are arranged around categories.	Informative or Persuasive	Best for categorizing information into easily understood categories; most commonly used pattern.
Causal Order	A two-part pattern that shows a cause to effect or effect to cause relationship.	Informative or Persuasive	Best for showing a direct relationship between an event and its repercussions.
Problem-Solution Order	Usually a two-part pattern where ideas are arranged as a problem followed by a solution.	Persuasive or Entertaining	Best for describing what is wrong and then proposing a method for correcting it.
Climax Order	A pattern where ideas are arranged so that they build to a climax or where a climatic ending introduces the factors which brought about that result.	Informative or Persuasive	Best for holding the attention of the audience by keeping them in suspense about an issue.

A TYPICAL FIRST SPEECH

For his first assignment Dan Cole was told to prepare a five minute introductory speech about himself. Dan was concerned, as he wondered what he could possibly say for five full minutes. However, Dan began by brainstorming and soon came up with a list of over 30 different ideas. He realized he couldn't possibly speak about all of them, but it gave him more than enough material to start.

Dan next wrote out his general purpose statement, which was *"to inform"* since he would be telling his classmates about something—himself. He next phrased his specific purpose statement: *"To inform my audience about myself."* Dan now needed to write out his central idea, but in order to do so he needed to come up with a few main points. He reviewed his

brainstorming list and saw that three clear general ideas stood out: he could talk about his family, a trip to Europe he took while in high school, and his future plans to have a career in business. He decided it was simplest to organize his speech in chronological order, going from the beginnings of his life as a child, to his trip in high school, and ending up with his future plans. Dan's planned speech now looked like this:

General Purpose: *To inform*
Specific Purpose: *To inform my audience by discussing my family, the trip I took to Europe, and my future career in business.*

Going back to his brainstorming list, Dan began to make a topic outline for each of this three main points. He didn't write anything in for his introduc-

family trips
summer job
stamp collection
antique cars
my sister Bev
best friend Pete
like to write poetry
dad's army career
mom's great Thanksgiving
    dinner
time I got lost in woods
my first year at state
    college
walks I take in early
    am.
my dream vacation
skiing in winter
breaking arm when 12
career as accountant
most embarrasing
    moment
brother named Ken
trophy won in 9th grade
my dog Blaze

want to own business
summer vacation at
    Lake Placid
girlfriend Sue
my V.W. bug
our family Christmas
my favorite book,
    Tale of Two Cities
car accident 2 yrs. ago
playing baseball
high school trip
    to Europe
visit to N.Y. City
jogging exercises
favorite restaurant
best rock group I ever
    saw
eventually get CPA
want to travel to
    Israel
hope to live in Florida

Figure 12.8
Example of Brainstorming.

I. If in about ten years any of you is looking to purchase any business machinery I am the person you want to see.

II. Family—always do my best
family traveled a lot—thrilled to go to Europe

Speak up!

III. Europe—more than expected
hope am successful to return to Europe

Slow Down!

IV. Business—prove challenging
open store in Phoenix

V. If any of you is traveling in Phoenix in ten years and need a word processing machine be sure to pay me a visit.

Pause Before End!

Figure 12.9
Typical Note Card.

tion, conclusion, or connectives yet, just put down as much information about himself as he could.

Dan now had more than enough information for a five minute speech; in fact he had much too much. He then began the process of shaping his speech by eliminating a lot of material. Once Dan had his ideas in order, he wrote out his conclusion, introduction, and a connective to join each of his main ideas. Dan's final step was to jot down on note cards his introduction, main points, transitional sentences, and conclusion. He was now set to practice his presentation. Dan was sure his speech would be a success.

CHAPTER SUMMARY

Giving a speech is a bit scary, a bit challenging, and a lot exciting. You might be asked to introduce yourself or someone else; to inform about something you know or demonstrate how something works; to tell an entertaining story or persuade people to do something. Regardless of the type, any speech can be prepared in ten easy steps. They are to: (1) select a topic; (2) decide on your purpose; (3) form a central idea; (4) analyze your audience; (5) research your topic; (6) support your ideas; (7) organize your speech; (8) connect your ideas; (9) prepare a conclusion; and (10) prepare an introduction.

Once you've prepared your speech you'll have to get ready to present it. This can be done in five simple steps. The are to: (1) create an outline; (2) word your speech; (3)work on your voice; (4) perfect your delivery; and (5) practice your speech.

Figure 12.10
As you practice speaking, your confidence will grow speech by speech.

There are four types of typical speeches you might be asked to present. You can introduce yourself by telling of an event and explaining how it shaped your life; you can introduce someone else by classifying their accomplishments into three or so categories; you can inform by leading your audience from one logical point to the next; or you can demonstrate a process by going from start to finish.

EXERCISES FOR REVIEW

1. Divide a sheet of paper into two columns. Label one column *"Effective in Speech."* Label the other column *"Needs Improvement."* As each of your classmates delivers their first speech jot down one or two comments about their presentation in each column. Be prepared to later discuss what you liked about their speech and what you think they need to work on.
2. If your first speeches are introductory, build a profile of each of your classmates. Keep track in a log of what they like and dislike, what interests and experiences they've had, and what they find especially challenging. You'll find this information will be very useful for analyzing your audience for future speech presentations.
3. Pair up with a classmate and mutually discuss your first speech assignment. Talk about how you're planning and preparing your speech; how you're organizing your ideas; the kind of introduction and conclusion you plan to use; and what types of examples and support you're going to bring in. Likewise, listen to your partner's ideas for his or her speech. Become a support person and sounding board for each other throughout the course.
4. Based on the patterns of organization chart in this chapter, explain which pattern you'd choose for each of the following topics:

   a. *fun in an amusement park*
   b. *describing a trip*
   c. *introducing someone*
   d. *why tuition is too high*
   e. *how to bake a cake*
   f. *how to catch fish*
   g. *how to stop smoking*
   h. *how to invest in stocks*
   i. *that UFO's really exist*
   j. *your favorite person*

   After you've chosen the pattern, in a sentence or two describe why you picked that particular method to get across your subject. Be prepared to discuss this in class.
5. Create a brainstorming list, like the one in the chapter. From the list pick out three ideas which could serve as main points for an introductory speech about yourself.

NOTES

1. Every time you give a speech you're in an act of self-disclosure. You reveal all those things which make you think and act like the person you are. See Leonard D. Goodstein and Scott W. Russell, "Self Disclosure: A Comparative Study of Reports by Self and Others," *Journal of Counseling Psychology* 24 (July 1977), p. 365.
2. If you want information from a special interest organization call 1–800–555–1212 for information—many organizations have a toll free number that you can call. Also don't be reluctant to ask the librarian or your teacher if you need help. Many times a few minutes spent asking a question can save a few hours of work.
3. The connectives referred to in this paragraph are internal previews, internal summaries, signposts, and spotlights.
4. The four-time remember rule is frequently mentioned by directors trying to help performers remember their lines.

Impromptu Topics

Pick one of the following quotations and give an impromptu speech on what the quote means to you. Speak for 3 minutes and use personal experiences and examples.

Beauty is a curse; virtue a blessing.

The tree that grows the straightest looks over the entire forest.

Roads with the most curves are the most interesting.

While politics makes strange bedfellows, the bed is often quite small.

The time one spends with oneself is like building a roof on one's house.

Time is a luxury only the young can enjoy and only the old can appreciate.

Innocence is a state of mind not a product of age.

The most vicious storm is often the most beautiful to watch and always the most often talked about.

The wise man reads both books and life itself.

Civilization is a suspicion that the other fellow may be right.

The shadows of life are caused by our standing in our own sunshine.

Our dilemma is that we hate change and love it at the same time; what we really want is for things to stay the same but get better.

Beautiful young people are accidents of nature. Beautiful old people are works of art.

Anxiety in human life is what squeaking and grinding are in machinery that is not oiled. In life, trust is the oil.

At 18, our convictions are hills from which we look: at 45 they are caves in which we hide.

The egotist always hurts the one he loves—himself.

A great city is one that handles its garbage and art equally well.

No one so thoroughly appreciates the value of constructive criticism at the one who is giving it.

There are two ways of spreading light: to be the candle, or the mirror that reflects it.

Men gossip less than women, but mean it.

To get high blood pressure go mountain climbing over molehills.

Middle age is when you don't have to have fun to enjoy yourself.

Each generation has to find out for itself that the stove is hot.

One way you can often do more for your child is to do less.

The fellow who leans on his family tree never seems able to get out of the woods.

A man doesn't live by bread alone. He needs buttering up occasionally.

A rumor is like a check—never endorse it until you're sure it's real.

The problem with competition is that it brings out the best in products and the worst in men.

Every society honors its live conformists and its dead troublemakers.

The next best thing to solving a problem is finding some humor in it.

We haven't got too much time left to ensure that government of the earth, by the earth, for the earth, shall not perish from the people.

A good conscience is a continual Christmas.

One thing that money alone cannot buy is the wag of a dog's tail.

Parenthood is the greatest single preserve of the amateur.

Most of history is just gossip that has grown old gracefully.

13

Presenting a Speech

Animation is the key to good delivery.

QUESTIONS FOR RETENTION

Before reading this chapter, ask yourself the following questions:

1. Which method of delivery should I use?
2. How can I use a visual aid?
3. What's the best way to persuade an audience?

Figure 13.1
People make judgements about what we have to say based largely on the effectiveness of our delivery.

Presenting a speech takes a lot of thought and planning. Just how do you want to deliver it? How can you use a visual aid? What do you need to know to persuade? The answers to these questions will be addressed in this chapter. We'll begin with one of the biggest concerns of experienced and beginning speakers alike - delivery.

DELIVERING A SPEECH

How do you want to come across? Serious but objective? Convincing and opinionated? Humorous and light-hearted? The answers to these questions are determined not so much on the words you use, as on the way you say them. How important is delivery? Consider Demosthenes, the famous orator of ancient Greece. When asked to name the three most important aspects of public speaking, he replied: "Delivery; Delivery; Delivery." Today almost all speech experts agree that delivery is very important.[1] How important? Several studies show that a skilled delivery makes a speech more understandable, memorable, and believable.[2]

Developing a smooth delivery takes years of effort and practice. And certainly, no one expects you to immediately be able to match the rhythmic cadence of a Jesse Jackson, the conversant ease of a Ronald Reagan, or the confident polish of a Geraldine Ferarro. But, with practice, you'll be able to turn a stiff talk into a finished speech. For gestures, eye contact, facial expressions, vocal inflections, and timely pauses gives any delivery a polished edge.

Bear in mind that a speech is more than just delivery. A dazzling delivery won't turn a senseless string of ideas into a great speech—but a good delivery mixed with a clear message equals a successful speech.

Styles of Delivery

Daniel Webster was one of America's greatest orators, molding the spirit of a still young nation for thousands of audiences. In 1820 Webster demonstrated his oratorical skills when speaking on the two-hundredth anniversary of the first settlement of New England; he spoke for nearly two hours, all the time barely glancing at his notes. A young student from Harvard wrote of his impression:

> *"I was never so excited by public speaking before I my life. Three or four times I thought my temples would burst with the gush of blood. . . . When I came out I was almost afraid to come near him. It seemed to me as if he was like the mount that might not be touched and that burned with fire. I was beside myself and am still so."*[3]

Daniel Webster wove such a spell on two generations of listeners. His delivery presented a combination of thorough preparation and recall, coupled with a colorful, almost dramatic delivery.

Daniel Webster wasn't alone. Throughout history many men and women have been able to give life to their ideas. Susan B. Anthony did so for women's suffrage; Martin Luther King for equal rights; Abraham Lincoln for the preservation of the union. Each of these speakers used far different styles of delivery, yet each were equally effective. This shouldn't be surprising, since the practice of delivery is a very individualized art—what works for one speaker may flop for another. That's why everyone must find what works best for them.

How do you find your own style? First, try to look and sound natural. If you appear overly dramatic imitating the style of a Daniel Webster, you'll seem less than sincere. Rather, *"talk"* with your listeners, using a conversational tone—as if discussing your ideas with a few close friends. Link the propriety of giving a speech with the naturalness of a conversation—weaving directness, spontaneity, animation, and emphasis all as one.[4] Sometimes it even helps to think of a speech as nothing more than an enlarged conversation.

Second, don't let your delivery call attention to itself. Distractions like excess movements, mumbling,

Figure 13.2
The best informative topics are those that you are knowledgeable about and enjoy discussing with others.

or speaking in a monotone make people pay more attention to your actions than your ideas. Likewise, an overly boisterous delivery matched with expansive, flailing gestures only causes listeners to wish they were someplace else. Fit you style with your purpose. Want to sound convincing? Be direct. Humorous? Try a well-timed pause. Wish to inform? Be clear and to the point. The best style is one that mixes purpose with personality.

Finally, practice a delivery that starts with the basics first, and moves to the frills second. Begin by using an easily understood voice, looking at listeners, and avoiding excess movement. Later blend in enhancing gestures, facial expressions, pauses, and vocal inflections. As you practice, you'll find that your style will take on a rhythm and tempo all its own. With the help of your instructor your delivery skills will grow assignment by assignment, speech by speech, day by day.

Methods of Delivery

Speakers can deliver a speech in four ways: read from a manuscript, recite from memory, speak impromptu, or speak extemporaneously. Let's review each in turn.

Reading from a Manuscript

A manuscript speech is written out word-for-word. It's often used when comments are made *"for the record"* and exact, precise wording is essential. Examples include a scientific report, legal proceeding, or Presidential address. The strength of a manuscript speech is in its accuracy—one misstatement by a President could turn a local concern into an international incident. A manuscript ensures, therefore, that a speech is both correct and accurate. Another advantage of manuscripts is the element of time. If a political candidate has ten minutes on television a manuscript ensures the message will be ten minutes, not nine and not eleven.

There are lots of disadvantages to manuscripts. Speeches that are read frequently sound bland and artificial. Many practiced speakers have difficulty speaking from a manuscript. Even Abraham Lincoln:

In his Senate campaign of 1858 Lincoln made more than sixty speeches. On several occasions he uncomfortably read from a manuscript. On one such occasion he apologized, saying: *"Gentlemen, reading from speeches is a very tedious business, particularly for an old man that has to put on spectacles, and the more so if the man be so tall that he has to bend over to the light."*[5]

Some speakers make working from a manuscript look easy. These people actually aren't reading, but only give the appearance of doing so. With them every word comes across as fresh and lively, every idea as clear and convincing. How can this be done? A former speech writer for President Johnson suggests readers should keep in mind the thought to be conveyed, their theme, and the mood to be expressed.[6]

The best advice? Don't speak from a manuscript unless absolutely necessary. However, if you must, type and triple space the manuscript, use one side of heavy quality paper, practice until you know whole lines at a glance, and rehearse thoroughly.[7]

Reciting from Memory

It wasn't uncommon for great orators of the past to memorize speeches two or three hours long! Fortunately none of us are expected to do that today. It's a rare occurrence that a speech is memorized, and then only for a special reason. For instance, in 1988 both presidential candidates memorized brief opening remarks before their debate. Not going to have a presidential debate on television? You might memorize a toast, eulogy, or oration for a speech contest. Outside of these rare occasions, however, a speech should never be memorized. It inevitably sounds canned and is little better than one read from a manuscript. Rather than being tempted to memorize, put your energy to work by practicing a natural extemporaneous delivery.

Speaking Impromptu

A speech with no preparation is called impromptu. Sometimes people can't help speaking *"off the cuff."* You might be asked to stand up and say a few words, present a contrary view at a meeting, or make a point in class. Whatever the cause, never plan on speaking impromptu, but always speak impromptu according to a plan.

What kind of plan? First, state the issue and give it a brief introduction; second, address the point you wish to make; third, support your point with some detail; and last, restate your main idea and wrap up your speech with a conclusion. By following a mental outline, an impromptu speech should be orderly, brief, and to the point.[8]

You've actually prepared for impromptu speaking all your life. Bring in anecdotes, familiar phrases, and personal experiences. Act like Ronald Reagan. He gives his seemingly off the cuff remarks a tailored, almost preplanned look.

Don't act surprised if you're suddenly asked to say a few words. Use recent events to help make a point. Next take a few seconds and think about what you want to say. Collect your thoughts and present your ideas in an order, like one, two, three. And remember that your remarks are spontaneous and shouldn't be compared to a prepared speech planned several days in advance. As Mark Twain said, *"It usually takes more than three weeks to prepare a good impromptu speech."*

Extemporaneous Speaking

Lots of people confuse impromptu and extemporaneous speaking. But, actually there's a big difference. Unlike speaking impromptu, an extemporaneous speech is always prepared in advance. When you speak extemporaneously you can use a few notes, but the precise working of your speech is saved until the moment of delivery. This gives extemporaneous speaking a touch of the natural.

Try and speak extemporaneously whenever possible. How can you master this technique? Try rehearsing until the speech starts to have a ring of the familiar. Feel free to alter, add, and eliminate ideas as you go along. You'll soon discover that your message shares the naturalness of a conversation, with the polish of a speech.

Most good communicators speak extemporaneously. For instance, John F. Kennedy found that this method let him quickly make changes in content, style, and manner at the moment of delivery.[9] Jesse Jackson says it gives him *"the bite of the moment."* And Barbara Walters says *"it just feels right."* Observe some accomplished speakers. How do they use their notes? What type of delivery do they use? Chances are you'll find almost all of them speak extemporaneously.

Why? To begin, this method makes it appear as though you're speaking off the cuff, while you're really presenting a prepared speech. Next, extemporaneous speaking gives you the flexibility to change as you go along—you're not tied to a script; you're not bound by memory. Finally, this method seems the most natural and conversational. And, after all, that's what effective speaking is all about.

Guidelines for Improving Delivery

Want to improve your delivery? Here are some guidelines to help.

Sound Conversational

Think of a speech as an extended conversation. How can you do this? First, think of your audience as a collection of individuals, rather than as a group of people. Second, liven up your delivery by being enthused, animated, and vibrant—bring intensity into your style. And third, be your natural self. Don't act; don't role play. When you play yourself, you'll come across as a sincere and real person.

Figure 13.3
Good speakers use effective gestures to emphasize their main contentions.

Work at Your Delivery

It's best to develop a regimen of practice. How? Go through a set of steps for each speaking assignment until they become second nature. Begin by practicing well in advance of the speaking assignment. Be sure to practice in small chunks of time—this works better than one long-winded session. Use a tape-recorder to check your voice, inflection, and tone. Try your speech out on a friend or classmate. Just prior to your speech, practice in a location similar to the one where it will actually be given—this helps lessen tension. Remember, a polished speech isn't the work of accident—it's the work of practice.

Start Your Speech with Confidence

Give your listeners a strong first impression. Appear at ease, slowly walk to the podium, and place your notes on the rostrum—never begin speaking until you're comfortably ready. Then wait a few seconds, get everyone's attention, and begin.

Deliver A Conclusive Ending

Never start to walk away from the podium until you've delivered the conclusion. Instead, state your conclusion, wait a few seconds, and then slowly walk back to your seat.

Directly Answer Questions

Sometimes speeches are followed by a question and answer session. Here are some suggestions: (1) make sure you understand the question before trying to answer it, if need be, repeat it first; (2) don't go overboard—keep your answers brief and to the point; (3) never answer a question if not sure of the answer, explain your uncertainty and give your best thoughts on the matter or simply say you don't know; and (4) think up some answers to likely questions in advance.

USING A VISUAL AID

One way you can help your delivery is to use a visual aid. Visual aids help make speeches more interesting, easier to understand, and simpler to remember.[10] How helpful are visual aids? One study found that when listeners just heard information they could only remember about 10 percent after three days, but when

Figure 13.4
Preparation and an ample variety of visual aids are the key to an effective, informative speech.

they both heard and saw that information they remembered much more, an amazing 65 percent.[11] No wonder it's often said that a picture is worth a thousand words!

This is why many people who speak on a frequent basis liven up their presentations with the use of slides, charts, graphs, models and other forms of visible support. For good speakers recognize that a well-placed visual can bolster their ideas, while sparking their message. Through the course of this chapter you'll learn how visual aids can add that *"thousand word"* spark to your speeches as well.

Understanding Visual Aids

And what exactly is a visual aid? The word visual implies something to look at and the word aid implies support. Consequently a visual aid is a way of supporting your ideas. If considering using a visual device ask yourself if it will help your message and clarify your ideas. Never use a visual aid just for the sake of using one—remember a good visual should only support a speech, never replace it.

One way visual aids help a speech is to give it clarity.[12] If you want to demonstrate a technique, show a relationship, or explain an event, a visual aid makes your ideas more striking, your images more clear. Here's how one student used a creative visual aid to illustrate his speech about the tragedy of Napoleon's invasion of Russia in 1812.

On the day of his speech Brian Conway carried a large box up to the front of the room. He then took out 42 dolls dressed as 18th century soldiers, which he neatly assembled into 14 columns of three each. With his audience now fascinated, Brian began his speech.

He first traced the historical events which led up to Napoleon's invasion of Russia. He then began talking of the march itself, the distance travelled, the obstacles encountered, the difficulties realized. Brian told that 422,000 troops marched into Russia, and that each doll represented 10,000 of those troops. Next he spoke of the diseases that plagued the soldiers—as he did he took several dolls and put them in the box. Brian then told of some major battles and minor skirmishes, and as he did swept several additional dolls into the box. Finally Brian spoke of the long march home through the Russian winter. As he discussed the devastation to the troops that the winter wrought, he pushed one doll after another into the box. At the end there was but one doll left as Brian said, ''Of the 422,000 troops who invaded Russia, only 10,000 ever returned home.''

No doubt, visuals make a speech more interesting. Certainly Brian's speech seemed more appealing to his audience because of his use of dolls—it made the tremendous loss of life seem especially real, glaring, and shocking. That's why using slides, charts, models, and graphs helps to rivet attention and hold interest.

Visuals also make a speech easier to recall. Brian's audience might not remember the exact number of troops lost in Napoleon's invasion, but they'll certainly remember that there was a disastrous loss of life. That point was dramatically etched in the minds of his listeners by that solitary doll left standing at the end of his presentation. Words tend to get lost in our memories, but images stay with us a much longer time.

Want to increase your credibility? Use a visual aid. People are impressed when they witness a speaker with an arsenal of visual support. Audiences rate speakers who use visuals as more credible, trustworthy and intelligent.[13] A creative, well-thought out visual aid not only does wonders for your speech, it elevates your image at the same time.

A final way visual aids help is to make the complex seem simple. A speaker trying to describe the space shuttle would be hard pressed to detail all its intricate facets and components. However through charts and a model, that same topic could seem much easier to follow. Teachers do this all the time by using charts, graphs, and illustrations to explain complex processes. This is because people learn through

sight. The *International Journal of Instructional Media* points out that we learn 1 percent through taste, 1 1/2 percent through touch, 3 1/2 percent through smell, 11 percent through hearing, and an astonishing 83 percent through sight![14] Let that 83 percent figure work to your advantage—let listeners not only hear your speech, let them see its content.

What types of visual aids can you use? Let's take a look.

Types of Visual Aids

Objects

Actual three-dimensional objects are an excellent way to demonstrate your ideas and give them added impact. You could bring in the equipment needed for skiing or mountaineering, a blood-pressure gauge, or a musical instrument. What better way to explain the different types of antique glassware than to bring in a sample of each kind? Or if you wanted to inform about some of the great recipes that can be made in a wok, what better way than to bring in the various ingredients and prepare various dishes right on the spot?

Living objects can also be used. A student who taught gymnastics brought in a few children to demonstrate. Another student explained dog grooming on her bull terrier. With all living objects, however, rehearse carefully making sure they're cooperative and aren't likely to steal the show. Also check with your instructor to see if it's okay to bring something in—some people might feel uncomfortable, for example, if your visual aid turns out to be six foot boa constrictor.

Some objects don't work as visual aids. Some are too small to be seen, others are too big to be lugged in, and a few may be straight out unavailable. A coin collection may be interesting to you, but impossible for your audience to see. While how to do body work on a car could be an engaging subject, it's a little difficult to back a car into most classrooms. And while you may want to discuss the art museum's collection of Indian pottery, the museum might not be too willing to loan it out. In each of these instances you could still speak on the subject, you'd just have to use another form of visual support.

Models

One way to demonstrate something that's too small, too big, or unavailable is to use a model. Models work exceptionally well in speechmaking because they're actual representations of the object you wish to discuss. One type is a small-scale model of a large

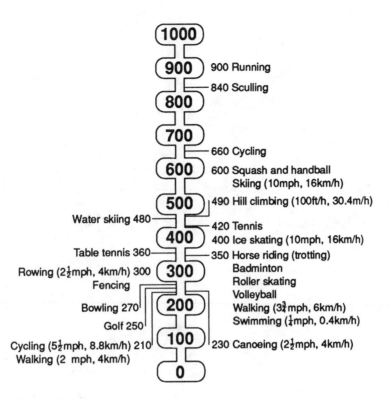

Figure 13.5
Calorie Consumption During Various Sporting Activities. This table shows the number of calories used by a 150 lb. person during one hour of activity.

object. A student gave an informative speech on the Challenger space shuttle tragedy by using such a model. Another student used a model of an Aztec temple to discuss the sophisticated architecture involved. And one student showed the stopping distance of cars traveling at a high rate of speed with model cars.

Another model is one which makes a small object appear larger. Science teachers and professors in medical school often use these to describe minute objects in great detail. For instance, one student described the structure of the human eye by using such a model.

A third kind of model is one which demonstrates an object that's unavailable. Often these are life-size. One speaker showed CPR on "Respiration Annie" the life-size doll. Someone else brought in a replica of King Tut's mask to describe the sophisticated craft work of the ancient Egyptians.

Charts

Charts are useful for presenting information in a compact, orderly form. They're particularly valuable when a large block of information needs to be summarized. The chart above shows the number of calories a person will use in one hour of various sports activities. Sometimes charts can be used in a series. The illustration on the

next page shows how this could be done to discuss common kitchen allergies. The chart depicts eight areas of concern. You could also use a chart to emphasize a particularly important point. For instance this speaker might list the allergy hot line number or an address where more information could be obtained.

Often it's helpful to make a graph and put it on a chart. Graphs help listeners understand figures and statistics. The line graph uses a horizontal and vertical scale to show a relationship. A pie graph uses a circle and shows a distribution in relationship to the whole. In a pie graph the *"pie"* represents 100 percent and each *"piece"* its appropriate share. A bar graph is an effective way of showing a comparison between two or more categories. These can be vertical or horizontal. Most math textbooks include examples of graphs—consult one to find the right graph for you.

Photographs

Photographs can serve as excellent visual aids. They are especially useful if the object you wish to discuss cannot be brought into class. One student used large photographs to describe the Hope diamond. Photographs can also be used to reveal a particular scene. A speaker displayed several photographs to

1. If you're allergic to one spice, you're probably allergic to others.
2. Allergic to wheat flour? Substitute oat or barley.
3. While preparing food, allergic people should wear rubber gloves with white cotton gloves underneath.
4. Fish is a common food allergen.
5. Use exhaust to get rid of cooking odors.
6. Use an air conditioner to reduce heat, which can cause or intensify skin sensitivity.
7. An electric range is preferable: you may be sensitive to unburned gas.
8. Young children may be sensitive to dust, mold, and insect debris which accumulate under and behind the refrigerator—clean area often.

Figure 13.6
Common Kitchen Allergies.

point out dangerous intersections and hazardous road conditions for her speech on road safety. Lastly, photographs can give a sense of realism to far away places. Whether you're speaking about Disney World or Damascus, a series of photographs can make these locations come alive for listeners.

Photographs should only be used if they're large enough for your audience to see—2 by 3 foot enlargements are the recommended norm. They should also be mounted on poster board for ease of handling. Many school audiovisual departments will enlarge negatives for you at a minimal cost. Never use a series of snap shots for a visual aid, however. If that's all you can get, you're better off having them converted to slides.

Slides and Filmstrips

What better way to show a large photograph than through a slide? Slides are the pet device of school recruiters, travel agents, and business lecturers. Slides allow for a great deal of flexibility, present a colorful image, and hold everyone's interest.[15] One student used slides to give a thrilling speech on white water rafting down the Colorado River; another showed interesting places to visit in Paris; and someone else presented the unique world of campus fashions.

Whenever slides are used certain factors must be taken into consideration. To begin, all slides must be carefully edited. If discussing your trip to Mexico, don't show your entire library of 200 slides, including 15 of your Aunt Matilda. Instead comb through your collection using the 10 or 20 that best support your topic. Next, carefully order those slides you've selected. Practice standing by the screen with a remote-control slide advance, using a pointer to emphasize particular points of interest. When using slides remember to never show one until ready to discuss it; rather fill in with a blank or one containing some appropriate commentary. And last, don't darken the room until your slides are ready to be displayed—it's even desirable to leave some lights on while showing your slides unless you discover that this washes out the image.

The rules for using a filmstrip are the same as those for using slides—this isn't surprising since a filmstrip is really nothing more than a series of slides connected together. Filmstrips are most useful if discussing a subject where you don't have any personal slides. For example, one student from Viet Nam borrowed a filmstrip from the library to deliver a speech on his former country. Another speaker used a filmstrip to show what to do in case someone is badly burned.

Drawings

Diagrams, cartoons, sketches, and other kinds of illustrations all can serve as splendid visual aids. They are relatively easy to make, and simple to understand. The Pentagon in 1991, for example, used drawings to describe bombing targets in Iraq. What could have taken hours of description was explained in a matter of minutes with the use of a few simple illustrations.

Many people are reluctant to use drawings because they feel they're not artistic enough. This should be of no concern. You don't have to be a Rembrandt or a Picasso to illustrate a visual for a speech. Feel free to use stick figures, circles, or basic squares to illustrate your ideas. For example, look at the diagram on the next page of fingerprints. The speaker who used this drawing wasn't an artist—all she did was copy the image out of a book on the subject. Her speech discussed how precise identifications can be made from a single fingerprint by examining its arches, loops, whorls, and composites. As you can imagine, this would have been an impossible task without the use of a visual aid.

Sometimes a speaker will use a series of drawings to show several steps in a process. In the other figure on the next page the speaker did this to show the six steps necessary to stay afloat.

Maps are popular visual aids. They're easy to prepare, and can be simply copied out of an atlas and enlarged for your speech. Speakers use maps to discuss specific geographical boundaries, weather conditions, shifts in population, voting patterns, and so on. One speaker used a map to show the percentage of

Every day this many men, women, and children are murdered in the United States.

Figure 13.7
Use of Numbers in Visual Aids. This form of visual depiction can convey to the audience the shocking reality of an issue much more effectively than just relating the raw number in the content of the speech.

land controlled by the military. His audience was surprised to learn that seven states—California, Nevada, Arizona, Utah, New Mexico, Alaska, and Hawaii—all have more than three percent of their land under military control.

Overhead Transparencies

Many classrooms include overhead projectors as standard equipment. This is because overheads help speakers to present orderly, thorough presentations. An overhead projector is a machine that shines light through a clear plastic sheet. Any images on the sheet will be enlarged and shown on a wall or screen. The advantages of using an overhead are that transparencies can be easily produced, permit the speaker to face the audience, and don't require the room to be darkened.

Audiovisual departments can make almost anything into a transparency at a nominal cost. However, be sure that the print is large enough to be clearly visible from 30 feet away. Also leave ample space and distance between details so as not to crowd all your information together. You can use the

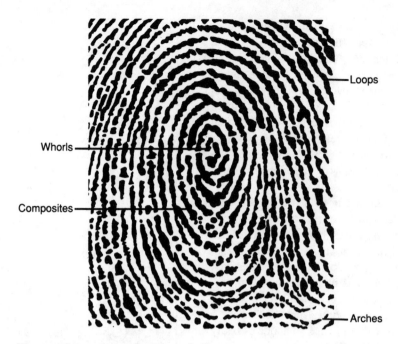

Figure 13.8
Enlarged Fingerprint. The intimate structure of an enlarged fingerprint can be examined through its arches, loops, whorls, and composites.

1. **Rest** Take a deep breath and sink vertically beneath the surface. Relax your arms and legs. Keep your chin down and allow fingertips to brush against knees. Keep neck relaxed and back of head above the surface.
2. **Get set** Gently raise arms to a crossed position with backs of wrists touching forehead. At the same time step forward with one leg and backward with the other.
3. **Rise, exhale** Without moving your arms and legs from the *get set* position, raise your head quickly but smoothly to the vertical and exhale through your nose.
4. **Inhale** To support your head above the surface while your inhale through you mouth, gently sweep your arms outward and downward and step downward with both feet.
5. **Sink** As you drop beneath the surface, put you head down and press downward with your arms and hands to arrest your fall.
6. **Rest** Relax completely as in Step 1 for 6 to 10 seconds.

Figure 13.9
How to Stay Afloat for Long Periods. Drownproofing can save your strength.

transparency either one of two ways. You can block out information with a plain sheet, moving it as you go. Or you can overlay one transparency over another as you develop your subject.

Films and Videotapes

Films are difficult to use. They take a lot of time to set up, require a darkened room, are troublesome to advance or reverse, and usually are too long for a classroom speech. Should you decide to use a film anyway, be sure and preview it first—*"Singin in the Rain"* isn't about the weather and *"42nd Street"* isn't a travelogue of New York City.

Videotapes are far superior. They can be precisely edited, are easy to fast forward or reverse, and can be shown in a lighted room. Oftentimes speakers use videos for just a part of their speech— one student used a small clip of a house catching fire to support her speech on fire prevention; another speaker showed a clip of a drum and bugle corps to support his speech about band choreography. The great thing about videos is that they have opened up subjects that were difficult to discuss in the past. For instance one student wanted to demonstrate how different aerodynamic designs reacted in a wind tunnel. By making a video he was able to capably explain this. Videos are readily available on all sorts of subjects, literally from aerobic dancing to zoom lenses. If searching for one, check your library or local rental store.

If you plan to use either a film or videotape be sure and clear it with your teacher first. Both require heavy equipment that has to be ordered well in advance. Also, some instructors prefer that students use some other form of visual support.

Tape Recorders and Record Players

Support need not be visual, it can be audio as well. But audio support works best when it's mixed with some kind of visual device. A speaker discussing bird calls displayed large photographs of a particular species while playing a sampling of that bird's call at the same time. Another student demonstrating a music synthesizer played a tape to show different techniques he had worked out at home. Sometimes audio support can be used as light background music to give an added affect. One woman presenting slides on Hawaii had Hawaiian music playing ever so softly in the background while she discussed our fiftieth state.

Yourself

Sometimes you can serve as your own visual aid. When this happens your body demonstrates your speech for you—by showing how to communicate through sign language, performing juggling tricks, riding a unicycle, demonstrating rap music and so forth. One student presented a speech on physical fitness. He explained each exercise while showing various fitness techniques. Not only did this inform his audience, but it kept their attention riveted on his speech at the same time. When you're the visual aid remember that it's usually not enough to just do something—you should also make your speech as *"visual"* as possible by wearing the appropriate attire and including auxiliary visuals such as charts or objects.

When demonstrating something coordinate your time carefully. Since many topics take a long time to develop, you might need to abbreviate some steps. For instance, a student discussing how to prepare beef stew would only slice up one carrot, explaining that the other nine were already sliced up in advance.

Guidelines for Using Visual Aids

Here are some things to keep in mind when using a visual aid.

Use Visual Aids that Support Your Ideas

Before deciding to use a visual aid ask yourself one important question: Does it help get across my content? If the answer is "no", don't use it. A beautifully drawn picture of a horse, for instance, would not add to a speech on people addicted to gambling. Always bear in mind that an unnecessary visual aid is not worth one word, little alone a thousand.

Only Use the Chalkboard if Necessary

Using the blackboard seems like a great way to visually support a speech. But in actual practice, it's the very worst type of visual aid that you can use. To start, chalkboards are awkward to write on, making whatever you prepare look sloppy and amateurish. Second, since classmates are all too familiar with seeing information displayed in this manner, it's the least likely way to grab anyone's attention. And third, writing on the board means you must turn your back on your audience. Even if you're able to prepare your visual on the board before class, it's still not going to look as appealing as a colorfully illustrated poster.

There are those few instances where the chalkboard might be used. If you're jotting down answers provided by your listeners, or teaching some kind of lesson, you may find that using the blackboard is essential. If writing on the board try using different colored chalks to give a more distinguished look. Before using the board, however, always, ask yourself if it's the best visual you can use.

Make Visual Aids Large Enough to Be Easily Seen

What good is a visual if most listeners can't see it? As simple as this seems, an awful lot of speakers make this mistake. Some people print letters that are too small, others fail to use contrasting colors that will stand out, and some try to squeeze too much information on one single poster. The result of all these errors is the same—the speaker may use an aid, but it's not a very visual one.

When preparing a visual aid always reflect on the size of the room, the arrangement of seats, and expected number of listeners. Make certain your visual can be seen by everyone, including the last person in the last row in the worst seat in the house. For charts or drawings use poster board at least 2 by 3 feet in size. Use dark ink and an extra wide marker to print bold crisp letters on a lighter surface. Make your letters at least 3 inches high, and don't cram all your information together. To test the visibility of your poster, view it from the same distance as your audience. Remember, a visual aid that can't be seen is worse than using no visual at all.

Make Your Visual Aids Simple and Neat

A visual aid should be clear and to the point. Speakers who overwhelm their listeners with visuals loaded with excess information only tend to confuse rather than clarify. And just what information should be included on a visual aid? Include only that which is absolutely necessary for a clear understanding of your subject. In short, the more basic your visual aid the better it serves your purpose. Extra details can be supplied in our content and don't need to be visually demonstrated.

A visual aid also needs to be neat. One that looks sloppy and hastily put together only turns off listeners. Simply put, a poorly done visual aid does more harm than good.

Display Visual Aids Where They Can Be Easily Seen

Place your visual where everyone can see it. Check the room out in advance. If you're using charts on poster board you'll need an easel or chalk tray to lean them on. Note if you'll need to bring along thumb tacks or tape to hold them up. If you'll need a table, electrical outlet, special lighting, or the room darkened, check this out in advance.

After you've decided on how to display your visual aids, figure out the best place for you to stand. A perfectly prepared visual aid can be rendered useless by a speaker standing in front of it blocking off part of the audience. Practice different positions until you find the one most suited for your topic. Also decide if you'll need to bring along a pointer, ruler, or pencil to point things out during your speech.

Don't Pass Visual Aids Around the Room

Avoid passing things around during your speech. If you do at least three people will be paying more attention to the aid than to you—the person who just had it, the person who has it now, and the person expecting it next. Nothing can cause as much commotion in an audience as a visual being passed hand to hand.

Of course you may want to use a handout. One student explaining string art (where pictures of yarn are made by following a design on canvas) gave each classmate a small piece of cardboard with dots and an attached string of yarn with a needle. By physically following her speech each listener was able to get a clearer understanding of her subject. But tread with caution in this area—only hand something out if you're certain it's the best way of supporting your speech and won't become a distraction.

Sometimes speakers want to give listeners a handout at the end of a speech—recipes, brochures, addresses of people to write and so on. If you do this, wait until the end—you don't want people looking at the handout when they should be listening to you.

Only Display a Visual Aid When It's Ready to Be Discussed

One student talking about cake decorating placed his finished model on the table as he started his speech. The result? No one watched him as he went through the steps of cake decorating—everyone's eyes were fixated on the beautifully decorated cake. Remember this lesson. Keep all objects out of sight until you're ready to discuss them. In this case the adage works, *"What's out of sight, is out of mind."*

Talk to Your Listeners, Not the Visual Aid

Some speakers become so intent with their visual aids that they forget all about their audience. While you'll want to periodically look at your aid, you always want the bulk of your eye contact to be directed toward your listeners. Of course if you're demonstrating something particularly hazardous, like carving a block of wood, concentrate on what you're doing—looking back at your audience once you've finished.

Consider Using Multiple Visual Aids

A good speech can be rich with visual aids. Feel free to incorporate charts, objects, models, or whatever else best supports your topic. For instance, one woman prepared various Jamaican recipes while wearing a traditional Jamaican costume, hanging several picturesque posters behind her, and playing a tape of some reggae music softly in the background. Another speaker used a model of a satellite along with several charts to explain his speech on the space program.

Prepare for the Unexpected

Whenever you use visual aids there's always the chance of something going wrong. Even the most minor problem can seem like a major disaster to an already apprehensive speaker. Therefore you need to head-off as many of these potential problems as you can. If you're using a projector always make sure you have ready access to a spare bulb. Using a video playback machine? Have it checked in advance—sometimes a loose cable or something similar can pose real difficulties. Using the chalkboard? Make sure there's chalk. Have several charts? Check if there's an easel or that you have tape to hang them up. Using slides? Make sure they're all in the correct order and are right side up.

Practice and rehearsal will alleviate a lot of potential problems. But some things can't be avoided. If the video playback machine malfunctions you'd better have an auxiliary plan in mind. Bring along some extra material to fill in just in case. A good speaker isn't only prepared if all goes as planned, but also knows what to do in case something goes wrong.

Practice with Your Visual Aid

Several of our guidelines have suggested one thing: become familiar with your visual aid. It's such an important point, however, that it bears repeating here. Rehearse using your visuals several times. Go through your speech before family or friends to see if there's anything you might have overlooked. Time your moves, practice your positions, perfect the moment when you'll introduce each visual device. A visual used properly makes a speech easier to deliver, more pleasing to receive.

Figure 13.10
Demonstrating something makes it clear to understand, more interesting to hear.

PERSUADING AN AUDIENCE

The most difficult thing for a speaker to do is to try to persuade an audience. Why? Because persuasion means getting people to think your way. Oftentimes this means changing opinions that have been built up over a lifetime. And no matter what your opinion, whether it be right or left, up or down, in or out, some part of your audience is likely to disagree. Abortion? Some accept it and some don't. Capital punishment? Some think it's right, others wrong. Euthanasia? Some think it's moral, others a sin. How do you convince people to think your way? This is the subject of our discussion.

Experts have concluded that a persuasive speech should do one of three things: (1) influence thinking; (2) reinforce views; or (3) motivate to action.[16] Let's take a look at each in turn.

Influence Thinking

One purpose of persuasive speaking is to get people to change their minds. For example, you might try to convince them that all diets don't work; that jazz is better than rock; or that airlines are unsafe. When your purpose is to influence thinking, you don't try to get listeners to take any action. Rather you're content to have them see a topic with new light.

How can you influence thinking? One way is to put yourself in the place of your listeners. Think like they think. Look at your ideas as if you've never heard them before. Play the role of a skeptical critic.[17] Have you left something out? Cover it. Is there an unanswered question? Answer it. Do you have a loophole in your argument? Refute it. By being a tough judge of your own thinking you'll be able to head off opposing arguments before they start.

Reinforce Views

Sometimes you want to reinforce already strongly held views. Lots of speakers do this every day: the minister preaches that sin is wrong; the football coach that it's important to win; the professor that class is important. So if people already agree with you, what's there to persuade? Reinforcing views means making people feel more committed to a view at the end of your speech, than they were at the beginning. Most people agree, for example, that smoking is unhealthy. But a speech on the dangers of smoking that's packed with facts can serve to only further strengthen this view.

Motivate to Action

Want your listeners to do something? Then you're motivating to action. Advertisers work on this premise all the time. Buy a Ford over a Dodge; use Colgate toothpaste, not Gleam; Pepsi tastes better than Coke. In a speech you can do much the same thing. Tell people to start exercising, stop drinking, or begin studying.

Getting people to start or to stop doing something is often difficult. Sometimes, however, if you present a reasonable request in an effective package you can find some satisfaction. Want people to be tested for A.I.D.S? Cite statistics to wake them up. Hope listeners will never drive drunk? Throw in a few illustrative stories. Convince people to give blood? Point out some useful comparisons. How can you give an added punch to your message? Be specific; tell people exactly what they can do. Explain where they can be tested for A.I.D.S.; who they can call if they've had a few drinks and need a ride home; and when the next blood drive will be held on campus. People respond best when given clear, explicit instructions.[18]

Once you've decided on your purpose you know *what* you want to do. Your next step is to figure out *how* to do it. This is what we'll discuss next.

Types of Persuasive Speeches

There are three types of persuasive speeches: those that use claims of fact, those that use claims of value, and those that use claims of policy. We'll review each.

Claims of Fact

Sir Edmond Hillary was the first man to climb Mt. Everest. The Sears Tower is the world's tallest building. Women live an average of seven years longer than men. Each of these statements is a claim of fact. Claims of fact like these are absolute and can easily be checked in any reference book.

But some claims of fact aren't so clear. They involve predicting an outcome, without the assurance that it's already occurred. A speaker could claim that crime will increase, that air bags will same lives, or that more research will lead to a cure for A.I.D.S. Each of these claims probably is true—but we don't know for sure. They only predict what could happen.

Other claims of fact reach into the past, rather than predict the future. You could argue that Columbus wasn't the first person to discover America, that Lee Harvey Oswald didn't assassinate John Kennedy, or that Franklin Roosevelt knew in advance of the Japanese plan to bomb Pearl Harbor. While you can find support for each of these claims, no one can say for certain that they're true—one could equally argue an opposing view.

Still other claims are speculative and theoretical. Are there UFO's? Was there a city named Atlantis? Did ancient astronauts visit the Earth? Claims like these force you to speculate. Yet they can be forcefully argued in a persuasive speech.

All claims of fact must be supported. Will increased research find a cure for A.I.D.S.? Cite expert testimony to back you up. Columbus didn't discover America? Prove it with documentation. UFO's do exist? Hit listeners with sightings and photographs.

What yardstick should you apply to your support? First, it must be truthful and accurate. Tell where you got your information, who said it, and what their qualifications are. Second, check your evidence to see that it directly supports your issue. If arguing that Oswald didn't shoot Kennedy, don't get sidetracked into discussing theories surrounding Sirhan Sirhan. Stick to your subject and the specific claim presented.

You can organize a claim of fact speech in several ways. One way is to use chronological order—presenting facts as they unfolded. Here's an example:

Specific Purpose: *To persuade my audience that the crash of the German zeppelin Hindenburg was due to sabotage.*
Central Idea: *Sabotage was the cause of the crash of the Hindenburg because of events that occurred before, during, and after the flight.*
Main Points: I. *Sabotage aboard the Hidenburg was feared before the flight due to several warnings.*
II. *Sabotage aboard the Hindenburg was feared during the flight because of several strange occurrences.*
III. *Sabotage aboard the Hindenburg was suspected after the crash because of the nature of the explosion.*

The most popular way to organize a speech using a claim of fact is to use topical order. With this order you would supply the major reasons why you believe something happened in the past, is happening currently, or is likely to happen in the future.

Specific Purpose: *To persuade my audience that the Vikings were the first to discover America.*
Central Idea: *Three reasons that support the theory that the Vikings were the first to discover America are that they were great sailors, they settled in Iceland and Greenland, and ruins suspected to be theirs were found in Canada.*
Main Points: I. *The Vikings freely sailed the Atlantic as early as 825.*
II. *The Vikings established settlements in Iceland and Greenland by 900.*
III. *Ruins suspected to be those of the Vikings were found in Canada.*

Observe that in each example the speaker's purpose is supported by using a claim of fact. Sometimes, however, you might want to take a fact one step further. When you do this you present a claim of value.

Claims of Value

When you try to convince listeners that one thing is better than another you're presenting a claim of value. This type of speech depends on facts, but also needs a qualitative judgment on your part. Should a lover be told if a person has a sexually transmitted disease? Is capital punishment justified? Are small colleges better than large universities? As these questions suggest, claims of value are dependent upon your own beliefs. After all, one person's *should* is another's *shouldn't*.

How do you persuade with a claim of value? One way is to get listeners to accept your values as valid. Tell your audience what standards you're applying. Supply concrete examples and logical appeals. Want to label all record albums with offensive lyrics? Tell listeners what you mean by offensive. References to sex? Drugs? Suicide? Satanism? How will they be labeled? Who will make the decision? What effect will it have? Questions like these must be addressed in any speech using a claim of value.

There are lots of ways to organize this type of speech. In the example that follows we use topical order. Here the speaker set out her values and then relates them to the topic.

Specific Purpose: *To persuade my audience that comic books are useful forms of literature.*
Central Idea: *Comic books are useful forms of literature because they have interesting plot lines, have thorough character development, and encourage children to read.*
Main Points: I. *Comic books are useful forms of literature because their plot lines are as sophisticated as those of many novels.*
II. *Comic books are useful forms of literature because they fully develop each leading character in the story.*
III. *Comic books are useful forms of literature because they encourage children to read.*

Another way to organize a speech using a claim of value is to use a variation of the problem-solution order. In this pattern your first point shows where a problem exits, the second why your solution is correct. Here's one:

Specific Purpose: *To persuade my audience that state run lotteries are ethically wrong.*
Central Idea: *State run lotteries are ethically wrong because they encourage people to gamble.*
Main Points: I. *State run lotteries make it too easy for people to wager.*

A. *Studies show that those people who can least afford it are most likely to purchase tickets.*
B. *Many people who are compulsive gamblers have gone bankrupt.*
II. *It's ethically wrong for states to promote gambling.*
A. *Society has a special obligation to protect the poor.*
B. *Society has an obligation to protect compulsive gamblers from themselves.*

Notice that in each of these speeches no action was demanded of the audience. This is because speeches of value only present an idea—listeners aren't urged to do anything. When you move to the next step and tell people they should or shouldn't do something, you're presenting our final type of persuasive speech—one that uses a claim of policy.

Claims of Policy

Speeches using a claim of policy are the most popular type of persuasive speech. They're easy to spot because they almost always use or imply the word *"should."* Here are a few examples:

> *Drunk drivers should lose their licenses for life.*
> *Students who cheat on exams should be expelled.*
> *The United States should reduce military spending.*

Observe how each of these topics sets out a specific course of action—they clearly say what should or shouldn't be done. Drunk drivers should lose licenses; student cheaters should be expelled; and the United States should reduce military spending. Therefore, speeches on policy always represent the opinion of the speaker—there's no clear right or wrong answer.

How do you support a speech using a claim of policy? You begin by building on a claim of fact. Prove what damage drunk drivers do, how many there are, and how many people they kill every year. Next, incorporate claims of value. Show that drunk drivers have forfeited their rights and that getting them off the road will save lives. Prove that your values are correct, and should be listened to.

A speech using a claim of policy inevitably asks listeners for passive or active support. Passive support means you want people to agree with you, but little else is required. Listeners might agree that drunk drivers should be taken off the road, but will do little unless they happen to be one themselves. **Active support** asks for much more. It demands that listeners get personally involved. They should report drunk

drivers, write legislators, and work to see this idea become law. Asking for active support? Don't be content to tell listeners to do something—tell them what to do. Research shows that when listeners are told exactly what to do they feel a closer bond with the ideas of the speech.[19]

A speech using a claim of policy should do four things. To begin, convince listeners that there's a need for a change in the first place. Show them that drunk drivers are a problem. Next, present a plan. Give specifics, tell them how drunk drivers will be caught and dealt with; what will happen to people who continue to drive; and how this law will be enforced. Third, prove that your plan is practical. Detail how it will work, what it will cost, and how it will save lives. Last, clearly indicate why your plan offers the best possible solution. Why is taking away a license for life better than revoking it for six months? Why is this superior to other ideas? Give proof and present facts to sell your idea.

There are several ways to organize a speech using a claim of policy. One of the simplest is to use a comparative advantages order. Here you compare your solution with another, showing why yours is superior. In the following example this is done comparing care in a hospice with that in a hospital.

Specific Purpose: *To persuade my audience that terminally ill patients should be sent to a hospice.*
Central Idea: *Terminally ill patients should be sent to a hospice rather than a hospital because hospices can better meet the psychological and medical needs of the patient.*
Main Points: I. *Hospice care is superior to hospital care in terms of meeting the psychological needs of the terminally ill patient.*
II. *Hospice care is superior to hospital care in terms of meeting the medical needs of the terminally ill patient.*

Another way you can organize your speech is to use problem-solution order With this order you would show the nature of the problem in the first point, and provide its solution in the second. Here's an example:

Specific Purpose: *To persuade my audience that the United States should improve the nation's railroads.*
Central Idea: *The nation's railroads are in terrible condition and need to be drastically improved.*
Main Points: I. *The nation's railroads are in terrible condition.*
A. *Many track beds are dangerous to use.*
B. *Much of the equipment is outdated.*

II. *We must solve the problem by improving our nation's railroads.*
   A. *We must immediately repair and replace many track beds.*
   B. *New cars and engines must be built to replace outdated models.*

The greatest challenge you'll face as a speaker will be trying to persuade an audience. But while it poses many complexities, it's also one of the most rewarding. For changing an audience's view, getting them to see an old issue in a new way, and causing them to think about the unthinkable gives you an awesome power. The power to persuade is a noble power indeed.

Figure 13.11
Careful preparation is a great confidence booster when delivering a speech.

CHAPTER SUMMARY

A speech can be delivered in four ways. You can read from a manuscript, recite from memory, speak impromptu, or deliver it extemporaneously. Of all these methods extemporaneous is greatly preferred. When delivering a speech you should sound conversational, work at your delivery, start with confidence, have a conclusive ending, and directly answer questions.

You can help your delivery by using a visual aid. Visual aids make a speech clearer, easier to understand, add to your credibility, and make the complex seem simple. There are many types of visual aids including objects, models, charts, photographs, slides and filmstrips, drawings, overhead transparencies, films and videotapes, tape recorders and record players, and yourself. You should use a visual to support your ideas; avoid the chalkboard; make visuals large enough to be seen; make them simple and neat; display them where they can easily be seen; resist passing them around; only display them when you're ready to; talk to your listeners, not the visual aid; prepare for the unexpected; and practice with your visual before the speech.

It's very difficult for a speaker to try and persuade an audience. Persuasive speeches either influence thinking, reinforce views, or motivate to action. The three types of persuasive speeches you can give are those that use claims of fact, those that use claims of value, and those that use claims of policy.

EXERCISES FOR REVIEW

1. Write a 200 paper explaining the four methods of delivery and times when each method might be used. Give some specific examples of occasions when one method would be preferred over the others.
2. Discuss the types of visual aids that could be used to present a speech about each of the following topics:
   a. *The sinking of the Titanic.*
   b. *A lesson on how to wash your clothes.*
   c. *The natural beauty of Alaska.*
   d. *How to invest in the stock market.*
   e. *How the national debt has increased over 40 years.*
   f. *The New York Marathon.*
   g. *How to build a bird feeder.*
   h. *The thrills and dangers of skateboarding.*
   i. *The collection of Ming glassware in a local museum.*
3. Plan on using a visual aid in at least one upcoming speech. Use a creative, well thought out visual device. After your speech discuss with a group of classmates how your visual helped your speech; how it was handled; and how it could be improved for next time.
4. Read the following speech topics and decide if they would be most suited for a speech whose purpose is to influence thinking, reinforce views, or to motivate to action. Then write a

specific purpose statement for each topic so it satisfies the purpose you've selected.

    a. That college is important.

    b. That ocean dumping must be stopped.

    c. That Jack the Ripper was not one, but several men.

    d. That everyone should register to vote.

    e. That family support is essential for success.

5. Below are listed five specific purpose statements for persuasive speeches. Decide for each one if it's a claim of fact, value, or policy. Be prepared to discuss your answers in class.

    a. To persuade my audience that Bigfoot really exists.

    b. To persuade my audience that pornography is morally wrong.

    c. To persuade my audience that all teachers should receive a drug test.

    d. To persuade my audience that Charles Lindbergh wasn't the first person to fly across the Atlantic.

    e. To persuade my audience that animal experimentation is ethically invalid.

NOTES

1. For years theorists have argued over the relative importance of style (how you say something) over substance (what you say). See for instance, Barbara Warnick, "The Quarrel Between the Ancients and the Moderns," *Communication Monographs*, 49, December 1982, pp. 263–276. One study suggests that style as characterized by delivery, appearance, and manner is more important than substance as characterized by the 1980 presidential debates, see, Goodwin F. Berquist and James L. Goldin, "Media Rhetoric, Criticism, and the Public Perception of the 1980 Presidential Debates," *Quarterly Journal of Speech*, 67, May 1981, pp. 125–137.

2. For two studies that support this phenomenon, see, W. B. Pearce and F. Conklin, "Nonverbal Vocalic Communication and Perceptions of A Speaker," *Speech Monographs*, 38, 1971, pp. 235–241; W. B. Pearce and B.J. Brommel, "The Effects of Vocal Variations on Ratings of Source Credibility," *Quarterly Journal of Speech*, 58, 1972, pp. 298–306.

3. Recorded observation of George Ticknor in Houston Peterson, *A Treasury of the World's Great Speeches* (New York: Simon and Schuster, 1965), p. 238.

4. The conversational style of delivery being the most effective is supported by most experts beginning with the classical text by James A. Winans, *Speech-Making* (New York: Appleton-Century-Crofts, 1938). For a review of current studies supporting listeners preference for the conversational mode, see, Erwin P. Bettinghaus and Michael J. Cody, *Persuasive Communication*, 4th ed. (New York: Holt, Rinehart and Winston, 1987), pp. 127–128.

5. Houston Peterson, *A treasury of the World's Great Speeches* (New York: Simon and Schuster, 1965), p. 497.

6. While former President Johnson is not remembered as a fluid speaker, he did become proficient in working from a manuscript, see, Jack Valenti, *Speak Up With Confidence: How to Prepare, Learn, and Deliver Effective Speeches* (New York: William Morrow, 1982), p. 129.

7. For a useful guide on how to speak from a manuscript, see, James C. Humes, "Read A Speech Like A Pro," in *Talk Your Way to the Top* (New York: McGraw-Hill, 1980), pp. 28–29.

8. For an excellent article on how to prepare for an impromptu speech, see, Peter Hannaford, "Why Off the Cuff Is Off the Mark," *Nation's Business*, May 1984, pp. 28–29.

9. James L. Golden, "John F. Kennedy and the 'Ghosts' " *Quarterly Journal of Speech*, 52, December 1966, pp. 356–357.

10. This is supported by much research. See, for example, Emil Bohn and David Jabusch, "The Effect of Four Methods of Instruction on the Use of Visual Aids in Speeches," *Western Journal of Speech Communication*, 46, 1982, pp. 253–265.

11. This has been shown in several studies, for instance see, Bernadette M. Gadzella and Deborah A. Whitehead, "Effects of Auditory and Visual Modalities in Recall of Words," *Perceptual and Motor Skills*, 40, February 1975, pp. 255–260 and Bella M. DePaulo et al., "Decoding Discrepant Nonverbal Cues," *Journal of Personality and Social Psychology*, 36, March 1978, pp. 313–323.

12. For a discussion of the relationship between ideas and visuals see, Sol Worth, "Pictures Can't Say Ain't," *Versus*, 12, 1975, pp. 85–108 and Edgar B. Wycoff, "Why Visuals?," *AV Communications*, 11, 1977, pp. 39, 59.

13. For support of this see, George L. Gropper, "Learning from Visuals: Some Behavioral Considerations," *AV Communication Review*, XI, Summer 1963, pp. 75–95.

14. Elena P. Zayas-Baya, "Instructional Media in the Total Language Picture," *International Journal of Instructional Media*, 5, 1977–78, pp. 145–150.

15. For a discussion of how to use slides in a visual aid speech, see, Richard Wiegand, "It Doesn't Need to be Dull to be Good: How to Improve Staff Presentations," *Business Horizons*, 28, July/August 1985, p. 42.

16. For a discussion of the purposes of persuasion to shape, reinforce and change listener responses see, Gerald R. Miller, "On Being persuaded: Some Basic Distractions," in Michael E. Roloff and Gerald R. Miller, *Persuasion: New Directions in Theory and Research* (Beverly Hills, Ca.: Sage, 1980), pp. 16–26.

17. Skepticism and heading off arguments has been treated in several studies. For the classic study on this see C. I. Hovland, A. A. Lumsdaine, and F. D. Sheffield, *Experiments in Mass Communication: Studies in Social Psychology in World War II*, 3 (Princeton, N.J.: Princeton University Press, 1949), pp. 201–227.

18. For motivation to action and specific directions, see Howard Leventhal, Robert Singer, and Susan Jones, "Effects of Fear and Specificity of Recommendation upon Attitudes and Behavior," *Journal of Personality and Social Psychology*, 2, 1965, pp. 20–29.

19. For a review of research on the theory of active agreement, see James P. Dillard, John E. Hunter, and Michael Burgoon, "Meta-Analysis of Face-in-the-Door and Door-in-the-Face," *Human Communication Research*, 10, 1984, pp. 461–488.

Name _____   Course _____

Speech Critique Sheet

Time Limit: 5 minutes   Speaking Notes: index cards

Sources Required: none written   Outline Required: yes (topic)

General Purpose: _____

_____

Specific Purpose: _____

_____

	1 Poor	2	3	4	5 Good
Choice of Topic: clear; introductory in nature					
Introduction: original; interesting					
Organization: follows logical progression, orderly					
Content: meaningful; topical					
Delivery: verbal and nonverbal elements					
Conclusion: clear; conclusive; original					
Overall Presentation: effectiveness; relevance					

General Comments:

Grade _____

Speech Outline

Time Limit   Speaking Notes Permitted:

Sources Required: Outline Type: Topic Sentence

General Purpose: _____

Specific Purpose: _____

_____

Title: _____

 I. Introduction:

 II. Main Point #1:

     A. Sub point #1:

     B. Sub point #2:

     C. Sub point #3:

     D. Transition:

 III. Main Point #2:

     A. Sub point #1:

     B. Sub point #2:

     C. Sub point #3:

     D. Transition:

 IV. Main Point #3:

     A. Sub point #1:

     B. Sub point #2:

     C. Sub point #3:

     D. Transition:

 V. Conclusion:

Name _____ Course _____

Speech Using a Visual Aid Critique Sheet

Time Limit: 10 to 15 minutes   Speaking Notes: index cards

Sources Required: 2 written   Outline Required: yes (topic)

General Purpose: _____

Specific Purpose: _____

_____

Title: _____

Visual Aid(s) Used: _____

	1	2	3	4	5
	ineffective			effective	
Presentation of strong introduction and conclusion					
Organization					
Variety of supporting materials					
Visual Aids: variety, handling, visibility, integration					
Clear Demonstration					
Animation for subject					
Credibility for subject					
Delivery: vocal quality, rate, duration, volume					
Nonverbal: eye contact, gestures, posture, bodily movements					

General Comments:

Grade _____

Speech Outline

Time Limit: Speaking Notes Permitted:

Sources Required: Outline Type: Topic Sentence

General Purpose: _____

Specific Purpose: _____

Title: _____

   I. Introduction:

  II. Main Point #1:

      A. Sub point #1:

      B. Sub point #2:

      C. Sub point #3:

      D. Transition:

 III. Main Point #2:

      A. Sub point #1:

      B. Sub point #2:

      C. Sub point #3:

      D. Transition:

 IV. Main Point #3:

      A. Sub point #1:

      B. Sub point #2:

      C. Sub point #3:

      D. Transition:

  V. Conclusion:

Name _____   Course _____

Persuasive Speech Critique Sheet

Time Limit: 5 to 10 minutes   Speaking Notes: index cards

Sources Required: 3 written, 1 interview   Outline Required: yes (topic)

General Purpose: _____

Specific Purpose: _____

_____

Title: _____

Before Speech: Point total ____   After Speech: Point total ____

Points shifted in position: ____   High points shifted in class ____

	1	2	3	4	5
Introduction					
Stated Credibility					
Logical Warrant Presented					
Ethical Warrant Presented					
Emotional Warrant Presented					
Speech Organization					
Evidence and Support					
Delivery					
Eye Contact					
Gestures					
Posture					
Persuasive Effectiveness					
Conclusion					

General Comments:

Grade _____

Name _____   Course _____

Sources of Information

General Purpose: _____

Specific Purpose of Presentation: _____

_____

Printed Sources:

Author: _____ Date: _____

Title: _____

Article Title: _____

Number of Pages Used: _____ Publisher: _____

Author: _____ Date: _____

Title: _____

Article Title: _____

Number of Pages Used: _____ Publisher: _____

Author: _____ Date: _____

Title: _____

Article Title: _____

Number of Pages Used: _____ Publisher: _____

Author: _____ Date: _____

Title: _____

Article Title: _____

Number of Pages Used: _____ Publisher: _____

Interview Sources:

Name of Person Interviewed: _____ Date: _____

Position or Title: _____

Reason for Expertise on Subject: _____

Read One of These Paragraphs Practicing Effective Delivery

1. From Herbert Spencer's Education—

    How to live?—that is the essential question for us. Not how to live in the mere material sense only, but in the widest sense. The general problem which comprehends every special problem is—the right ruling of conduct in all directions under all circumstances. In what way to treat the body: in what way to treat the mind: in what way to manage our affairs: in what way to bring up a family: in what way to behave as a citizen: in what way to use all our faculties to the greatest advantage of ourselves and others—how to live completely? And this, being the great thing which education has to teach. To prepare us for complete living is the function which education has to discharge.

2. "Beck Put to Flight"

    Mister Beck, on one occasion had just risen in the House of Commons with some papers in his hand, on the subject of which he intended to make a motion when a ruffian member who had no eye for the charms of eloquence rudely started up and said, "Mister Speaker, I hope the honorable gentleman doesn't mean to read that large bundle of papers and to bore us with a long speech as well." Mister Beck was so enraged as to be incapable of utterance and absolutely ran out of the House. On this occasion, Judge Selwin remarked that it was the only time he ever saw the fable realized—a lion put to flight by the braying of an ass.

3. "The Old Chart"

    The lodgekeeper found an old chart written in a peculiar chapter. After careful study he was able to make it out and learned from it that a choice and rare old treasure chest was buried four or five feet underground on the very spot where the new school house stood. He was sure he could find it if he obeyed directions, however, and following several trials at last he did unearth it. But as he was lifting it out, the box fell to pieces and the contents fell back into the hole.

4. "The Painter"

    Once upon a time there was a painter who divided his life into two halves. In the one half he painted potboilers for the market, setting every consideration aside except that of doing for his master—the public, something for which he could get paid money on which he lived. He was great at floods and never looked at nature except in order to see what would make most show for least expense.

    The other half of his time he studied and painted with the sincerity of Giovanni Bellini, Rembrandt, or Holbein. He was then his own master and thought only of doing his work as well as he could regardless of whether it would bring him anything but debt and abuse. He gave his best without receiving so much as thanks.

    He avoided the temptation of telling either half about the other.

14 Argumentation and Debate

Debate is the practice of skilled argument.

QUESTIONS FOR RETENTION

Before reading this chapter, ask yourself the following questions:

1. What is debate?
2. How can I prepare for a debate?
3. How can I win a debate?

Figure 14.1
Debating before others is both exciting and challenging.

Debate has a revealing history and an exciting present. What impact has debate had on our history? In 1858 a little known lawyer named Abraham Lincoln engaged Stephen Douglas in a series of debates over the issue of slavery. Lincoln's words galvanized the nation, and just two years later helped elect him the sixteenth President of the United States. Without the famous Lincoln-Douglas debates this probably never would have happened. Think of some more recent famous debates. Kennedy and Nixon, Carter against Reagan, Bush versus Dukaukis, Bentson and Quayle. Each of these debates propelled one candidate to victory, and pushed the other to defeat.

Not planning on running for President? Debate training is still of tremendous benefit. The skills you'll learn in debate—researching an issue, preparing an argument, refuting evidence, cooperating with a teammate—will all prove of tremendous value throughout your lifetime. But the one skill debate teaches above all others is the ability to communicate under pressure. How do you answer a question? How do you shoot down a point? How do you use evidence to back you up? These questions are only satisfied by being tested under fire. And for that you must experience debate firsthand.

UNDERSTANDING DEBATE

What is a debate? It's an exchange of conflicting views. One side presents one argument, the other one with a contrary view. For example, say two teams are debating the issue of requiring air bags in all new cars. One team would argue that air bags would save lives and should be required. The other side would argue that consumers should have the right to decide if they want air bags, and they shouldn't be required. Who's right? That's for a judge—or panel of judges—to decide. That's why a debate always involves two teams, a question, and someone deciding who should win.

The place all debates begin is with a question. After all, both teams have to know what to disagree about. The question is called a proposition, and that's our next subject to review.

The Proposition

A proposition is a judgment expressed in words. It can be accepted as correct, or argued as wrong. For instance, if a student says, *"I think I'll get an A in Speech class,"* that's a proposition. We could agree that the student is right, or try to prove her wrong. Or, a classmate could say, *"I think English is more useful than biology."* This statement could also be argued either way. If someone said, *"I think colleges should offer more courses to help students get jobs,"* we could likewise say *"yes"* or we could think *"no."*

While each of these statements are propositions, they're different types of propositions. The example, *"I think I'll get an A in Speech class,"* is a proposition of fact. We can easily prove at the end of the semester if the student was right, of if she was wrong. The statement, *"I think English is more useful than biology,"* is a proposition of value. This isn't as easy to verify as one of fact. Whether English is more valuable than biology could be argued for hours without resolution. Often propositions of value are used for discussion topics because they can so easily be discussed. Our last statement, *"I think colleges should offer more courses to help students get jobs,"* is a proposition of policy. These types of statements are harder to verify. People could effectively argue both sides of this issue—some could say they should; others could say they already do; and others could say this isn't the function of a college. Because both sides can be argued so effectively, propositions of policy are usually used for debates.

A proposition shouldn't be biased to give one side an unfair advantage. The proposition, *"Smoking is hazardous to one's health,"* for example, would be a poor topic for a debate. One side would clearly have an easier time supporting their case. If the topic was reworded, however, to *"Smoking should be banned in all public places,"* we'd have a much fairer topic. Now both sides could argue their positions with equal effectiveness. How do you avoid debating slanted issues? By making sure every proposition is worded in such a way that both sides start on an equal footing.

Debate propositions are always worded so that one team—the affirmative—has to prove the proposition true. They always begin with the words, *"resolved that."* Here are a few examples.

> *Resolved that capital punishment should be abolished.*
> *Resolved that drugs should be legalized.*
> *Resolved that women should be drafted in the military.*

Look at these propositions. Notice that each presents an issue with two clear sides. One could argue that capital punishment is or isn't right; that drugs should or shouldn't be legalized; and that women should or shouldn't be drafted. Observe, too, that each topic presents a change in present policy. Capital punishment isn't abolished, drugs aren't legalized, and women aren't drafted. This is done intentionally because one team (called the affirmative) always suggests change, while the other (called the negative) defends the way things currently are. You'll also notice that each proposition only suggests one change. It's clear that the debate would be about capital punishment, drugs, or women being drafted. The topic, *"Resolved that we should abolish capital punishment and legalize drugs,"* wouldn't work because it presents two issues. The key word in every debate topic is *"should."* Should means *"implied or ought to be done;"* therefore, debate topics don't require that a team prove the government would legislate their plan, only that it could.

Being in a debate means being part of a team. Let's see what this means.

Debate Teams

Every debate needs two teams. One is the affirmative, the other the negative. The affirmative team presents a plan that suggests a change from the present system. The negative, on the other hand, argues against the plan and suggests that there's no need for such a change. Suppose, for example, the topic *"Resolved that we should permit euthanasia for the terminally ill,"* was being debated. The affirmative would present a plan that we should permit euthanasia (mercy killing) and the negative would argue against the plan, saying we shouldn't permit it. The affirmative always presents a plan for change, the negative always argues against the proposed change.

Bear in mind that the affirmative has the **burden of proof.** That is, they must prove to a judge that their suggested plan is better than the present system. The negative has the **burden of rejoinder.** They must defeat the plan by raising doubts about its advantages. Sometimes a negative team agrees that some change is needed, but never agrees that the affirmative suggestion is the way to do it. To do so would mean to forfeit any chance of victory.

Who wins? If the judge feels the affirmative plan is superior to the present system, the affirmative. If s/he feels the negative has raised sufficient doubt about the plan's advisability, the negative. In a debate there's no such thing as a tie, but if such a theoretical tie did exist, the negative would win. The affirmative must always show that their plan is clearly superior, not just as good.

Most debate teams consist of two members each, although some teams may have three or more. Each team member speaks twice, giving one constructive speech, and one rebuttal toward the end. Frequently a cross-examination format is used, where each debater also has the opportunity to ask questions of a member of the other team.

While we'll discuss the exact order of speaking and responsibilities of each speaker later, one point should be made now. The affirmative always presents first and last. The opening speech sets out the affirmative plan. The last speech summarizes why the affirmative believes they should win. How does it work? Briefly, the affirmative team suggests a reason for a change, and a plan to meet that change. The negative argues against the need for a change, and points out weaknesses in the plan. Whichever team seems most convincing wins the debate. Sounds exciting, doesn't it! Let's see how it works.

Format of Debate

All debate speeches are carefully timed by a timekeeper. Each debater first presents a constructive speech which is seven minutes long. There may be a question and answer session after each speech, which usually runs two minutes. The debate concludes with each speaker giving a three minute rebuttal. Here's how it looks:

1st Affirmative Constructive Speech	7 minutes
1st Affirmative Questioned by 2nd Negative	2 minutes
1st Negative Construction Speech	7 minutes
1st Negative Questioned by 1st Affirmative	2 minutes
2nd Affirmative Construction Speech	7 minutes
2nd Affirmative Questioned by 1st Negative	2 minutes
2nd Negative Construction Speech	7 minutes
2nd Negative Questioned by 2nd Affirmative	2 minutes
1st Negative Rebuttal Speech	3 minutes
1st Affirmative Rebuttal Speech	3 minutes
2nd Negative Rebuttal Speech	3 minutes
2nd Affirmative Rebuttal Speech	3 minutes

How can you remember who goes when? Here are some hints. First, keep in mind that both teams alternate—first the affirmative, then the negative, and so on. Second, notice that the person doing the questioning is never the person who is due to present the next speech. If your debate didn't have a question and answer session, the order would be the same, only the questioning sessions would be eliminated. Finally, observe that the affirmative-negative order in the constructives, reverses to negative-affirmative in the rebuttals. This is how the affirmative team gets to speak both first and last.

Who keeps the time? In debate the timekeeper is just as important as the judge. This person follows the debate while holding up time cards signifying the amount of time each speaker has left. For a constructive speech the timekeeper would start with card 7, after one minute go to 6, finally to 1/2, and end at *STOP!*. For a question session it would begin with 2, for a rebuttal at 3. When the *STOP!* card flashes the speaker may finish the sentence, but should stop talking within a few seconds. What happens if the debater keeps talking? The timekeeper will yell, *"STOP!"* at which point the person must stop speaking, or be penalized by the judge.

As already mentioned, all debates are evaluated by a judge. In classroom debates usually a panel of five judges of classmates hear a debate and render a decision. Of course, all judges must be impartial. When judging they erase all personal feelings, opinions, and friendships. The decision must be based strictly on which team did the better job of debating. Likewise, judges must decide independently—they can't discuss what others think, or how they're voting. Usually judges come up and announce how they're voting with a brief analysis. The team which receives the most votes wins—with five judges a team would need at least three votes.

Judging is tough business—after all, you can't vote for both teams, and you can't have a tie. One easy way to help make this decision is to add up points, the team with the highest total wins. Observe the sample ballot on the next page. Notice that each speaker can receive up to five points in six different categories. Analysis means how well they looked at the argument; reasoning and evidence means how effectively they backed up their ideas; organization means how logical their thinking was to follow;

Debate Evaluation

Affirmative 1 ______________ Negative 1 ______________

Affirmative 2 ______________ Negative 2 ______________

Check the column on each item which, according to the following scale best describes your evaluation of the speaker's effectiveness, and indicate the rank for each speaker in the space following his name.

1—poor 2—fair 3—adequate 4—good 5—superior

	1st Affirmative 1 2 3 4 5	2nd Affirmative 1 2 3 4 5	1st Negative 1 2 3 4 5	2nd Negative 1 2 3 4 5
Analysis				
Reasoning and evidence				
Organization				
Cross-exam				
Refutation				
Delivery				
	Total ______	Total ______	Total ______	Total ______

Team Ratings: Affirmative: poor fair adequate good superior

Negative: poor fair adequate good superior

Comments:

1st Affirmative rank ( ) 1st Negative rank ( )

2nd Affirmative rank ( ) 2nd Negative rank ( )

In my opinion, the better debating was done by the ______________
affirmative or negative

____
judge's signature

Figure 14.2
A Sample Ballot.

cross-exam means how well they asked and answered questions; refutation means how precisely they shot down opposing arguments; and delivery measures the smoothness of their presentation. With six categories of five points each, the most a speaker could receive would be thirty points. Simply add up the total points for both speakers. If, for example, the affirmative team totaled 55 points (25 for the first, 30 for the second), and the negative 53 (23 for the first, 30 for the second) the affirmative would win by two points! Bear in mind, however, that when you're judge you can do whatever you want. You can amend, alter, or ignore point totals as you wish. After all, you're the judge! It's a good idea to write some commentary on your ballot, since these are usually given to the teams after the debate. In your comments include major definitions, the plan, and key arguments raised against the plan.

Now that we understand how a debate's decided, let's see how it's prepared.

GETTING STARTED

Preparing for a debate takes time and patience. In almost all cases you'll be given ample time, the patience is up to you. How much time? Usually a few weeks, sometimes more. How do you start? By examining the proposition, establishing a plan, and gathering information. We'll discuss each in turn.

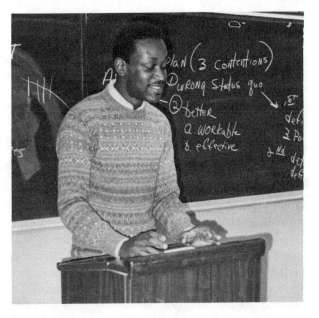

Figure 14.3
A well organized presentation often wins in debate.

Examining the Proposition

In debate you might be assigned a topic, pick one from the list at the end of the chapter, or make up your own. Whichever you do, both teams must agree to take opposing sides. Must you feel strongly about the side you're proposing? Not at all. In intercollegiate debate, for instance, teams reverse positions with every other debate, arguing affirmative in one round, negative in the next. Of course we all feel strongly about certain issues; but recognize that debate teaches us to argue effectively, not to win over our personal point of view.

Once you've decided on a topic, you and your teammate need to examine it closely. How is it worded? What does it say? What needs to be done? Some of these answers are provided in the topic itself; since all propositions imply both a problem and a solution. If debating the question, *"Resolved that we should permit euthanasia for the terminally ill,"* for example, we could quickly see the problem—the use of euthanasia. Likewise it includes a solution—allow it for the terminally ill. In this way the topic becomes immediately clear.

Your next step is to look at all key terms. Terms like *"we,"* *"euthanasia,"* and *"terminally ill"* will all need to be carefully defined. How do you do it? While a dictionary is a good place to start, it's only a beginning. Check out medical dictionaries, resource books, and legal dictionaries. Just the right definition can give just the right twist to your topic. If, for example, we define *"terminally ill"* as *"incurable,"* we'd give it one slant. If, however, we define it as *"without any known cure"* we'd be looking at it in a considerably different way.

Both teams should copy all likely definitions on index cards. The first affirmative will need to state all key definitions in the first constructive speech—but the negative may either accept or reject those definitions. If rejected, the negative will need to provide another definition, explaining why it's preferable. This happened in a recent debate on prayer in school. The affirmative defined prayer as a *"moment of silence."* The negative rejected this, saying prayer means a *"practiced ritual."* Who was right? That was for the judge to decide, after hearing the rest of the debate. But, by copying down all definitions both teams can get a clear focus of the topic at hand.

The final step when evaluating a proposition is to ask two questions: (1) What is present policy in respect to this issue, and (2) What kind of change is needed? In our example on euthanasia both teams would learn that it's considered illegal in the United States, but is allowed in certain Scandinavian countries. Therefore, the topic clearly represents a change in current policy. The second question is where both teams will certainly clash. The affirmative will argue that this alternative is needed for the terminally ill, the negative will point out reasons why it isn't. Once both teams understand their topic, they're ready to move on to reasons.

Establishing Reasons

All too often a team will select a topic and then quickly jump into preparing an argument. This is a big mistake. Teams need to think about the issue, talk it out, and do some background reading. During the first stages it's especially useful to read information on both sides of the question. What better way to understand the arguments of the opposing team than to look at it from their vantage point? Once you've clarified the question, defined some key terms, and exposed yourself to background information, you're ready to establish your reasons.

What are your reasons? They're the cornerstone of each constructive speech. Simply put, they explain why you feel a certain way about your subject. Let's, for example, look at some possible reasons for the topic: *"Resolved that we should permit euthanasia for the terminally ill,"* from the affirmative point of view.

Proposition: *Why we should permit euthanasia.*
Reason 1: *It would eliminate unnecessary pain and suffering.*
Reason 2: *It would save families of the terminally ill tremendous expense and financial ruin.*
Reason 3: *It would preserve medical resources for those patients who can be saved.*

The negative team would also come up with some reasons why euthanasia shouldn't be allowed. Here they are:

Proposition: *Why we shouldn't permit euthanasia.*
Reason 1: *There's always the hope of a cure.*
Reason 2: *Life is sacred, and we have no right to take it.*
Reason 3: *It would be difficult to decide who should make such an important decision.*

Why did each team come up with three reasons? Because in a debate the affirmative will present a plan with three distinct points. The basis of these points is often built right in the reasons. The negative created three reasons, because they'll need to defeat each affirmative point. Sometimes, however, teams come up with more reasons. This way the affirmative team could pick the three points they feel would be the strongest. Likewise, the negative wouldn't know for sure what the plan of the affirmative was. By thinking up more reasons, and then creating an argument for each one, they can better handle anything the affirmative comes up with.

Often a debate hinges on **need** and **workability.** Is there a need? And is the plan workable? The affirmative must clearly show that their plan is needed, and that it is workable. Conversely, the negative must show just the opposite. Here's what both teams might come up with:

Affirmative	*Negative*
Resolved that we should permit euthanasia for the terminally ill.	Resolved that we shouldn't permit euthanasia for the terminally ill.
Is there a *need* for euthanasia?	Is there a *need* for euthanasia?
Yes	No
1. Too many people suffer from incurable diseases. 2. Many diseases are incurable. 3. Medical costs often ruin a families' finances. 4. Medical resources are needed for saving curable patients. 5. Medical insurance rates keep getting higher because of terminal illness. 6. Government programs like Medicare are going broke.	1. There are many effective drugs which relieve pain. 2. New cures are being discovered every year. 3. No value can be placed on a human life. 4. All patients are saveable until they die. 5. Medical insurance companies are actually making a great deal of money. 6. The government needs to put more money into Medicare instead of other programs.
Is the plan *workable?*	Is the plan *workable?*
Yes	No
1. New drugs can make death painless. 2. Patients could decide for themselves if they wished to die. 3. When the patient is unable to decide, a next of kin and a doctor could make the decision. 4. Euthanasia has been used in other cultures previously. 5. People have a right to choose their own destiny and may commit suicide anyway. 6. Euthanasia is already being used in some hospitals, people just don't realize it.	1. Who can prove that these drugs make death painless? 2. Many times the patient is in a coma or unable to think logically. 3. The next of kin may have selfish reasons and the doctor might cooperate. 4. Today we value life more than in the past. 5. Society has the obligation to protect people even against themselves; and suicide is against the law. 6. There is little proof of euthanasia being used and we don't need to encourage it further.

Are these lists complete? Probably not. With thought and analysis both teams could surely come up with additional arguments for their side. Of course, reasons, in and of themselves aren't enough to prove a case. For this you need evidence, and this is our next subject of discussion.

Collecting Evidence

Every point in a debate must be supported with evidence. Evidence serves as the foundation to your plan, as the underpinning to your ideas. It's best to start researching early, even before the complete development of your plan. You might find, for instance, that there's a new definition of life—determined by brain waves rather than heart beat. The affirmative could argue that euthanasia would only be applied when there was a minimum level of brain waves. The negative could counter that someone with such a minimum level of brain waves wouldn't be suffering from pain in any case. Clearly, the discovery of such new material enlightens the thinking of both teams.

You begin building an evidence file by putting information down on index cards. Usually larger cards, 4 by 6 or so, are preferred. Label each card on the top with a specific category. For a typical debate you might have half a dozen categories—definitions, pain and suffering, moral considerations, cost factors,

Pain and Suffering

"During my course of treating hundreds of terminally ill patients I have heard many ask to be put to death. I wish we had mercy killing."

Nancy C. Martin
nurse at St. Agnes Hospital, New York City
from: *Newsweek*, "Mercy Killing,"
January 17, 1985, p. 38.

Figure 14.4
Sample File Card.

countries allowing euthanasia, and so on. Why are labels important? Because in a debate you and your partner may have to access a card in a few seconds—after all, much of your speech will be created as the other team is speaking. Also, in debate there aren't *your cards* and your *partner's cards*—there are only the *team's cards*. By labeling cards they can be placed in categories and quickly located.

Be sure to only include one piece of information per card. The best way to organize a speech in debate is to stack your cards in the order you'll need them. If you've put too much on a card, it confuses and make organization difficult. Debaters frequently read quotations, cite statistics, and give precise examples. This is the kind of material you want on each card. Keep your information direct and to the point—cutting out ideas that are off topic. Remember that in a debate time is valuable. Observe the card above. Notice it's labelled with a general heading, has the full quote, tells where the quote was found, and states the position of the person making the statement. Why is all this important? Because an incomplete quote can be disastrous. Few things are as embarrassing as someone using part of a quote only to have the opposing team complete it to their benefit. Likewise always state the person's name and position, unless it's a nationally known figure. The name Nancy Martin means nothing, but nurse Nancy Martin gives her view instant credibility.

Review the way to do research in Chapter Ten. Once you're prepared to collect information, look for three types: examples, statistics, and opinion. **Examples** use one or more instances to illustrate a point. **Statistics** supply information with mathematical precision. **Opinion** includes quotes and paraphrased statements by people in the know. Mix and mesh all three types as you develop your speech. Clear reasoning, backed by compelling evidence, makes a strong argument.

Types of Evidence

Most debates are packed with evidence using examples. One type compares one thing with another. Here's a sample:

> *Author John Smith recently wrote, "Euthanasia is the same as capital punishment. Whether you kill someone by mercy killing or the electric chair, the result is the same. Each serves its purpose for society and is necessary."*

Another type of example uses a real-life case. Here's one:

> *"For weeks Mary Johnson watched her daughter suffer in pain. Finally she took the only action she could—she put her to rest."*

Sometimes examples pack a wallop when taken from the observations of others. For instance:

> *"Every year more and more doctors are coming to the realization that we need corrective euthanasia as a final act of medical responsibility."*

Statistics pack a punch. They come in the form of percentages, raw numbers, and measurements. Here's one using a percentage:

> *"85% of all doctors and medical professionals recently polled by* People *magazine support the need for euthanasia."*

By using raw numbers, the same statistic can be presented this way:

1,895 doctors and nurses recently polled supported the need for euthanasia.''

Sometimes the result of a scientific test makes a point statistically. Here's one:

"A correlational coefficient of .95 was found between doctors and nurses who support the need for mercy killing.''

Which statistical form works best? Probably statistical testing if presented in an understandable way. Percentages also work because they're easy for most people to grasp. Raw numbers usually aren't as effective because there's no way to gage an adequate comparison. 1,895 doctors and nurses out of how many? 10,000?

Opinion evidence can take the form of direct quotes, indirect quotes, and paraphrased statements. These two examples use a direct quote:

Dr. John Moss said, "We need euthanasia more than ever before.''
For the first time the Medical Association stated, "We should legalize euthanasia.''

Indirect quotations take part of a statement to make a point. For example:

Dr. Hyman Peters, speaking at a recent association dinner said, "We need euthanasia . . . It's very important that we support those who want mercy killing.'' Others have also agreed, "We want euthanasia as soon as possible.''

Sometimes indirect quotations don't give the precise words of the quote. When statements are paraphrased, the original comment is put in the words of the debater:

"Countless doctors have been quoted as supporting mercy killing. This briefly reports the comments made by Dr. Peters at a recent conference.''

What's the strongest type of opinion evidence? That which uses a direct quote. Indirect quotations and paraphrasing are somewhat weaker since they're interpreted by the reporter.

Your next concern should be the quality of your evidence. Is it valid? Does it sound reliable? Will it be believed? Let's review evidence quality.

Quality of Evidence

How can you measure the strength of your evidence? One way is to measure it against five questions:

1. *Who says? A source from the government? From a special interest group? Is it objective?*
2. *Where did s/he say it? Was it published in a reputable magazine? A special interest publication?*
3. *Why did s/he say it? Was it during a political campaign? Did the person have a special interest in the issue?*
4. *When did s/he say it? Recently? Has the person's opinion changed since making it?*
5. *Is it meaningful? Does it really say what I think it says? Can it be interpreted both ways?*

If you measure all your evidence by these five questions you should be assured of being on solid ground. Of course, always be somewhat wary. A great quote from a nurse might sound impressive, but not if she's voicing a lone opinion out of a staff of one-hundred. If you're the toughest critic of your own evidence, you can be assured it will stand up against the test of the other team.

Once you've collected your evidence, you're ready to develop your plan. Let's see how this is done.

PREPARING A PLAN

The plan is the why, the what, and the how of a debate. Why is the plan needed? What will it do? How will it work? Each of these questions must be satisfactorily answered by the affirmative team. Remember that the negative doesn't have a plan, their only job it to defeat the affirmative plan that's presented. Therefore the affirmative team must present as tight a plan as they can, minimizing weaknesses where ever possible.

The *why* of a plan is it's need. In the first speech the first affirmative speaker must clearly show why things aren't as good as they should be. This is called establishing need, as was demonstrated earlier. The *what* is the plan itself. Every plan consists of three points, which set out the ways the need will be corrected. This plan must also be presented early on in the first affirmative speech. It is against this plan that the negative will focus their attack. How important are these three points? Generally if the negative is able to raise sufficient doubt about any two of them, they win the debate. On the other hand, if the affirmative successfully defends any two, they win. Of course both teams work on all three points, since you never can tell how a judge will read a debate—many times what you think you've won you've lost, what you think you've lost, you've won. The *how* is the implementation of the plan. This is almost always presented by the second affirmative speaker, since the first affirmative almost never has time to get into it. Often a negative team will focus much of their attack on this workability part of the plan. On the euthanasia debate, for example, the negative would want to know who would decide to terminate a life, what procedures would be followed, and what safeguards would be put in place. Other frequent questions about the implementation of a plan include cost, effectiveness, and practicality.

Creating a plan takes a lot of energy and creativity on the part of the affirmative. They should never rush into a plan, but study the issue carefully, sifting over every fact before deciding on their three points. Needless to say, this plan must be kept top-secret. If the negative were to discover the plan, they could just load up on evidence to knock it down. The element of surprise gives the affirmative their advantage. The advantage to the negative is that it's always easier to criticize an idea, than come up with one yourself.

The first affirmative presents the three points of the plan right after definitions. The points should be clear, logical, and orderly: *"point number one is, point number two is, point number three is."* Remember the negative team has to copy down the plan and begin loading up on evidence to defeat it. Occasionally a debater will mumble the plan, losing a point or two in the process. While this frustrates the negative, it devastates the affirmative. For if the negative team can't catch the entire plan, the judges can't either. In this case, the negative just hammered away on the one point they heard. Needless to say, they won the debate five to none.

Try to word each point of the plan in parallel language, so they're easy to follow. The clearer the points, the more focused the debate. Here are some examples of plans:

Topic *Resolved that police roadblocks should be abolished.*
Point 1: *Police roadblocks should be abolished because they are an invasion of privacy.*
Point 2: *Police roadblocks should be abolished because they are ineffective in catching drunk drivers.*
Point 3: *Police roadblocks should be abolished because they take police officers away from dealing with more important crimes.*

From this plan we can see that the affirmative will attempt to prove that roadblocks violate a person's right to privacy, are ineffective in catching drunk drivers, and take police officers away from dealing with more important crimes. The negative would need to argue that roadblocks are not an invasion of privacy, are effective in catching drunk drivers, and don't take police officers away from more important tasks.

Topic: *Resolved that all companies should have the right to give their employees a drug test.*
Point 1: *Companies have the right to give a drug test because employees who use drugs are ineffective workers.*
Point 2: *Companies have the right to give a drug test because employees who use drugs endanger the safety of coworkers.*
Point 3: *Companies have the right to give a drug test because employees who use drugs endanger the public.*

In this plan the affirmative sets out to show that companies should have the right to test for drugs because employees who use drugs are ineffective workers, endanger coworkers, and endanger the public. The negative would need to argue that employees who might use drugs don't endanger coworkers or the public. They also might argue that drug tests are invalid, unreliable, and an invasion of one's right to privacy.

Topic: *Resolved that the District of Columbia should become the fifty-first state.*
Point 1: *The District of Columbia should become a state because residents don't have equal representation in the Congress.*
Point 2: *The District of Columbia should become a state because otherwise it can't receive state aid.*
Point 3: *The District of Columbia should become a state because residents deserve more autonomy from the federal government.*

Should Washington, D.C. become a state? The affirmative plan suggests it should because it doesn't have representation in Congress, doesn't receive state aid, and deserves more autonomy from the federal government. The negative would argue that Washington has nonvoting representation in Congress, receives other types of aid, and as the seat of government shouldn't have autonomy.

Each of these plans sets out a course of action. If the affirmative is successful in showing why the plan is needed, what it will do, and how it will work, they'll win the debate. The job of the negative will be to defend against each of these plans. Let's see how the negative goes about its mission.

NEGATIVE STRATEGIES

What's a good negative team? It's a negative team with an affirmative mind. Negative teams need to ask, *"How would we argue this issue if we were the affirmative?" "What would our three points be?"* Questions like these help a negative team prepare by predicting what points the affirmative might come up with. Of course it's impossible to exactly predict a plan—that's why a negative should prepare for several likely points.

Once the negative has thought of several main issues, it needs to collect evidence to defend the present system. If the present system isn't perfect—it seldom is—be prepared to admit it. But, likewise, be prepared to show why it's better than anything else. As a negative you can always be sure the affirmative will be out to tear into the status quo. You're first obligation is to minimize that damage by showing things aren't as bad as they seem.

Your next step is to prepare an attack for each point. What are the implications if the plan was adopted? Would it really solve the problem? Is it the best solution? Questions like these get you to focus on the plan like a shark after bait. An adage for negative teams is *"hit the plan, hit the plan, hit the plan."* Keep on the attack, backing up your reasoning with hard evidence.

The weak link of many affirmative plans is in its implementation. How will it work? What will it do? How much will it cost? Where will the needed money come from to fund it? Questions like these drive affirmative teams crazy. For any plan, no matter how well conceived, has certain weaknesses. Your job is to expose those weaknesses. How do you do it? Compare the workability of the plan with the present system. Will it work as efficiently? Will it really solve the problem? When held to such a comparison, most plans fall short.

One key to successfully arguing the negative side is organization. As a negative speaker you can't have a prepared speech in advance. After all, how can you prepare for a plan you haven't even heard yet? Therefore your evidence has to be orderly, easy to reach, and straight to the point. Likewise you have to know your issue well enough that you can quickly get your thoughts together for the attack. Most good negative teams are aggressive—they go after the affirmative plan tooth and nail. When a negative team gets defensive, and lets the affirmative turn the tables on them, they almost always lose.

A final strategy is to use common sense. Many debaters are surprised to learn how far they get by reasoning with the judges. Explain in your own words why something doesn't make sense; how the plan falls short; and why things shouldn't be changed. Judges respond to clear thoughts, expressed with strong information. Back up your ideas, but don't become overburdened with evidence. A debater who just reads one fact after another soon loses everyone. Mix reason with fact and the result should be positive.

What are your precise responsibilities as a debater? This is the next area we'll discuss.

RESPONSIBILITIES OF EACH DEBATER

In debate each participant plays one of four roles; s/he is either a first or second affirmative, or a first or second negative. Roles can't be switched during a debate—for instance one couldn't give a first affirmative constructive speech, and a second affirmative rebuttal. Your roles are fixed from start to finish. What should you do in your particular role? Let's take a look:

First Affirmative

In some ways the first affirmative has the easiest job in the debate—after all this is the only speaker who can prepare his or her speech in advance. But being a first affirmative also carries with it awesome responsibilities. The speech must be perfectly timed to seven minutes. If the speaker fails to support the third point by running short of time, for example, the affirmative teams starts out at a real disadvantage. That's why it's important to practice this speech until it's timed just right. Most first affirmative speakers read their speech from a manuscript, but also know it by heart. Their delivery should sound natural, their information appear precise.

What needs to be included in the speech? It should begin with a greeting to the judges, other team, and audience. Next should be a statement of the proposition. This follows with key definitions, the three points, and a general statement of what the affirmative will attempt to prove. All of this should take under two minutes. The speaker should then address the need for the plan for about two minutes. The final three minutes are spent by restating each point and supplying a minute's worth of explanation to support each one. The speech should close with a statement that your colleague will detail how the plan will work. If any time is left, it should be used summarizing the basic position of the affirmative team. Here's the order of what should be covered:

Introduction

1. *Greet judges, other team, and audience*
2. *State the proposition*
3. *Define all key terms*
4. *State the three points of the plan*
5. *Briefly explain what the affirmative will attempt to prove in the debate*

Body

1. *State the need for the plan, back with evidence*
2. *Restate first point and reasons for it*
3. *Restate second point and reasons for it*
4. *Restate third point and reasons for it*

Conclusion

1. *State that partner will present details of plan*
2. *Summarize basic position of affirmative team*

First Negative

Chances are that after the first speech everyone will be pretty impressed with the affirmative plan. It's up to the first negative to pull the pendulum back. That's why the first position is the key spot on the negative team. How should the first negative start? Begin by greeting the judges, affirmative team, and audience. Next state your acceptance or rejection of key definitions. If you take issue with a definition, explain why, and state your preferred interpretation of the term. Follow by showing that there isn't a need as the affirmative presented one. The bulk of your presentation will involve taking each point one by one and attacking it with evidence. If the affirmative raised a concern, knock it down: if they offered an idea, hit it hard; if they mentioned a solution, push it aside. Conclude the presentation by summarizing why you believe the negative position is correct. Of course, you won't have all the workings of the affirmative plan to criticize, your partner will have to do that.

What's the best way to prepare this speech? Have some ideas on need and likely arguments thought out in advance. But the majority of your speech will have to be worked out as the first affirmative is speaking. As each point is mentioned quickly collect evidence cards related to that area—of course your colleague can help you do this as well. Put some ideas together, and extemporaneously tell why your view is right. By the time you're done, you should

have put some serious dents in the affirmative plan. Here's the order of what you should include:

Introduction

1. *Greet judges, other team, and audience*
2. *Accept or reject definitions*
3. *Argue that there's no need as argued by the affirmative*

Body

1. *Attack point one of plan with evidence*
2. *Attack point two of plan with evidence*
3. *Attach point three of plan with evidence*

Conclusion

1. *State general position of negative team*
2. *Summarize key arguments against affirmative plan*

Second Affirmative

This speaker needs to pull the momentum of the debate back to the affirmative side. Part of this speech can be prepared in advance. This would include a discussion of how the plan will be implemented. But much of the speech will have to be quickly thrown together as the first negative is speaking. The likelihood is that you and your partner were probably able to pretty well predict what arguments the negative would raise, but there are surprises. What if they challenge a key definition? What if they ask a few rhetorical questions? What if they find a flaw in one of the points? All of these questions might arise. The second affirmative, therefore, must pull evidence cards and quickly put some persuasive ideas together.

The first job of the second affirmative is to argue definitions if any were challenged—if not consider it a dead issue, concluding the affirmative definitions were accepted. Next review the three points and supply new evidence supporting each one. This should diffuse much of the damage done by the first negative. All of this should take about three minutes. Your remaining time should be spent outlining the affirmative plan. How will it work? Where will it be implemented? When will it occur? Who will carry it out? Supply the answers to each of these questions in the details of your plan's workability. Following are, in order, the responsibilities of the second affirmative:

Introduction

1. *Defend definitions if they've been challenged*
2. *Review three points of plan and support with new evidence*

Body

1. *Present details of how plan will work*
2. *Establish how plan is superior to present system*
3. *Clarify why plan is needed*

Conclusion

1. *Summarize key elements in workability of plan*
2. *Knock down major arguments raised by negative*

Second Negative

This speaker has the advantage of seeing the unwrapped package. Now it's clear what the plan is, how it will work, and what it will do. It's up to the second negative to sink the affirmative ship. How is this done? By hitting the plan and its implementation. By the time the second negative is done, the affirmative team should be as woozy as a boxer in the fifteenth round.

You should start by hitting each point with evidence and argument. Spend about a minute on each one, highlighting key weaknesses as your team sees them. Concentrate your remaining four minutes on the implementation of the plan. You're the first speaker who can really cut it to ribbons. Point out obvious flaws; show where it won't work; question likely weaknesses. If you undercut the workings of the affirmative idea, you destroy the plan altogether. How can you prepare to do this? As the workings of the plan are revealed gather key bits of evidence; collect your thoughts; and come up swinging. An aggressive attack can undue the most persuasive of plans. Here's the order of what you should do:

Introduction

1. *Attack point one with evidence*
2. *Attack point two with evidence*
3. *Attack point three with evidence*

Body

1. *Show that plan won't work*
2. *Point out imperfections in workability of plan*
3. *Suggest obvious weaknesses in implementation of plan*

Conclusion

1. *Summarize major weaknesses as you see them*

When the second negative is done, all constructive speeches are concluded. What remains are the rebuttals—short speeches given by each debater at the end of a debate. All rebuttals have much in common. Let's see what that is.

Rebuttal Speeches

In a rebuttal each speaker wants to highlight key arguments, reiterate the main points, and summarize why his or her team should win. The rebuttal is not the place to bring up new ideas; it is the place to underscore those key issues that floated to the surface. Most debates end up balancing on a few key points. Accordingly, both teams need to convince the judge that their side is correct. A rebuttal is usually closed with the statement, *"And that's why the (affirmative) or (negative) should win this debate."* Here are some things to include:

Introduction

1. *State main overall position or objection*

Body

1. *Answer all key questions raised by other team*
2. *Defend or attack all three points*

Conclusion

1. *Summarize what has been covered*
2. *State why your team should win*

Cross Examination

Often a debate includes a question and answer session following each speaker's constructive speech. Several key questions should be prepared in advance. It's a good idea to review the types of questions that can be asked in Chapter Eight. You'll find that branching questions work particularly well. You also can ask *"yes"* or *"no"* questions. However, make sure your line of questioning leads to a point—don't just string several unrelated questions together. There are a few things to bear in mind about questioning in a debate, however. First, keep your questions short, don't waste your valuable two minutes trying to get a question out. Word them crisply and directly. Second, don't ask too many open-ended questions that let an op-

Figure 14.5
Phrasing just the right questions in just the right way is the key to making a point in cross examination.

ponent ramble on endlessly. Phrase questions so answers are kept relatively short. Third, don't use this time to make a speech—use it to question, not hypothesize. Finally, don't let your adversary turn the tables on you. Sometimes a clever opponent will answer a question with a question. A careless questioner will then start answering, instead of asking! Never let this happen. Make it clear you're up there to ask questions, not answer them.

What do you do when being questioned? Be polite and keep your composure. Don't take tough questions personally, remembering that you're debating issues, not personalities. Give reasonable answers, and don't look evasive. Avoid trap questions that might paint you in a corner. And if you give an unwise answer, admit it, don't let it go unchecked. A respectful person, supplying honest answers usually comes out looking good in this part of a debate.

How should you act in a debate? In the final section we provide some suggestions.

DEBATE ETIQUETTE

Debate is a nobel pursuit. Debaters may legitimately clash over issues, but should only do so with respect and courtesy. Here are some *"rules of behavior"* to keep in mind.

Seating Arrangement

One team sits at a table on the left of the podium, the other on the right. Tables are usually arranged at a forty-five degree angle facing the audience and the podium.

General Procedure

When it's a person's time to present, s/he should gather all materials and proceed to the podium. Begin speaking within several seconds and deliver the speech toward the audience, not the other team—although occasional glances toward the opposing side is allowable.

Time Between Presentations

How soon should you approach the podium when the person proceeding you is finished speaking? Just ten or so seconds. Once it starts, a debate moves quickly, so be ready to promptly move to the podium when it's your turn to speak. This isn't the time to hunt for notes or whisper to a teammate. Judges may penalize you if there's more than a several second delay.

General Behavior

The only person who has the right to speak is the one at the podium. While at your team's table don't answer questions, don't make comments, and don't shout remarks. If something is said that you don't like, wait until it's your turn to speak to respond. Likewise don't send negative nonverbal signals—grimaces, faces, gestures and the like.

Conversing with a Teammate

Sometimes you might want to whisper to a teammate during a debate. This is okay so long as it's done infrequently and kept to a whisper. Don't plan on having an extended conversation with a teammate, however. When a member of the other team is speaking you should be carefully listening, taking notes, and gathering evidence. How do you take notes? Use the **flow sheet** at the end of this chapter. It's a simple way to keep track of everything that's said.

Cross Examination Period

If you're to question a member of the other team, approach your side of the podium. If being questioned, move slightly aside, to your side of the podium. Therefore, both participants should end up facing each other at a forty-five degree angle. Questioning should begin with a greeting using proper names, for example, *"Good day, Ms. Johnson."*

Overall Politeness

A debate means being respectful to the other team. Never use a sarcastic tone, make cutting remarks, or personal references. Keep the debate focused on the issue being debated. An insulting attitude demeans everyone.

Remember the Team Concept

Speak as a member of a team. Don't say *"My feelings are,"* say *"My colleague and I feel."* Bear in mind that you win or lose a debate as a team, not as an individual. Likewise support your teammate. If s/he takes a stand you're obligated to support it; you can't disown it saying, *"Well that's her idea, not mine."* If it's her idea, it becomes *your team's* idea.

When the Debate's Over

Once the last speaker is finished both teams should meet at the midpoint of the room and shake hands. Thank each other for a good debate; then return to your seats to hear the judge's result.

Debate is an exciting activity. When you thoroughly prepare, cooperate with your teammate, and exert a positive attitude you'll surely find it a worthwhile experience. Frequently students enjoy their debate so much they're quick to ask, *"When's my next debate!"* Hopefully you'll feel much the same way.

CHAPTER SUMMARY

A debate is an exchange of conflicting views. It begins with a proposition, which is the question to be debated. The issue is divided into two sides, the affirmative and the negative. Debate follows a rigorous process, whereby each team presents in alternating order. The affirmative speaks both first and last. All debates are carefully timed and the decision is rendered by a judge.

The first step in preparing for a debate is to examine the proposition. The next step is to establish the reasons for the team's position. Teams should then go about collecting evidence. Evidence should be recorded on index cards and should include examples, statistics, and opinion. All material collected should be of high quality.

The plan is the why, the what, and the how of a debate. A good plan should consist of definitions, an establishment of need, and three clear points. The negative should argue against the plan by showing the plan isn't needed and won't work. Each speaker has set responsibilities. The first affirmative clearly states the plan, while the second affirmative tells how it will work. The first negative argues that there's no need for the plan, while the second negative tells why it won't work. All speakers summarize their main ideas in the rebuttal.

Etiquette is very important in debate. Debaters should sit on opposing sides of the room, be ready to speak soon after the proceeding speech, be polite, only whisper to a teammate, never speak out of turn, and congratulate the other team at the debate's conclusion.

EXERCISES FOR REVIEW

1. Go through the list of debate topics at the end of this chapter and pick several that you believe might make for an interesting debate.
2. Prepare an outline detailing the responsibilities of each speaker. Be sure to list the primary responsibilities of each debater.
3. Choose a member of the class to serve as your debate partner. Then meet with a pair of other students who will oppose you in class. Agree on a topic and on which team will argue affirmative, and which will argue negative. Then begin researching your issue and developing your team's strategy.
4. Read about a famous debate in history. Then write a 200 word paper discussing the debate and the impact that it had at the time.
5. Meet with a group of four or five classmates and talk about what needs to be included in a good affirmative plan. Sketch out several possible plans for some of the topics listed at the end of this chapter.

Overtones of Speech Sounds

Psycholoanalyst Sigmund Freud believed that all symbols, and accordingly all language, are extensions of the body and have message significance. Symbols could be identified with the body, for instance, the mouth, breasts, and penis. Thus, the letters that are used in language could be interpreted as representing these organs. When Freud used a psychoanalytic interpretation of a dream he would interpret a person diving into a pool as a desire to return to the womb and so forth. By using these dimensions of language Freud was able to draw a line between communication and all behavior.

Recent theorists, including speech pathologists Clyde Rousey and Alice Moriarity believe that the sounds of a word are extensions of bodily functions. For instance, the harsh k sounds at the beginning and ending of the word ''cock'' make the word sound very aggressive. The more elongated sound of the word ''stream'' make it seem more seductive and peaceful. People who use words that have a great deal of harsh articulations such as k, t, d, and p, may be seen as being overly hostile and sexually aggressive. People who use the labial sounds of m, n, oo, and u may be seen as more seductive and gentle. Research by Rousey has shown that a careful analysis of various language sounds can be a useful tool in the diagnosis of people suffering from various psychological problems or with difficulties in interacting with other members of society.

See: Clyde Rousey and Alice Moriarity, *Diagnostic Implications of Speech Sounds: The Reflections of Developmental Conflict and Trauma* (Palo Alto, California C. C. Thomas, 1966).

Topics for Debate

1. Resolved that all children should be fingerprinted.
2. Resolved that the electoral college should be abolished.
3. Resolved that prostitution should be legalized.
4. Resolved that drugs should be legalized.
5. Resolved that we should reinstitute the military draft.
6. Resolved that women should be allowed to serve as combat infantry.
7. Resolved that marijuana should be legalized.
8. Resolved that all states should have capital punishment.
9. Resolved that all schools should have sex education.
10. Resolved that prisoners should be given no luxuries.
11. Resolved that juveniles who commit murder should be executed.
12. Resolved that the United States should ban all future immigration to this country.
13. Resolved that prayer should be allowed in public schools.
14. Resolved that children with A.I.D.S. should be prohibited from attended classes with noninfected children.
15. Resolved that we should censor all pornography.
16. Resolved that companies should be allowed to give employees a drug test.
17. Resolved that euthanasia should be permitted for the terminally ill.
18. Resolved that all animal experimentation should be abolished.
19. Resolved that abortion should be made illegal.
20. Resolved that smoking should be banned in all public places.
21. Resolved that drunk drivers should lose their licenses for life.
22. Resolved that all people seeking a marriage license should be tested for A.I.D.S.
23. Resolved that state lotteries should be abolished.
24. Resolved that ads for alcohol should be banned from television.
25. Resolved that English should be made the official language of the United States.
26. Resolved that all musical recordings should be rated for suitability for children.
27. Resolved that air bags should be required in all new cars.
28. Resolved that the United States should limit all imports from Japan.
29. Resolved that Lee Harvey Oswald did not act alone in the assassination of President Kennedy.
30. Resolved that anyone caught selling drugs within 100 yards of a school should receive life imprisonment.
31. Resolved that parents should be held accountable for the vandalism of their children.
32. Resolved that marriage should be legally recognized between homosexuals.
33. Resolved that adopted children should have the right to locate their birth parents.
34. Resolved that all Americans should be required to serve two years of compulsory public service.
35. Resolved that the sale of tobacco products should be banned.
36. Resolved that all Americans should be required to recycle their garbage.
37. Resolved that police roadblocks should be abolished.
38. Resolved that violence on television should be reduced.
39. Resolved that the federal government should eliminate funding of all obscene art.
40. Resolved that obscene musical performances should be banned.
41. Resolved that children should be required to go to school twelve months a year.
42. Resolved that social security should be made voluntary.
43. Resolved that gambling should be banned.
44. Resolved that women reporters should not be allowed in men's locker rooms.
45. Resolved that teachers should have the right to physically punish children.
46. Resolved that the space program should be abolished.
47. Resolved that panhandling should be banned in all public places.
48. Resolved that the police should have the right to remove all homeless people from public locations.
49. Resolved that affirmative action programs should be abolished.
50. Resolved that religious cults should be banned.
51. Resolved that the sale of alcohol should be prohibited.

Flow Sheet

Proposition _____ Other team members _____ and _____

First Affirmative	*First Negative*	*Second Affirmative*	*Second Negative*
Definitions:	Definitions:	Plan:	Objections to Plan:
1.	1.	1.	1.
2.	2.	2.	2.
3.	Need Defense:	3.	3.
Need:	1.	Implementation:	Workability:
1.	2.	1.	1.
2.	3.	2.	2.
3.	Attack on Plan:	3.	3.
Plan:	1.	4.	Disadvantages:
1.	2.	5.	1.
2.	3.	Re-establish need:	2.
3.	Attack Details:	1.	3.
Plan Details:	1.	2.	Need Defense:
1.	2.	3.	1.
2.	3.	Comparative Advantages:	2.
3.	4.	1.	3.
Cross-Exam Answers:	Cross-Exam Answers:	Cross-Exam Answers:	Cross-Exam Answers:
1.	1.	1.	1.
2.	2.	2.	2.

Debate Evaluation

Affirmative 1 _____   Negative 1 _____

Affirmative 2 _____   Negative 2 _____

    Check the column on each item which, according to the following scale best describes your evaluation of the speaker's effectiveness, and indicate the rank for each speaker in the space following his or her name.

1—poor   2—fair   3—adequate   4—good 5—superior

	1st Affirmative 1 2 3 4 5	2nd Affirmative 1 2 3 4 5	1st Negative 1 2 3 4 5	2nd Negative 1 2 3 4 5
Analysis				
Reasoning and evidence				
Organization				
Cross-exam				
Refutation				
Delivery				

Total _____   Total _____   Total _____   Total _____

Team Ratings:

Affirmative: poor   fair   adequate   good   superior

Negative: poor   fair   adequate   good   superior

Comments:

1st Affirmative   rank ( )   1st Negative   rank ( )

2nd Affirmative   rank ( )   2nd Negative   rank ( )

In my opinion, the better debating was done by the _____
                                                    affirmative or negative

_____
judge's signature

Individual grade _____
team grade _____

Sources of Information

Topic of Debate: _____

My team is the Affirmative Negative (Circle one) and our basic position is: _____

_____

Printed Sources:

Author:_____ Date: _____

Title: _____

Article Title: _____

Number of Pages Used: _____ Publisher: _____

Author:_____ Date: _____

Title: _____

Article Title: _____

Number of Pages Used: _____ Publisher: _____

Author:_____ Date: _____

Title: _____

Article Title: _____

Number of Pages Used: _____ Publisher: _____

Author: _____Date: _____

Title: _____

Article Title: _____

Number of Pages Used: _____ Publisher: _____

Interview Sources:

Name of Person Interviewed:_____Date: _____

Position or Title: _____

Reason for Expertise on Subject: _____

Appendix and
Answers to Exercises

Name _____ Course _____

Correct Answers to exercise on Page 13

Test of Knowledge

Circle the correct true or false answer for each question:

1. (T) F Most of our communication time is spent listening.
   Yes, 70%.

2. T (F) An extemporaneous speech is one given with no preparation.
   No, has minimal; no preparation is impromptu.

3. T (F) A good tension reliever when speaking in public is to hold a pen or paper clip.
   No, causes a distraction.

4. (T) F The study of speech communication dates back to ancient times.
   Yes, over 4300 years ago.

5. (T) F We can comprehend (listen) at a faster rate than we can speak.
   Yes, two or three times quicker.

6. (T) F It is important to consider time limits when preparing a speech.
   Yes, always.

7. (T) F How you say something is more important than what you say.
   Yes, tone and expression communicate a great deal.

8. (T) F Most actors and experienced public speakers have some nervousness before speaking before an audience.
   Yes, just about everyone does.

9. T (F) When preparing a speech your first step should be to prepare an outline.
   No, first decide on general purpose.

10. (T) F First impressions are very important in interviews.
    Yes, extremely important, especially the first 30 seconds.

11. (T) F Eye contact is important in all interpersonal interactions.
    Yes, determines trust and interest.

12. (T) F The average American spends more time reading than writing.
    Yes, reading is 16%, writing 9%.

13. (T) F Gestures can help to bring out what you want to say.
    Yes, they help a lot.

14. T (F) The proper way to close a speech is to say "I thank you."
    No, original conclusion is needed.

15. T (F) Effective communicators are born, not made.
    No, that's why you're taking this course.

16. T (F) Feedback should have no effect on the way we communicate with our listeners.
    No, always use feedback for information.

17. (T) F Most Americans spend about 70% of their waking time communicating with others.
    Yes, the average American spends 7 out of every 10 waking hours communicating.

18. T (F) All messages either inform or entertain.
    No, the three purposes are to inform, persuade, or entertain.

19. (T) F Research shows that communication is essential for most lines of work.
    Yes, the Dept. of Labor suggests that communication is essential for 80% of all jobs.

20. T (F) The greatest fear of most Americans is the fear of snakes.
    No, it's the fear of speaking before a group, according to 41% of all people polled.

Answer to Definitions of Communication on page 24.

3 is 1st
8 is 2nd
10 is 3rd
7 is 4th
5 is 5th
2 is 6th
9 is 7th
1 is 8th
4 is 9th
6 is 10th

Scoring Key for NASA Moon Survival Task on pages 141 and 142.

Your individual and group score may be determined by subtracting the difference between your score and the correct score listed below. The higher the score, the worse you did—a perfect score would be 0.

(15) Box of matches . . . little or no use on moon
(4) Food concentrate . . . supply daily food required
(6) 50 feet of nylon rope . . . useful in tying injured—help in climbing
(8) Parachute silk . . . shelter against sun's rays
(13) Portable heating unit . . . useful only if party landed on dark side
(11) Two .45 calibre pistols . . . self-propulsion devices could be made from them
(12) One case dehydrated milk . . . food, mixed with water for drinking
(1) Two 100-pound tanks of oxygen . . . fills respiration requirement
(3) Stellar map of moon's constellation . . . one of principal means of finding directions
(9) Life raft . . . CO^2 bottle for self-propulsion across chasms, etc.
(14) Magnetic compass . . . probably no magnetized pole; thus useless
(2) 5 gallons of water . . . replenishes loss by sweating, etc.
(10) Signal flares . . . distress call within line of sight
(7) First-aid kit containing injection needles . . . oral pills or injection medicine valuable
(5) Solar-powered FM receiver-transmitter . . . distress signal transmitter, possible communication with mother ship[74]

Index

A

Alliteration, 68
Animal communication, 16–19
    ants, 17–18
    bees, 17
    chickens, 17
    crickets, 16
    dolphins, 17
    geese, 17
    primates, 18–19
    sea gulls, 17
    tree toads, 16
Anthony, Susan, 4, 86, 210
Antithesis, 68
Appearance, 84, 189
Argumentation and debate, see debate
Aristotle, 38, 176
Articulation, 80–81
Asian dialect, 83–84
Attitudes, 179
Audience analysis, 172–189, 194–195
    adapting to, 184
    collecting information, 181–183
    demographics of, 176–178
    environment, 180–181
    form, 187–188
    public speaking, 193–194
    thinking of, 178–180
    types of, 175–

B

Bacon, Francis, 50
Baer, Bugs, 65
Bales, Robert, 129
Barnlund, Dean, 23
Barriers to communication, 24
Becker, Boris, 6
Beliefs, 179–180
Berlo, David, 39
Black English, 82–83
Bomb shelter exercise, 139
Bonaparte, Napoleon, 174
Bradshaw, Terry, 6
Brainstorming, 131, 203–205
Brokaw, Tom, 78
Burns, George, 46
Bush, George, 4, 61

C

Career communications, 108–121
    benefits, 4–5
    complaints of bosses, 115
    electronic recruiting, 121
    interviewing, 110–116
    listening, 46
    oral reports, 116
    situations, 20
    telephone speaking, 117–118
Carson, Johnny, 7, 80
Carter, Jimmy, 82
Cash, Johnny, 78
Castro, Fidel, 6
Central idea statement, 193–194

Characteristics of communication, 23
Churchill, Winston, 6, 60, 65, 67, 78
Cliches, 66
Climax, 69
Communication
    animal, 16–19
    barriers to, 24
    characteristics of, 23
    concern sheet, xiv
    definition of, 24–25
    elements in, 33–36
    human, 19
    levels of, 21–23
    models of, 38–42
    process of, 32–33
    purpose, 19–20
    situations, 20–21
    transactional nature of, 37–38
Conclusions, 196
Connectives, 196–197
Connotative meaning, 62–63
Cornell system, 51
Cosby, Bill, 61, 78
Cosell, Howard, 78
Cuomo, Mario, 4, 201
Dance, Frank, 40–41
Darrow, Clarence, 47
Debate, 234–254
    constructive speeches, 245–247
    cross examination, 247–248
    etiquette, 248–249
    evaluation sheet, 253
    evidence, 241–243
    flow sheet, 252
    format, 238–239
    plan preparation, 243–245
    proposition, 237, 239–240
    reasons, 240–241
    rebuttals, 247
    speaker responsibilities, 245–248
    strategies, 245
    teams, 237–238
    topics, 251

D

Definition of communication, 24–25, 258
Delivery, see speech delivery
Demosthenes, 8, 200, 210
Denotative meaning, 62
Dewey, John, 130
Dialect, 75, 81–84
    Asian, 83–84
    Black English, 82–83
    Spanish, 83
    regionalisms, 75
Dienstag, Eleanor, 199
Discussion topics, 137–138
Disraeli, 192
Distance, 86–87
    intimate, 86
    personal, 86
    public, 86
    social, 86
Downs, Hugh, 82
Douglas, Stephen, 236

Turner, Tina, 78
Twain, Mark, 7, 60, 70, 80, 199, 212
Tyson, Mike, 61

U

Understatement, 67

V

Valenti, Jack, 85
Values, 180
Verbal communication, 76–84
    articulation, 80–81
    dialect, 81–82
    pauses, 80
    pitch, 79
    pronunciation, 81
    rate, 79–80
    variety, 84
    volume, 79
    worksheet, 91–92
Verbs, 69
Visual aids, 202, 213–221
    charts, 215
    critique sheet, 229

drawings, 217
films, 219
filmstrips, 216–217
guidelines, 219–221
how to use, 213
models, 214–215
objects, 214
overhead transparencies, 217–218
photographs, 215–216
record players, 219
slides, 216–217
tape recorders, 219
yourself, 219
Voice, 78–82, 199–200
Voice-prints, 186
Volume, 79

W

Walters, Barbara, 7, 61, 78, 212
Washington, George, 50
Webster, Daniel, 79–80, 210
Weaver, Warren, 39
Wilson, Woodrow, 85
Wolf spider, 26
Words, number used, 171

NOTES

NOTES

NOTES

NOTES